CORRUPT EXCHANGES

SOCIAL PROBLEMS AND SOCIAL ISSUES

An Aldine de Gruyter Series of Texts and Monographs

SERIES EDITOR

Joel Best

Southern Illinois University at Carbondale

CORRUPT EXCHANGES
Actors, Resources, and Mechanisms of Political Corruption

Donatella della Porta and Alberto Vannucci

ALDINE DE GRUYTER
New York

About the Authors

Donatella della Porta is professor of local government on the Faculty of Political Science at the University of Florence. Her earlier books in English include *Social Movements, Political Violence and the State, Policing Protest* and *Social Movements: An Introduction.*

Alberto Vannucci is a postdoctoral fellow in the Department of Political Science at the University of Pisa. He has written three books in Italian one with Professor della Porta; this is his first book in English.

Copyright © 1999 Walter de Gruyter, Inc., New York
All rights reserved. No part of this publication may be reproduced or transmitted in any form or by any means, electronic or mechanical, including photocopy, recording, or any information storage or retrieval system, without permission in writing from the publisher.

ALDINE DE GRUYTER
A division of Walter de Gruyter, Inc.
200 Saw Mill River Road
Hawthorne, New York 10532

This publication is printed on acid free paper ∞
Library of Congress Cataloging-in-Publication Data
Della Porta, Donatella, 1956–
    Corrupt exchanges : actors, resources, and mechanisms of political corruption / Donatella della Porta and Alberto Vannucci.
        p.   cm.
    Includes index.
    ISBN 0-202-30574-0 (alk. paper).—ISBN 0-202-30600-3 (alk. paper)
    1. Political corruption.   2. Political corruption—Italy.
I. Vannucci, Alberto.   II. Title.
JF1081.D45   1999   FEB 2 2 1999
364.1'323—dc21   98-39625
                                                                          CIP

Manufactured in the United States of America
10 9 8 7 6 5 4 3 2 1

To Alessandro Pizzorno,
who inspired our research

"Bribe it," Yossarian said.

"Bribe it!" Milo was outraged and almost lost his balance and broke his neck again. *"Shame on you!"* he scolded severely, breathing virtuous fire down and upward into his rusty mustache through his billowing nostrils and prim lips.*"Bribery is against the law, and you know it. But it's not against the law to make a profit, is it? So it can't be against the law for me to bribe someone in order to make a fair profit, can it? No, of course not!"* He fell to brooding again with a meek, almost a pitiable distress. *"But how will I know who to bribe?"*

"Oh, don't you worry about that," Yossarian comforted him with a toneless snicker as the engines of the jeeps and ambulance fractured the drowsy silence and the vehicles in the rear began driving away backward. *"You make the bribe big enough and they'll find you. Just make sure you do everything right out in the open. Let everyone know exactly what you want and how much you're willing to pay for it. The first time you act guilty or ashamed, you may get into trouble. "*

Joseph Heller, Catch 22, London, Corgy Books, 1964, p. 283

Contents

Acknowledgments

This book reports on three different pieces of research. the first research was conducted by Donatella della Porta at the European University Institute in Florence; the second constitutes Alberto Vannucci's Ph.D. and post Ph.D. research at the faculty of Political Science of the University of Pisa; and the third was led jointly by the two authors under the sponsorship of the Consiglio Nazionale delle Ricerche, under the Special Program on the Public Administration. Donatella della Porta worked on the final revisions of the book during a sabbatical year at the Wissenschaftszentrum in Berlin with a grant from the Alexander von Humboldt Stiftung. We wish to thank all these institutions for their logistic support, and our colleagues and mentors Sabino Cassese, Raimondo Cubeddu and Alessandro Pizzorno for their scientific advice.

Some results of our research have been discussed at the following meetings: the Joint Sessions of European Consortium for Political Research in Leiden (April 1993); the conference on "Illegalità-legalità e ceti emergenti nel cambiamento delle società europee" organized by the Istituto di sociologia internazionale in Gorizia (October 1993); the international conference on "Corruption and Democracy" at the Observatoire du Changement Social en Europe Occidentale in Poitier (November 1993); the Conference on "Tangentopoli e la crisi del sistema politico italiano," organized by the Robert Schuman Center at the European University Institute in Florence (January 1994); the Conference on "Reconstituting Italy: Sources of Pathology and Forces for Reform," at the Center for European Studies at Harvard University (February 1994); the workshop on "La crisi dei partiti in Italia," organized by the Istituto Gramsci of Turin (May 1994); the Annual meeting of the Association for the Study of Modern Italy (London, November 1994); the International Conference on "Democracies between Crisis and Reform. Comparing Italy and Belgium" held in Brussels (September 1995); the International workshop on "Political Corruption" in Nottingham (May 1996); the International Conference on "Political Corruption" at the University of Salford (November 1996); the International Conference on "Political Corruption in Western Europe: Austria, Belgium, Italy and Franco Compared" in Brussels (December 1997); the Joint Sessions of the European Consortium for Political Research in Warwick (March 1998); the International Conference on "Public Trust and Governance in the Trilateral

Democracies" in the Bellagio Study and Conference Center of the Rockfeller Foundation (June 1998). We are grateful to our colleagues who organized and participated in those occasions—among them, Arnaldo Bagnasco, Jean Cartier-Bressons, Martin Bull, Giacomo Costa, Arnold Heidenheimer, Paul Heywood, David Hine, Francesco Kijllberg, Jean-Francois Médard, Henri Mendras, Yves Mény, Leonardo Morlino, James Newal, Susan Pharr, Bob Putnam, Vincent Wright, Lieven de Winter—for very stimulating discussions.

The authors are obliged to all those who helped them collect the thousands and thousands of pages, mainly judicial materials, on which much of their research is based. Among the judges who helped us, special thanks go to Gherardo Colombo, Michele Del Gaudio, Antonio Di Pietro, Piercamillo Davigo, Filippo Grisolia, Francesco Greco, Fausto Izzo, Giovanni Leonardi, Guido Lo Forte, Leonardo Guarnotta, Marco Maria Maiga, Rosario Minna, Fabio Napoleone, Guido Papalia, Vittorio Paraggio, Luca Pistorelli and Ottavio Sferlazza. For her help in the collection of parliamentary sources we are grateful to Dottoressa Emilia Lamaro. Moreover, we are profoundly indebted to the dozens of interviewees who trusted us not only with their time, but also with their confidence.

This work derives from a constant—fruitful and friendly—collaboration between the two authors. Alberto Vannucci has collected and excerpted most of the judicial materials; Donatella della Porta has run the case studies of three Italian cities, mainly based on in-depth interviews. In a long (almost endless) procedure, all the chapters have gone back and forward from Florence to Pisa and vice-versa, until both authors were satisfied with the results. For the record, Donatella della Porta has produced the final version of chapters 3, 4, 5 and 6; Alberto Vannucci the final version of chapter 1, 2, 7, 8. The conclusion was jointly written. John Donaldson translated the whole manuscript with competence and care. Richard Koffler at Aldine de Gruyter gave good advice (not only linguistic) about the translation of our Italian production for an international public. We hope it was worthwhile.

1

The Market for Corrupt Exchange:
An Introduction

When Bettino Craxi rose to speak in the Chamber of Deputies on July 3, 1992, he was a political leader in grave difficulty. And yet immediately after the elections of April 7, Craxi, leader of the Italian Socialist Party (Partito Socialista Italiano, PSI) since 1976 and prime minister of the longest-lived government in Italy's postwar history—from 1983 to 1987—had appeared set for a return to the premiership. He was backed by a political alliance known as the CAF, after the initials of its leading exponents (Craxi himself, outgoing premier Giulio Andreotti, and the party secretary of the Christian Democrats, Arnaldo Forlani). The CAF, however, turned out to be a failure, achieving not one of its objectives. To understand why, it is necessary to take a short step back in time, to February 17, 1992. In Milan, Mario Chiesa, Socialist city councillor and president of a municipal home for the elderly, the Pio Albergo Trivulzio, was arrested while accepting a small bribe. The man responsible for the arrest was Antonio Di Pietro, the Milanese assistant prosecutor who would later become a national hero. Thirty-five days later, Chiesa began to collaborate with the magistrates, setting off a chain of confessions that resulted, shortly after the election, in indictments against a great many businessmen, bureaucrats, and politicians, all of them closely associated with the country's ruling political elite. As a result of the massive wave of popular indignation produced by the scandal, Forlani was unsuccessful in his bid to be elected president of the republic (one of the objectives behind the CAF) and the new president, Oscar Luigi Scalfaro, was persuaded not to offer Craxi the premiership. In the meantime the "mani pulite" ("clean hands") investigations spread to other cities and ever closer to national centers of power. Although most of the political parties were implicated in the scandal, Craxi's Socialist party was from the outset the hardest hit. In the summer of 1992, as the party's Milanese exponents fell one by one, the investigation approached the national leadership.

Craxi was still an influential figure when he took the floor of the Chamber on July 3. His speech, to all intents and purposes an act of self-incrimination (the magistrates later called it an "extrajudicial confession of the offenses [he had] committed"), sketched out a political line of defense that he would stick to firmly throughout the following months and years. In more general terms, his attempt to play down the significance of the scandal with the generic declaration that "everybody knew" what was going on came to sound like an indictment of the functioning of the democratic system itself.

"The political parties," Craxi claimed, "have been the body and soul of our democratic structures. . . . Unfortunately, it is often difficult to identify, pre-

1

vent, and remove areas of infection in the life of parties. . . . Thus, under the cover of irregular funding to the parties cases of corruption and extortion have flourished and become intertwined. . . . What needs to said, and which in any case everyone knows, is that the greater part of political funding is irregular or illegal. The parties and those who rely on a party machine (large, medium, or small); on newspapers, propaganda, promotional and associational activities . . . have had, or have, recourse to irregular or illegal additional resources. If the greater part of this is to be considered criminal pure and simple then the greater part of the political system is a criminal system. I do not believe there is anybody in this hall who has had responsibility for a large organization who can stand up and deny what I have just said. Sooner or later the facts would make a liar of him." (TNM:87–88)

The mani pulite *investigations continued and Craxi was backed into an ever tighter corner until, on January 12 the following year, the decisive blow—in the shape of a first, richly documented request to parliament for authorization to proceed against him—was struck. The testimony of numerous businessmen and members of his party confirmed the former premier's personal involvement in the administration of corruption. The party treasurer "presented him with the 'budget' for illegal funding from business" and "obtained his approval for it." Craxi in person urged party members holding office in the public administration "not to sit there keeping the seat warm, making it clear that they were expected to procure votes and funds for the party from the exercise of their functions." He reminded one entrepreneur that "'you had to put two billion on the table to get into the game', 'getting in' referring to the possibility of being considered for public contracts." Craxi also gathered information on corrupt activities of opponents within his own party so that he "could keep them in line" (CD, 13 January 1993, no. 166, p. 48; CD, 5 March 1993, no. 210, pp. 8, 14). Forced to resign as Socialist party secretary on February 11, 1993, and violently confronted at every public appearance, Craxi took refuge in his villa in Hammamet, Tunisia, a few months later. He continues to reside there with an international warrant for his arrest and prison sentences adding up to twenty-four years hanging over his head.*

In its development, the "clean hands" investigation brought about the most serious political crisis in the history of the Italian Republic, quickly extending to the uppermost levels of the political and economic system. In a matter of months, the magistracy had opened a breach on a scene of corruption and political illegality without precedent in the history of the Western democracies, involving the entire political class of the country and broad sectors of its business community. The investigation reached the highest levels of the public administration and affected most areas of the state's activity. More than five hundred former parliamentarians were implicated, many former ministers, five former premiers, thousands of local administrators and public functionaries, the army, the customs service (responsible for investigating financial crimes in general), the main publicly owned companies and even sectors of the magistracy itself. The equilibrium that had long characterized Italian politics was swept away. After forty-five years of uninterrupted government the country's largest single party, the DC, was eclipsed along with its leaders, accompanied by the other parties of the ruling coalition, the PSI included. Craxi was not alone in facing criminal charges. Both Forlani and Andreotti were also indicted, the latter for association with the Mafia. An idea of the sheer size of the investigation can be gleaned from the statistics for corruption and extortion accusations: between 1984 and 1991 the average ran at 252 cases a year involving 365 individuals; between 1992 and 1995 it increased to 1,095 cases involving 2,085 individuals. In the last of these years 1,065 accusations were made involving 2,731 persons.[1] Between 1992 and October 1996, the public prosecutors of Milan alone produced 2,319 requests for judicial action related to corruption crimes (Procura di Milano 1996) (see Figure 1.1).

In what follows, we will introduce our research based mainly on the results of those investigations. In the first part, we discuss the relationships between corruption and the crisis of democratic values, explaining also why we focus, although in a comparative perspective, on the Italian case. In the second part, we attempt to define and outline the main theoretical approaches to political corruption. In the third part, we present some methodological choices and summarize the contents of the volume.

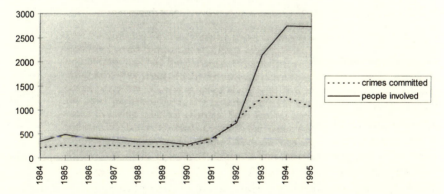

Figure 1.1. Official statistics on corruption in Italy, 1984–1995. Elaboration from ISTAT, Rome.

1.   CORRUPTION AND DEMOCRACY

1.1.   The Italian Case in Context

The speech by Craxi quoted above can be read as a dramatic admission of democracy's fragility in the face of corruption. It was made before the parliament of a democratic state governed by the rule of law. A democratic state, however, that both the magistracy and public opinion had come to suspect of systematically violating the law. Some commentators have compared this speech with that of Mussolini on January 3, 1925, in which he proudly proclaimed his "political, moral, and historical responsibility" for the murder of the Socialist deputy Giacomo Matteotti by a fascist gang in June 1924. Matteotti had condemned Fascist electoral fraud and violence and it was feared that he would make further revelations about the nascent regime's illegal activities. Comparisons between Craxi and Mussolini are not new. His autocratic disposition, arrogant self-confidence, and the "cult of personality" he fostered within his own party led some cartoonists to portray Craxi after the style of the dictator who ruled Italy from 1922 to 1943, black-shirted, his jaw jutting high and forward. The comparison between the two also reveals a more telling analogy, however: both speeches were symptoms of a serious crisis of the democratic regime. Mussolini's was made at a moment when the very survival of the democratic model was under serious challenge and it represented a decisive step toward the long and brutal dictatorship that Italy was later to experience. Craxi's speech was made in a very different context. The Berlin Wall had fallen and socialism in Eastern Europe had collapsed in 1992. Democracy was celebrating its global triumph. The Western political regime appeared both intrinsically superior and a universal model for political life.

Yet at the very moment of its triumph the democratic model is being convulsed by a series of perceived tensions. Western governing elites are facing a set of increasingly thorny problems: the decline of political participation; the crisis of the principle of electoral representation and of the traditional political parties; a growing lack of confidence among citizens in the functioning of the political system and in their political leaders; difficulties in controlling or influencing more complex economic processes; the crisis of the welfare state; the spiraling cost of political activity; and the questioning of "democratic values." Corruption is one of the most acute expressions of triumphant democracy's unresolved problems. At the same time, through its reverberations in an increasingly skeptical public opinion it has contributed to an awareness of the seriousness of these problems. By publicly admitting the generalized nature of corruption in political funding in his speech, Craxi was also confirming that the governing elite had both known about and participated in this ubiquitous illegality. The ceaseless scrambling for money dominated the day-to-day activities of many political leaders to such an extent that it is necessary to consider the corruption market in order to understand the real motivations behind public policy and action in Italy in recent decades.[2] In this sense corruption appears both a cause and an effect of the serious political crisis that beset Italian democracy in the early 1990s. Although certainly unique in the size of the phenomenon and its political repercussions, Italy is not an isolated case. Concern about the problem of corruption has emerged in an increasingly large number of countries in these years.

These processes of degeneration have caused a crisis in the dominant paradigm in both academic and political considerations of corruption. Until recently, in fact, corruption was presented as a phenomenon characteristic of developing countries,[3] authoritarian regimes,[4] or, at the outside, "Mediterranean" societies in which the value system favored clientelism, vertical relationships, or neopatrimonialism.[5] In such a context, according to the structural functionalist perspective, corruption has a number of positive functions: "greasing" bureaucratic and political mechanisms that would otherwise block development, modernizing the political system, lessening recourse to political violence, and favoring social integration and economic capital formation.[6] It follows that in more developed countries corruption should be marginal, caused by a few "black sheep" or a gap between restrictive laws and more permissive practices, and should have few serious consequences. In advanced democracies in particular, the media's function in informing and censuring, and the political control exercised by citizens should prevent corruption from exceeding certain physiological thresholds.

In recent years, however, the thesis of an inverse correlation between corruption and economic and political development (and therefore democratic "maturity") has been frequently and convincingly challenged. Countries with a long democratic tradition such as the United States, France, Belgium, and Great Britain have all experienced a combination of headline-grabbing scandals and smaller-scale cases of misappropriation.[7] Corruption increasingly appears a problem common to most if not all democracies. Popular control has proved ineffective and the perception that corruption, while concealed, is widespread has fueled a general distrust of and dissatisfaction with politics, public institutions, and the governing elite. The Transparency International's corruption index that ranked fifty-four countries according to the degree of diffusion of corrupt practices (see Figure 1.2) found that a number of democratic countries (among them Italy, Belgium, Spain, and Greece) were in the highly corrupt group of countries and that many others (France, Japan, Austria, and the United States, for example) were intermediate.[8]

Moreover, political corruption appears to be on the rise. This can be observed, for instance, looking at the patterns of the evolution of corruption practices in some of these countries, according to Transparency Inter-

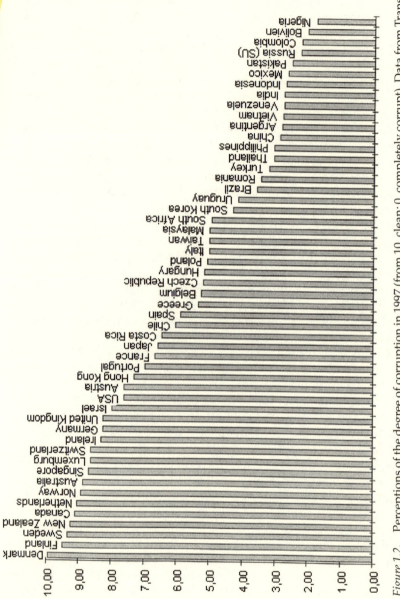

Figure 1.2.　Perceptions of the degree of corruption in 1997 (from 10, clean; 0, completely corrupt). Data from Transparency International and Göttingen University 1997)

Corruption ranking trends: 1980-1997

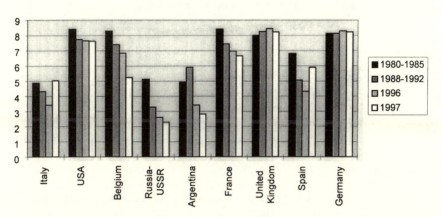

Figure 1.3. T.I. corruption ranking trends from 1980 to 1997 (from 10, clean; 0, completely corrupt).(Data: elaboration from Transparency International & the University of Göttingen 1997)

national rankings, as represented in Figure 1.3. It appears that corruption has increased—taking on new forms—rather than decreasing or being eradicated, insinuating itself into the increasingly complex relations between state and market, feeding off the changing needs created by new mechanisms of political consensus formation ("politics as spectacle") and the crisis of political activism, and taking advantage of new techniques of mediation and management of the financial resources for corruption.[9]

The recent democratization of Eastern Europe actually appears to have created an increase in corruption (e.g., Russia, Hungary), with many of them moving closer to the highly corrupt group. Also in Latin America (e.g., Brazil, Argentina, Chile) corruption has apparently increased its scope after the move toward democracy throughout the region, sometimes changing its features with the inclusion of private businesses as a new component in an old network of political clientelism (Little 1992; Rehren 1997). In relation to the democratic transition in Eastern Europe, Rose Ackerman notes that

> democracy and the free market are not invariably a cure for corruption. A shift from authoritarian to democratic rule does not necessarily reduce payoffs. Rather it redefines the country's norms of public behavior. A country that democratizes without also creating and enforcing laws governing conflict of interest, financial enrichment, and bribery, risks undermining its fragile new institutions through private wealth-seeking. A country that moves to

liberalize its economy without a similar reform of the state, risks creating severe pressures on officials to share in the new private wealth. (1996:365, see also 1994)

In addition, during transitions to democracy

> the newly prescribed rules are too complex to be enforced, and thus "ritualization" and re-interpretation in practice differs from what is written. Rituals and imitations of exemplars from modern countries are highly developed, but cultural patterns are based on friendship and family ties, not on rational choice and legal provisions. Actually, without re-interpretation, the state cannot function; thus, this is the way the society adapts the abstract proclamations to reality. (Kregar 1994:57)

In this situation, the very definition of corruption is the object of symbolic struggles that involve "conflicts over: the boundaries between public and private roles, institutions, and resources; the boundaries between state and society; the distinction between individual and collective interests and rights; the distinction between politics and the administration; and conflict over the proper extent and limits of market, bureaucratic, and patrimonial processes of allocation" (Johnston 1996:333).

The market approach that dominated in the eighties does not suffice to reduce political corruption. In fact, the very *privatization* of public enterprises produces occasions for corruption (Rose Ackerman 1996). Some characteristics of the new tendency toward a "light state"—such as the lack of training or guidelines in decentralized management or budgetary responsibilities, the opportunity offered by privatization and managerial discretion, the pressure for output-led performance, the development of a management culture within a public service context—may endanger public ethics. Concern has been expressed "to ensure that traditional public sector values are not neglected in the effort to maximize economy and efficiency" (Doig 1996:47–48). Moreover, market *globalization* increases the number of international transactions in which

> expedients that foster corruption are numerous: protectionist regulations that the exports seek to circumvent . . . in which political or administrative authorities are in a position to cash in; obligation when obtaining a contract to use the service of brokers who are too often concerned with creaming off a compulsory "commission," tied loans, obliging the recipient state to use these funds in the creditor country; intervention of the public authorities in the negotiation and conclusion of contracts, especially when supplier and client are themselves members of the public sector in their respective states. (Mény 1996:317)

The victory of the democratic political model on a world scale has been paralleled by that of the free market economic model. Although democracy and the market are often considered coessential, corruption is a symptom of subterranean friction between the two. Every state sets boundaries between *internal* and *external* power, the first derived from the legitimate exercise of legal authority, the second from control of market resources: "corruption is then defined as activity which tends to overstep or move the line " (Pizzorno 1992:14). What is corruption, after all, if not the application of market logic to relationships whose terms are fixed, according to democratic procedures, by public authority? However, the extension of the price system to legal procedures and rights is not only contrary to democratic values, it also obstructs the correct functioning of the market itself. As Arrow notes,

> [The] course of the law itself cannot be regarded as subject to the price system. The judges and police may indeed be paid, but the system itself would disappear if on each occasion they were to sell their services and decisions. Thus the definition of property rights based on the price system depends precisely on the lack of universality of private property and the price system. (Arrow 1972:357)

When the law, conflict resolution, the protection of rights, and all those other public goods that are a necessary complement to the market system themselves become the object of corrupt dealing and exchange, then that minimum of predictability and regularity that allows economic actors to profitably engage in their business is removed.

Further, corruption (to be found in any political system) undermines a number of democracy's fundamental principles. As Pizzorno notes, "corruption tends to act upon those conditions of political activity without which democracy is not democracy at all: the principle of transparency, and what might be called equality of political rights, equal access to the state for all citizens" (1992:17). Corruption is secret by definition and public decisions affected by it therefore violate the principle of transparency. As a result, corruption undermines the political control exercised by citizens, which "depends precisely on the greater or lesser extent to which the actions of the supreme power are offered to the public, are visible, knowable, accessible, and therefore controllable" (Bobbio 1980:186). Furthermore, the arbitrary decisions of corrupt agents produce inequality of access to the benefits of state action and "citizens will feel they count only insofar as they *know someone or can contact someone* who will render access to the machinery of state possible" (Pizzorno 1992:21, emphasis added).

As will become clear from our research, moreover (see particularly Chapters 2, 3, and 4), corruption tends to modify the nature as well as the outcome of the competition for votes that lies at the heart of the democratic process. It encourages the selection of politicians for their lack of scruples and the skill they display in reinvesting the resources accumulated through illegal activity: money, electoral support, trust, information, etc.

Money plays an increasingly important role in modern, postideological politics, and it is frequently the candidate with the most to spend on an electoral campaign rather than the one with the weightier political program who triumphs. Money from payoffs and illegal contributions can be employed in acquiring votes, thereby setting off an inflationary spiral that intensifies the financial pressures on *all* participants in the political contest, encourages recourse to corruption, and rewards those able to gain access to positions of power, which permit them to augment even further the resources they derive from corruption. For these reasons, corruption *in* a democracy is always the corruption *of* a democracy, something not true of other political systems.

The negative consequences of corruption are felt throughout society. As will be seen later (see particularly Chapters 5, 6, and 7), corruption gives rise to a whole succession of social costs. Some of these are easily amenable to direct measurement in economic terms, such as the inflated cost of public works and services, inefficient contractor selection, and the waste of those resources used in concealing illegal activities and obtaining political rents (or "rents" obtained through political decisions and protection). Besides these more easily measurable ones, corruption also has other long-term negative consequences. On the one hand, the spread of corruption within the public service introduces elements of inefficiency, where the primary purpose of an operation becomes the generation of payoffs. On the other, the confidence of those in an organization not directly involved in corruption is undermined, leading to generalized inefficiency. At the level of the political system as a whole, the spread of corruption erodes the support and trust of citizens in democracy, in public institutions in general, and in the political class in particular (Johnston 1986:142, 1982:172ff.). Italy, probably the country that has suffered the most widespread corruption in Europe, has regularly and easily topped the periodic comparative opinion polls conducted by Eurobarometer on levels of dissatisfaction with the functioning of the political system (see Figure 1.4).[10] Distrust, as predictable, increased with the beginning of the *mani pulite* investigations on corruption

An analysis of the dynamics of corruption (developed in Chapter 9 in particular) further indicates that this illegal activity feeds off itself: "the critical attitude towards the non-corrupt in a corrupt society is a main mechanism behind this snowball effect" (Elster 1989a:268). Where there is corruption the noncorrupt are led to collude with it, or at least accept it, in order to obtain political advantage. The generalization of such practices, and the very attempt to combat them through denunciations of the "climate of corruption" (Myrdal 1968:409), strengthens the idea that where so many others are doing so, it must be correct to engage in corruption. Corrupt agents deliberately introduce conditions of unpredictability and inefficiency into public affairs in order to facilitate corruption. These condi-

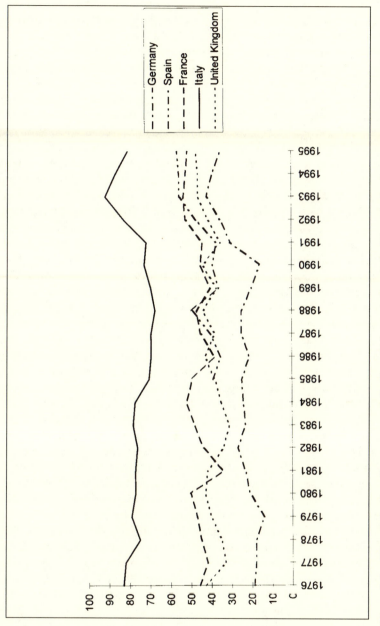

Legend:
- - - Germany
· · · · · Spain
– – – France
—— Italy
· · · · · · United Kingdom

Figure 1.4. Dissatisfaction ("not very satisfied" and "not at all satisfied") with the functioning of democracy. Elaboration from Eurobarometer trends, 1974–1995, Brussels.

tions then spontaneously reproduce because those initially hostile to such practices are excluded. Moreover, a "bad" collective reputation of public administrators creates "more incentives to engage in corrupt activities than if they had always behaved honestly," determining even for newcomers a vicious circle "where the new generations suffer from the original sin of their elders" (Tirole 1996:3). The more widespread the phenomenon becomes, naturally, the greater the economic and social costs shouldered by the entire community for the exclusive benefit of a small clique of corrupt individuals. As shown by the Italian case, corruption can become a pervasive phenomenon, multiplying its perverse effects and leading a country to a serious political, institutional, and economic crisis.

The multiplication of political scandals produced an increased sensitivity to the issue of corruption. In 1993, Transparency International, an international NGO, was created with the task of representing for the fight against corruption what Amnesty International has represented for the struggle against human rights violation. The basic assumption of Transparency International is that corruption is mainly exported from the "First World" to the developing countries. As its president warned: "Corruption has become one of the most devastating obstacles to economic and social development in the developing countries" (Eigen 1994:65). Multinational firms have been accused of spreading political corruption to the Third World, in particular "through the expectations of officials in the low corruption environment. If they are quick to learn that these firms know to bribe, and may pay you if you have some valuable information or decision-making power, their change in behavior may be rather sudden" (Andvig 1996:20). A number of international conferences—among others, seven International Anti-Corruption conferences and five Ethics in Public Services conferences—testify to the growing concern with political malpractice. The struggle against corruption was the main topic of the presidential opening speech at the IMF–World Bank Annual meeting and is under examination in such international bodies as G7, the European parliament, and the European Commission (Commissione delle Comunità Europee 1997). Recently, some countries, among them Great Britain, adopted a law similar to the U.S. Foreign Corruption Practices Act, which, approved in 1977, was subject to harsh attacks in the eighties (Rosenthal 1989). In 1996 the International Chamber of Commerce (ICC) adopted new rules of conduct on extortion and bribes in international transactions (ICC 1996). The following year the Organization for Economic Cooperation and Development (OECD) approved a Recommendation on Bribery in International Business Transactions, which calls on member countries to make the bribing of public officers a crime (OECD 1997).[11]

In our research, we used the Italian case to analyze those interlinked factors that influence the spread and characteristics of corruption in democratic regimes. Our focus on Italy is justified not only by the large dimension the phenomenon reached in this country, but also by its unparalleled public exposure thanks to the judicial inquiries. Besides denouncing what both media and politicians have come to describe as the crisis of the "First Italian Republic," such judicial inquiries provide in fact an enormous amount of material for the analysis of what can be defined—paraphrasing Bachrach and Baratz (1970)—as the "other face of power." Reviewing the information that has emerged from the *mani pulite* inquiry since 1992 and that slowly accumulated in earlier judicial inquiries, it is possible to reconstruct certain aspects of that "invisible" level of Italian politics that has had such an important influence on the "visible" one. The Italian case can therefore be considered as a sort of magnifying glass for the analysis of more general patterns of corruption in democratic systems. Notwithstanding this focus on a single national case, we will use the available scientific research on other democratic countries to develop cross-national comparisons.[12]

1.2. The Roots of Italian Corruption

The past fifty years of Italian history has been marked by numerous sensational scandals (Galli 1991; Turone 1992), through which corruption has been brought to light (only to be swiftly covered up again in many cases). The frequency and magnitude of these scandals has noticeably increased in the past twenty-five years, culminating in the recent political upheavals caused by the *mani pulite* corruption investigations, which have produced the deepest political crisis in the history of the Italian republic. The perception of widespread illegality in administration of public power by Italian bureaucrats and politicians has thus found significant confirmation. The exposure of what had been the "hidden face" of public power demonstrates that the market for corruption has, for many years, represented the determining factor for a vast range of (frequently illegal) activities based on the appropriation of public resources by state functionaries, a group of entrepreneurs benefiting from political protection, and actors from the criminal world.

As the scandal about the covert masonic lodge P2 (see Chapter 6) had already begun to reveal in the eighties, the concealed dimension of public activity, and corruption in particular, has exerted a crucial influence on public policy since the immediate postwar period. In the 1950s, relations with leading politicians and the higher echelons of the bureaucracy were monopolized by *Confindustria* (the industrial employers' association) and the electric companies, which generously financed pro-Western public exponents. A sort of competition to obtain a privileged position through corruption developed then between the private and public sectors of industry. Eugenio Cefis, former president of ENI (Ente Nazionale Idrocarburi, the public body responsible for industrial politics in the oil market), has since stated:

> It was decided after the war that the state-owned sector had to compete on
> an equal footing with the private sector. The private sector financed the polit-
> ical parties, and how! They even used the contributions we in the state sec-
> tor paid to *Confindustria*. You understand, they used our money to obtain
> decisions that favored them and damaged us. Were we supposed to just
> stand back and watch? (*L'Espresso*, 22 November 1991, p. 41)

Moreover, Italy's history presents the circumstance of a powerful monetary *input* originating abroad. Immediately following the war, Italy was
contested terrain between the two dominant world power blocs and it was
from them that the two principal Italian parties, the Christian Democrats
(Democrazia Cristiana, DC) and the Italian Communist Party (Partito
Comunista Italiano, PCI), took their political lead. Huge sums of money
arrived from both the United States and the Soviet Union to finance the
political life and electoral activities of the parties (Colby and Forbath
1981:86–87). The drying up of American subventions to the DC and the
advent of the center-left in the 1960s coincided with the beginnings of the
policy of large-scale nationalization and growing public intervention in
the economy. From then on, covert activities concentrated on this field of
public action, in which the curbs and controls on an administration geared
to the (often openly illegal) accumulation of political funding were
steadily being eroded. Their deposits abroad allowed the main parties to
develop strong and costly apparatuses, with a network of local headquarters, publications, and paid personnel, creating in this way economic
needs that could not be easily reabsorbed. Part of the budget of public entities therefore became the "property" of government exponents, who nominated their own men to the positions of command. In these years of
notable expansion in the area of public entrepreneurial activity, a bounti-
ful flow of bribes arrived from major public enterprises such as ENI and
IRI (Istituto per la Ricostruzione Industriale, the public body in charge of
industrial development). From its creation in 1952, ENI was a generous
financial benefactor of prominent political figures.[13] The paradoxical situation thus arose of public agents spending public money on other corrupt
public agents, to overcome the hidden influence of private entrepreneurs.
ENI in this way managed "to condition even the most prominent members
of the political class and to determine important governmental decisions
in internal and foreign policy, in exchange for substantial patronage of
government offices, political factions or members of parliament, Christian-Democrat or otherwise" (Perrone 1991:33).[14]

The concealed accumulation of financial resources for political activity
was intensified, then, through the (mal)administration of public power.
The "legitimation" for demanding (greater or lesser) kickbacks also
depended on electoral results, thus creating incentives to spare no financial effort in that area. With the early scandals concerning IRI's secret

funds, more caution was required in the utilization of public resources in the 1970s. *Confindustria* was becoming an increasingly articulated organization and was no longer capable of handling both relationships with the political world and the clandestine lobbying of the bureaucratic apparatus in a manner satisfactory to all enterprises. On the other hand, the exponential growth of politicians' financial needs—at the local level as well, following regional decentralization—demanded ever greater resources. Payoffs climbed to astronomical levels: from the 7 billion dollars transferred by the Banco Ambrosiano to a secret account of the PSI in 1981, to the 150 billion paid to principal government exponents in the early 1990s for the Enimont affair.[15]

To augment the flow of financial resources and diminish the risks, politicians entered directly into the running of public agencies, further extending their sphere of direct political control. Thus, according to Cefis, beginning in the 1970s "the new government philosophy [toward ENI] was to get deeply involved in its running (even intervening in the appointment of top managers) and not simply to provide general directives and effectuate the necessary controls" (*L'Espresso*, 6 June 1993, p. 68).[16] The system of bribes seems to have expanded dramatically between the end of the 1970s and beginning of the 1980s. According to the entrepreneur Vincenzo Lodigiani, the simultaneous presence of the various circumstances described above made it "necessary for the parties to open a direct 'line' with entrepreneurs who intended entering the world of public supply and contracting" (TNM:41). In this market for corruption the opposition too would sometimes be involved in covert bargaining, either in order to advance protected firms or occasionally, in more recent years, also to receive bribes. As a leading political administrator of DC in Milan, Maurizio Prada, observes: "The development, growth and rationalization of this system of illegal financing came at the moment the traditional ideological confrontation between the parties declined and the time of consociationalism began. . . . It became much easier to treat financing problems together" (PM:25). The system of corruption by this time had thoroughly infected every sector of the state, local, and central administrations, public agencies and enterprises, the military apparatus, and the bureaucracy, including the judicial power.

This clandestine political market created a structure of invisible norms more powerful than the laws of the state (see Chapter 9). The latter could be violated with impunity, while anyone who challenged the conventions of the illicit market would meet with certain punishment. Those occupying the principal public roles moved around easily within this pervasive system of hidden exchange, legislating and directing the affairs of the state and of public entities (della Porta 1992, 1996b). At the same time, they acted as guarantors for the functioning of the illegal market, which directed every public action of any economic importance. The careers of politicians and public functionaries depended on their ability to create networks of clandestine contacts and to invest the proceeds of corruption politically. On the other side of the market, citizens' and businessmen's lack of trust in the impartiality and efficiency of public action augmented the demand for purchasing favors. In these circumstances, the interests of all actors involved lay in accepting the status quo, receiving or paying bribes, rather than in denouncing corruption, despite the fact that some of them might be aware of the disastrous effects of such behavior on the collectivity.

2. A THEORETICAL MODEL FOR UNDERSTANDING POLITICAL CORRUPTION

2.1. What Is Corruption?

The term corruption has assumed different connotations in different historical periods. In a classic conception, political corruption indicated the degeneration of the political system in general: for Machiavelli, it was the destruction of citizens' virtues; for Montesquieu, the perversion of a good political order into an evil one; for Rousseau, the inevitable consequence of the very struggle for power. [17] Later, political corruption started to be considered a specific pathology rather than a general disease (Friederich 1972:135):

> [I]ronically, as the scope of politics has broadened, our conception of corruption has narrowed. Society has become secularized and fragmented; many, are seen more as arenas for contention among groups and interests than as embodying any coherent system of values; and ethical issues in politics revolve more around maintaining the fairness of that competition than around the pursuit of fundamental moral goals . . . "corruption" now refers to specific actions by specific individuals. (Johnston 1996:322)

In the modern sense of the word, the presence of corruption requires a limited power: "Modern conceptions of corruption are based on the idea of explicitly public roles endowed with limited powers and bound by impersonal obligations" (ibid.:327). Accordingly, corruption refers to the abuse of public resources for private gain, through a hidden transaction that involves the violation of some standards of behavior.[18]

To understand the logic of corruption, it is necessary to analyze the relationship existing in any organization between the *agent*, the person delegated to take decisions, and the *principal*, on whose behalf that agent acts.[19] There is corruption:

1. When there is a secret violation of a contract that, implicitly or explicitly, specifies a delegation of responsibility and the exercise of some discretionary power.

2. When an *agent* who, against the interests or preferences of the *principal*, acts in favor of a *third party*, from which he receives a reward.

A relation of this kind can exist even in the private sector, for example, between the manager and the stockholders of a company: When the manager sells secret information to a competing firm, we have an instance of *private* corruption. Focusing on political and bureaucratic corruption in a democratic regime, we should add a third element of the definition:

3. The principal is the state, or, better, the citizenry.

The functioning of a democratic government can in fact be conceived as a system of principal-agent relationships between electorate, elected officials, and bureaucrats.[20] The "contract" that public administrators stipulate with the state—and therefore with the citizens the state represents—imposes respect for certain rules restricting the discretionary power of the agent, universally adopted for limiting the potential conflict between the private interests of the agent and those of the principal (i.e., the public). We have a corrupt transaction when a public agent does not respect these rules because of the intervention of a third party, the corrupter.[21] The latter induces the public agent to surrender the resources connected to his role (decisional power, privileged information, protection) in order to obtain—or increasing his probability of obtaining—property rights upon a political rent. In exchange for these resources, the third party offers to the public agent a quote of the value of such political rent, typically in the form of a bribe. Corruption involves a violation, in favor of the corrupter, of the rules that should enforce respecting the principals' interest.

Behind every corrupt exchange there are then three subjects: principal, agent, and corrupter. As Johnston says, this approach "shifts the focus of analysis from individual actions judged against external (and, at times, static) standards to the significance of officials and clients' conduct within an institutional and political setting" (1996:326). In our analysis, although focusing on the relationship between public agent and third party in corrupt exchange, we will also address the consequences of those activities for the principal, that is, for the collectivity. Even with these specifications, the term *corruption* continues to be applied to a large variety of phenomena, and it is therefore necessary to distinguish between different types of corrupt exchange. As for the actors involved, bribery can implicate politicians or bureaucrats, at the local or at the national level. Moreover, the corrupt exercise of power can advantage subjects as different as an individual, a family, a group of friends, an ethnic group, an institution, or a political party. Also the resources exchanged can be various: the gain can be a direct or an indirect one, it can involve money but also other utilities or services, the exchange of commodities may be simultaneous or delayed, the value of the goods may differ. As for the structure of the corrupt exchange, it changes according to the degree of continuity and stability of the relationships, the number of actors involved, the role of protective agencies, and the presence or absence of extortion. The basis of loyalty that allows for the development of a corrupt exchange varies from personal friendship to party membership. The degree of deviation from the norms can be more or less serious, according to standards set both by the law and/or by public opinion.[22] In what follows, we will analyze the different types of corrupt transactions, from simpler ones to more complex networks of exchange in a "systemic corruption," when "the illicit becomes the norm and . . . corruption so common and institutionalized that those behaving illegally are rewarded and those continuing to accept the older norms penalized" (Caiden and Caiden 1977:306).

2.2. Theoretical Perspectives on Political Corruption

Since corruption is a deviation from norms that involves a hidden exchange between a public agent and a third party, a main question to be asked is, What causes, or allows for, differences in the diffusion of such deviation? Why do the degrees of corruption change in time and space? Explanations address different analytical levels. Together with the already mentioned functionalist approach, three main explanations for political corruption have recently developed:

1.   The first approach, sociological in nature, looks at differences in cultural traditions and values. The central focus is on the so-called moral cost, which reflects internalized beliefs, such as *esprit de corps*, the "public spiritedness" of public officials, political culture, and the public attitude toward illegality. We can define moral cost as the utility lost because of the illegality of an action; it therefore increases with the presence of a value system that supports a respect for law.[23] For an individual "the moral cost is lower the more ephemeral appear to him those circles of moral recognition that provided him with positive criteria for respect for the law" (Pizzorno 1992:46). An individual is going to suffer a higher cost when both in his own perspective and those of his peers corrupt behavior involves a violation of values—such as "public"—that are deeply internalized. From an interactionist perspective, motivations are a social construction, determined by the expectations of significant others and generalized expectations of society as a whole (Coleman 1987). Variations in moral costs can therefore explain the different responses of individuals to similar occasions for corruption: "[P]eople in a given society face the same institutions but may have different values" (Elster 1989a:39). In this perspective, Pareto noticed, "the differences [between countries] are to be found in the

substance, that is in the sentiment of the people; where they are more (or less) honest, there we find a more (or less) honest government" (Pareto 1916:625).[24] It is therefore possible that, given similar institutional conditions, the levels of political corruption will vary with the average moral attitudes among the citizens and the public administrators.

2. From an economic perspective, instead, an individual *rationally* opts for corruption when the institutional system of incentives and opportunities makes this activity subjectively satisfying: "A person commits an offense if the expected utility to him exceeds the utility he could get by using his time and other resources at other activities. Some persons become 'criminals,' therefore, not because their basic motivation differs from that of other persons, but because their benefits and costs differ" (Becker 1968:172). As with other behaviors involving deviation from laws and/or norms, individual decisions to participate in corrupt exchanges depend upon the probability of being discovered and punished, the severity of the potential punishment, and the expected rewards compared with the available alternatives. Political economists have singled out some factors that influence the individual calculus to participate in political corruption (Rose Ackerman 1978). There are the opportunities and incentives for corruption: those institutional forces determining the costs of political mediation; the ease with which new actors or groups can enter the system and the probability of electoral defeat; the overall level of state intervention in the economic and social fields; the degree of discretion involved in public acts; the relative efficiency of the various administrative and political controls; the forms of political competition; the types of market where corrupt exchanges develop. At the individual level, the more a politician needs money in order to obtain political power and the more an entrepreneur needs political protection, the higher will be the marginal value expected from corruption. Furthermore, the lower the probability of being denounced or buying a "lemon" from the partner, of being discovered and sanctioned by the judiciary power, and the lower the penalties for corruption, the less will be the expected costs of getting involved in illegal exchanges.[25]

3. The third approach is still based on rational choice, but in a game theoretical framework. From this perspective, the choice between corruption and noncorruption depends upon not only individual preferences and the institutional context, but also on the strategic interaction with the choices of other individuals. In fact, the more widespread is corruption, the lower the risks of being denounced for those who decide to engage in illegal practices, and the higher the price to be paid by those who try to remain honest and thereby get marginalized. The very diffusion of corruption reduces its moral costs: "[W]ell, if everybody seems corrupt, why shouldn't I be corrupt?" (Myrdal 1968:409).[26] The skills and information

concerning the most effective methods for creating relations of corruption accumulate with time, while the simple expectation that corruption is widely practiced induces a growing number of individuals to employ it. Vice versa, when corruption is marginal, the search for a reliable partner is a difficult one.[27] Relying on similar assumptions, game theorists indicate the possibility of multiple equilibria—with high and low densities of corruption—in the corrupt market.[28] Therefore, "people may have similar values, within and across societies, and similar institutional structures and yet, for accidental reasons, end up in different equilibria" (Elster 1989a:40). We can add that even differences in values among similar countries may be explained by the evolution of different social norms in equilibria, as virtuous or malicious parties tend to reinforce reciprocal (mis)trust, cooperation (or defection), (un)civic-mindedness, reciprocity, i.e., value systems that are more or less favorable to corrupt practices.[29]

Different hypotheses could be developed on the relative importance of institutional assets and cultural values on the actual density of corruption (Pizzorno 1992:42–43). Suffice it to say that the level of political corruption in a given country will be determined not only by the expected economic costs and benefits, but also by the distribution of moral costs in society, and that different possible equilibria may be determined by individual interrelated choices. In order to understand corrupt exchanges, we therefore have to look at the institutional and cultural constraints on violation of the contract between the public administrator (the agent) and the state (the principal). As we shall see in this volume, however, we have to look also at the production and reproduction of some additional resources that are necessary for the development of corrupt exchanges, among them trust, illegal skills, political protection, informal norms, and consensus. These resources bring down the cost of illegal exchanges, by reducing their material risks as well as their moral costs. In our analysis, we shall try to integrate sociological and economic models. Although this is not an easy task, we believe that only by considering these diverse sets of variables will we be able to improve our understanding of the complex functioning of the corruption market

2.3. The Structure of Corrupt Exchanges

In our approach, corruption is the result of a network of illegal exchanges. Sometimes corruption involves a simple exchange between two actors, a corrupter and a corrupt agent (or "the corrupted"), who derives some discretional power from his (implicit or explicit) contractual agreement with a principal (see Figure 1.5).

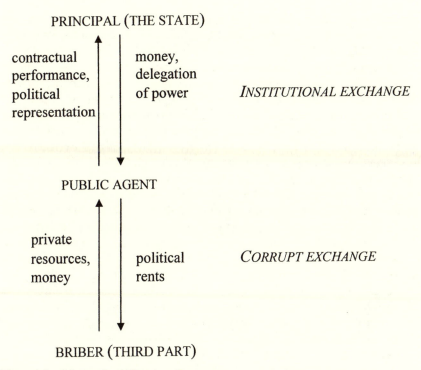

PRINCIPAL (THE STATE)

contractual performance, political representation | money, delegation of power | *INSTITUTIONAL EXCHANGE*

PUBLIC AGENT

private resources, money | political rents | *CORRUPT EXCHANGE*

BRIBER (THIRD PART)

Figure 1.5. Network of illegal exchanges.

As we are going to see, the relationship between the corrupted and the corrupter may sometimes be made easier by the intervention of a middle-man, while its repetition over time favors the formation of trust between parties. Where corruption is widespread it often involves groups of administrators and businessmen, who between themselves negotiate the size of the bribe and the public resolutions to be taken. On the one side, associations of public actors include various figures with different roles, whose coordination in reaching administrative decisions that can be exchanged for bribes is indispensable: particularly, we find public admin-istrators (both those in elected positions and those with party appoint-ments), career administrators and party functionaries. On the other side, cartels of businessmen reach agreements on a series of public decisions, which they must demand from the politicians: they collect money and hand it over to political cartels, who in turn offer them privileged access to the decisions and distribute the money between politicians. Often middle-men intervene to establish contacts between the two parties, to conduct the negotiations, and to transfer the bribe money. In this more complex web of exchanges, bonds of trust are established that allow the corrupt exchange to be brought to a conclusion. This structure of exchanges is shown in Figure 1.6.

Corrupt exchanges do not involve, however, only the public administrators and private entrepreneurs who directly participate in them, but also other actors, who although not directly taking part in the sharing out of the political rent, nevertheless obtain other favors in exchange for resources they control. If we look at Figure 1.6, for instance, we can notice that the corrupt politicians, in order to acquire decisional power, need the *consensus* of the voters, a consensus that they can obtain via clientelistic exchange. Moreover, the actors in the corrupt exchange need "cover-ups"; in other words, they must minimize the likelihood of being reported and investigated. With either threats or favors, the corrupt politicians must erect a wall of silence around their illicit dealings. They therefore exchange favors with a series of actors—the bureaucracy among them—who might otherwise jeopardize their illicit activities. Since trust is not always sufficient to enforce illegal agreement, and to avoid individuals exiting from the covert exchanges, *coercion* may be needed as an additional resource. Organized crime is therefore often an actor from whom corrupt politicians buy the resources of physical violence they need to punish "lemons," free-riders, or those who threaten to denounce the corrupt system (see Figure 1.7).

In our study, we will aim first of all at a "thick description" of corrupt exchanges, of the networks of actors involved in them, and of the resources they use. Our assumption is in fact that, in order to understand the causes and consequences of corruption, we need a clear picture of the

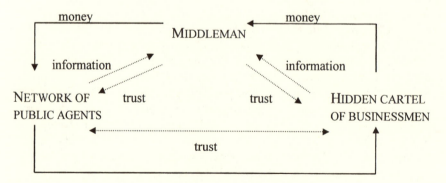

Figure 1.6. Complex web of exchanges involving middlemen.

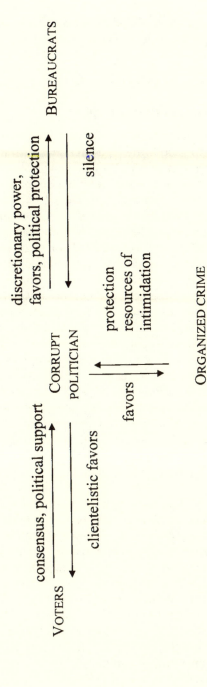

Figure 1.7. Role of organized crime in illegal exchanges involving corrupt politicians.

characteristics of the phenomenon—in other words, before we can investigate the "why" of corruption, we must know, in detail, the "how."

3.   HOW TO STUDY POLITICAL CORRUPTION

3.1.   Empirical Research on Political Corruption

In our research we aim at analyzing in greater detail the structure of corrupt exchange, by examining both the characteristics of the actors who
directly engage in it and the resources they exchange. But how do we
study corrupt exchanges? What are the potential sources of empirical
research on corruption? The construction of causal explanation about
political corruption is hampered by the difficulty of measuring the frequency of corrupt exchanges. As in any form of crime, the official statistics—based on police or judicial sources—include only the visible part of
the phenomenon. Not only therefore do they underestimate the amount of
corruption, but there is no reason to believe that the visible part of the ice-
berg is representative of the submerged part. On the contrary, it would be
safe to hypothesize that the distribution of the "discovered" corrupt
events and their characteristics are influenced both by the investigative
strategy of the state's repressive apparatuses, as well as by the degree of
tolerance for illegal activities among certain social groups, or within public opinion at large. These problems are even more serious for a crime that,
like corruption, often has no visible victims, while the potential risk for
those who denounce a corrupt action may become, as we will see, quite
high. Recent experiments with indexes of corruption based on experts'
perception of the phenomenon face serious criticism in terms of their reliability. This means that any attempt at building explanatory models of
political corruption would confront the difficulty of accurately measuring
the dependent variable.

If, however, we shift our concern from the causes to the mechanisms of
political corruption, judicial materials represent a very rich source. In
order to describe the dynamics of corrupt exchange, we made in fact abun-
dant use of the trial records, including interrogations and documents, of
about one hundred cases of political corruption, which occurred in Italy in
the eighties and the nineties. In sampling these cases we followed two criteria: (1) we included all the most important cases of political corruption
for which the preliminary sentence had already been passed; (2) we tried
to use examples of corruption in different geographical as well as administrative areas. Our cases are therefore a significant, although not representative sample of political corruption in Italy. To these judicial materials
we added those referring to four hundred requests for judicial action

against members of parliament (which arrived at the chamber between May 1992 and July 1993) for crimes such as corruption, corruption with extortion on the part of the public actor, violation of the law on party financing, and criminal and Mafia association. The judicial material was catalogued according to a coding scheme that included about ninety categories. The in-depth analysis of judicial materials was supplemented by the information retrieved from a ten-year press archive, formed of more than 2,500 articles from dailies and weeklies.

With the aim of controlling the "generalizability" of our cases we also analyzed the yearly reports from 1987 to 1992 of the *Corte dei conti* (the Audit Court) to the parliament; the acts of the three parliamentary committees on the masonic lodge P2, the Mafia, and reconstruction efforts after the earthquake in Irpinia; the acts of the Florentine city council committees formed to investigate misadministration in 1983; and the annual reports of the ombudsman for the Tuscany Region from 1991 to 1993. The introduction of these additional sources not only gave us the possibility of collecting new information, but it also allowed us to compare the functioning of different institutions for oversight of public administration.

Conscious of the limitations of all these sources, we supplemented them with about sixty semistructured interviews with experts from both the public and the private sector. Politicians, bureaucrats, entrepreneurs, trade unionists, and judges were among our informers on the dynamics and characteristics of corrupt exchange. Most of these interviews referred to in-depth case studies on the development of political corruption in three cities, chosen in order to be representative of different geographical and political contexts: Savona in northern Italy, Florence in the center, and Catania in the south.[30]

Prior to proceeding to our analysis, a methodological note is in order. Since some of the judicial proceedings have not yet concluded, our study relies upon very rich, but yet not complete documentation. Moreover, our firsthand descriptions of corrupt exchanges are often biased by individual defense strategies: thus, the entrepreneurs tend to present an image of corruption as the result of greedy politicians, while the latter accuse the former of distributing bribes in order to avoid market competition. As mentioned, we tried to reduce the shortcomings typical of our sources by triangulating the description of the different actors, and adding information coming from actors external to the corrupt exchanges. However, when reading the excerpts from our documents or interviews, keep in mind that they do not neatly mirror the reality, but represent its distorted image. A last observation: in reporting information from different sources we are not interested, of course, in individuals' penal responsibility; the statements referring to individuals involved in illegal action are therefore to be considered not so much as a judicially based truth, but more as wide-spread images about the dynamics of corruption.

3.2. The Structure of This Book

The book is organized around the analysis of the resources that are exchanged and of the different actors who take part in political corruption.

Business politicians, illegal brokers, protected entrepreneurs, and party-appointed bureaucrats exchange resources on the illegal market, altering the institutional system of interactions between the state and the market. As we are going to see in Chapter 2, by manipulating or violating the rules established to oversee the behavior of public agents, they are able to produce political rents, increasing the amount of money the state pays for a service, or reducing what the "protected" entrepreneurs have to pay to the state for a public service. The control of property rights on rents is thus exchanged with corrupters, through the exercise of power, reserved information, or political protection.

Chapter 3 describes the characteristics of an actor—the "business politician"—whose presence spreads with corruption. Corruption, in fact, operates on the motivations for choosing a political career, the "emergence" of political skills, and the aggregations among politicians. Using the additional resources they accumulate during corrupt exchanges, business politicians take over the control of political parties.

As we will argue in Chapter 4, the diffusion of political corruption is related to the characteristics of the principal collective actor of a political system: the party. In particular, corruption transforms the structure of the parties by creating and strengthening a "hidden" structure, organized around illegal activities, which tends to become more powerful than the visible party structure and bureaucracy. In this hidden side of politics, the parties assume an important function: they enforce corrupt exchanges by socializing the individual to illegal action, selecting the public decisions in which illicit rents are easier to produce, and acting as warrantor for the illegal transactions.

Corrupt agents intervene in the system of control of political corruption. Since incentives to corruption grow with the less probability that they will be discovered and punished, systematic corruption tends to destroy— as we will argue in Chapter 5—the functioning of the mechanisms of control internal to the state apparatuses (such as administrative bodies or the magistracy). In particular, the corrupt politicians, to avoid administrative controls, will try to involve public bureaucrats as well as magistrates in illegal exchange, paying for their connivance with political protection in their careers as well as a share of the bribes.

Together with the business politicians and political parties, other actors take part in corrupt exchanges, mediating between the corrupters and the corrupted. As we will see in Chapter 6, since corruption is a crime and corrupt transactions must therefore remain secret, at least to the public and the police, those acting as mediators have to possess particular skills in illegality. Brokers in the corrupt market trade privileged information when occasions for illegal exchanges arise and when people are available to participate in them. This privileged information is often exchanged inside hidden networks—for instance, deviant masonic lodges—which foster the development of bonds of loyalty between the various actors taking part in political corruption.

Corrupt exchanges, of course, also involve private actors, mainly entrepreneurs, since they often have stronger interest in public decisions and more resources to influence them. While entrepreneurs usually present themselves as victims of politicians, in most of the cases—as we will state in Chapter 7—they also derive advantages from illegal activities. With different strategies, entrepreneurs who work in the public sector try to ensure political protection—which they can either buy each time they come in contact with a public administrator, or try to gain on a more continuous basis. In both cases, political protection produces in fact political rents, from which the bribes are taken.

Moreover, being illegal, corrupt and collusive exchanges find favorable conditions where the use of force is not under the monopolistic control of the state. Where organized crime is strong and deep rooted, it provides corrupt politicians with resources of violence that can be used to enforce the illegal pacts. As will emerge in Chapter 8, organized crime and corrupt politicians are linked to each others by a pact of reciprocal protection: while the mafiosi offer (the threat of) violence and electoral support, the politicians reward them with public resources (such as public contracts) and protection against the investigative state apparatuses.

As we are going to discuss in the concluding chapter, there is a vicious circle in the interaction between corruption and other political pathologies (such as inefficiency, clientelism, and the political protection of organize crime), in which each of them facilitates the development of the other. The result is a progressive erosion of both material public resources and symbolic political resources, (legitimization) which may end up—as happened in the Italian case—in the breakdown of the regime.

NOTES

1.   As these statistics signal, the number of people involved in political corruption grew more than proportionally to the number of cases, revealing the existence of more complex networks of corrupt exchanges. By December 1993, four hundred judges (i.e., about 5% of the Italian judges) had participated in the investigations on political corruption (Nelken 1996b:111).

2. As Scott notes, if "the study of corruption teaches us anything at all, it teaches us not to take the political system or a particular regime at its face value. . . . Here coalitions that could not survive the light of day, government decisions that would set off a public outcry, elite behavior that would destroy many a political career are located. . . . For most nations at some point in their history, and for many nations today, however, the surreptitious politics of this arena is so decisive that an analysis which ignored it would be not simply inaccurate but completely misleading" (1972:2).

3. On corruption in LDCs (less developed countries) see, among others, Bayley (1966), Waterbury (1973, 1976), Somjee (1974), LeVine (1975), Beenstock (1979), Epko (1979), Gould (1980), Médard (1982), Wade (1982, 1985), Gould and Amaro-Reyes (1983), Ward (1989), and Wilson (1991).

4. There are a number of theoretical works dealing with corruption in socialist systems. See, for example, Kramer (1977), Schwartz (1979), Simis (1982), Montias and Rose Ackerman (1980), Liu (1989), and Harris (1989). Sands (1990) offers a pessimistic perspective on the short-run effects of economic reforms on bureaucratic corruption in China.

5. This is the case with the concept of "amoral familism," which Banfield used to describe certain characteristics of the value system dominant in Italy, and the South in particular: "In a society of amoral familists, the claim of a person or institution to be inspired by zeal for the public rather than private advantage will be regarded as a fraud" (Banfield 1958:95).

6. Suggested by Huntington (1968), Merton (1957, 1972), Leff (1964), and Nye (1967), among others, and in a number of recent economic analyses, e.g., Beck and Maher (1986) and Lien (1986). For critical reviews, see Ben-Dor (1974) and, more recently, Cartier-Bresson (1997b, in particular 52–55).

7. A survey of seven democratic countries can be found in della Porta and Mény (1997a). See also Little and Posada-Carbò (1996), Ridley and Doig (1995), Levi and Nelken (1996), and Bakker and Shulte Nordholt (1996). A study of the evolution of corruption in Israel indicates that illegal practices have adapted to economic and political modernization (Werner 1989). Political scandals have also taken place in countries traditionally considered as having low levels of corruption. To give only one example, in Great Britain two government ministers have been forced to resign in the past ten years after accusations of using their parliamentary office for private gain.

8. This attempt to produce a global comparative measure of corruption is based on ten different surveys that collected information from businessmen, risk analysts, journalists, and the general public. It is not immune to criticism, however, being based on data far from homogeneous in nature and relating mainly to international commerce. A discussion of the general issues involved in the measurement of corruption can be found in Malec and Gardiner (1987).

9. An increasingly common form of corruption is described by Thompson (1993) as mediated corruption, mediated, that is, by the democratic political process. It differs from conventional corruption because (a) the gain the politician receives is political, not personal and illegitimate in itself; (b) the way in which the benefit is provided by the public official (not the benefit in itself) is improper; (c)

the democratic process is damaged by the connection between the gain of the politician and the benefit of the private actor.

10.   As Heidenheimer notes, "the deep-rootedness of corruption in the Italian political system is a by-product of the lack of trust among its citizens and between citizens and the state" (1996:339).

11.   In this context, however, countries may themselves face a "prisoner's dilemma." Even if everybody prefers a situation with no international corruption to one of generalized corruption, the situation is more favorable for a country that, as opposed to the others, does not prohibit foreign corrupt practices, thus providing its enterprises with a competitive advantage. And even if all governments adopt restrictive laws, a similar prisoner's dilemma may apply to the implementation of the norms. For this reason, international supervising agencies may be indispensable for the fight against international corruption.

12.   Concentrating our attention on democratic countries, we will be able to keep a series of variables related with the political system and the level of modernization constant (Lijphart 1975; Sartori 1979). On the problems of comparative analysis of political corruption, see Scott (1972).

13.   Eugenio Cefis, who succeeded ENI's first president, Enrico Mattei (killed in a suspicious air accident in 1962), recalls that the latter "said more than once that before giving money to the parties, they should ask three times for it, and then only 25–35 percent of the sum demanded should be paid. In Mattei's philosophy, moreover, the payoff had to be proportional to the benefits derived by ENI" (*L'Espresso*, 6 June 1993, p. 68).

14.   A competition developed between the different parties to gain control of that money. As the former secretary of the Socialist party, Giacomo Mancini, recalls: "I realized that the bosses of the publicly controlled firms mistreated us in comparison with the DC. I quarreled with the president and the general director of IRI . . . which had offered a ridiculous amount of money, and eventually I succeeded in obtaining a total of 300–400 million lira" (*La Repubblica*, 20–21 August 1992, p. 7).

15.   In 1991 the public company ENI—for 4,200 billion lira—bought back shares of the chemical company Enimont, which had been previously created by the merger of the two leading public and private chemical companies. The decision to nationalize the Italian chemical industry was taken on very favorable terms for the private partner Montedison, guided by its manager Raul Gardini: ENI paid 1,650 lira per share, although the average market value was 1,374 lira. By way of compensation, Gardini (who committed suicide in 1994, as the scandal emerged) paid bribes totaling 150 billion lira to all the principal political leaders and parties in the ruling coalition.

16.   This strategy bore its fruits: ENI's financial director, Florio Fiorini, has admitted paying 10 billion dollars per month to the four principal government parties between 1970 and 1980, for a total of 1,500 billion lira (*La Repubblica*, 17 February 1993, p. 2).

17.   Different insights about the "corruption of the body politic" in Thucydides, Plato, Aristotle, Machiavelli, and Rousseau are presented in a unified framework in Dobel (1978).

18. Similar definitions have been proposed by Key (1936), Huntington (1968:59), Benson, Maaren, and Heslop (1978:xiii), and Nas, Price, and Weber (1986:108). Corruption has been characterized as a behavior that deviates from the public interest (Rogow and Lasswell 1966), from legal norms (Nye 1967), or from some other publicly sanctioned moral standards or norms (Berg, Hahn, and Schmidhauser 1976). According to Philp (1997), any definition of corruption pre-supposes an implicit notion of noncorrupt politics, and this implies normative judgments about the proper scope of politics. The meaning and mechanisms of corruption may then vary with the nature of the political system, making compar-ative analysis more problematic. For reviews of social science literature on politi-cal corruption, see Deysine (1980), Clarke (1983), Benson and Baden (1985), Belligni (1987), Andvig (1991), della Porta and Mény (1997b), and Cartier-Bresson (1997a). For a wide collection of essays on this topic see Heidenheimer (1970a) and Hei-denheimer, Johnston, and LeVine (1989).

19. More generally, we have a principal-agent relationship when there is an asymmetric distribution of information between two (or more) contracting parties, prior or subsequent to their agreement: "The *principal* (or *uninformed player*) is the player who has the coarser information partition. The *agent* (or *informed player*) is the player who has the finer information partition" (Rasmusen 1990:134).

20. Among those who have studied corruption as a violation of a contract between an agent and a principal are Banfield (1975), Rose Ackerman (1975, 1978), Klitgaard (1988), Pizzorno (1992), Franzini (1993), and Groenendijk (1996).

21. If there is general agreement on considering corruption as an abuse of pub-lic roles, it is much less clear where the boundaries of the concept should lie (Gar-diner 1993). Of course, there could be uncertainty, when the principal is collective as in democratic politics, in the definition of the principal's preferences. Could not the public interest be better served by corrupt practices than by respect for ineffi-cient procedures? On the other hand, the norms that rule the behavior of public agents—particularly those which prohibit accepting bribes—are based on the assumption that, when the agent violates them, there is a strong risk that this will endanger the general interest. As Markovits and Silverstein observe, "Liberal democracies seek both to ensure the separation of the private and the public realms and to overcome (or hide) their ambiguity over the use of political power. . . . The liberal's inherent distrust in political power is lessened by a political process defined by strict rules, procedures and public scrutiny. . . . To the liberal, the process *is* the public interest" (1988:6). The liberal faith in rules as limits to power, however, may conflict with the democratic justification of political activities that, in order to achieve general ends of equality or social welfare, may lead to an increase of political power, with its exclusive, secretive, and potentially corruptive implications (Cubeddu 1994).

22. As Heidenheimer (1970b) observes, it is more difficult to suppress the phe-nomenon when the judgments about corruption expressed in society and in the political system do not coincide. See also Padioleau (1975).

23. Rose Ackerman (1978) considers moral cost as a kind of fixed cost that derives from breaking the law, while Johnson (1975) and Alam (1990) employ the similar concept of "aversion to corruption." Economists assume moral cost as given and consider economic incentives and opportunities for corruption; we think

instead than it can be seen as the expression of an agent's *preference for legality,* and that it may vary over time and for different groups. Qizilbash (1994) presents a model of "moral character" using a formal definition of temptation to describe agents that can be continent or incontinent, so influencing their corruption choices.

24. At a descriptive level, some elements of particular ("not civic") culture have been considered as constituting a favorable background for the diffusion of Mafia, corruption, and clientelism: "amoral familism" and emphasis on instrumental friendship are among them (for instance, Banfield 1958). These explanations have been used in particular for Third World countries as well as Southern European democracies. The risks of these cultural explanations are hypersimplification and self-referentiality (Heywood 1997; Magatti 1996). In our explanation, we will in fact try to go beyond the stereotype referring to specific cultures, trying to analyze the social and political characteristics that interact with the development of some value systems.

25. Goel and Rich (1989) demonstrated the importance of these "economic" variables to explain changes in the observed levels of corruption.

26. It should be remembered that these different sets of variables—moral costs of and economic incentives for corruption—are not independent. As illegality becomes common practice, the codes of behavior condemning corruption may be weakened by the adoption of a "situational morality" (Chibnall and Saunders 1977:151). Moral costs may be considered the expression of "moral conventions": beliefs in certain general principles (such as trust in others or respect for the law) accompanied by the expectation that they are recognized and shared by (at least large number of) others. These conventions will be stable, forming an equilibrium only where their social consequences—the sum of the resulting actions—are compatible with the expectations that shape them. Otherwise, if the actual results do not match expectations, the adaptation of the latter may bring about a change in the conventions themselves. If moral adversion to corruption is conditioned by the (more or less corrupt) behavior of others, the expectation that corruption is widely practiced becomes self-fulfilling, not simply as a result of rational calculation, but also because the moral barriers to that activity are lowered as processes of self-legitimation come into operation (Hirschman 1982).

27. As Andvig noted, in fact, "One of the major reasons why corruption frequency stays low, when it is low, is the transaction cost involved if one attempts to bribe in a society where bribing is rare. Think of a situation when the developer knows that only one of hundred officials is likely to ask for a bribe. If he then offers a bribe he would have to expect a long search to find one to bribe. Given the expected search costs, it will not pay to offer a bribe. Looking at the other side of the market: if only one of hundred developers is willing to bribe you, why then ask for it? In this case only one of 10,000 meetings between officials and businessmen is likely to give rise to a bribe" (1996:18).

28. Multiple equilibria refer to the amount of the bribes (Cadot 1987), the number of corrupt exchanges (Lui 1986), or both (Andvig and Moene 1990). Murphy, Shleifer, and Vishny (1993) single out a model of multiple equilibria in levels of corruption and income.

29. The same applies to similar regions within the same country, such as North and South in Italy, according to Putnam's (1993) analysis of comparative civic-

mindedness. In other words, there may be multiple equilibria in models of social customs, which can persist even if disadvantageous to the individual—being rationally accepted—when there is a loss of reputation for disobedience: "In one of these equilibria the custom is obeyed, and the values underlying the custom are widely subscribed to by members of the community. In the other equilibrium the custom has disappeared, no one believes in the values underlying it, and it is not obeyed" (Akerlof 1980:751).

30.   For more information on these interviews, see della Porta (1992:Chapter 2).

2

The Resources of Corruption

The Municipal Transport Company (ATM) is Milan's largest publicly owned concern and second only to the city local government itself in the number of people it employs. Operating in the urban transport sector, it has a work force of 11,700, a turnover of 1,100 billion lira and a deficit of 186 billion lira. In October 1986, Customs Service telephone interceptions relating to an entirely different matter recorded a suspicious conversation between one of the company's functionaries and an entrepreneur. Further telephone interceptions produced proof that led to the arrest of five of the company's leading managers in October 1989. A small notebook recording corrupt transactions was subsequently found during a search of one of the managers' homes. Bribes had been paid on every small-scale contract for supplying the company over a fifteen-year period (in all more than two thousand contracts). Uniforms, brushes, badges, mats, toilet paper, seat covers: the contractors paid bribes on everything the ATM bought. The payoff ranged from 2 to 10 percent depending on the sector involved and the entity of the contract. A total of more than 5 billion lira was paid in bribes.

In the whole fifteen-year period not a single denunciation or hint of internal controversy had disturbed the well-oiled machinery of corrupt exchange. Those bureaucrats whose position meant that they would inevitably become aware of the corruption of others were gradually brought within the system. A careful and precise division of the proceeds of corruption existed,"each person being due a predetermined percentage. . . . Calculations were precise to a ridiculous extent. Even a handful of lira would be shared out" (TAM:82). A high degree of reciprocal trust regarding fulfillment of promises and payment of "debts" was demonstrated by the fact that these illegal funds were deposited in a common pool prior to distribution. This was confirmed by "the existence of accounts for 'ongoing situations,' demonstrating that the original undertakings persisted over time and could wait before being fulfilled".

The company managers—who were politically appointed—appeared helpless in the face of this vast and organized system of corruption. In reality, as the mani pulite *investigations a few years later would make clear, they were party to it. The president of the ATM, Maurizio Prada, a Christian Democrat, Sergio Radaelli, a Socialist and former vice-president, Giacomo Properzij, Christian Democrat and former president, and a number of other administrators and entrepreneurs were arrested in May 1992. It was discovered that while bribes on contracts under 100 million lira went to the functionaries, the politicians took a percentage on contracts above that amount. Once again, the division of the proceeds was carefully and precisely regulated. Between 1980 and 1991 more than 30 billion lira was channeled into the party system from companies that supplied the ATM. Radaelli stated that "an agreement for dividing such payments existed between the various parties in Milan on the basis of which 25–27 percent was due to the Socialist Party. . . . He kept the PSI's share and passed the rest on to Prada to be shared out among the other parties"*: 25 percent to the DC, 25 percent to the PCI, and 12.5 percent each to the PSDI and the PRI (CD, no. 6, p. 10).

The politicians who managed the ATM transferred some of the money they received in bribes to their parties or, as the price for protection of their careers, to the political bosses who could influence nominations to the offices they held. Prada admitted paying over a third of his share of proceeds from bribery, formally due to the Christian Democrats, to the Socialist party for precisely this reason: *"I found myself in an awkward position when, shortly after assuming the presidency of the ATM there was a change in the ruling group on the municipal council. I found myself in a minority position and had to guarantee support by using this means as well"* (L'Espresso, 21 June 1992, p. 25).

The entrepreneurs who paid bribes in their relations with the ATM received a number of resources in return: *"information on the names of competitors . . . for each contract"; "information on the prices submitted by them so that they knew how much to bid on any occasion"; "inclusion in the list of suppliers of a particular product known to and favored by the company, facilitating the establishment of contacts and the reaching of agreement"; "absence of any checks on the consignment of the materials"*; in short, *"the bribes paid to functionaries constituted the money price for help in winning the contract"* (TAM:87–89). On some occasions corruption was used to guarantee the stability of cartel agreements between the firms participating in public tenders, tenders being awarded to each firm in rotation. The ATM's corrupt functionaries also offered protection against the vagaries and inefficiency of the public bureaucracy in return for payment of a bribe, *"preparing the orders and other such obligations, and generally making a whole series of unavoidable bureaucratic procedures easier for the corrupter "* (TAM:95).

The politicians who managed the ATM also provided services to guarantee success in public tendering or protection against the snares associated with the public bureaucracy's inefficiency. One entrepreneur stated that having *"received an order from the ATM I was called by Gianstefano Frigerio, the DC's local political secretary. . . . He informed me that a cash donation to the party he represented would be opportune. At first I refused . . . but then realized that if I dug my heels in there could be repercussions, particularly as far as payment was concerned"* (TM:81). In some cases bribery became a kind of *"insurance policy"* in relations with the public administration. An entrepreneur claimed that he had paid 800 million lira to Prada and Radaelli, *"as the representatives of the corrupt political system," "to be able to get on with the work in peace and avoid unnecessary delays in payment"* (CD, no. 6, p. 10). Another entrepreneur recalled: *"We realized that we needed political-entrepreneurial protection to have any chance of finishing the work successfully, to avoid pretexts for obstruction and delay. . . . I tried therefore to identify the leading representatives of the political system . . . realizing that this was the only way to ensure a certain amount of tranquillity to see the project through"* (TM:143).

As the case of ATM in Milan illustrates, corruption networks may become very complex and widespread.[1] Can a rational motivation be found behind such a generalized participation in the corruption system? Any individual who participates voluntarily in a market exchange obtains a gain equal to the difference between the value attached to the "commodity" received and that relinquished. On the other hand, as Coase (1937) first stressed, we have to consider the costs that are unavoidably connected with the performance of any transaction, as for instance in the negotiation of an agreement and in its realization.[2] Where the value of this surplus exceeds the transaction cost for both parties, it can be expected that the exchange will take place to their mutual satisfaction, other circumstances permitting. The same logic applies also to exchanges taking place in the corruption market, but this presents some peculiarities. First of all, transaction costs are usually higher than in legal markets (Bardhan 1997:1324). Such activities as the search for a counterpart, the negotiation of an agreement, the exchange of "goods," and the implementation of the agreement are extremely expensive since they involve two risks: an *external* one, such as being denounced or being discovered by control agencies; and an *internal* one, such as being cheated by the counterpart without the possibility of resorting to a legal protective agency. The second characteristic is that the corrupt agent does not invest his own resources, but resources belonging to the public body of which he is part. Instead of using these resources according to the rules, the corrupt agent exercises an informal property right on these resources, selling them as if they were his property.[3] In this chapter we will look more closely at the areas of public intervention where occasions of corruption may emerge. Then we will analyze "commodities" that flow from the public to the private sector (influence over decisions, information, protection) and vice versa (bribes, influence on mass media, patronage favors). We will finally look at some of the resources that, as "inputs" in a productive process, are required by corrupt agents in order to initiate and successfully conclude hidden exchanges.

1. CORRUPTION AS A MARKET FOR POLITICAL RENTS

Corruption may be related to a market for political rent where property rights are exchanged. In general terms, "property rights of individuals over assets consist of the right, or the power, to consume, obtain income from, and alienate these assets. . . . The rights people have over assets . . . are not a constant; they are a function of their own direct efforts at protection, of other people's capture attempts, and of government protection" (Barzel 1989:2).[4] Actually, "governments operate by assigning, reassigning, modifying, or attenuating property rights" (Benson and Baden 1985:392). State activity, like market exchanges, modifies the structure of property rights. Transactions in markets, if voluntary, advantage all the parties involved, although in different measure according to the degree of competition in the market and the related bargaining power. The modification of property rights imposed by state coercive power might instead be disadvantageous, or more or less favorable for private parties, depending not only on impartial procedures, but also on the discretionary choices of public agents. Potential corrupters are interested in those public decisions that assign benefits or impose costs; in other words, those decisions that modify to their advantage the system of *property rights* to resources administered by the state—or subject to state regulation—through the activity of its bureaucrats or political representatives. The difference between the value assigned by private parties to such resources and what the state's bureaucrats or representatives effectively pay (or receive) in order to acquire (or to release) property rights on them is, in economic terms, a *rent*. We will call it *political rent* when it is created through the use of political power.

For example, both control of public spending and the right to license (permitting or not the exercise of certain private sector activities) produce restrictions in access to public benefits and the enjoyment of private resources, thus creating conditions of scarcity politically. The state then produces opportunities for obtaining such scarce property rights, which are assigned to citizens on the basis of decisions and procedures controlled by public agents. Just like market-produced resources, these represent a legitimate source of enrichment. People thus have an incentive to influence to their advantage this discretionary allocation of rights on political rents—even through corruption.

Rose Ackerman (1978:61–63) distinguishes three general areas of public intervention that are vulnerable to corruption:

1. *Private provision of goods and services required by the state.*   In this case the political rent is created by the decision of the state to pay more for private resources than their value for the seller in the most remunerative alternative use. The rent, which is equal to this difference, is then partly given as kickback to the public agent who has influenced the favorable decision. Tenders for goods and services by the state or public bodies, paid above the current market price, can be included in this category.

2. *The sale or distribution of goods and services administered, produced, or previously owned by the state.*   The political rent is created by the state accepting *less* for the property or resources than the private purchaser or recipient would be willing to pay. In this case, too, the rent is equal to the difference in value, and part of it is assigned to the corrupt agent. The sale of publicly owned goods for less than the market price or the granting of concessions and licenses that guarantee a particular profit can be considered here. In certain cases, such as an urban planning program that increases the value of a particular piece of real estate, the public measure

adopted should be inspired by the general interest, and should not foresee any payment in exchange: for the owner of the land the entire increase in value represents then a political rent.

3. *The imposition of sanctions or decisions creating costs.* The political rent in this third case comes from the power to escape punishment or costs and is equal to the anticipated loss for the private interest (i.e., the maximum he is willing to pay in order to avoid it). Governments can impose costs on private parties by the legal expropriation of profits created in the market:

> "In order to protect these returns, private owners have an incentive to strike bargains with legislators, as long as the side payments to politicians are lower than the expected losses from compliance with the threatened law. (The payments need not be bribes; they might be contributions for political campaigns or in-kind donations of services and property, for example.) A politician thus can gain by forbearing—for a price—from exercising his right to impose costs on private actors that would reduce rents from capital they have created or invested themselves" (McChesney 1987:103).

Obviously, officials who have the power to uncover and sanction actions that violate existing regulations can also threaten such a loss. There can be an exchange between the right (or power) of the agent (not) to impose the cost—following the state's procedures—and the property right of the corrupter on the part of the rent that is saved. This is the case of a customs official, for example, who overlooks fiscal irregularities, thus allowing the guilty party to avoid paying the fine anticipated by the law.

Corruption is then connected with the *exchange of property rights to rents created through the political process*: "Corruption is actually just a black market for the property rights over which politicians and bureaucrats have allocative power. Rather than assigning right according to political power, rights are sold to the highest bidder" (Benson 1990:159; see also Jagannathan 1986). As one entrepreneur declared, "In essence, businesses asked politicians to help them to obtain work and the politicians asked a sum of money in return" (CD, 18 May 1993, no. 366, p. 7). In this perspective:

1. Behind every act of corruption lies either a modification of the structure of property rights to particular resources (imposed and guaranteed by the state) to the advantage of the corrupter, or of its maintenance notwithstanding a legal obligation or a power to alter it in a way unfavorable to him.

2. By means of a hidden transaction, corrupter and corrupted share property rights to the political rent thus created. The corrupted official in fact obtains a part of that rent in return for his services, which aim to guarantee (or at least increase the chances of) the granting of those property rights, usually in the form of a bribe.

All else being equal, the greater the resources that pass through the hands of politicians or functionaries, the greater the opportunities for corruption:

> the greater government interference in private matters the greater will be its use and abuse; the more the material to be exploited the more that can be generated from it. . . . The governing class appropriates the property of others not only for its own use but also to give a part to those of the governed who ensure its power with both arms and cunning; with the help that a client provides a patron. (Pareto 1916:635–36)

A positive correlation between corruption and the size of government (measured by public spending) emerges from one recent analysis of the United States (Goel and Nelson 1996).[5] However, the magnitude of public intervention is not the sole factor influencing the spread of corruption. There are cases, such as the Scandinavian countries, where large-scale public intervention in the economy and society is accompanied by low levels of corruption, according to Transparency International rankings.

Actually any system of public decision-making can create opportunities for corruption, since it alters the structure of property rights. This can occur just as easily in a state that reduces the extent of its activities (even in one that limits itself to mere regulation or prohibition of certain behaviors) as in one that expands it. Rose Ackerman notes, for example, that "[c]orruption originates from the forms of monopolistic power created in the state apparatuses by both an excess or a lack of regulation" (1994:67). Individuals may resort to corruption to obviate the effects of a weak state or underdeveloped market, seeking protection from politicians and functionaries whose degree of autonomy is increased by the uncertainty or absence of rules. The *collapse* of the state, or its *abandonment* of certain areas of activity may also fuel corruption through a weakening of controls and the creation of uncertainty over private property rights. The process of restoring private property in the former Soviet Union and in the other socialist-bloc countries has led to numerous cases of misappropriation (Kaufmann and Siegelbaum 1997; Mendras 1997; Warszawski 1993; Popescu-Birlan 1994), as did the privatization and market deregulation processes in Western Europe or in Latin America (Manzetti and Blake 1996; Saba and Manzetti 1997), where the divestiture of government-owned assets created occasions for corruption involving high-ranking government officials.[6] The present section has suggested that opportunities for corruption arise from the various forms of public activity that create rents; these are present (although to differing degrees) in any state, whether it is laissez-faire or interventionist. Corruption can also be present in market relations wherever the distribution of information between the contracting parties is asymmetrical.[7] The idea that corruption can be defeated by the state withdrawing in favor of the market may thus prove illusory:

> While it is true that *perfect* competition in *all* markets will prevent corruption, deregulation will almost never lead to the resumption of a market resembling the competitive paradigm. Indeed, many of the market failures that justify government intervention are the very same conditions that generate corruption in the absence of intervention. Thus scale economies, externalities, and products which are unique or of uncertain quality all create incentives for employees to enrich themselves at company expense. Deregulation may simply mean the substitution of a corrupt private official for a corrupt public one. It is not at all obvious that this is an achievement. (Rose-Ackerman 1978, p. 207)

Moreover, while neoliberals claim that excessive state presence is responsible for the contemporary explosion of corruption, for others deregulation and "virulent attacks on state intervention, the welfare state, and the bureaucracy" have lowered the moral costs of corruption by blurring the "lines of distinction between collective and individual interest and between the public and private spheres" (Mény 1996:315).

It is not just the *extent* of property rights in political rents that is important, but also *how* they are assigned. The more *predictable* the identity of future beneficiaries of public decisions, the greater the convenience of corruption. Thus, if an impartial procedure (drawing lots, for example) is used to assign such rights rather than a discretionary decision there will be weaker incentive for corruption.[8] In addition, the more general and broadly applicable a decision, the fewer the opportunities for corruption because the cost and difficulty of collective action increases with the number of individuals who may benefit from the distribution of a rent. Each will have an incentive to free-ride, taking advantage of the corruption employed by the others (Olson 1965). Where only a few individuals are affected, on the other hand, the use of corruption to influence political decisions becomes much easier.

2. THE COMMODITIES OF CORRUPT EXCHANGE

In the present section an empirical dimension will be given to the observations made above. The aim of a corrupter is to obtain property rights on political rent: what concretely are the "services" the corrupted official provides to achieve this result? A first resource is decisional power: either a discretionary decision assigning a benefit or influencing the outcome of a public procedure or inaction. At times the corrupted official limits himself to the provision of *reserved information*, increasing the corrupter's chances of obtaining a benefit. Let us now examine these resources more closely.

2.1. Influence over Political Decisions

Once taken by the competent organs, political decisions are binding on the entire community. Based on the institutional regulations governing the procedures and modes of exercising public power, the decisions thus adopted are applied to and enforced on a collectivity, regardless of whether they are taken by one, few, or many. They are *collectivized* decisions: "Collectivized decisions are political in that they are (a) sovereign; (b) without exit; and (c) sanctionable" (Sartori 1987:215). They are *sovereign*, in the sense that they take precedence over any contrasting rules or directives not deriving from a higher level of public power itself; they are *binding*, reaching out to the frontier that territorially defines citizenship; they carry a *sanction*, backed by the legal monopoly of the use of force.

Corrupters seeks to influence such exercise of public power to their advantage by paying a bribe. The most direct way to do so is to identify an interlocutor in a position to influence the decision-making process to ensure the assigning of the property rights in question. Two possibilities exist: (1) the corrupt occupies a public position endowing him with *discretionary power*; (2) the person who is given the bribe is in a position to *influence* the actions of the occupier of the public role to which the decision is officially delegated.

Discretionary authority needs to be understood in its broadest sense. Even porters can on occasion accelerate or retard the transfer of a document from one department to another if they wish. In certain public agencies in Rome, for example, porters received minibribes of between fifty thousand and four hundred thousand lira in return for this service (VICM:3). Naturally enough, the "price" of illegal services increases as the level of power rises: "The amount of the bribe depends on the importance of the position and the risk run by the politician," declared Adriano Zampini, broker in corrupt exchanges (Pansa 1987:113).

In certain cases bribes may be paid to individuals who can influence the decision-making process *independently* of their formal position within the public administration. This would be the case of a politician with the power to nominate or revoke his "representatives" within a certain body. Gabriele Serriello, an entrepreneur interested in the privatization of refuse collection in Naples, did not approach those responsible at the local level, but national-level Neapolitan politicians. He explained: "Everyone knew it was they who decided on the realization of any major projects concerning Naples and that the wishes of local bodies were neither determining nor conclusive" (CD, 20 April 1993, no. 297, p. 2).

The destination of bribes, then, reflects the corrupter's perception—formed over time—of the distribution of public power. For example, an individual who no longer holds public office may still ask for a bribe to influence the decisions of a given body. Thus, Gioacchino Platania, one-time vice-president of the Managing Board of the Catania USL 35 (*Unità sanitaria locale*—Local Health Board) demanded and obtained 50 million lira from an entrepreneur although he had already left office. The entrepreneur in question later stated: "He told me that the situation was the same as before. I gave him [the money] because he said that *it was he who still decided in the USL*" (ACA:103, emphasis added).

When a given institutional power is in the hands of a single agent, corruption is much simpler and less risky.[9] Frequently, however, such powers are exercised by a plurality of individuals—within an elected assembly, for example, or a bureaucracy—or even by all citizens, during an election or referendum.[10] When a number of people can influence the final decision without being able to take it independently, it is important for the corrupter to know the *number of agents involved in making the decision* and the *scale of diffusion of information* concerning it. In order to know *who* should be bribed and *how much*, the corrupter must estimate the influence each individual has on the public choice and the risk of being denounced to the magistracy.

Where decisions are taken collegially, the interest of the corrupter turns to the majority's decision. Quite obviously, the involvement of many agents in the public decision-making process increases the transactions costs for the briber. On the other hand, as Tullock (1980, 1990) remarks, there is sometimes a surprising gap between the extremely small size of the bribes paid and the rent collected by the briber (see also Chapter 9, p. 204). The "bargaining power" of the latter can sometimes be reinforced by certain characteristics of democratic politics: if each "legislator" expects the majority of others will approve a certain proposal, then he will be willing to accept even a very small bribe in exchange for his vote, which becomes (in his perspective) almost uninfluential. The briber will then try to strengthen similar expectations, obtaining the approval of the proposal he is interested in merely with a series of many tiny "kickbacks" (Rasmusen and Ramseyer 1994). In fact, voting procedures introduce a coordination problem in the bribe collection among public agents who cannot enforce agreement with one another, collecting the full (or a substantial portion of the) political rent they assign through their decision.

Coordination problems in bribe gathering are often balanced by disciplined factions and political party organizations: "[I]n the past few decades Japan's Liberal Democratic Party (particularly its so called Policy Affair Research Council, where important policies were made and payoffs were coordinated behind closed doors) has been quite successfully in centralizing bribery and raking off billions of dollars' worth in the process" (Bardhan 1997:1327). The actual "value" of parties in influencing voting procedures is linked not only to their weight (i.e., the number of representatives' votes they control), but also by their position in the political spectrum. For instance, the PSI with less than 15 percent of the vote, was often decisive in local politics for the formation of both left and conservative majority coalitions. As a consequence, its members assumed a role disproportionate to the party's electoral strength, while their services acquired enormous value in the market for corruption. Concerning the party's then administrative secretary, Balzamo, an administrator of the Techint company, Paolo Scaroni, said: "[H]e made it quite clear that paying the PSI, to all intents and purposes the fulcrum of both individual public bodies and the party system as a whole, was indispensable for an entrepreneur to remain in the market" (CD, 5 March 1993, no. 210, p. 24).

Generally, corrupters are more willing to "do business" when a particular individual or political group retains a strong grip on a given institutional power. In fact, the expectation of political stability over a period of time renders repeated transactions more advantageous, by reducing uncertainty over "investing" time and efforts on the wrong person. The ex-managing director of Montedison, Carlo Sama, explained the division of the bribery money vis-à-vis the expected growth in the political influence of the Socialist party:

> Cusani . . . informed me that half of the funds to be raised (between 67 and 75 billion lira) would be given to the PSI in the person of its political secretary, the Right Hon. Bettino Craxi. In that period, the early months of 1991, the PSI's leader cut a very charismatic figure and it was considered advisable that he should be given particular consideration in view of the power he held and that of his party. This power in Italian politics was considered likely to increase. (CDEM:13)

The simple fact of belonging to an organization considered capable of exerting a lasting political influence heightens the *quality* of the "commodity" being sold. Normally, there is a certain time lag before a political decision produces the anticipated effects. During this time, a change of mind or *a change of the person holding office* remains a possibility. This factor of uncertainty emerges from the situation described by the entrepreneur Giorgio Li Pera:

> [Two managers of the Fondedile firm] told us that they had reached an agreement with the Right Hon. Rino Nicolosi for awarding the said tender to the firm. . . . The period was one of serious crisis in the regional government. All the assessors had resigned and Nicolosi took on all the assessorships. Later, after the crisis had been resolved, the Right Hon. Lombardo became assessor for culture. He did not at all like the fact that a tender that was under the authority of his assessorate had been "dealt with" by Nicolosi and the agreement between Fondedile and the latter came to nothing. (CD, 11 June 1993, no. 417, p. 6)

On the contrary, the risk that an agreement will be defaulted on increases where a politician's position is judged unstable or transitory.[11] A change of political personnel thus represents a critical moment for the corrupter, who can no longer be sure that sums paid in the past will be acknowledged or that he will find the same amenability as before. This is confirmed by the entrepreneur De Mico: "One of the least savory aspects of entrepreneurial activity was connected with changes in personnel at the higher levels of the 'power' conditioning it. Having already had to satisfy the desires of one functionary, at a certain moment another took his place. While beginning affably by admitting that he was aware we 'had already contributed,' he would point out that 'it was he who was there now'" (PROM:720). Where contacts can be consolidated with the same individuals, the entrepreneur avoids having to renew the initial effort of exposing his illicit intents, gaining their trust, and forming a capital of common knowledge.

Influence on power decisions takes also the form of a *veto power*, that is the capacity to delay or block decisional powers that are initiated or led by others. The complexity and the risks of the corrupt transaction are proportionally increased: "Sometimes the bribee cannot deliver not because he wants to cheat, but because there is a multiple veto power system in operation, which makes centralized collection of bribes in exchange for guaranteed favors very difficult. One high official in New Delhi is reported to have told a friend: 'If you want me to move a file faster, I am not sure if I can help you, but if you want me to stop a file I can do it immediately'" (Bardhan 1997:1324). By exercising these interdiction powers, some actors—politicians or bureaucrats—may enter the game with some capacity for negotiation in the division of the bribes (see also Chapter 5). To avoid paralysis, and the discontent of the corrupter, an agreement based on the division of benefit may be convenient. In this way, the intensity that arises from conflicts of interest, which are hotly contested in the visible political arena, is reduced.[12] According to the former mayor of Reggio Calabria, Licandro: "Political conflicts, even at the visible level, represent the most convincing and effective way to obtain money, since they induce those who have to pay to do it in a faster and more substantial way" (Ciconte 1994:160). As we shall see in Chapter 4, collusive agreement among parties and diverse political actors neutralizes this source of conflicts and turbulence in the corruption market.

2.2. Restricted Information

Besides discretionary decisions, the attribution of a political rent can depend on the outcome of a public procedure, generally designed to guarantee impartial treatment. In this case knowledge relating to certain stages of the procedure or to decisions influencing its course, which are restricted in their diffusion, represents a valuable resource. Corrupt exchange may then consist in passing *privileged information* to the corrupter, thus allowing him to increase his probabilities of being the final beneficiary.

When there is a tender, information may relate to aspects of contracting procedure that should remain secret to guarantee the regularity of competition. There is a huge number of cases in Italy of corrupt agents providing information on the minimum and maximum prices for exclusion from a tender set by the commission, the average offer set by as a "fair price" (and which should be approached as nearly as possible), or on particular aspects that would be privileged in evaluating projects.[13] To give just one example, two members of the Parma public health unit USL adjudication commission were held to have acted illegally by "providing information favored firms with project guidelines before they had actually been deposited" (CD, 22 March 1993, no. 233, p. 2).

Naturally, the more opaque and uncertain the course of arriving at a decision, the more valuable the information concerning it is to the corrupter. If the norms regulating public decisions are technically complex, having a "reliable" interpretation may be sufficient to conquer a privileged position in the public sector market. The ex-director general of the Ministry of Health, Duilio Poggiolini, provided such information in return for payment:

> The pharmaceutical companies came to me for "advice" because I was the only one who could explain the rules, and in particular the mechanisms relative to homologation of medicines in Europe. . . . In other words, having helped to create them, *I could give the correct interpretation of the said rules.* I have no problems admitting that this *information was crucial for the pharmaceutical companies* since it allowed them to adapt to the complex and continually evolving European norms. (*L'Espresso*, 28 November 1993, pp. 25–26)

Information concerning the future plans of an administration can also become a commodity for exchange. To draw an analogy with the private market, such information allows an entrepreneur to "anticipate" the future direction of demand and to defeat competitors. In the public market, however, we are dealing with "public preferences," whose concrete expression is often delegated to politicians. An entrepreneur participating in a tender for the privatization of refuse collection in Pescara was helped in this way by the municipal secretary of the PSI, Paolo D'Andreamatteo:

> We required someone who could inform us of the various problems of the service. D'Andreamatteo procured us a meeting with the Director of Municipal Public Hygiene, Engineer Di Cintio, who assigned one of his employees to take us round the various districts of the city and explain the problems associated with them. However, we also needed to know approximately what might be considered a just price and here too we were helped by D'Andreamatteo. (CD, 11 June 1993, no. 417, p. 6)

While the exercise of a given power leaves definite traces, passing restricted information can be easily concealed and is therefore more difficult to demonstrate in a court of law. Where the result will be the same, therefore, a corrupted official can be expected to prefer passing information allowing the private party to obtain a benefit in a formally legitimate manner to a more visible distortion of the decision-making process. From the corrupter's point of view, the value of the information (which by its very nature can be shared) depends on the number of people in possession of it. When information is sold to more than one corrupter in a fraudulent manner, or by more than one public agent without the others being aware, the "commodity," no longer being an exclusive possession, becomes a "lemon." While knowing the secret "number" (the minimum acceptable price decided by a public official) can guarantee the awarding of a contract, this may, as one Florentine entrepreneur asserted, be "an open secret." "I know because . . . when the envelopes with sealed offers were opened we realized that more than one of us had paid for the 'number' of the same tender" (*L'Espresso*, 18 June 1989, p. 29). Thus, restricted information "devalues" in proportion to its diffusion. When all the private parties have paid to have it, the relative advantage is canceled out.

3. POLITICAL PROTECTION

On some occasions entrepreneurs or other private actors engage in bribery not to obtain a specific advantage but rather a more general political protection of their rights, either within corrupt exchange or in everyday relationships with the state. Political guarantors have the power to prevent or settle disputes arising with regard to both legal and illegal activities: bribes unpaid, services promised but not performed, the nonfulfillment of contracts, or inadequate protection of rights through state inefficiency.[14] Those acquiring protection reduce the uncertainty involved in future transactions, counting on the fact that someone will intervene on their behalf should any problems arise. Such uncertainty is extremely high in both the illegal corruption market and in relations with a state sector characterized by inefficiency and/or a lack of transparency in decision-making. The present section will attempt to answer two questions: (1) What kinds of protection are acquired through bribery? (2) What forms does bribery in this arena take?

3.1. The Changeable Forms of Political Protection

The Protection of Corrupt Exchanges. Illegal by definition, there can be no legal recourse for settling disputes within the corruption market. The risk of being "sold a lemon" in such a situation can become extremely high, also because the transaction is nonsimultaneous in nature and one party must rely on the word of the other. Having secured their payoff, politicians might fail to deliver what they promised; an entrepreneur, having won the contract, may forget to pay the bribe promised.[15] A case in point is the experience of Antonio Gregni, an entrepreneur seeking to persuade the Sicilian Region to buy him out of his failing enterprise: "[H]e made payments amounting to about 350 million to a regional deputy powerful enough to be known as 'the boss.' He turned out to be a 'delinquent' who, after making 'a lot of promises,' 'stole [Gregni's] money'" (CD, 4 October 1992, no. 98, p. 5). Nor are entrepreneurs necessarily more "honest." As one Ansaldo manager recalled: "Let's just say the money was promised but then we stalled, asking to pay in installments" (*La Repubblica*, 30–31 May 1993, p. 15). Fear of being sold a lemon may result in otherwise profitable transactions being passed up, and a demand for protection will arise. By handing a *third party* the power to sanction agreements and intervene to discipline the market, both corrupted and corrupters protect themselves from any improper behavior by the other party. Where this demand meets someone both willing and able to satisfy it, a portion of the money from the corruption market will go to this external guarantor who, being a sort of "judge," has the power to resolve disputes and impose sanctions. In such cases the bribe is split into two parts, each having a distinct destination and paying for a distinct service. Correspondingly, such a market is organized into two levels: in the first, specific benefits are exchanged with bribes; in the second, the Milanese magistrates remarked:

> Those who demanded (or received at least) these sums retained only a part, and that not always. More often they were also sent on to other more powerful politicians who, regardless of whether they held public office, were or would be guarantor on those directly responsible for success in the tender and in the management of the contract, because of their influence over those who did. (CD, 13 April 1993, no. 266, p. 2)

To ensure that difficulties did not arise, agreements were sometimes made dependent on the presence of a guarantor. When the broker Adriano Zampini offered a bribe in exchange for the purchase of a property of his by the commune of Turin, the assessor responsible replied: "Could be interesting, but we'll have to find a guarantor . . . someone who can link everybody up. . . . You might speak to Enzo [Biffi Gentile, the deputy mayor] about it." The Turin magistrates noted that "by the term guarantor . . . Zampini means someone in a position, on the one hand, to ensure that the entrepreneur actually pays the bribe; on the other, that the public functionaries would act 'accordingly,' ensuring a satisfactory outcome to the whole operation" (QGT:362).

Disputes might arise over agreements for sharing out bribes among a number of politicians or over the subdivision of public works among a cartel of entrepreneurs, paralyzing the market and risking that it might come to the magistrates' attention. As will be seen below (in particular, Chapter 4), these forms of protection could be supplied by a variety of political actors: influential individuals, party factions, or official party bodies or organizations.

Protection from Other Corrupt Agents. Even a gang of extortionists has an interest in maintaining exclusive control over their victims, preventing others from taking advantage of them: "Protection is primarily against the one who offers it, but it has to include protection against rival taxing authority" (Schelling 1984:185). A similar process occurs in the corruption market: more powerful politicians protect their "clients" against demands for bribes from others because in doing so they can collect a greater amount with lower risk. Thus, in a context of widespread corruption *one* person may be paid simply in order to avoid paying many and paying continually. The entrepreneur Angelo Simontacchi claimed, for example, that "paying at the level of the national secretariat allowed [him] to refuse the demands of individual local politicians" (*Il Giornale*, 14 January 1993, p. 4). [16] The protection of some individuals increasingly directs the attention of the less important figures within the world of corruption to those remaining, thus heightening the desirability of a long-term protection "contract." A spontaneous demand for political protection can then emerge, under the subjection to a leading "authority" in the corruption system, which is preferable to the persistence of an "anarchistic" equilibrium, where an undesirable bribe request may be expected from every public agent.[17] Of course, when somebody in the political-administrative context has bought an effective safeguard against widespread corruption, low-level corrupt agents tend to concentrate their attention on those who did not pay any bribe. Although this form of protection bribery may begin with the imposition of a "cut" from a certain number of reluctant victims, it can then create a chain of voluntary requests for "protective umbrellas" from those who initially remain without defense against an increase in demands for bribes.[18]

Political Protection against State Inefficiency. The growth of the public sphere has multiplied the occasions where citizens or businessmen have an interest in asserting their right to certain public services or resources, or in entering contractual relationships with the state. Lack of confidence in the efficiency and impartiality of official procedures may then give rise to a demand for political protection.[19] By paying bribes to those with long-term influence over the exercise of public power, corrupters hope to prevent contention with the state or to resolve such contention in their favor.

When the *public* and *impartial* protection offered by the state's laws is uncertain or ineffective, the *private* and *selective* protection offered by a given center of power may appear more convenient and effectual. The entrepreneur Fabrizio Garampelli explained:

> Knowing that civil lawsuits can go on for more than six years the Commune of Milan put an incredible weapon in the hands of public officials (political and otherwise) when, five or six years ago, it abolished the possibility of arbitration, a means of resolving the situation in a matter of months. For that reason construction companies could not evade certain demands, demands that were not, probably, specific to the one job but more general, coming from a contract that probably was not strictly linked to that particular job. ("Un giorno in pretura," RAI 3 TV, 22 February 1993)

Administrative inefficiency leaves both entrepreneurs and citizens in a position of uncertainty about the time that business affecting them will take (in addition to the uncertainty regarding its outcome). Administrators thus acquire arbitrary power, which permits them to obstruct even quite legitimately anticipated decisions without running any particular risk. Their discretional power and informational advantages make them able to threaten to deny (or to delay) due rights, in order to collect bribes. If private parties have sufficiently frequent contact with public institutions, therefore, it will be in their interest to find longer-term protection, avoiding "regulatory blackmail" (Mogiliansky 1994).[20] The entrepreneur will look for an influential political partner who will be paid on a regular basis in return for wide-ranging protection from state inefficiency. The entrepreneur Vincenzo Lodigiani noted:

> Thousands of problems can and do arise in the awarding of contracts and supplies and all the way through the contracting process. . . . Enterprises are therefore under the necessity of preventing the legal representatives of public bodies, or someone acting for them inside such bodies, from making their lives difficult. . . . Rather than continually submit to the phenomena described above Lodigiani sought to protect himself by negotiating directly with the center, the national secretariats of the parties. (TNM:42)

Political Protection from Competition.   It is unlikely that political protection will be accorded indiscriminately to anyone willing or in a position to pay for it. A politician who did not select among those demanding protection would find it difficult to ensure they all received preferential treatment. Moreover, the inability to reconcile incompatible requests would increase the risk of denunciations being made by dissatisfied clients. Third, as

Shleifer and Vishny emphasize, "keeping corruption secret requires keeping down the number of people involved in giving and receiving bribes" (1993:615). Competition among bribers, on the other hand, increases the price of corruption as the following account, by an entrepreneur, makes clear:

> I got in touch . . . and said I was willing to pay a bribe. . . . He stated that he could not guarantee anything as there were other firms interested and I realized the offer I had made was not high enough. When I informed [another manager of the same firm] he got angry with me because I had not made a higher offer, of 5–6 percent. He told me not to bother, he would take care of it. (TRIM:78)

Beyond a certain point, however, for the corrupt administrator the advantages of competition tend to diminish, since there is a limit to the size of the bribe that can be paid. It can be assumed, therefore, that each center of power has a precise interest in *limiting* the number of corrupters to whom they offer protection.[21] According to the manager of the Ligresti group, for example, the group paid 7 billion lira to the PSI in the expectation that they "would be included in a *small circle* of entrepreneurs who had demonstrated their friendship toward the Socialist Party" (*L'Espresso*, 6 December 1992, p. 60, emphasis added). Entry into the protection market was encouraged by the perception of important economic advantages for those who could secure their place. Nevol Querci, extraordinary commissioner of Inadel stated: "It is true that in recent years a circumscribed group of about 20 entrepreneurs has emerged . . . who, on the one hand, contributed to covering the expenses of the DC and PSI and on the other received favored treatment where real estate was to be purchased" (TNM:76). According to Gambetta, insofar as there are those who *remain excluded*, any payment made solely for the purpose of inclusion in a protected market is not extortion:

> In a protected market a potential dealer faces a cost of entry higher than the cost which would be strictly necessary were the market not protected. From the point of view of the entrant, this may look like extortion. But from the point of view of those dealers already buying protection, the extra cost imposed on the new entrant is precisely one of the reasons they pay for protection: to deter new competitors. (1993:31–32)

Under normal conditions total *freedom of entry* into the market for political protection does not exist. Those who arrive too late, do not inspire trust, or are simply not liked, therefore, will find themselves frozen out. Thanks to the protection they receive from competition, entrepreneurs operating in the public sector are able to obtain higher profits than they would otherwise—in other words, a political rent (see Chapter 7).

4.   THE CORRUPTER'S RESOURCES

An extremely large range of resources is available as commodities of exchange to an individual engaging in corruption. In the popular imagination bribery is associated with an envelope full of folded bank notes that conceals, or at least camouflages, illegal payments. Corruption trials have revealed that this form was indeed widely practiced, a newspaper or a box of chocolates on occasion taking the place of the envelope. With the increasing amounts of money being paid, overnight bags were later needed rather than the traditional envelope.[22] That practice in its turn becoming common enough to arouse suspicion, cardboard boxes or plastic bags might be employed instead. The director of ANAS (*Azienda nazionale autonoma strade*—National Road Authority), Antonio Crespo, recalled: "What to do with all those cases and overnight bags? And besides, it worried me that the employees might suspect that they contained money. I was forced to suggest that the money should be put in cardboard boxes or plastic bags, both of which can be disposed of easily" (*La Repubblica*, 14–15 March 1993, p. 16). A bank transfer can notably simplify the corrupter's task, particularly when the bribe is a very large one. While precluding the risk of interception during a cash transfer, it nevertheless leaves traces that can provide the magistracy with incontrovertible proof of a transfer of funds, the obstacles of banking secret and cross-border judicial cooperation having been overcome.[23]

Money is the medium of exchange par excellence in the corruption market, as in any other. However, in some cases barters also take place, the value of the asset offered by the corrupter being less than the political rent acquired.[24] The president of the Serenissima motorway was paid with a gate and a washbasin for his house rather than the usual money bribe (VIV6:4). Passing off a bribe as a "gift" reduces the risk of penal sanctions and at the same time the moral cost, alleviating the unpleasant feeling of breaking the law. A supplier to the Milanese ATM admitted that "he felt ashamed of having to go to the company's offices with an envelope full of money so he began to pay in gold sterling. He felt relieved psychologically. It seemed like offering a present rather than the price of corruption" (Barbacetto and Veltri 1991:181).[25]

It should be added that, as the unit in which the power of the person receiving it is measured, a bribe also acquires a sort of "symbolic " connotation. As Hobbes observed:

> The Value or Worth of a man, is as of all other things, his Price; that is to say, so much as would be given for the use of his Power: and therefore is not absolute; but a thing dependant on the need and judgment of another. . . . And as in other things, so in men, not the seller, but the buyer determines the Price. For let a man (as most men do,) rate themselves as the

highest Value they can; yet their true Value is no more than it is esteemed by others. ([1651] 1968:151–52)

In fact, the real *quality* of the otherwise impalpable "commodity" exchanged—the power to influence public decisions or to protect economic activities—is sometimes difficult to ascertain for both the buyer and the seller, but it can nevertheless be quantified approximately in economic terms: the market value of the bribe usually received (or passed on to others). The amount of the bribes passed on to other political actors also permits implicit acknowledgment on the part of the receiver of the giver's importance. Mario Chiesa observed, "When your referent accepts a contribution from you personally, then you've made the jump. The passage of money seals the unwritten pact at the basis of politics. . . . You've arrived among those who count." The politician's awareness of his power is reinforced, favoring identification with the elite: "You feel that you belong to a restricted group, which can be relied on in everything and for everything; a sort of inner circle. The bribe is the consecration of your belonging to the group" (Andreoli 1993:62).

When corruption is widespread, privileged information concerning the "prices" charged by public agents spreads within circumscribed groups, providing orientation as to their power, and—completing the circle— directing successive flows of bribery toward them. When Mario Chiesa received his first bribe he felt gratified more for the recognition of his importance than for the money itself: "I felt 100 percent a politician; from head to toe. But not because I had more money in the bank. I felt like a real politician because I was finally free from a kind of tutelage" (ibid.:58). Agatino Licandro, Christian Democrat ex-mayor of Reggio Calabria, makes the same point:"The way things stand in politics nowadays, you can either ask for money or they bring it to you. The higher up you are, the more you're able to ask or they have to bring you" (Licandro and Varano 1993:222). Consequently, the more money you are brought, the more power you appear to have. Accepting smaller bribes may block the possibility of promotion to more important political positions, partly because there is less money to buy the benevolence of those who count, but also because one will be considered of little importance and as a consequence overlooked. Of a politician who refused a bribe he considered inadequate, Licandro commented: "I understood the difficulty of his situation. *Everyone's importance depends on the size of the bribe offered* and at 10 million he felt he was being treated disrespectfully" (ibid.:58–59, emphasis added).

An additional resource is political-electoral support, a vital resource for all politicians. In fact, bribery can be translated into *benefits in terms of image*, the corrupter ensuring the benevolence of the media or funding propaganda. Some Milanese politicians convicted for corruption "made their wishes quite clear in this regard and in certain cases went so far as to compel the firm [Icomec] to subsidize private offices, election campaigns, and periodicals" (PRIM:62). In particular, companies involved in the mass media system can exchange a resource that is particularly valuable to politicians, and at the same time can be easily concealed. According to the ex-regional secretary of the Lombardy DC, Gianstefano Frigerio, the relations between his party and Fininvest—which controlled three TV channels—were "particularly positive and constructive," and indeed Fininvest

> has always helped the party at both national and local level with contributions in kind, as you might say, *through their television channels*. In every election campaign Fininvest provides the party in Milan and Lombardy space on television and in the mass media for party propaganda. . . . Secondly, the company offers free space on television and in the newspapers for a series of candidates particularly friendly toward them, choosing the candidates strongest in political terms and providing them with television coverage. This robust aid has created a *cordial disposition* toward Fininvest's industrial activities in the DC. (*L'Espresso*, 9 May 1993, p. 76)

The firms involved in corruption also represent fertile ground for the placement of clients indicated by politicians. The Milanese magistrates noted that "the choice of the enterprise that should win the tender was based above all on the guarantee of political support they could assure through the activity awarded by the tender and the implicit formation of clientele derived from it" (CPDM:101). Luigi Bosso, for example, managing director of Napoletanagas, took on personnel on the basis of the importance of the politician making the request: "When I take on personnel I choose the persons indicated by all the parties with whom I have relations. For the higher level politicians, the faction chiefs of the majority parties, the general rule is to keep them happy . . . in order to have their support. They can influence those within their party who occupy administrative positions" (*La Repubblica*, 19 December 1993, p. 4).

In this way corrupt politicians extend their influence into the private sector as well, giving rise to a triangular exchange permitting the allocation of public goods to be transformed *directly* into political support (Figure 2.1).

As we will see in Chapter 9, clientelism and corruption are thus mutually reinforcing. The possibility of creating a durable political following through these employment channels means that the success of the firm is also desirable for the corrupt politician. The firms run the risk, however, that personnel taken on in this way will have little desire to work and their political protection will therefore be an unsustainable burden. Gabriele Serriello, a Neapolitan manager, stated: "I was obliged to hire innumerable people by the DC and PSI, all strongly recommended. They had no desire whatsoever to work and were incompetent in the majority of cases. In the end it was too much: the labor costs, for that kind of personnel, were too high. . . . So they asked for money and I paid it" (*La Repubblica* 16

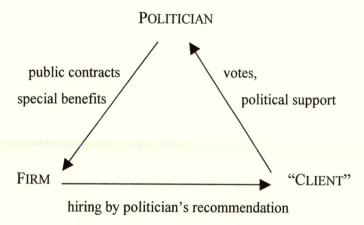

Figure 2.1. Influence of corrupt politicians on the private sector.

March 1993, p. 8). Instead of hiring a hundred clients little disposed to work, Serriello preferred to pay 1.3 billion lira in order to obtain the 350 billion lira tender for the privatization of municipal refuse collection.

When bribes are paid as a price for political protection, they often look like a sort of "tax burden." Clearly, the different forms of protection described in the preceding paragraph are often interwoven, both in reality and in the expectations of those paying for guarantee. Bribes charged for this more general protection rather than a specific service become, to all intents and purposes, a tax paid to political protectors, either at a fixed rate or in proportion to profits. This form of payment also has the advantage of reducing the possibility of criminal proceedings, since it is harder to prove that it is in fact illegal. This fact had not escaped Bettino Craxi; according to the entrepreneur Ottavio Pisante:

> De Toma [the PSI's exactor] told me Craxi had identified about 20 major Italian firms who, if they wanted to survive in business, would have to commit themselves to making regular cash payments to the PSI, in the order of about two billion a year. . . . In other words, Craxi realized the penal dangers of associating levies of money with individual tenders and intended to forfeit them against annual contributions. (TNM:83)

In Germany also, long-term relations of protection between certain major enterprises and the political parties (with money being channeled through huge annual contributions or "donations") served to reduce the risks associated with direct bribery for *specific* political favors or decisions: "The long term funding strategy of the corporations was aimed at 'cultivating' the political scene in such a way as to make outright corruption superflu-

ous. . . . In good part, this strategy may certainly be said to have succeeded"
(Blankenburg, Staudhammer, and Steinert 1989:924).

The sums of money paid by "contributors" then become a kind of
"insurance policy" taken out against the difficulties and obstacles that
may arise for those maintaining periodic relations with public bodies—a
"contract" to be taken up only where required: to unblock a particular
dossier, silence an overzealous inspector, or speed up a given operation.
Having won the tender to construct a sports complex, the entrepreneur
Romagnoli encountered just these kinds of difficulty and decided to seek
political protection:

> Having won the contract we were forced to recognize that there were mal-
> contents and objections. . . . We realized that we needed political-entrepre-
> neurial protection to have any chance of finishing the work successfully and
> avoid pretexts for obstructionism and delay. . . . I therefore tried to identify
> the leading representatives of the political system . . . realizing that this was
> the only way to ensure a certain amount of tranquillity in order to see the
> project through. They told me that they had the power to intervene with the
> traditional political parties but drew my attention to the fact that these par-
> ties needed money. (TM:142–43)

A protected entrepreneur is able to confront his political and bureaucratic
interlocutors without undue worry. In return, as Vincenzo Lodigiani
recalled:

> Both Citaristi and Balzamo told me, not long after the middle of the 1980s,
> that it was necessary to agree to a contribution that Lodigiani (like all the
> other companies, incidentally) would pay to the DC's and PSI's coffers,
> systematically and regularly, independent of individual tenders or
> orders. . . . In return they guaranteed, on behalf of their parties, that the nec-
> essary steps to prevent any obstructionism would be taken with those
> responsible for Lodigiani's orders. (TNM:43)

5.   THE "BUSINESS OF POWER"

Corrupt politicians and bureaucrats often possess and exhibit resources
that are useful in order to reassure corrupters of their capacity to influence
public decisions, the sincerity of their offer, and their personal reliability.
The corruption market, like any other, is in fact populated by fraudulent
"salesmen." No corrupter, no matter how inexperienced, will give money
to anybody demanding it. Rather, he will seek to identify someone who
will be able—due to information in his possession, the position he holds,
or his reputation—to complete the corrupt transaction successfully. As we
have seen, corruption turns the power to administer public resources into
a commodity of exchange. In such business a number of resources are

nevertheless necessary in order to provide more efficiently, i.e., at lower cost, the services required by corrupters. As in the automotive industry, a combination of several inputs—labor, capital, raw materials—is necessary in order to supply the cars that are the final output of the productive process, these resources are "inputs" for the "manufacturing" of corrupt acts. This explains the importance that blackmail information, reputation, and intelligence-gathering activities assume in the market for corruption.

5.1. Information and the Power to Blackmail

Corrupt agents require different types of information in order to render their services in a convincing manner. Possession of privileged information, in fact, permits them to simplify contacts with those interested in doing business, select reliable partners, obtain the silence of other actors concerning their illegal activities, or intimidate whoever might wish to withdraw from agreements made. Here the information is not, as in the cases considered in the preceding section, the commodity exchanged, but rather is a precondition that permits the conclusion of the transaction with less risk.

The agent who demonstrates a thorough knowledge of what goes on behind the scenes in the public decision-making process may easily overcome eventual misgivings on the part of the interlocutor. For instance, the ex-assessor of the Commune of Milan, Epifanio Li Calzi, apparently vaunted his knowledge of confidential information before a group of businessmen interested in dividing up public contracts. One entrepreneur specified: "Li Calzi was perfectly informed of the point where the dossier for each hospital was, and let us know it. He indicated what work would be given to the so-called general enterprises, those considered among the fifty most important in Italy. He also informed us of the division of the work that had been decided between them" (TM:52). Possession of reserved information is very useful in this persuasion effort, as observed by an entrepreneur:

> "He insisted a great deal on his importance and he was certainly convincing. He was extremely well informed about all the tenders, when they had been awarded, and who had won them. He told me things that were highly confidential and that not even I, who was part of that world, could have found out. He told me, for example, that a certain contract would shortly be tendered, financed for a certain amount, and other highly confidential information. . . . Obviously I would not have given him any money if I had not been sure of his power within the world of public contracting" (UIS:590).

Information concerning someone who is involved in illegal activities or who has not informed the authorities on becoming aware of them can be used to influence his behavior. To create a patrimony of such compromising information requires espionage activities, which may be delegated to specialists. According to Roberto Arlati, an ex-policeman turned armed escort for bribery payments, the broker Agostino Ruju "was a good collector of information because his (legal) office was frequented by officers of the *Carabinieri*, police, and Customs Service; by members of the military and civil secret services as well as by magistrates and important businessmen. He would put his interlocutors at ease and then worm useful information out of them." Such information can be put to use immediately, as the same witness noted: "Frequently Ruju asked me to give the Right Hon. Craxi 'confidential memos,' news about the delicate questions of the moment; on judicial or financial matters, for example, or on individuals who might be of interest to him" (*L'Espresso*, 9 June 1993, p. 58–59).

Possession of compromising information permits the imposition of one's own wishes or the blocking of unfavorable decisions. In other words, it is a *source of power*, an effective instrument for influencing others involved in corruption or safeguarding one's corrupt practices, strengthening *omertà*. Interviewed during the *mani pulite* scandal, a PSI parliamentary deputy asserted: "Bettino Craxi is still very powerful in the party. A lot of people owe him and others are scared of him. A lot of others are under his thumb because he knows what they got up to" (Pansa 1994:259). Thus the sharing of information concerning corruption creates a widespread "power of interdiction." In turn the mechanisms of political competition are neutralized and relative positions of power stabilized. As shown by forty-five years of Italian politics, blackmail becomes the invisible cement of a political class condemned to a lengthy and forced cohabitation. In this context, anyone making a hasty move or attempting to impose too quick a decision is exposed to the risk of a scandal. This explains the particular role the secret services play in a corrupt system, where they easily become the instruments of various factions in the collection of blackmail information. For example, some dossiers from the Italian intelligence agency have been found in luggage sent from Italy to Bettino Craxi's refuge at Hamamet (*La Repubblica*, 8 April 1997, p. 13).

5.2. A Reputation for Influence

A corrupt politician sells resources connected with his power to take decisions within the public administration. The extent and stability of his power, however, cannot always be estimated exactly. One concern of the purchaser will be for the quality of the services being acquired. It is a matter of trust, but in this world trust becomes a particularly scarce commodity. The ex-managing director of Montedison, Carlo Sama, recalled that "during the elections of 1992 the Ferruzzi group also was contacted by various politicians who, as is usual in these cases, get 'friendly,' flattering the businessman and asking for cash contributions; boasting about their political activity and their willingness to take into account the interests of the business group from which they are asking money" (CDEM:22). These insinuating attempts at self-promotion do not demonstrate the capacity of politicians to maintain in time their promises of future gains. To gain the potential corrupter's trust is not easy, particularly in a context like Italy, where the process of decision-making is frequently opaque and complicated by a plurality of interventions. The corrupt politician or bureaucrat, like agents dealing in other commodities with similar characteristics, must pay close attention to his *reputation*.[26] The ability to create a favorable impression as to one's capacity to deliver corrupt services provides the seller with a "credit of trust" and he will no longer be obliged to prove his influence and reliability at each transaction.

In love, as in relations of power, the "quality" of the goods being offered is uncertain and as a consequence reputation takes on particular importance. Great seducers seem aware of this and tend to display and publicize their conquests. In *Dangerous Liaisons*, the Marquise de Merteuil makes the following confession to the Vicomte de Valmont:"Even before I met you I desired you. I was seduced by your fame. " In a less poetic context, a similar power of seduction is exercised by a reputation for influence, individuals in search of recommendation and protection being particularly vulnerable.

A reputation attracts clients, extending the power that underlies it. Take the example of the Christian Democrat ex-minister Remo Gaspari and his client machine: "His favorite phrase is 'Find me a single individual from Abruzzo who asked to speak with me and didn't.' . . . There is always a queue in front of his door. In the summer the procession transfers to the Sabrina di Vasto hotel where the more intimate obtain audience beneath the beach umbrella. Legend has it that in a single day Gaspari managed to receive 250 voters and take note of as many requests for his help" (Messina 1992:26–27). The fact that such requests are numerous both reinforces the reputation of the boss and guarantees the support necessary to sustain the client network. This is a form of natural publicity, spreading the fame concerning the actions of more important politicians independently of their will. The activities described so far relate to clientelist exchange, but corrupters are similarly attracted by reputation. Information about the effectiveness of interventions (notwithstanding their illegality) is circumspectly circulated. One entrepreneur claimed: "I should specify that it was well known in entrepreneurial circles that to be paid promptly it was necessary to 'go through' Patrizi [a functionary of the ANAS]. I did so too on a number of occasions" (TRIM:53). Further, the more that aspiring corrupters throng around a public agent, the higher the "price" the latter can demand for the decisions he makes. And, as already observed, higher prices in turn reinforce the reputation concerning the quality of corrupt services.

In the political arena a reputation for being powerful overlaps, at least in part, with the actual possession of power. As Thomas Hobbes noticed:

"Reputation of power, is Power; because it draweth with it the adherence of those that need protection" ([1651] 1968:150). The politician with a "good name" is not forced to demonstrate his capacity to enforce decisions on every occasion. When there is a widespread expectation that he has the power to reward or punish certain actions, people will behave accordingly, seeking to meet his interests. Their *image* of the distribution of power contributes in determining their actions (Stoppino 1982:26).[27] If someone possesses a sufficiently robust reputation, few people will dare to challenge the power underlying it. As for other commodities with similar properties, such as protection, "[I]ts benefits are enormous since once a reputation exists in the protection trade, it is scarcely necessary to produce the real thing. Reputation, as long nobody challenges it, *is* the real thing" (Gambetta 1993:144). Thanks to his reputation for being powerful, a corrupt politician can save on"production costs " of his services. It follows that, if a politician's reputation proceeds him, he may not actually need to do anything in order to influence public decisions as he desires. An employee of ANAS, for example, was called urgently to the Ministry of Public Works to request that he favor a particular firm that "the Minister had at heart because . . . it was well known that it was in the sphere of influence of Minister Pomicino" (APN:21).

Arrogance is also connected with maintaining a reputation for influence. An entrepreneur, Antonio Colombo, recalled that Polverari, a corrupt official,"was supposed to come at 10:30 but came at 12:30 instead. I had the impression that he had a triumphant look, as if he was saying to himself 'Look, I've humbled Colombo.' With Polverari even the fact of being late, however habitual, could be made into a sign of power insofar as I was forced to wait for him" (CD, 4 January 1993, no. 154, p. 7). The corrupt politician who demonstrates arrogant self-assurance can silence opposition and advertise himself as an authoritative partner for clients, the latter increasing in number in proportion to his reputation.[28] As summarized by a cartoonist, in this context the politician's attitude is: "But how can you be sure you've got power, unless you abuse it?" Besides, displaying an overbearing or haughty attitude suggests a lack of fear, inducing the other party to accept without resistance the demands of the politician.

Once power and money are symbolically associated, even the most glaring ostentation of wealth becomes a form of selective "advertising" directed to potential corrupters. The flaunted frequenting of an increasing number of fashionable circles and expensive night clubs, a predilection for expensive clothes, cars, and homes, reassure the corrupter that bribes will presumably be accepted and put to good use. In recent years many Italian politicians have exhibited clear signs of their corruption, even when greater discretion would have been easy: the continuous occupation of expensive hotel suites, luxurious rooftop apartments, and yachts flaunted before the press. At the same time they have displayed a scornful indifference to criticism and suspicion. Such behavior was not limited to highly visible national-level politicians, however. From the 1980s, a number of provincial bosses began to flaunt their newfound wealth, *advertising* to all intents and purposes the fact of their corruption. Sergio Restelli, for example, the personal secretary of the socialist leader Claudio Martelli, boasted a "white Porsche, a home of 300 square meters in the Parioli district, and another among the rustic scenery of Villa Borghese" although he had no private professional position whatsoever. He admitted the advertising function of this ostentation: "I undoubtedly left open the idea that I could be corrupted" (*La Repubblica*, 22–23 August 1993, p. 12).

The value of having a reputation emerges clearly when it begins to fade. If people cease to believe that a politician is powerful, his real power diminishes dramatically, just as a financial enterprise no longer trusted by its investors goes bankrupt. A corrupt official finds himself in trouble when his "customers" impose lengthy negotiations for each transaction or threaten to turn to others. The politician must employ the means at his disposal to induce obedience or mete out punishment when his power is resisted. This is a very costly activity, but also carries a more subtle risk: that in the meantime those means have evaporated, that "friends" no longer recall past favors, that support promised does not materialize, or the majority counted on has dissolved. A simple incident, or episode that diminishes the widespread regard for his authority, is often sufficient for others to consider themselves free to disobey too.[29] For example, notwithstanding an impressive personal success at the polls in the administrative elections of 1985, Carlo Tognoli, the ex-mayor of Milan, found himself in difficulty due to opposition from the Craxi faithful. This challenge began a chain reaction, which led to a more serious political defeat, as Mario Chiesa recalls: "Tognoli was clearly in difficulty. . . . Also, being in deep water he could not depend on the unity of his supporters. The result: he found himself in a minority at the meeting [of the provincial directorate of the PSI]. A few hours later, another setback": Chiesa himself, Tognoli's right hand, was removed from the list of future assessors and he too thus found himself in a difficult position, not so much for the episode as such but for the effect of being "flunked" on *his* reputation. "Many of the people I had contacts with began to make extremely dangerous comments, which could be translated as the following: if Tognoli didn't back Chiesa there's no reason we should give him a hand. In the future configuration of power we'll be left out, just like him" (Andreoli 1993.71–72).

5.3. A Reputation for "Honesty"

For all actors involved in corrupt exchanges, a reputation for "honesty" may be useful. A certain degree of *cooperation* is in fact required by agents in the corruption market since, as we have already observed, in such illegal dealings there is a higher risk of being cheated by others.[30] The basis for cooperation may indeed be fragile: in the absence of a protective agency that has the power to sanction "lemons," even the most advantageous trade risks failing. Not trusting the politician, the corrupter will prefer to avoid having to pay while the former will avoid committing himself for no return. Anyway, there are some *rules* that help distinguish who can be trusted and who, presumably, cannot. Individuals who trust each other and prefer an "honest" exchange to a swindle will respect the terms of the contract, to their mutual advantage. In this type of business, anticipation of the intentions of the interlocutor play a fundamental role, and the ability to *instill trust* is at least as valuable as *trusting* (Dasgupta 1989:82). A personal relationship of trust predating the secret transaction can influence, therefore, the choice of partner. Antonio Crespo, ex-director general of ANAS recalled: "Around the end of 1989 and the beginning of 1990 the minister [of Public Works], Prandini, asked me if I could collect donations from certain entrepreneurs that were not for the party, not for the party secretariat that is, and give them directly to him. . . . A week later he asked me again, *because he couldn't trust anybody else.* At that point I could not refuse" (*Panorama* 28 March 1993, p. 44, emphasis added). Any indication of the trustworthiness of one's interlocutor can be important. Kinship, common political affiliation, or masonic links, for example, are recognized as important sources of trust.

When it is not abused, trust can become an effective lubricant of the exchange mechanism. Where transactions are repeated over time, rather than occasional, an additional motive for forsaking the immediate gain of a "lemon" for long-term gains emerges.[31] Whoever does not stick to the corruption agreements can in fact be punished by exclusion from future transactions. Thus the fulfillment of the agreement is guaranteed by an interest in continuing a fruitful exchange relationship.[32] In what amounts to a "guide" to corruption, the broker Adriano Zampini maintained: "Don't ever think of cheating others, not even for fun. *The consequence of being caught would be the end of the relationship*" (Zampini 1993:113, emphasis added). A politician can punish a "dishonest" attempt at corruption, for example, by denying access to the benefits distributed by the public bodies under his influence in the future. In the course of a heated negotiation that was secretly recorded, a broker warned an entrepreneur—interested in having a piece of land declared buildable—of the danger of reprisals:

> You have to honor the commitment. If you say, *I'll give you the six million when I see the building regulation plan* and then you don't pay you might as well shoot yourself. . . . Afterwards, every time you have to deal with the Commune, the Province, or the Region or whatever, they throw it out. Theoretically if you wanted to say goodbye, thanks very much, I'm not giving you the money. . . . Don't think it's so easy to say "So, I managed to cheat them." (*L'Unità*, 4 April 1992, p. 7)

Especially when the exchanges are repeated with many individuals (who can acquire information on the "correctness" displayed in previous dealings), the reputation of being trustworthy takes on its value. A "good name" can be won by respecting commitments made: "The value of the reputation in the future is always more than what can be had by taking advantage of it in the short run" (Kreps 1990:532). The effects of losing, or failing to gain, a reputation for trustworthiness are devastating: "[A]lthough a reputation for honesty may be acquired slowly, it can generally be destroyed very quickly" (Dasgupta 1989:79). Following the above rule is particularly advantageous for agents who have prospects of long-term participation in the corruption market, and need therefore to gain the trust of potential clients. The "ten commandments of a successful corrupter" formulated by the broker Adriano Zampini state: "Above all, if you want to have a minimum of credit as a corrupter it is necessary to honor commitments and be as precise as a Swiss watch. If 10 million must be paid at 10 o'clock on the 10th of November you have be there five minutes early with not a sixpence less than the sum agreed" (*L'Espresso*, 18 November 1984, p. 40). According to ex-Minister De Lorenzo's secretary, Giovanni Marone, in some case "offers of money were not even taken into consideration because the persons making them were not to be trusted. There was a queue of people willing to pay waiting outside the door of the Ministry and the party offices" (*Il Giornale*, 13 January 1995, p. 10).

6. THE RESOURCES OF CORRUPTION: A SUMMARY

Corruption transforms the exercise of public authority into a sort of "power business." In this chapter the main resources involved in corrupt exchange have been analyzed. First we concentrated on the "output" produced by corrupt functionaries: property rights to political rents. Then we examined the different ways in which that output could be provided to corrupters. As we saw, the services of corrupt politicians and functionaries can take different forms, depending on procedures and decision-making mechanisms. Every area of public intervention can be involved, through exchanges that imply a discretionary decision assigning a political rent, the inaction of the public agents, or the selling of restricted information. In some cases, a selective and private protection of property rights of private actors, based on a credible promise to influence future political decisions, develops.

In exchange for these services, corrupters pay a portion of the rent received in the form of a cash bribe, or in other private resources that have particular value for the corrupt politician: influence over the mass media or voters, for example. The form of payment preferred by the politician depends on several factors. If the politician's aim is the reinvestment of the resources produced by corruption in electoral support rather than personal enrichment, then using corrupting firms to place clients is probably less risky in penal terms, while the expected return (the support of beneficiaries and their families) is quantitatively limited but secure and persistent. Taking bribes, on the other hand, increases the personal wealth of the corrupt politician but its use for acquiring support is less certain: depending on propaganda costs and on the *current price* for buying votes, corrupt politicians can create only short-term (even if wider) support. Presumably, the first strategy will be preferred by politicians with better prospects of staying in power, the second by those fast rising and unscrupulous politicians "on the make," the so-called *rampanti* (della Porta 1992:189), whose time-horizons, for that very reasons, are more limited in time (see Chapter 3).

In Section 5, we examined some of the resources that public agents can use to reduce friction in illegal dealings. These resources can in fact lower the costs of "producing" corrupt services and transferring property rights on the commodities exchanged. For a corrupter, for instance, acquiring a precise idea of the decision-making power is sometimes impossible, or too expensive. Being aware of this, unscrupulous politicians and other shadowy figures have an incentive to offer their services, counting on the difficulties of distinguishing between "serious" and fraudulent offers. We have seen how information, blackmailing power, and reputation for influence and "honesty" allow corrupt agents and corrupters to orient themselves, among contrasting signals, in search of partners who are trustworthy and powerful enough to furnish the services requested.

It should be noted that the different resources of corruption are linked to one another in various ways, the same being used sometimes as "commodities" for exchange and sometimes to reduce "production" or transaction costs in such illegal dealings. We have also shown how a symbolic nexus may emerge between them. For example, in certain cases the dimensions of a bribe become a recognizable measure of the "market value," and therefore the *quality*, of an otherwise unmeasurable political resource such as the ability to determine public decision-making. Where every public decision is associated with a particular sum of money in return, then not taking bribes will be considered not as honesty but rather as a lack of power, weakness, or incompetence. Thus a member of Milan PSI considered his far from brilliant career to be, in his own words, "a consequence of being considered a cretin by fellow party-members because incapable of stealing" ("Un giorno in pretura," RAI 3 TV, 22 February 1993). A lavish style of conducting politics, as well as one's private life, becomes an index and expression of power as well as wealth, which can attract and reassure "clients." At this point, however, money is no longer sought simply to gain power, nor power simply to get rich: the one is mirrored in the other and both are multiplied.

NOTES

1.   Another example of a public structure dominated by systemic corruption is presented by Sherman (1978), with reference to police departments in the United States.

2.   Basically, transaction costs are related to the coordination and incentive problems that must be borne by the parties involved in a transaction. As Kreps remarks, there are several sorts of transaction costs: "*Ex ante costs* are incurred before the transaction takes place. If the transaction is to be governed by a written contract, the contract must be drafted. Whether governed by a contract or simply by verbal commitments, the terms of the transaction must be negotiated. *Ex post costs* are incurred in consummating and safeguarding the deal that was originally struck" (1990:743).

3.   The enduring nature of these illegal earning opportunities, as Jagannathan observed, "implies the creation of intangible property rights within these systems" (1986:127). The discretionary choice of a politician to "sell" his decision-making power will be rational if the net advantage anticipated is greater than that which could be got from legally exercising that power, or, more generally, if no more remunerative use exists for the resources employed in corruption.

4.   These property rights refer to *scarce* goods (material or otherwise): "Property rights are understood as the *sanctioned behavioral relations* among men. . . . These relations specify the norms of behavior with respect to goods that each and every person must observe in his daily interactions with other persons, or bear the cost of nonobservance" (Furebotn and Pejovich 1974:3).

5.   Several indices of economic freedom on over fifty countries also show a significant negative correlation with the Transparency International index of corruption (Chafuen and Guzman 1996). Tanzi (1994) and Acemoglu and Verdier (1997) emphasize the contribution of pervasive public sector and government intervention to the spread of corruption.

6.   In Great Britain the Audit Commission, responsible for the appointment of external auditors for local government and the National Health Service, has emphasized that many of the changes that accompanied the Conservative party's program for reducing the size and cost of government increased the risks of fraud and corruption. Problems arose in the postprivatization phase, particularly after 1987, when the "government introduced legislation and structural reform across the public sector to ensure the introduction of internal markets, transfer large parts of the civil service from the Whitehall framework into Next Step agencies, and devolve substantial amounts of financial responsibility to the deliverers or the purchasers of services" (Doig 1996:48).

7.   The public as well as the private sector may in fact be interested by the problem of "contractual opportunism": "To say that individuals are opportunistic means that they are self-interested with guile. If it will further his own weal, an opportunistic individual will break any of the commandments" (Kreps 1990:744). In all principal-agent relations (see Chapter 1) an opportunistic individual can break his word, engage in misrepresentation of what he knows, and refuse to divulge information that another person lacks when the other person asks him to give up that information.

8. Even in this case, however, corruption is still possible if bribes are paid for a fraudulent drawing procedure. For instance, to freeze one little ball immediately before putting it among others to be drawn, as described by the corrupt politician Mario Chiesa, could guarantee its "casual" choice during the official procedure for the selection of the members of an important public committee (Andreoli 1993:43).

9. Each single corrupt transaction carries high *fixed costs*, that is, costs that do not vary with the amount of resources exchanged. The greater the number of agents involved in the decision-making process, therefore, the greater the number of corrupt exchanges that are necessary, involving higher risks and costs for someone seeking to influence their jointly taken decision.

10. Bryce, who defines corruption as "those modes of employing money to attain private ends which are criminal or illegal because they induce persons charged with a public duty to transgress that duty and misuse the functions assigned to them," puts voters alongside elected representatives, functionaries, and judges as among those who can be corrupted: "The bribery of voters is a practice from which few countries have been exempt" (Bryce 1921:477–78). It is possible to corrupt citizen-voters willing to sell their vote, but the uncertainty of its outcome increases with the size of the electorate, given the difficulty of buying the necessary votes and controlling whether the votes bought are actually given.

11. The form of payment adopted sometimes seeks to limit such risks. According to Agostino Licandro, ex-Mayor of Reggio Calabria, "The bigger firms were careful not to hand over all the money in a single payment. They were worried about paying an administration which could fall from one day to the next given the instability typical of the South. An instability business itself causes: where I come from a mayor is 'disposable.' When conditions foster new business possibilities and new consortia wish a larger slice of the cake they [the mayors] are thrown out to make way for others" (*L'Espresso*, 11 October 1992, p. 54).

12. As we shall indicate in Chapter 5, bureaucratic veto power is exercised in particular through the action of the control bodies, or thanks to the possibility of delaying public decisions.

13. From an analysis of 396 episodes of corruption in Italy covered by the press during the period from 1976 to 1986, it emerges that 36.6 percent refer to public contracting procedures, 28.1 percent to building permits, and 10.9 percent to recruitment in public bodies (Cazzola 1988:74). A similar study conducted in the United States obtained similar results: of 372 cases of corruption covered by the press 30.1 percent were related to public contracting procedures, 22.3 percent to building permits, and 12.1 percent to personnel recruitment and promotion (Gardiner and Lyman 1978:7–8).

14. For a more extensive analysis of several forms of political protection in the market for corrupt exchange see Vannucci (1997a, 1997b).

15. Boycko, Shleifer, and Vishny (1995), analyzing privatization processes in Russia, emphasize how the nonenforceability of corruption contracts in courts usually makes control rights on the "goods" and services exchanged uncertain and arbitrary.

16. According to Buchanan, the overall level of crime and the amount of resources that must be devoted to law enforcement decline when organized crime has a monopoly: "Monopoly in the sale of ordinary goods and services is socially

inefficient because it restricts output or supply. The monopolist uses restriction as the means to increase market price which, in turn, provides a possible source of monopoly profit. . . . If monopoly in the supply of 'goods' is socially undesirable, monopoly in the supply of 'bads' should be socially desirable, precisely because of the output restriction" (1908:119). According to this argument, monopoly-based corruption also would be *socially* preferable to a situation where it is practiced by a large number of independent actors because the overall extent of the corrupt activities would be less.

17.   In a similar way, Olson explains the fact that in the 1920s in China people preferred warlords who were stationary bandits, continuously stealing from a given group of victims, to roving bandits who soon departed: "If the stationary bandit successfully monopolizes the theft in his domain, then his victims do not need to worry about theft by others. If he steals only through regular taxation, then his subjects know that they can keep whatever proportion of their output is left after they have paid their taxes. Since all of the settled victims are for him a source of tax payments, he also has an incentive to prohibit the murder or maiming of his subjects. . . . The monopolization of thefts and the protection of the tax-generating subjects thereby eliminates anarchy" (1993:568). In the case of corruption, however, the "output" shared with "bandits" is not generated by productive activities: it is instead a political rent deriving from state activities influenced by the same "monopolist authority" In other words, such resources are often "stolen" from the public, making these protective agreements much more convenient for both parties involved.

18.   Where this expectation of protection is not met, protest quickly follows. The public sector manager Zamorani recalls that Pizzarotti, an entrepreneur, "complained about the lack of intervention from the center to deal with local party politicians, it being implicit that he had paid or promised to pay sums of money to the center and, notwithstanding that, he was still meeting with resistance in the periphery" (*La Repubblica*, 6 October 1992, p. 17). In fact, the effective supply of such protection permits to the bribed person the "internalization" of the costs and risks of decentralized bribe-taking, deriving from the simultaneous presence of many independent corruption rackets, as the reduction of the risks of being caught through intertwined judicial inquiries. Moreover, decentralized corruption tends to increase the rate of bribes, for example, in the case of many corrupt officials with multiple veto power who can use it to present their own bribe requests independently.

19.   The inability of the state to enforce impartiality in procedures relating to the benefits of public action thus increases corruption and the demand for political protection. Such a process has been observed in Russia in the crisis of transition from the socialist system: "Now criminal acts are on the increase. A sense that anything goes has taken root at the same time as faith in the help and protection forthcoming from the state has been eroded" (Loïma 1993:26).

20.   Agatino Licandro, the former mayor of Reggio Calabria implicated in the investigation, claimed that this was the case of enterprises operating in the public contracting market: "They prefer a permanent relationship. All of them. Because it's less risky. There is no need to start from the beginning on each occasion, with the trouble of locating the right individuals and running the risk of being sold a lemon" (Licandro and Varano 1993:83).

21.   Even in a hypothetical "free entry" equilibrium—when a group of producers has no (legal, moral, economic) barriers to entry into the corruption system—bribery can affect the competition among firms, reducing their number and guaranteeing rents, which are partially given to officials as bribes: "differences in the cost structure of firms create surpluses that an individual corrupt official can milk. This gives a motivation to all officials to demand bribes. This will drive the most inefficient firms out of business, enhancing the profitability of other firms, in turn making it possible for corrupt officials to demand larger bribes, and so on. This does not lead to the eventual extinction of all firms, because when the flow of payments from firms to officials reaches a high level, the officials are no longer willing to risk losing the source of their bribe income" (Bliss and Di Tella 1997:1004, 1995).

22.   The installments in which a bribe was paid could depend on the amount that would go in such bags. The 2 billion lira paid by De Mico to the government minister Nicolazzi was divided into four installments because "no more would go in a 24-hour bag" (PROM, 258).

23.   From 1992 until 1997 the *mani pulite* judges requested 657 rogatory letters of foreign magistracy, only 210 of which have received an answer (mainly negative) (*La Repubblica*, 12 March 1998, p. 6).

24. Judicial inquiries in France have revealed the heterogeneity of the means used by corrupters to bribe public officials: presents of all kinds, money loans not repayable, the settlement of debts, financial benefits in businesses, the offer of sexual relations (Fougére 1984).

25.   In modern corruption, however, a symbolic payment or gift as a manifestation of deference to patrons is generally not enough. Thus, Rocco Cornacchia, an entrepreneur, "due to his habit of bringing small gifts of bread and mushrooms from Altamura for the administrators was told by Bellomo [the functionary responsible for collecting bribes] that if he wanted to be treated the same way as the other firms he would have to contribute a great deal more than bread and mushrooms, which they could buy for themselves anyway" (UIB:12).

26.   In each case the exchange takes place in conditions of asymmetric information, one party having greater knowledge of the qualities of the commodity. This situation was first studied by Akerlof (1970), taking the example of the market for used cars. The risk of acquiring a "lemon" from the dealer may induce the purchaser (less informed than the former as to the true condition of the product) to forsake purchase. In that case, however, the dealer would prefer to sell a good used car, furnishing guarantees of that intention. If his business survives, this information will spread among consumers, creating the possibility for profits in the future. Thus building a *reputation* for honesty will be more beneficial than taking the immediate advantage of swindling the customer.

27.   Some political scientists limit the definition of relations of power to cases where there is a causal relationship between the *intentional* behavior of a holder of power and of those subject to that power. This would exclude reactions that anticipate the behavior of the holder of power, such as those used above to exemplify the force of reputation, which are included in broader definitions of power. For a discussion, see Dahl 1967:197–200.

28.   A predatory attitude, which is very costly when viewed in isolation, may be rational when considering its effects on reputation. If expectations on the politician's future behavior are based on his past actions, predation may be useful to deter potential political competitors and to draw clients (Milgrom and Roberts 1982).

29.   This may explain the violent reaction politicians occasionally display over seemingly unimportant questions, when they are aware that yielding might obfuscate the image of power that surrounds them. Umberto Colombo, president of ENI (*Ente nazionale idrocarburi*) for only four months before resigning due to his complete political isolation, engaged in a personal (and losing) battle with the vice-president, Leonardo di Donna, who was backed by the leadership of the PSI. He was warned by Eugenio Cefis, a former president of ENI, that it "was a battle [he could not] win." "He explained to me, for example, that Craxi could not abandon people like Di Donna who had been so valuable to the party. According to Cefis, if Craxi had been forced to sacrifice Di Donna he would have lost credibility and run the risk that many others no longer considered themselves protected" (*Panorama*, 9 May 1993, p. 7).

30.   As Axelrod remarks, "most forms of corruption are welcome instances of cooperation for the participants but are unwelcome to everyone else" (1984:22).

31.   Above a certain threshold trust can produce cooperation, in the illegal exchange, between corrupters and those they corrupt. Even in a "prisoner's dilemma" interaction, in fact, the indefinite repetition of the game generates multiple equilibria in strategies of mutual defection or conditional cooperation (which imply failure or success of the illegal exchange) (Axelrod 1984). Cooperation can be achieved when each party's expectations converge on a cooperation equilibrium—or, in other words, when both trusting in the cooperation of the other find it convenient to cooperate.

32.   Put another way, the choice to cooperate is conditional on the cooperation of the other party. According to the "tit for tat" strategy, the arrangement is respected so long as the other party does so and is abandoned on the first sign of "betrayal" (see, e.g., Axelrod 1984; Taylor 1987).

3

The Business Politicians

The "repentance" and confessions of one man, Mario Chiesa, were the starting point of the mani pulite investigations. Having obtained a degree in engineering, Chiesa went to work at the Sacco Hospital in Milan, on a six-month contract and there, in 1972, he joined the Socialist party, setting up a workplace section. First of all, his political affiliations appear to have brought him good fortune in his job at the hospital. After a series of contract renewals he was appointed section head following a closed competition. His position in the hospital administration then aided his rise within the Socialist party. Indeed he himself admitted that his election as secretary of one of the party's Milan sections "derived exclusively from the fact that almost all the members of the section were employees of the Sacco [Hospital]" (TM:16). In 1980, his prestige within the party reinforced, Chiesa was elected to the provincial council with twenty-two thousand votes, first becoming leader of the Socialist group and later transport assessor. He ran again in 1985 and was successfully reelected, at the top of his party's list, but he was not reappointed as an assessor. In compensation, in February 1986 he became president of the Pio Albergo Trivulzio nursing home (also known as the Baggina). Appointments to such a position, and to places on the management boards of public bodies, were officially a matter for the city council but in reality they were made at the behest of the political parties.

In order to retain his position as administrator of the Trivulzio, Chiesa resigned as provincial assessor for school buildings, a post he had also obtained in 1986. He remained a provincial councillor until 1990 but himself recalled his "absenteeism" in the role: "I rarely took part in council sessions. They only brought me in when there were loans to be voted" (L'Espresso, 18 June 1992, p. 14). One reason for preferring the administrative position was given, implicitly, by Chiesa when he spoke of his disillusionment with the lack of real power of representative bodies. He told the magistrates: "At the end of the 1970s I was an active militant and a supporter of the party current led by the then mayor, Carlo Tognoli. He made a political investment in me by putting me up for the provincial elections. I was successfully elected but found that even minor political positions like the one I had reached were largely empty, simply serving to legitimate the real sources of decision-making and power: the party secretariats and their bidding" (TM:56).

On the other hand, Chiesa was able to accumulate money and power through his position on the board of management of various public bodies. In fact, according to the Milan magistrates Chiesa imposed payment of bribes on both contracts of supply and the services he provided, negotiating and collecting payoffs personally. During the investigation one Baggina supplier described his relations with Chiesa from their first contact ("He told me I had won the tender and that it was time to pay a sum of

money in exchange. He very arrogantly insisted that a certain sum was due him")
through the prosecution of their relationship: "[H]e wouldn't put up with any
delays. Frequently, I remember, he would insult me simply because I was a couple of
days late in handing over money. . . . He once accused me very loudly, so that even
the secretaries could hear, of being a 'bum' and a 'good-for-nothing' and he threat-
ened to 'kick me out' if I didn't do what he demanded " (MPM 1992:86–87).

Besides this arrogance, however, the entrepreneur also noted a certain capacity
for management: *"The payoff was always in cash and frequently took place in his*
office. He used to pull down the blinds to prevent anybody seeing what was going
on. [He] immediately put the money in an envelope he kept at the foot of his desk. He
was very methodical and attached a Post-It memo to each bundle of notes indicating
the sum. He wanted the money properly sorted and got angry if it was in a mess"
(TM:31). These managerial capacities were not shown only in the collection of
bribes. Chiesa made a point of drawing the magistrates' attention to what he considered the positive side of his administration: *"I would like to start by saying that my*
responsibility in relation to the charges against me notwithstanding, I worked very
hard to transform the Trivulzio. I remember that when I arrived the Trivulzio was
just a place people went to die and there was a smell of urine everywhere. Between
1986 and 1991 at least 500 new beds were added in new wards, 420 of them for long-
term rehabilitation. These figures exemplify the positive aspects of my management"
(L'Espresso, 18 June 1992, p. 16). Chiesa was also highly skilled in using his position to distribute favors. He explained: *"A nurse wanted her son taken on? Fine, we*
got to work on it. A comrade had been evicted and needed somewhere to live? OK,
we would try and get him a council house. A hospital doctor wished a transfer to
another unit? Right, we would put pressure on the hospital administration. I became
very popular in this way. Years later I met an old comrade and was delighted to see
that in his wallet he still had a santino, one of the little cards with my name we dis-
tributed at election time" (Andreoli 1993:42–43).

The magistrates seized more than 15 billion lira between official bank accounts,
safety deposit boxes, shares of stock, real estate companies, government bonds, and
property shortly after Chiesa's arrest. A large part of the proceeds of bribery were
plowed back into political activity, particularly into ensuring that the party confirmed his position (Chiesa was in his third term of office when arrested). Chiesa
claimed he had helped out others in the party, handing out millions of lira, particularly at the outset of his career. He then stopped forwarding money to the party in
1989 when, as he saw it, he had *"acquired an authoritative and autonomous position*
within the Milan PSI" (TM:25). Boasting that he controlled 20 percent of the membership of the party's city federation and that he was responsible for the election of
32 out of 120 ward councillors, Chiesa declared: *"In Milan I personified a current*
within the party with its own funds, organization, and personnel" (TM:19). As he
doggedly explained to the magistrates, in part bribery had to be transformed into
votes in order to guarantee renewal in office by the party. *"In substance, to under-*
stand the reasons why I should expose myself personally in the mechanism of bribery
it is necessary to understand that I did not remain president of an organization like
the Trivulzio simply because I was a good technician and a good health manager but
also because in a certain way I was a force to be reckoned with in Milan, having a
certain number of votes at my disposal. To acquire what amounted in the end to
7,000 votes I had, during my political career, to sustain the cost of creating and

maintaining a political organization that could amass votes right across Milan."
These blocs of members and votes were then put at the service of influential party
leaders in return for a new term of office. Chiesa explained during one interrogation:
"I had to maintain my political structure in the city, a structure articulated not only
through via Castelfidardo and later via Soresina [his headquarters] but also a whole
series of circles and sports clubs throughout the city. Only the ensemble of these var-
ious activities allowed me to count politically, through preferences votes that could
be utilized either for myself or for other candidates" (L'Espresso, 18 June 1992, p.
19). In fact, according to Chiesa it was he who organized the electoral campaign of
Bettino Craxi, the party secretary, in 1987. In 1990, again, he relinquished an asses-
sorship in the city council in return for the reconfirmation of his position at the PAT,
putting his votes at the disposal of Vittorio Craxi, son of the national secretary Bet-
tino, and Paolo Pillitteri, former mayor of the city.

As this brief description indicates, political corruption has specific consequences on the political class, the way in which political careers evolve, the
capabilities required of a politician who participates systematically in corrupt exchange, the motivations that push individuals to get involved in
politics. In this chapter, we discuss these questions, by defining an ideal-
type of the "business politician" as one possessing the abilities necessary
for the functioning of the system of corruption. As we shall see, situations
of widespread corruption facilitate the emergence of a political class characterized by very low moral costs for illegal activities. At its turn, in a sort
of vicious circle, this political class, occupying all the important positions,
perpetrates and enlarges political corruption.

In what follows, the results of our empirical research will be used to illus-
trate some of the attributes of a special type of business politician, which
we will define as "boss of the public body." In Section 1, we will define some
preconditions of the emergence of the political boss in the crisis of the mass
party. In Section 2, we will analyze the skills in illegality, as a factor that
facilitates these new political careers. Moreover, as we will see in Section 3,
the business politicians use their *networking abilities* to create support and
complicity. In Section 4, we will, from a comparative perspective, discuss
the effect of political socialization on the "moral cost" of corruption. The
characteristics of politicians' reference groups, the presence or absence of
socialization in civic values, and the "moral quality" of political life are
indicated—following Pizzorno (1992); della Porta and Pittorno (1996)—as
factors defining and influencing individual calculation in relation to
involvement in corrupt transactions.

1.   THE EMERGENCE OF THE BUSINESS POLITICIANS

How do people like Mario Chiesa succeed in occupying political space?
Our research indicates that corruption spreads out in periods of transfor-

mation in the political parties, when a political class with strong ideological convictions is substituted by individuals viewing politics as just another "business." This comes out most clearly from a reconstruction at the local level of the history of the political party most deeply involved in the recent Italian scandals: the PSI. In the two local federations we analyzed in more detail—Savona in Northern Italy and Florence in the center—the transformation of the party that led to its infiltration by a class of politicians with little sense of civic morality was already under way in the immediate postwar years. Gradual abandonment by part of the working-class base was accelerated sharply when the left wing of the party split to found the Socialist Party of Proletarian Unity (Partito Socialista di Unità Proletaria, PSIUP) in 1964. A militant of the period described the social and organizational transformations of the party as follows:

> The history of the Savona PSI . . . has two distinct phases. First, starting from 1943, the heroic period of clandestinity, and the post-Resistance years, many of the party's militants coming from its ranks. . . . In this period militants came from disparate social groups: antifascist lawyers, for example. There were also many workers, who would later leave with the breakaway of the PSIUP and the transformation of the party. At the time the PSI had a strong nucleus of railway workers, students, workers from Italsider, and the other big factories in the *Savonese* (which was a heavily industrialized zone). So much so that in the first elections after the war the PSI had more votes than the PCI. An intermediate period followed, the influence of the Resistance remaining strong. However, after that there was an authentic generational break. (Interview SV6)

As in Savona, in Florence the breakaway of the PSIUP led to a draining of membership in the party branches, weakened contacts with the trade union movement, and significant electoral losses. According to a party leader:

> The break in the Florentine PSI came in 1964, when the trade unionists left. In fact, to find a Socialist assistant secretary to the *Camera del Lavoro* [Trades Council] they had to dig up an old comrade who had done the job before the war. The most pro-Communist element went with the breakaway, but also the most proletarian and popular. . . . The proletarian component quit; the enlightened bourgeois element became a minority. . . . Gaps thus opened that were slowly filled with personnel coming from the PSDI [Partito Social Democratico Italiano—Italian Social Democratic Party]. With the losses and the rupture practices changed a lot. (Interview FI7)

In both cities the organizational weakening of the party coincided with a growing presence at all levels of government and a consequent mutation in the motivations of militants and leadership. If in the immediate postwar period the PSI had recruited from the ranks of the partisans, in the 1970s its functionaries came from the middle class. At the very moment material resources were becoming the principal ones distributed within the party, the power base of the leadership was tending to shift outside the party itself. At the time influence within the party depended on positions occupied in local government bodies or in parliament. In order to obtain these positions it was necessary to develop an *ad personam* electoral following, particularly from expanding social groups such as the new middle classes. In the 1960s and 1970s "emerging" social groups were attracted to the party. In both Savona and Florence the growing importance of the construction industry led to the development of privileged relations between socialist officials and such social groups as proprietors of vacant land, entrepreneurs in the building industry, architects, and engineers. The power of attraction exercised by the PSI on these groups appears to have derived from the availability of posts in local government, which expanded rapidly in the mid-1970s in particular.

Generational turnover meant that a new leadership would exercise the power acquired at the local level. A new political class that formed in the wake of the first experiences of government replaced the prewar political class, which had maintained its power within the party through traditional political resources (such as the charisma associated with participation in the Resistance). This new political class consolidated its power through the occupation of party-appointed positions in the public sector, positions that permitted "business politicians" to organize their careers around the private appropriation of public resources. Business politicians, in fact, lined their pockets through bribery and the exploitation of their political power in other activities, particularly where that power furnished them with an edge over competitors. In the first place, political connections facilitated the acquisition of career positions within the public sector bureaucracy. If these positions proved sufficiently productive of unlawful earnings, then the relations they enabled within illegal markets also produced advantages in legal activities.

For corrupt politicians, the party became the source of upward mobility. While following different institutional itineraries and with varying degrees of success, the careers of the administrators implicated in the investigations considered did indeed reveal common tendencies, summed up by many of the interviewees with the colorful neologism *rampantismo*—an Italian neologism that can be translated as being "on the make." In the first place, our business politicians generally entered politics *without prepolitical resources*—that is, they entered politics with little money, prestige, and/or power. Their careers frequently began from "near the bottom." As in the case of Chiesa, a picture of "obscure social origins" and, at the same time, scant ability or professional qualifications is fairly common also for the descriptions of other business politicians. Many of the politicians involved in a scandal in Savona were described in our interviews as "on the make" types: "an impoverished young man with neither art nor part, without education" (Coisson 1983:15), "a two-cent adventurer," "an architect on the make, without scruples" (Interview SV3). One Florentine politician's "obscure origins" were mentioned, while of another the judges remarked: "[H]e has no well-defined occupation" (QGF:61). Many of these new leaders were described as "not overly scrupulous," out for "personal gain" or "power for its own sake," "ambitious professionals attracted by the chance of allying themselves with whoever, irrespective of their slogans or ideas, is actually in power" (della Porta 1997:241; see also 1996a, 1997).

Second, while displaying differences, their career paths were all of a "party" nature, sharing their *determination by political affiliation*. There are examples of public administrators' careers following the quite traditional path from trade union or party hierarchy to political appointment in the public sector, and on to elected administrative office. Posts in the public sector furnish the clientele necessary to be elected to local councils, from which control over the local party federation can also be tightened. Less frequently careers are conducted wholly within the party machine. Here we find the figure of the "lieutenant" who builds up his own power in the shadow of a boss: the power of administrative secretaries or the personal secretary of a political leader was often emphasized by interviewees. The common feature is that career depends on party membership and there is little sign of specialization or the development of administrative skills.[1] To give just an example, the former president of a welfare agency candidly confessed his ignorance of administrative laws and regulations: "The moment to tender the first contract arrived"—he declared to the judges— "and I asked how things worked. I was told that there would be a commission and that those competing had to reach a certain sum, represented by the average of the offers. *I didn't know exactly how it worked, but I guessed something would happen and that somebody would thank me with cash*" (TM:122, emphasis added).

Careers in elected bodies are combined with those in party-controlled appointments in local public organizations, with very little specialization on the basis of professional background—a driver can be found running a hospital, for example—and also little coherence in moves made within the public administration itself. The hierarchy of different political posts is quite unlike the traditional one: being a "simple deputy" (a *peones* in parliament) is less attractive than a good position in a local council or the presidency of a local public body. According to our interviews, entering the national parliament was sought only when (at least) an undersecretaryship was guaranteed or if an urgent need for parliamentary immunity existed. A position as a party functionary becomes increasingly unattractive while the administration of public bodies offers the possibility of building up resources "for oneself" rather than in the name of the party.

Third, *political activity facilitates success in other professional activities.* Obviously this is not something new for careers in politics, particularly at the local level. What appears peculiar, however, is the kind of entrepreneur or professional for whom political activity serves to improve his economic market position. Traditionally, doctors or lawyers, for example, have used their professional clientele to get elected to public administration. In our case, it seems instead that politics serves to gain privileged access to public resources, on which the professional career was based in the first place. Thus, political career and economic activities, in particular those rendered more "profitable" precisely through control of public power, become intertwined. Political activity often serves primarily in obtaining a post at some level of the public bureaucracy.[2] Such positions not only allow the rounding out of earnings, but also act as a counterweight to the swings of fortune that occur in elected office. In the Catanese case, not only were careers of hospital doctors described as "political," insofar as they were dependent on political protection, but positions in the bureaucracies of publicly controlled organizations were also mentioned, in the Savona case, for example, ranging from provincial tourist boards to the public housing body (*Istituto Autonomo Case Popolari*, IACP). For others, a career in politics helps boost professional or commercial activities. Thus, we encountered architects or hoteliers who had become local administrators, and therefore were enabled to pursue their professional activities in particularly advantageous conditions.

Finally, it can be noted that the money from corruption is frequently invested in consultancy firms in the hope of being awarded loosely controlled public contracts. To give just one example, the Liguria administrators involved in a political corruption case in the 1980s specialized in speculative ventures in the construction sector, making substantial personal real estate investments, for the most part through third parties or front companies (UIS:217). These companies are useful to the corrupt politician's career in many ways: they permit the self-attribution of privileges, are used to launder the proceeds of corruption, conceal bribes as mediation costs, and ensure material security should judicial difficulties compel a forced exit from politics.

In brief, the importance of *belonging to a political party as the means of upward mobility* is a common denominator of the careers of business politicians. In this sense, business politicians closely resemble one formulation of the famous Weberian category, the "professional politician" (Weber 1919): those entering politics with no prepolitical resources and for whom politics is therefore the sole avenue to upward mobility (e.g., Gaxie 1973; Mastropaolo 1984). If belonging to a political party is the principal resource of business politicians, they nonetheless make use of others necessary for the organization of corrupt exchange.

2. SKILLS IN ILLEGALITY AND POLITICAL CAREERS

As it emerged in our reconstruction of the career of Mario Chiesa, business politicians specialize in "operating in the shadows" and dedicate the greater part of their time to illegal activities—such as contacting businessmen, and demanding, negotiating the amount of, and receiving bribes. Illegal activities, corruption among them, require knowledge of the "rules of the game." As a corrupt administrator recalled, "Normally people think that corruption is just about money flitting from one pocket to another, a simple, uncomplicated matter like a vulgar theft. In fact, it is not. It's really difficult to explain the way the world of corruption works. You need a lot of patience to understand its different (and frequently complex) mechanisms. It's not like a series of burglaries: *there are rules and relations, fixed conventions; a whole language of nuances and accents that assume all the solemnity of a written contract*" (Licandro and Varano 1993:18, emphasis added). A distinctive "jargon," exclusive to initiates, allows unlawful requests or exactions to be communicated and at the same time avoids the danger of exposing oneself too far. In fact, even where corruption was the rule, it was never mentioned openly. The initial approach took stereotypical forms: "And there's nothing in it for us?" or "Speaking of the party's necessities and the usual practice as far as businesses helping to cover them is concerned" (from a businessman's evidence in CDEM:119). The following description by a Milanese entrepreneur, who approached a Socialist representative on the board of a public company seeking work for his firm, is sufficient illustration: "I tried to point out the advanced techniques used by the firm I represented. *I noticed immediately that [he] was getting impatient and irritable.* Within a few minutes he made me understand what he wanted with phrases like '*the message has been passed on . . .* to furnish rolling-stock *one has to follow the normal procedure.*' . . . In short, he made me understand that if we wanted the contracts we had to pay 5 percent of their value in bribes" (*Panorama,* 5 July 1992, emphasis added). In the phase of negotiating the amount to be paid, a wide range of terms was adopted: "reimbursement of expenses," "compensation," "gratuity," "bonus," "organizational contribution," "premium" in the language of the public officials;"disbursements," "political expenditures," "additional costs," "obligations," "the X percent rule," "unspecified expenses" in that of the entrepreneurs.

In corruption as in other illicit markets, knowledge of the techniques required to minimize the risk of denunciation is also required. To give one example, the ex-mayor of Reggio Calabria described the "professionalism" required in preparing bribery money in the following terms:

> I opened the bag and bundles of 100,000 [lira] notes fell out. It was all perfectly prepared and I should know, I used to work in a bank; all used notes

but none too damaged. Bills nobody could ever identify; it would have been impossible to trace them. An expert job. Whoever was responsible was a specialist; they really knew what they were doing. The bands on the money were as anonymous as the envelopes and the briefcase. Nobody could ever have proved anything. The whole thing betrayed solidity of organization, efficiency, shrewdness, and professionalism. I thought to myself: "These people do nothing else." (Licandro and Varano 1993:33)

Since organizing corruption is no easy task, business politicians must spend a lot of their time and energies in keeping illegal activities secret and avoiding being "had" by the other side in the deal. As Susan Rose Ackerman observes, in fact, "[Corruption's] very illegality produces inefficiencies, since resources are wasted in keeping transactions secret and in enforcing anti-bribery statutes" (1978:8). Our research describes a universe in which a great deal of time is spent establishing and maintaining the "right contacts," seeking information or guarantees, and transmitting or receiving remuneration. Mario Chiesa recalled with apparent pride: "The waiting room of my office was always full of supplicants, entrepreneurs, cap in hand . . . and willing to wait unsuccessfully for hours" (Andreoli 1993:55). Also revealing is the testimony of the ex-head of procurement for Milan's public transport company (ATM), Claudio Provini: "There was a competition to gain our, the functionaries', favor and oust competitors already introduced. In this context it was necessary neither to compel nor to persuade but simply a matter of choosing the best or most recommended offer" (*Panorama*, 21 April 91, p. 68).

If corrupt exchange requires discretion, business politicians, as other actors in illegal marketplaces, have an interest in acquiring a semipublic reputation for arrogance. Descriptions of corrupt administrators stressed their exhibitions of aggressive and menacing behavior. The following passage from an interview with a doctor indicates that certain public administrators had a widespread reputation as "high-handed" among the hospital's suppliers:

The representative of a large pharmaceutical firm told me that one day the president of the hospital called him in, a mountain of files on the desk in front of him, and said "You represent firm X. From a memorandum I have here on the desk it appears that the invoicing for your firm is 340 million. Now, we're a bit behind here, but anyway, it's 10 percent. That makes 34 million." The representative says, "Sorry, I don't understand. What do you mean?" The president replies arrogantly, "If you don't understand have it explained to you and then come back. We're serious people here." It was the president himself who pulled the strings. He personally called in the people. (Interview CT1)

As we mentioned in the previous chapter, while at first sight it might seem to elevate the risk of denunciation, a reputation for arrogance is also useful in certain respects in the organization of corruption. Having a reputation as "tough" or "authoritarian" and for making arbitrary decisions heightened the perception among entrepreneurs of the risks involved in resisting the demands of corrupt officials. High-handedness gave the impression of a power as absolute as it was arbitrarily exercised, increasing the businessman's fear because it led him to believe that "a change of humor [on a corrupt politician's part] would have been enough for me to lose the work" (MPM:85). In fact, arrogance simulates greater power than is actually possessed and thus permits the amplification of the range of connections maintained and the extension of real power. What Pizzorno (1992:25–26) has called the "vicious circle of arrogance" is thus completed: exhibition of the capability to be arbitrary creates a reputation for being powerful, concentrating the demand for favors and creating support that can then be used in the political system to extend actual power.

3.   NETWORKING ABILITIES AND CORRUPTION

Skills in illegality are not the only qualities demanded of the business politician. It is true that a number of abilities normally rewarded in traditional politics are superfluous for the careers (brilliant or otherwise) of our business politicians. Administrators involved in corruption trials did not have great reputations as ideologists or orators: to give just one example, it has been said of the ex-president of the Liguria Region, Alberto Teardo, involved in a scandal in 1983: "[H]e did not speak in public. Public meetings of the PSI were held but he never intervened" (Baget Bozzo 1985). Moreover, they appear to have little respect for the "visible" sites of politics: it has been observed, once again in relation to the ex-president of Liguria Region, that "he had already reached a record for absenteeism in the regional assembly, and on one occasion sent a tape recording of the resolutions to be passed" (Coisson 1983:16). Generally speaking, business politicians have no professional training that would allow them to fulfill the tasks required by public administration. Nominated on party grounds, public sector administrators perceive their position as a reward for loyalty to a particular political leader and as a means of increasing their own financial resources or those of their political patron. This was well illustrated by one of the politicians implicated in the Milan investigations, who told the magistrates: "When the PSI nominated me as a director of the ECA [a public body] everyone told me that others had done well out of it, even though the salary was only 280,000 lira a month. . . . In encouraging me to take the post, they knew very well what benefits came with it: not only the car and the secretary, but *the concrete possibility of 'setting oneself up,' of providing for one's old age* as well" (in MPM:159, emphasis added).

Our business politicians, however, are well endowed in terms of other capacities traditionally considered valuable for a political career: the ability to *network*, forming relations, creating bonds of trust, and encouraging mutual obligations and favors.[3] If networking is rewarded in traditional politics, in a system of widespread corruption it is not solely directed to the augmentation of personal power but also to the creation of the necessary "cover"—within one's own party, the other parties, civil society, and public institutions.

A first circle of connivance permitting the reproduction and expansion of corruption is constituted *within the party system*, where a sort of reciprocal "protection" is created involving both "corrupt" and "not corrupt." In our research, we observed, first of all, that few denunciations for corruption to the magistracy were presented by representatives of the political parties. What processes lead to the "protection" of corrupt politicians both by their own and by the other parties? What resources do corrupt politicians exchange with those who are not corrupt in order to obtain the widespread connivance they enjoy?

In the first place, the corrupt politician gains complicity within his own party by offering, in return for connivance, the blocks of "delegates" required in interfactional competition. The management of relations within the party on the part of "corrupt" politicians was described in our interviews as "pragmatic" or "cynical." The absence of "ideological preconceptions" in the management of alliances between different factions, for example, ensured the corrupt Savona politicians the "protection" they needed in the national leadership of their party. One member of the group told the judges: "Practically . . . we transferred arms and baggage from one faction to another" (*Il Secolo XIX*, 17 April 1985). The instability of alliances between party factions also increases the blackmailing power of the corrupt politicians, who can approach the faction to whom they are indispensable at a given moment and obtain connivance and protection. The picture that emerges from the Savona case is confirmed—as we saw also at the beginning of this chapter—by Mario Chiesa, who revealed: "With the proceeds of the bribes I paid the subscriptions of members of my section and when the various party offices had to be renewed, I controlled a block of party members and votes that I put at the disposition of the party and in particular of those candidates indicated by my principal referent. Likewise, I put my block of members and votes on the table when my own position was to be renewed or I was to move to a new one" (TM:118–19).

Business politicians are also very *pragmatic* in their distribution of funds within their party, in order to spread the circle of connivance. "Pragmatism" in political management also assists corrupt politicians to obtain the silence and complicity of the other parties, including those not directly involved in corruption. This silence, in fact, is "bought" through the sharing of the bribes or the exchange of political alliances for tolerance of corruption. A "pragmatic" conception of politics increases the openness of corrupt politicians to different kinds of alliances. For example, the president of the Liguria Region implicated in the Savona scandal was respected as a dependable ally. According to a leader of the Communist party: "His concrete conception of politics gave him the possibility of being very open on the question of alliances. . . . If he did not have a direct interest himself, he gave way to the other parties" (Interview SV3).

As the story of Mario Chiesa presented at the beginning of this chapter already indicated, beyond the party system, too, many business politicians had been able to construct a large network of personal supporters, constituted by *clients* and "friends" in local elites. Through a "generous" and "discerning" management of favors—made possible by a conception of public resources as personal property—corrupt politicians obtained collusion in civil society. In the first place, these public sector bosses created exclusive relationships with groups of entrepreneurs, designed to finance both their own careers and, naturally, the party system.[4]

According Mario Chiesa, the growing costs of the party organization were met thanks to deals with particular entrepreneurs: "Certain economic sectors, especially those involved in construction, are symbiotically linked to the public authorities in order to ensure continuity of business. As is well known, they pay bribes in return" (TNM:23). The case of an "on the make" funeral director, someone described as having gone from a cardboard suitcase to a fast car (Andreoli 1993:22), illustrates this symbiosis perfectly. Chiesa remarked of him: "He became a natural ally and was pleased by my growing political success. He made a point of displaying in public his connection with [me] and the fact that he assisted [me] in everything, even when this meant paying from his own pocket. He forced his employees to join my branch of the party, filled the halls with carnations for party gatherings, and paid for electoral dinners" (Andreoli 1993:22). As this makes clear, bribery and electoral support are neither mutually exclusive nor independent. It may be in the interest of an entrepreneur who finds himself in an advantaged market situation through bribery to create a stable relationship with his political counterpart and thus vote for, and have elected, the person with whom he is involved in corrupt dealings. Corruption can therefore become a means of creating electoral support, even among those from whom bribes are demanded and who, at the same time, are made to feel that they require a powerful sponsor.

It is the desire to increase the flow of money coming from bribery that induces corrupt politicians to escalate the activity and spending of the bodies they control (see also Chapter 9). By doing so they multiply opportunities for distributing the favors with which they procure support from the "respectable," as one person interviewed put it. In order to increase the flow of bribes they must spend more public money, particularly in those sectors where the illegal returns appear highest. A number of politicians involved in recent corruption investigations stressed their "dynamic" image, a self-representation that also offers a "moral" justification of corruption. The description given of an eminent colleague by a Calabrian administrator makes the point nicely:

> He really is convinced that he always pursued the general interest with abnegation and public spirit. He had a theory. Reggio was in competition with the other cities, Calabria with the other regions. Securing investment, even through corruption, served the interests of the population and contributed to the prosperity of the city. Paris was worth a mass, and public works were worth a bit of bribery even if by doing so the system was perpetuated. He said: "That's the way it is. Otherwise we have no public works, no employment and no help for the less well-off." (Licandro and Varano 1993:71)

In addition, portrayals of public sector bosses commonly stress their "power to corrupt": the capability to grant favors to large numbers of individuals, privileging those sectors and groups that offer the greatest "compensation" in terms of support and connivance. They created personal support through the management of public resources thanks, as the judges of Savona remarked, "to small connections and favors (career promotions, transfers, allocation of housing or loans, assorted licenses and authorizations, small gratuities, and prebends, etc.)" (UIS:148). Indeed, many of the politicians involved in the investigations spent a large part of their time creating this kind of personal consensus. This emerges clearly in an interview given by the neighbor of the former president of the Liguria Region, of whom he said: "The Region's car came every morning at half past eight exactly to take him to Genoa, but never left before ten o'clock. I was curious to know why. Well, he would go down at eight-thirty precisely, but he didn't leave. He was in a corner of the courtyard or in the car, listening to clients, favor-seekers, recommended persons, the party comrade dragging his son along to meet the comrade-boss" (cited in Bocca 1983:9). Similarly, an interviewee stressed the "corrupting power" of the president of the Sicilian hospital already mentioned: "He invited magistrates or their wives to teach in the schools of specialization, offered consultations to important members of the professions, attached himself to Catanese professional and entrepreneurial circles, elevated corruption to the rule" (Interview CT1).

Corrupt politicians, once more through concealed regulation of favors, are also able to obtain the connivance of the media. The intrusion of political influence appeared particularly dangerous in the field of the media. Investigative journalism, in fact, constitutes an essential deterrent to corruption. Besides contributing directly to the exposure of illegal practices, the media also represents the *filter* through which knowledge of corruption is divulged. The public's idea of the gravity of a scandal (and therefore its possible electoral consequences) depends on the *quantity* and the *kind* of information provided by the media. Links between politicians playing institutional roles and the press and television, whether the result of secret understandings or of proprietorial pressure, represent a serious contamination of the democratic political process (for instance, Rossi 1993:107). As for television, for a long time in Italy the monopolistic public channels were under strict political control, which thwarted any attempt to develop an investigative journalism. The development of private channels, often under political "tutelage," did not change the situation. Research on the way television news handles corruption revealed, in fact, that political scandals were frequently "covered up" (Cazzola 1988). During our research, we noticed that—before the *mani pulite* investigations—the local press rarely dramatized political scandals.[5] On the contrary, they seemed often to breach both professional ethics and their interest in selling copies in order to protect local administrators involved in episodes of corruption. In this case also, the "corrupting power" of business politicians—through private employment of public resources and the strategy of favor distribution—allows them to procure the connivance of the press. One person interviewed concerning the Catanese case remarked:

> The president of one USL managed to involve *La Sicilia* [the leading local newspaper] in this chain of collusion. *La Sicilia* would never attack him, given the deal he arranged for its proprietor. In fact, the president had the USL rent a villa, which had been bought for peanuts by the newspaper's proprietor, as its administrative offices. Instead of using the thousands of rooms in the different hospitals for administrative offices, the president of the USL rents this villa. . . . After a horrible refurbishment—no more than 50 million [lira]—he managed to rent this villa (which cost a billion) for 350 million a year, almost a million a day. (Interview CT2)

As the ex-mayor of Reggio Calabria explained, this strategy aimed above all at creating collusion between the controllees and their potential controllers: "In a word, I paid everybody: the politicians, the upright state functionaries who were meant to be controlling the validity of my administrative decisions, even a State Audit Court magistrate. And naturally I paid the journalist considered the most influential of the city, whose articles got both the majority and the opposition parties moving and who pulled the strings of quite a few influential magistrates at the Court of Justice" (Licandro and Varano 1993:3).

The business politicians also constructed networks of support among the employees of the bodies they managed.[6] Personnel expansion, accompanied by a brazen use of any and every law allowing the requirement of impartiality in hiring to be circumvented, permitted entourages of faithful vassals to be created. The bodies in which corruption was most wide-spread were also those in which clientelist hiring practices were most common, often in favor of party activists. Taking two examples, according to witnesses the Metropolitana Milanese (MM) was "used as a reservoir for political appointments, comrades who collected a wage from the MM without even clocking on" (Andreoli 1993:51), while in the airport authority "everyone taken on was hired on political grounds: mayors, assessors, and councillors from the hinterland, and also party leaders, in order to get their and their followers' support" (ibid.:132).

Finally, bribery money gives greater opportunities for creating a large electoral clientele insofar as it permits more effective organization of the political machine of individual bosses. The management of public bodies also allowed corrupt relations to be formed with certain professional categories, often themselves possessing an autonomous capacity for constructing electoral clienteles. Doctors provide a typical example. As Chiesa himself recalled, "In via Castelfidardo I met with actual or aspiring heads of unit, looking for my support in winning promotion or obtaining a transfer" (ibid.:31). This political protection could be repaid in cash: "In the Fatebenefratelli hospital a system of bribery was in force. A job as head of unit could cost as much as 100 million [lira], paid by the interested party to the right person" (ibid.). Alternatively, it might be repaid in clients: "There isn't a hospital head of unit who hasn't made a more or less public profession of political faith; even extremely able doctors. Merit counts very little on the career scale. You get on if you have party connections. *It isn't because you are a luminary of the profession that you become a head of unit, but because you can guarantee votes on the appropriate occasion*" (ibid.:84, emphasis added).

As we mentioned describing the career of Mario Chiesa, networking appears to be favored by two seemingly contradictory character traits highlighted in the interviews: arrogance, which we already mentioned, and sociability. The portrayals of the ex-president of the Liguria Region appearing in the newspapers immediately after the scandal broke dwelt on the contradictions of someone "famed as an artist of command, implacable with his adversaries, extremely devoted to his friends" (Lerner 1983:67); "very different images and memories remain [of him] in the *Savonese*. There are those who remember him as a hard and methodical boss, 'one who wore both belt and braces' and others who remember him as a benefactor, 'I owe everything to Alberto'" (Bocca 1983:9).

For our politicians, politics is a business based on the distribution of favors in exchange for connivance. The administrators implicated in corruption cases tend to present their actions as perfectly normal, albeit not conforming to a "utopian" ideal of democracy. Significantly, of one of the administrators involved in the trial concerning Villa Favard in Florence the public prosecutor observed: "[H]e has always acted on the belief that receiving payoffs for the party was legal, politically laudable, and in no way morally reprehensible" (*La Nazione*, 27 February 1986). Looking at the justifications of the defendants during trials, a relevant common feature is their presentation of themselves as "children of the political system," in no way different from their less unfortunate "colleagues."[7] Their actions (including bribe-taking) originated from the requirements of politics; not an idealized version of politics but real, actual politics. In the picture presented by the "corrupt," "real" politics is a *costly business* given that an election campaign, it is assumed, will cost several hundred million lira. In a conception of politics defined by them as "modern," "payoffs" are seen simply as a form of sponsorship by particular interest groups. The closing address of the ex-president of the Liguria Region's defense lawyer is once more illuminating: "This trial originates in the demands of politics: what is wrong with a private individual deciding to finance a politician? The construction firms providing finance had their convenience. The reality is that we are not very advanced, little developed, in the rear as far as democracy is concerned. We have a long tradition of fear and diffidence toward public figures. But look at America! There, the lobbies sponsor politicians" (cited in *L'Unità*, 3 August 1985).

In addition, politics is characterized by a continual exchange of *favors*. Thus it is asserted that the contributions were "gifts" given not in return for illegal action but rather for "favors." "Gifts" and "favors" are then defined as expressions of "friendship" and "solidarity," terms often used during interrogations. Arrogance thus shades into a particular conception of *generosity*, as the distribution of "favors" to "friends": one of the administrators implicated said, "I've always given" (*L'Unità*, 16 March 1985). Delays and inefficiencies in the administrative system provide additional justification: to "speed up the process" for a "friend" becomes "legitimate defense" against the inefficiency of the system. Indeed, the constant exaltation of "friendship" renders the corrupt transaction ethically praiseworthy. Many of our business politicians would agree with a Sicilian DC 'boss' who confessed: "I can admit to having a fault. . . . I am human. If I am somebody's friend, I help them" (cited in Leone 1988).[8] Finally, this conception of politics and of friendship allows those implicated to distinguish between criminal behavior (which is not their case) and a practice described as "unorthodox" or a "shortcut." "Gifts," "favors," and expressions of "solidarity" are considered "innocent " behavior so long as third parties are not directly harmed. From this idea of politics the corrupt create an image of themselves as generous, altruistic, and efficient. In short, in the cases examined, there is a conception of politics as "business" and an argument that public service is in no way incompatible with private gain, even when the latter is obtained outside "the visible rules of the game."[9] Actions, while "unorthodox," can be justified as necessary to reach a legitimate goal.

4. HOMINES NOVI, PATRIMONIALISM, AND THE MORAL COSTS OF CORRUPTION: A CONCLUSION

Political corruption transforms the political class. It operates on the motivations for choosing permanent political activity, on the capabilities demanded of political personnel (and therefore the criteria upon which they are selected), and on the aggregations in which those personnel are organized. In fact, the presence of corruption will be accompanied by the dissemination of a particular type of politician: the *business politician*. In particular, a good proportion of these new politicians will base their power on the control of public bodies—they will become *public sector bosses*.

The spread of corruption and the emergence of a new political class, the business politicians, whose characteristics we have attempted to define here, are interacting processes. The politicians considered in the present study certainly belong among those, according to the noted definition of Weber (1919), who "live by politics," seeking extrinsic or instrumental advantages. They are "professional politicians," and more particularly in one of the definitions given for the term, politicians who view politics as a means for achieving upward social mobility (Mastropaolo 1990:58–59).[10] As was observed in Section 1, the crisis of the ideological mass parties brings about a lowering of the barriers to illegal behavior. In this situation, a political class motivated prevalently by ideology is displaced by individuals who view politics primarily as a business.

In which situations does this political class emerge? The classic studies of local power in the United States identified the preconditions for a reduction in the moral quality of the political class in the accession to power of particular emerging groups. In his famous study on New Haven, Connecticut, Robert Dahl (1961) singled out, on the basis of the social origins of those occupying positions of institutional power, some distinct stages in the passage from oligarchy to pluralism, from the concentration to the dispersal of the most relevant political resources. The first was characterized by the predominance of the *patricians*, a ruling class possessing all the resources of power (wealth, education, and social status) and enjoying high legitimacy. With the extension of suffrage and the secret ballot, the power of the patricians diminished and that of the *entrepreneurs*, wealthy but lacking in social prestige and education, increased. Their popularity (linked to their identification with the dominant value system) notwithstanding, the entrepreneurs were few in number. With continuing industrialization and the consequent immigration of new ethnic groups, the road was opened to the *ex-plebs*, who had neither wealth nor instruction but were able to build a following among the new immigrants. The entry of the ex-plebs brought about a transformation of the political ethos: "Political leaders and their followings combined to use the political system in order to eliminate the handicaps associated with ethnic identity rather than to reduce disadvantages stemming from the distribution of resources by the existing socio-economic order itself" (ibid.:33). It was in this phase that corruption developed, since the new political leaders, themselves often from ethnic groups discriminated against, began to offer protection in return for electoral support:

> Since political leaders hoped to expand their own influence with the votes of ethnic groups, they helped the immigrant overcome his initial political powerlessness by engaging him in politics. Whatever else the ethnics lacked, they had numbers. Hence politicians took the initiative; they made it easy for immigrants to become citizens, encouraging ethnics to register, put them on the party rolls, and aided them in meeting the innumerable specific problems resulting from their poverty, strangeness, and lowly position. To obtain and hold the votes, the political leaders rewarded them with city jobs. (ibid.:34)

According to Dahl, however, the integration of these ethnic groups into the community reduced the power of the ex-plebs.

Other students of local power very explicitly link the lowering of the moral quality of the political class to its social origins, describing a kind of class ethos. According to such hypotheses, while the middle class sees local politics as a service to the community, emphasizing the public virtues of honesty, efficiency, and impartiality, the lower classes prefer political clientelism and corruption, from which they receive the particularistic protection they need. Edward Banfield and James Q. Wilson in particular have argued that

> the middle class ideal sees local politics as a cooperative search for the concrete implications of a more or less objective public interest, and interest of the community "as a whole." The logic of the middle-class ideal requires that authority be exercised by those who are "best qualified," that is, technical experts and statesmen, not "politicians." The logic of the middle-class ideal implies . . . particular regard for the public virtues of honesty, efficiency, and impartiality; and a disposition to encourage the consumption of "public goods" like schools, parks, museums, libraries, and by extension, urban renewal. . . . The old-style politics of the boss and machine is, and no doubt will remain, highly congenial to the lower class. (Banfield and Wilson 1967:330)

Contrary to what emerged in the aforementioned studies of the American political machines, in our research we found that the spread of corruption is not related to the rise of ex-plebs who supplant the middle classes. Rather, it develops when politics begins to attract chiefly those individuals who are able and willing to derive personal benefit from the control of public resources. We noticed in fact that the crisis of the PSI developed when the working-class membership abandoned the party, and a new middle class entered it, occupying positions of power. This new political class was characterized, as we stressed, by a "business" approach to politics, in the sense that political involvement was considered as a way to enrich oneself. A similar conception has been noted also in other times and countries. As Raymond Wolfinger observed in his research on New Haven, "Patronage inevitably creates a cadre of activists for whom politics is a way to make money, not a means of striving for the good, true, and beautiful" (Wolfinger 1973:95).

Our business politicians can, however, be described as *homines novi,* whose entry into politics, from the Roman Republic onward, is considered as having raised the tolerance threshold of deviation from the established norms. According to Banfield and Wilson's analysis of American cities, for instance, the greater propensity of newcomers to involvement in political corruption can be explained by the need of new entrepreneurs and political bosses to break into a world that tends toward their exclusion. Once they have "arrived," these same social groups become defenders of the new order. In part taking up these hypotheses, Alessandro Pizzorno has recently suggested that the *homines novi* are more susceptible to participation in corruption because the detachment from prior reference groups entailed by entry into politics lowers the moral cost of behaving illegally. According to Pizzorno,

> entering politics, the "new men" tend to break with what still binds them to their roots or, leaving aside metaphors, to detach themselves from the reference groups in which they were socialized. Politicians who belong to the socially dominant classes and have therefore been socialized in reference groups whose morality is the same as that of legal authority, on the other hand, continue to view their actions as being judged and rewarded according to the criteria of those groups and therefore conform to their norms. (Pizzorno 1992:45)

Monetary rewards gained through corruption, in fact, can be enjoyed in a socially satisfying manner only if this does not lead to stigmatization by an individual's reference groups.

As our research indicated, if "desocialization" leads to greater openness to corruption, it should be added that the environment in which the individual is "resocialized" also plays an important role. In fact, the corrupt politicians are stronger in their competition with their noncorrupt colleagues, since the former can also invest in their political career the material resources and the network of clients accumulated on the illegal market. Using the additional resources they accumulated in illegal markets, the business politicians took over the political parties, prevailing in the competition with their "honest" colleagues. In this way they transformed the very rules of politics. The diffusion of corruption therefore altered career paths: traditional channels such as individual distinction and covert channels substituted ascent through the party bureaucracy or specific technical knowledge. In Section 2, we saw that the sphere of covert politics rewarded those "talents" most valuable for organizing corruption. The business politicians possessed, in fact, those *skills in illegality* necessary to organize illegal business (ibid.:23). Moreover, the actors who moved within the system of corruption created and contributed to the diffusion of a set of rules that, accompanied by a jargon confined to the initiated, allowed corruption to minimize the risks of denunciations. If the moral obligation to conform to shared values normally pushes in the direction of legality, it is turned on its head where political parties become loci for the diffusion of a normative system that rewards rather than condemns unlawful behavior. The *willingness* to become involved in corrupt transactions, that is, its *moral cost*, changed. As Pizzorno observed:

> The theory that members of these new strata (whether the "homines novi" of the Roman Republic, the Irish, Italians, and Jews in turn-of-the-century America, or our *rampanti,* leaving aside a thousand other examples) are more disposed to corruption comes from a series of commonsense considerations. The first is that those new to power—whether exercising it or seeking to influence it—are presumably more covetous since they set out from a lower level of personal wealth. . . . This is not, however, the whole story. "New men" entering politics tend to sunder the connections with what remains of their roots, repudiating the reference groups in which they were social-ized. . . . [W]hen the relation is lost with the circle of persons who enable the real, subjective and not monetary, measure of the gains to be enjoyed, the guide for individual conduct becomes uncertain, at least until another refer-ence group begins to operate. (ibid.:45)

As we are going to see in the next chapter, for the uprooted politician, the political party represents an important socializing agency to illegal practices.

However, other qualities demanded of the business politician are in cer-tain respects little different from those of the traditional politician: most prominently, the capacity to build up connections, to establish strong ties of trust, to encourage the exchange of favors and create reciprocal obliga-tions, and to grasp the least acknowledgeable motivations of individuals. Normal and corrupt politicians both move in a landscape where friend-ship, generosity and reciprocity, gossip, fellowship, and brotherhood con-verge. The description of the Italian modern bosses of corruption quite resembles those emerging in other national cases. Most of our bosses would have shared the statement of a New Haven boss, who explained: "I do a lot of things for people. I keep working at it. . . . People come to see me, call me at home at night. . . . I just keep piling up good will. . . . I'm always building up loyalty. People never forget" (Wolfinger 1973:84). In fact, generosity and loyalty toward friends have been described as characteristic of the American city bosses of the beginning of the century (Zink 1930:18–21). The biography of one of the most influential Japanese politicians, Tanaka Kakuei, minister and prime minister from 1957 to 1985, clearly illustrates that the characteristics we singled out for the Italian boss are also widespread in other countries.[11] Like the Italian boss, Tanaka, a leader of the Liberal Democratic party until the Lockheed scandal and that of his own group, also managed to remain in power for many years, notwithstanding the many scandals, thanks to his ability to build a rich political machine and distribute favors. His electoral success is related to the privileges attributed to his electoral constituency, in Niigata, with a steady increase in the central government budget allocation oriented to that province. As Chalmer Johnson observed, "During the mid-1960s Tanaka's personal wealth also began to grow. . . . [H]e began to set up a series of *yureigaisha*, or 'ghost companies'—firms without employees or offices that traded endlessly and profitably in real estate, particularly real estate that was soon to be the site of a government-built power plan or bullet-train right-of-way or reclamation project" (1995:191). A lot of this money was used to buy consensus: "What Tanaka's discerning eyes saw above all was that money was indeed the mother's milk of politics and that whoever controlled the largest amount of it in the political system, controlled the system. Everybody needed money—for reelection campaigns, for his faction, for entertaining and cultivating the bureaucrats who made the vital decisions" (ibid.:193). Involved in a corruption scandal, Tanaka defines himself as a scapegoat, as he "believed that he did not do anything out of the ordinary and that his political opponents changed the rules on him in this particular case" (ibid.:198).

In fact, research on different countries indicates a strong link between political corruption and patrimonialism. In the studies dealing with corruption in Third World countries, corruption has been linked to their patrimonial character defined as "not simply to the persistence in social relationships generally of personalistic principles of kinship, clanship and clientship, but, more crucially, to their inevitable invocation in dealing with the state" (Theobald 1996:13).[12] In Spain, where political corruption became in the nineties "the single most salient issue in Spanish politics" (Heywood 1995:726; see also Pérez-Diaz 1996), commentators explained its development with the traditional emphasis on *amiguismo*, involving the use of brokers in relationships with the public administration (Heywood 1997:70–71). Studies of corruption in Portugal recalled the long-lasting presence of caciques, "influential local bosses such as priests, lawyers and others who were able to offer to the government in power bundles of votes from their local community" (Magone 1996:9), and a neopatrimonial structure and culture, inherited by the democratic state, emerged in 1975. Many political scandals emerged in Greece, under the so-called "patrimonial socialism" led by Andreas Papandreou (ibid.). As for Japan, another country in which corruption appears to be quite widespread, a persistent weakness of the concept of public good—which only recently and imperfectly has been distinguished from that of the private good of those in power (Bouissou 1997)—has been often quoted. The Japanese *giri*, that is, the traditional obligation to ensure an equilibrium between gifts made and received, contributed to the diffusion of bribes, as well as clientelistic voting; the tradition of offering a "gift of presentation" to a person who is going to take care of a dossier easily slips into corruption (ibid.:168). In postcommunist Eastern Europe, widespread corruption, in particular during the privatization of state enterprise,[13] has been linked to the lack of a modern conception of public administration. In particular, corruption in Russia seems to rely upon a deep-rooted fear of the public bureaucrat, which brings about submission and the attempt to buy his favors (Mendras 1997:120). Corruption in the former French colonies in Africa was facilitated by the development of personalized relationships between the African leaders and their counterparts in France (Médard 1997). In fact, as Michael Johnston observed, the very notion of corruption is related to three important developments: "*the emergence of a degree of political pluralism*, that is, the existence of 'intermediary groups' beyond the sovereign's personal or patrimonial control, that can make politically meaningful demands; the definition of *bounded political roles*, with impersonal, limited powers and obligations; . . . [t]he rise of a *'system of public order'*: a relatively durable framework of social and legal standards defining practical limits of behavior by holders of government roles, and by those who seek to influence them" (Johnston 1994:11).

In conclusion, the development of corruption requires the advent of a political class that has internalized a particular set of behavioral norms. Particular subcultures are created whose operational codes, partially overlapping with the official value system, reduce the moral cost of participation in political corruption (Chiesi 1995:136–38). Socialization in political corruption leads to the internalization of a set of values analogous only in appearance to the value system regulating legal activity. In particular, business politicians often stress the importance of *friendship*, understood instrumentally as a relationship based on the exchange of favors. In fact, such networks of relations simultaneously create the possibility of organizing and successfully concluding illegal transactions, protection from denunciations, and the electoral support required to further individual careers and maintain the party system.

NOTES

1.   For Italy at least, the cases studied here do not appear anomalous. According to a quantitative study on local public bodies, "the scarcity of 'institutional-

administrative' careers might lead us to conclude that in recent years there has been a kind of 'improvisation' in power" (Cazzola 1991:114–15; see also Bettin and Magnier 1989, 1991).

2. According to the data collected by Bettin and Magnier (1989:114, 131), 27 percent of town councillors in Italy are public employees, while in the South a full 37 percent are permanently employed in public administration.

3. That networking activity absorbs a good part of politicians' time has also been confirmed for Germany (Scheuch and Scheuch 1992:50–52).

4. On the political protection of entrepreneurs, see also Chapter 6.

5. Compare della Porta 1992:272–80. On the evolution of political scandals, cf. Sherman (1978).

6. On the interaction of politicians and bureaucrats in the corrupt market, see also Chapter 5.

7. In a similar way, U.S. vice-president Spiro Agnew, who had to resign from office in 1973 for allegations of bribery during his time as Governor of Maryland, "protested that what he had done had been normal practice in Maryland for years" (Williams 1996:7).

8. It should be specified that this friendship is "instrumental," i.e., each member of a dyad acts as a potential connection to individuals outside it, as opposed to "emotive," which supposes a relationship between ego and other that satisfies the emotional requirements of both (see Wolf 1966:10).

9. Also according to a study of a British scandal, the moment judicial proceedings begin the individuals involved are forced to reclassify their earlier behavior, elaborating justifications (or "neutralizations") (see Chibnall and Saunders 1977:141). Criminological studies on white-collar crime singled out such neutralization techniques as denial of harm, reaction to unjust laws, adherence to particular rules of the game, and transfer of responsibility to a large and vaguely defined group (among others, Sutherland 1949; Clinard 1952; Cressey 1953; Chibnall and Saunders 1977; Geis 1968; Clinard and Yaeger 1980; for a review, Coleman 1987; Ruggiero 1996a).

10. Alfio Mastropaolo (1990:58–59) distinguished two further connotations of the category of "professional politician." The first is based on "time" dedicated to politics, referring to "long distance" politicians, i.e., those remaining in politics over a long period and who therefore have to give up their private occupations (e.g., Herzog 1975; revisited recently by Scheuch and Scheuch 1992). The second concentrates on political "technicians," individuals who have acquired "skills" in either party management (party bureaucrats), accumulation of power (Schumpeterian entrepreneur), or particular policies (single-area party experts). Empirical research has underlined the diffusion of *technokratisch denkender* politicians (Derlien and Mayntz 1988).

11 In a similar vein, the English entrepreneur John Poulson, implicated in a scandal of notable dimensions, showed a great ability to build up personal contacts, satisfying demands and doing favors and generally showing himself affable and friendly (Doig 1984).

12. The survival of corruption even after democratization has been explained by the presence of a "soft state," i.e., "a state that fails to supersede personal, family, ethnic and tribal loyalties. Many elected presidents or democratically

appointed officers do not perceive the boundaries between state and private finances. . . . This 'soft state' is perpetuated in new democracies because political institutions are usually very weak" (Pinheiro 1994:38).

13.   On corruption and the crisis of postcommunist states, see Holmes (1996).

4

Political Parties and Corruption

Sicily's second largest city, Catania, has frequently been described as one of the worst administered in Italy, characterized by a weak economy and the virulent presence of a criminal element that has long enjoyed political and institutional protection (e.g., Fava 1991). As a lengthy list of political scandals testifies, administrative ineffi- ciency was accompanied by a whole succession of illegalities. The principal episodes of misgovernment in the 1950s and 1960s concerned the building boom, which took place in the total absence of urban planning. In the 1970s the magistrates carried out numerous investigations into the management of local public bodies, the attention of the national media being drawn when the administrations of city and province in their entirety had their passports withdrawn. More than a hundred judicial investi- gations took place in the 1980s into every aspect of the Catania public administra- tion, from the city council to the provincial council, the universities, local health ser- vices, the magistracy, and the carabinieri *(La Repubblica, 3 December 1987). At the beginning of the 1990s, twenty-seven of sixty city councillors and eight of twelve assessors were involved in ongoing criminal prosecutions (Fava 1991:144, 155).*

An uninterrupted Christian Democrat supremacy characterized local politics until 1992. The long undisputed boss of the local party, Antonino Drago, has been described as the principal architect of the "clientelist mass party" (Caciagli et al. 1977:Chapter 4). For the greater part of the 1960s and 1970s Drago controlled a party machine based on a clientelist exploitation of the forty-four DC sections of the city. The hierarchical structure within the party provided for "membership cards' bosses" controlled by the section secretaries, all faithful Drago supporters. Every membership boss aspired to the position of section secretary, and the section secre- taries to find a post in local government. This "strong" party structure gradually disintegrated, however. The section secretaries developed autonomous power bases within the public administration and mutinied against Drago. As one interviewee noted, "the system went into crisis when the power of certain elements could no longer be coordinated with that of others. Drago could not maintain control. His machine went crazy because his lieutenants became poles of attraction with enough power to drain resources but without the force to impose a new set of rules. The monocentric, imperial system existing within the DC was replaced by a polycentric one composed of colonels who all wanted to be emperors" (Interview CT9).

This highly corrupt system developed during a period when national control over the local federation was particularly weak. First, a "clean-up" was obstructed by national faction leaders who needed the backing of the membership controlled by their southern allies in order to win power in the party nationally. Second, there was a per-

ceived risk that any censure from the center might produce significant losses in polit-
ical personnel and therefore of votes. And indeed, "when the DC tried to clean up its
lists there were a lot of defections to minor parties and entire blocs of votes went with
them" (Interview CT8). The fragmentation of the party system was furthered by the
fact that for many local administrators switching from the DC to a minor party could
be a means of increasing their personal power. "Being in a small party magnifies your
power of interdiction, in fact. Because government relies on coalition, someone with
5,000 votes in a party with 60,000 like the DC has to negotiate, but a bloc of 3,000
votes in a party that gets 7,000 makes you one of the dominant forces" (Interview
CT8). The criteria used to select candidates for the party's lists accentuated this cen-
trifugal tendency. According to one party insider, future local administrators were
chosen "without any prior vetting, no serious checks on their ideological loyalty [to
the DC] or their public and private behavior. Sometimes new affiliates were dragged
in from among the discontents of the other parties or from the middlemen and vote
procurers who appeared during the frequent elections. As time went on, vote procur-
ers assumed the role of their erstwhile employers, forming another stratum of vassals
in their turn" (Nicolosi 1989:335). The twelve administrations that succeeded one
another in the short period between 1978 and 1988, ending with the suspension of the
city council and changes amounting to "an earthquake" in the composition of public
administration (Cazzola 1991:102), testify to the extremely high levels of conflict
between local administrators, whether of the same or of different parties.

The roots of the crisis of the "Drago model" of party organization have been iden-
tified as lying in the institutional appropriation practiced by the parties, or rather
by particular factions within them. In the words of one local politician, this had
"very serious consequences. Their diasporas, conflicts, divisions (often resulting
from immoderate or supposedly unsatisfied ambition), excessive parochialism and
fragmentation into groupings and subgroupings (with the consequent proliferation
of arrogant, pretentious petty bosses) were brought within the institutions them-
selves" (cited in Nicolosi 1989:90). Controlling the party machine was considered
important in the DC only insofar as it gave access to the public administration. The
power of local administrators increased in comparison with party functionaries, in
step with their ability to control the public resources required by clientelist politics.
One politician closely linked to the DC dubbed this the "Coco model," after the
mayor who led the original mutiny of Drago's subordinates. "The Coco model was
based on the hegemony of institution over party: all political mediation took place
inside the institutions. The other parties also got involved. Their leaders decided to
abandon the party structure for public institutions. . . . A cultural factor also played
a role. In the south you count only insofar as you bring in resources and it was as
part of a public institution rather than as a party secretary that you could do this.
The parties therefore became marginal, ceasing to be sites of mediation and decision-
making"(Interview CT8). Excessive party power appears all the more dangerous in
a situation of economic weakness. There is "no pressure from a civil society wholly
dependent on the public sector and the politicians. The battle against misgovern-
ment and inefficiency is not perceived, and micronegotiations at an individual level
are preferred. It is a society in which nobody expects anything to happen, in terms of
change, unless it comes through 'friendship'. . . . At the level of the political class,
power is employed where it is created. If you have a position of authority, granting

licenses say, you do so in exchange for a personal favor" (Interview CT8). In any case, all those interviewed agreed that political administrators were not only incompetent but also that they were totally uninterested in good administration: "Everything depends on the politicians: means, organization. . . . But the point is, what interest do the politicians have in ordinary administration? None at all" (Interview CT3).

Within this fragmented power system the Communist party, the principal opposition party, has been accused of maintaining a silence on the "moral question" in exchange for the presidencies of a number of local and regional commissions. Similarly, the trade unions are said frequently to have tolerated administrative abuses in exchange for advantages such as control over certain administrative operations or a share for "red" cooperatives in public contracts. As a trade unionist interviewed during the research said: "Of course I believe it when they say the PCI (of which I am a member) had an interest. It had an interest in inclusion. And to what end? The provision of [public health service] meals was controlled by a cooperative with links to the PCI. In other words, there was an agreement to share things between the cooperatives. The cleaning side was controlled by a Christian Democrat cooperative while the provision of hot meals (worth about a billion lira a year) went to one close to the PCI" (Interview CT2). He continued: "The unions limited their interest to personnel: assumptions and transfers. . . . Having managed to get that slice of power over assumptions and transfers, and therefore being able to respond to requests from current and future members, they never sought control over procedures relating to contracts of supply. The areas of influence were divided up as follows: if ten people were to be taken on, half were for the politicians, half for the unions" (Interview CT2).

As this tale of a city indicates, political corruption, as a means by which money influences politics (Key 1936), is clearly influenced by the characteristics of the principal actor in the political system: the party. Samuel Huntington, in particular, has linked the development of corruption to party weakness during phases of growing political participation. Corruption spreads in those specific paths to modernization in which popular participation in political decision-making is not immediately accompanied by a strengthening of those institutions that should filter and direct collective demands: "the weaker and less accepted the political parties, the greater the likelihood of corruption" (Huntington 1968:71). Apparently in contradiction with this hypothesis is the widespread belief that corruption is favored by the ubiquity and omnipotence of the parties, powerful and well-organized political machines capable of controlling civil society and the market. In Italy, *partitocrazia*, a concept derived from the political science literature, has been taken up in the press and in political debate to stigmatize the ills of the "First Republic."

In what follows, we will discuss some issues of particular relevance for an analysis of the interaction between political parties and corruption. In Section 1, we look at the hidden structures of the parties themselves. In

Sections 2 and 3, we describe the changing role of the political parties in the situation of systemic corruption, focusing in particular on the function of political parties as "guarantors " of illegal exchanges (Section 2) and on the distortion in institutional policymaking that corruption brings about (Section 3). In Section 4, we look at the development of "consociational" agreements between different political parties—mutual pacts of reciprocal protection against scandals. In Section 5, we compare our results with the information available on other countries, focusing especially on the central question of the cost of politics in present-day democracies. In particular, we would emphasize that previous interpretations have concentrated prevalently on the "visible" side of the party, neglecting what has taken place in the "hidden" party structure.

1. THE "HIDDEN" STRUCTURES OF THE PARTIES

The postwar period in Italy saw the rise of two mass political parties capable of creating social integration on a subcultural basis: the Communist party (PCI) and the Christian Democrat party (DC). Taking up the distinction made by Sigmund Neumann, it can be said that in the postwar period the replacement of parties of individual representation (composed of "notables," displaying low levels of mobilization and concentrating their activity in preelectoral periods) by parties of integration (aimed at integrating social groups, organized through "ancillary" associations and in which the members represent the principal organizational resource) was completed.[1] Up to the 1960s, the Socialist party (PSI) had an organizational structure formally similar to that of the Communist party. Using Duverger's (1961) well-known categories, we can say that the main Italian political parties gravitated toward an organizational structure based on territorial sections, open to outsiders and therefore suited to mass participation and the recruitment of a heterogeneous membership. In the decades that followed, there was a strengthening of the power of the party leadership at the expense of the rank-and-file membership. The subcultural roots of DC and PCI progressively weakened as they transformed themselves in the direction of Otto Kirchheimer's (1957) "catchall" parties: ideologically diluted, addressing themselves to all, open to interest groups, and increasingly centralized. The Socialist party with its local feuds, party notables, and profound fragmentation represents an exception with respect to the above two parties, approaching the model of *caciquismo mediterraneo*: "a model," as Sapelli has remarked (1994:121), "with numerous leaders and their personal followings continually torn between the scarcity of material resources and the overabundance of short-range and strategically shortsighted political resources." During the eighties, however, Bettino Craxi's secretaryship seemed to represent "a move toward an *autocratic and monotheistic clientelism* with abundance of resources acquired by the savage extension of illegal control of the markets" (ibid., emphasis added).

Compared with these views of the organizational structures of the political parties, the investigations of political corruption bring out an important new element: the growth of hidden structures that transformed the political parties—as in the case of the DC in Catania—into aggregations of conflicting local bosses, more interested in business than in politics. First of all, the growth of corruption has led to an *ever-diminishing prestige of visible as opposed to invisible political positions.* In the new hierarchy of corrupt politics, national positions have lost relevance with respect to those of the periphery: careers no longer lead from periphery to the center (see also Chapter 2). To give only a couple of examples, while the ex-president of the Liguria Region scorned those who accepted the position of *peones* in parliament (della Porta 1992), Mario Chiesa, the first administrator to be implicated in the *mani pulite* inquiry, described the appointment of the former Milan mayor Tognoli as a minister without portfolio as a sort of "punishment": "Tognoli was humiliated in the field, reduced first to the level of regional secretary and then called to a ministry, the Urban Areas, which didn't even have its own seat" (Andreoli 1993:144).

1.1. Party Cashiers

Positions connected with clandestine financial transactions acquire greater importance. In fact, secret structures were constituted within the parties, devoted to the gathering and administration of illegal funding. As we mentioned in the previous chapters, public service bosses founded their careers on the bribes they collected. Moreover, a fundamental role in organizing the business of corruption was played by those, in the course of recent scandals, the press referred to as "party cashiers." While occasionally to be found as administrative secretaries of parties, more frequently they occupy "informal" positions, recognized only within the invisible organizational structures that exist inside the parties. Their careers are founded on the party's confidence in their ability to bring in contributions, legally or otherwise, and to manage them in an "honest" and "reliable" manner. Such individuals were described in the following terms to the Milan magistrates:

> Each party has referents responsible for controlling the allocation of contracts, maintaining the contacts with the different companies, and collecting bribes, or having them collected. They also try to place trusted politicians on the boards of the various bodies, who then negotiate directly with business-

men [thus] veiling what are really prearranged deals on bribery with formally legal agreements and legitimation. (*Panorama*, 12 July 1992, p. 27)

The cashier's function, in fact, is to organize both the legal and illegal
financing of his party. In doing so he must mediate between and coordinate a plurality of networks composed of different kinds of actor. Referring to a Milan CD cashier, the magistrates remarked: "President of the
municipal transport company and Regional Administrative Secretary of
the DC, he ran what amounted to a complete administrative structure for
the money businessmen paid for the awarding of public contracts. This
money served to cover the enormous expenditure of the DC and its individual leaders. He was therefore well known in political circles, and particularly within the DC, as a receiver for illegal funds. Funds that he thereafter distributed for the purposes already indicated" (CD, 8 February 1993,
no. 184, p. 5). At the municipal level, these cashiers coordinate the activities of public sector administrators belonging to their party and, in contact
with the national cashier of their party, they maintain the connections
between center and periphery. Their role, moreover, goes beyond the
boundaries of their own party, taking in mediation between the various
parties involved in the system of corruption. According to a Socialist
cashier, "[E]ach referent of the party reports to the national administrative
secretary, who prepares provisional and final balances of receipts, and
works with the administrative secretaries of the other parties to control the
flow of illegal funding. All this was communicated to the political secretariats of the parties, for the obvious reason that party activity had to be
organized according to the resources available" (CD, 13 January 1993, no.
166-quarter, p. 47).

Besides coordinating the activities of the various actors involved in corruption, the cashier system also limits the amount of compromising information in circulation. It is the cashiers, in fact, who maintain relations with
those who gravitate in the orbit of the political parties in search of favors,
in particular, entrepreneurs operating in the public sector. Although in no
way official, the position they hold is well-known to businessmen, who
turn to them for resolving technical or bureaucratic difficulties regarding
public contracts. As a Milanese PSI cashier explained, when proceeds from
bribery were handed on to political referents, explanations were neither
requested nor given: "When I handed over the money . . . I didn't say anything and nobody asked. Total secrecy was an established practice. . . . You
don't tell the person receiving the money where it comes from; it's usually
obvious anyway, since in a system of generalized consociation everyone
knows even if they pretend not to" (TM:60–61). This was confirmed by the
DC cashier in the same city: "I never told those receiving the money where

it came from. They didn't ask and I didn't say. . . . Payments were always in cash, and everybody acted out their part without asking embarrassing questions" (CD, 31 July 1992, no. 83, p. 7).

Naturally, this "confidentiality" concerning the origin and distribution of bribery money heightens the power of the cashiers, frequently the only ones who possess a detailed knowledge of the mechanisms and regulations governing its allocation. For this reason, party cashiers, in order to acquire a favorable "reputation" in the market of corruption, must adhere to a particular conception of *honesty*: respect of the obligations assumed in illegal transactions, obligations not subject to legal ratification, naturally, and whose violation cannot be legally punished. The importance of this sense of honesty emerges, for example, in the following description of the national administrative secretary of the PSI: "a man of honor who personally saw to his obligations and therefore, for reasons of uprightness and personal prestige, consigned in person the money due to the local branches" (CD, 23 February 1993, no. 202 bis, p. 12).

1.2.   An Invisible Structure

The various actors were connected, often across party lines, in an *invisible organizational structure*. As happens in illegal systems, however, the degree of vertical centralization these networks were able to attain seems to have been quite low. The evidence of politicians involved in judicial investigations offers a picture of the system of corruption as a multiheaded collection of networks gathered around individual bosses, with only a few points of coordination from above. This image is well-illustrated in the declaration of Loris Zaffra, regional secretary of the PSI in Lombardy, who described the functioning of his party to the magistrates thus:

> Inside the Socialist party the position was complicated in that there were no institutionalized economic referents. There was terrible confusion, with a plurality of referents each directing his own area. The party's institutional organs were concerned exclusively with current expenditure. This parcelized administrative structure corresponded to an analogous structure in the field of political decisions, in the sense that it was not so much the party that counted in decision-making as the single possessors of power, including economic power. There were not factions in the party but these reference groups, which also represented pressure groups. The running of the administration had nothing to do with formal positions because reference was to the person and not the position. So the economic referent could move from one office to another according to the movement of the people who counted most. Also, there was little substantial coincidence between real and formal functions: for example, local functionaries were not paid by the federation but by their political referent through informal, but substantial payments

which did not appear in the party's public financial statements. (Andreoli 1993:37)

In these circumstances, the parties fragmented into numerous groups based on blind, if temporary obedience to a boss—what Mario Chiesa called *falangi*. The power of each boss rested on a nucleus of faithful followers, with a clanlike solidarity that Chiesa describes thus: "The *falange* was the nucleus. About eighty people, a respectable number in a party like ours, by now lacking in militants. Each member of the *falange* could count on the support of about ten friends. I had an extremely fraternal relationship, of absolute communion, with the *falange*" (ibid.:21).

Alongside the reduction in power of the official party leadership, the *traditional structures of the party lose significance*. In the first place, as a result of political corruption the personal secretariats of individual bosses acquired a growing importance. A fundamental step in the career of any business politician, in fact, was the creation of a private "headquarters," a personal secretariat, often disguised as a research center or some form of enterprise. The function of these restricted spaces in the life of parties permeated by corruption is explained by the Milan ex-administrator Mario Chiesa. Already in 1974, he recalls,

> I had my private office as well. In the city-center, in via Castelfidardo. A long way from Quarto Oggiaro. Two rooms on the ground floor of Number 11. A table for meetings, a telephone, an office for the secretary. The transformation of the PSI from a party of militants to a party of clients made finding via Castelfidardo necessary. The section, even when normalized and run by loyal comrades, wasn't a suitable place for a certain kind of politics. For example, I couldn't call restricted meetings in the section. If a member of the rank and file, passing and seeing the lights on, was tempted to come in, I would have had to change subject. If he didn't and felt marginalized because he hadn't been asked to attend, then he would have been less friendly at the opportune moment. *A visual control on your activity has heavy costs.* (ibid.:29, emphasis added)

As emerges clearly from this testimony, the reasons for creating personal secretariats lie precisely in that minimum of control that the visible structures of the party imply. If the organization of the system of corruption required more discrete sites, the sections were not, however, shut down: on the contrary, in Milan the eighties saw an exponential growth in the membership of the some sixty sections of the PSI, which passed from an average of one hundred to five hundred or even one thousand members. While growing in size, the sections changed function, becoming the sites for assembling "paper members [*falsi tesserati*], ready for making up the numbers at meetings and demonstrations and disciplined participation at section, ward, or municipal congresses" (Mario Chiesa, ibid.:35). Clubs and (fake) research institutes mushroomed around party bosses, responding to their need to escape any internal democratic control, and create flexible and less visible structures (della Porta 1992:202).

1.3. From Militants to Clients

The emptying of the role of the sections has been explained, in part, in relation to the transformation of the social bases of the parties, particularly in the case of the PSI. As mentioned in the previous chapter, from the 1960s, while the estrangement of the working-class base of the party was reflected in a weakening of organization, the coalition power of the PSI—translated into a number of posts in the public administration far greater than its effective electoral strength—drew toward the party many "emergent" social groups interested in expanding the volume of their affairs through political protection. As "internal" witnesses confirm, "In the ranks of PSI, but not only, militants left and clients joined, people who might be very intelligent but who saw the party as a shortcut to personal goals. In the space of a few years a genetic mutation took place: comrades willing to work gratis for the *feste dell'Avanti* were harder and harder to find" (Andreoli 1993:33).

These "genetic" transformations in the composition of the party were actively accelerated by the business politicians, who used their power precisely to distance the remaining militants. In Savona, for example, the gradual marginalization of the groups of the Socialist Left was pursued with means not excluding physical violence, at least according to the evidence given to the magistrates (UIS:123–45). In the Milan Socialist party also, a progressive process of expulsion or absorption of all internal opposition, culminating in the 1980s, has been mentioned. As Chiesa emphasized: "The comrades of the Socialist Left, who theorized a strategic agreement with the Communist party, were targeted. If they worked at the Sacco [the hospital Chiesa controlled], I threatened to transfer them. If they had a *distacco sindacale* [leave for union activities], I tried to get it revoked" (Andreoli 1993:20). The same resources that served for the organization of covert exchange appear also to have been useful for promoting the power of the corrupt bosses within the party. Once more according to Chiesa, "The left of the party, which had one of its power-bases in the Sacco, was slowly converted. After all, whoever was against me had a hard time. And to those who supported me, I offered friendship and favors" (ibid.:128).

The money coming from *tangenti* (bribes) seems to have been indispensable for marginalizing the opposition, building *falangi* of followers, and competing with other bosses in the battle for the division of the spoils. In terms of party structure, all this leads to a monetarization and parcelization of power, the reduction of internal loyalty to a minimum, and the transformation of the party into a series of networks in a permanent state of internecine war. This system, as Chiesa revealingly concludes, referring to the situation in Milan in the 1980s, is extremely inflationary:

> A nasty habit predominated: even a ward councillor or a candidate for the most modest public office knew not to spend a penny of their own money but to solicit the notable of the moment to finance their election campaign. In return they would promise absolute loyalty. The notable would accept without question for fear that, with a hundred thousand lira note, some competitor might grab a contact and a packet of votes. Frequently money would be asked not for the party but for the individual. Sometimes a banal demand for cash to cover pointless expenses was hidden behind a request for a contribution to pay the rent of the section. But, and this is the point, it would have been dangerous to refuse these demands. Your nearest rival was always there, ready to close not one but both eyes in order to satisfy the most outlandish requests. The money circulated. Really circulated. A lot of it. Every leader was out for himself and saw his neighbor as an enemy. The gathering and administration of resources was strictly tied to increasing one's own political weight. *A network of parallel power centers, eternally at war with each other, was formed inside the PSI* (Andreoli 1993:35–36, emphasis added).

If the illustrations given up to now have involved the PSI, the picture that emerges from the investigations of political corruption is similar also for the other parties involved in the scandals (as our initial examples, referring to the Sicilian DC already indicated). According to one of the judges who led the *mani pulite* investigation, Piercamillo Davigo, "A lot of the illicit founds were used by the politicians of the different fractions to buy party membership cards. . . . These membership cards were used to established power relations inside the parties. . . . The parties were transformed into joint-stock companies, where bribes were used to buy shares in order to acquire the possibility to be reelected" (Davigo 1993:11). The corrupt political parties as they developed in Italy certainly do not correspond very closely to the definition of mass parties or that of catchall parties. One cannot speak, in fact, either of an opening to the rank and file or of a centralized power of the leadership (della Porta 1992:211–50; della Porta and Vannucci 1994:Chapter X). The parties disintegrated, but not into traditional ideological factions. Rather, hidden structures were created within them and used by each boss in order to acquire power by investing in the power game the money obtained through illegal activities.

2. THE ROLE OF THE PARTY IN CORRUPT EXCHANGES

Up to now we have discussed some hypotheses concerning the organizational structure of the political parties. Corruption also has effects on the *role* played by the parties. The diffusion of covert exchange is possible, in fact, only thanks to the parties' assumption of certain particular functions. When political corruption becomes systemic, the political parties sanction covert transactions, rewarding those who collaborate and punishing those who are not willing to play the corrupt game. Like all illegal transactions, the corrupt transaction is characterized by a particular deficit of trust: in fact, while the law protects the contracting parties in a legal transaction against possible transgressions, in illegal markets other actors must assume the role of guarantor. The political parties—or what is left of them—represent one of these actors whose function is to reduce the costs and risks of illegal business.

2.1. Socialization in Illegality

The party system is transformed in the first place into a system of *socialization in illegality*. As criminologists observed long ago, "criminal behavior is learned in interaction with other persons in a process of communication" (Sutherland and Cressey 1974:75). In the case of political corruption in Italy, this communication process developed in particular inside the political party. The corrupt party provides socialization to the rules of the (illegal) game, permitting the system of covert transaction to expand. Politicians already "introduced" to the rules of the illegal marketplace introduce others in their turn. Loyalty to the party serves in obtaining appointments, which are then paid for in the distribution of the money acquired through corruption. A Lombardy regional councillor revealed: "Bringing in money for the party was a way of getting on, gaining the trust of the bosses. And my boss wasn't just anybody. . . . Pulled in his wake, I would have had a brilliant career" (*Panorama*, 12 July 1992, p. 54).

The corrupt party "places" its men in various positions of responsibility in public bodies; in return it demands that they "conform" to the "rules," utilizing those positions not only for personal enrichment, but also for (illegal) party financing. As Nevol Querci, Socialist MP and president of the INADEL (a public body), declared to the magistrates:

> It was the national leaderships of the DC and PSI themselves that gave me the green light to buy the buildings in question from companies that had shown themselves friends of the parties (attentive regarding contributions). . . . I knew, and know, that the key positions in particular bodies (the INADEL among them) are filled by people the parties trusted *to take the burden of obtaining contributions for the party itself*; in any case, *I knew that any change of mind on my part would immediately lead to my marginalization and the loss of my position* (*Panorama* 1993, p. 76, emphasis added).[2]

Through the parties' assumption of this role in socializing to corruption, the system of covert transactions expands. The politicians already introduced to the rules of the illicit market in their turn introduce the others.[3]

An illustration of the functioning of these mechanisms of extended involvement comes from the investigation of corruption in the Provincial Council of Bari. According to the judicial documents, the bribes paid for contracts allocated by the Provincial Council were divided among all the councillors of the PSI, all of whom thus found themselves implicated: "One of the first cuts of money was distributed, 30 million each, to all the members of the group. This decision was taken during a meeting of the group in which it was decided, among other things, to give the same amount to the members of parliament" (TRIB:42). The division of bribes among all councillors of assemblies served to create a generalized complicity; moreover, in this way the party leadership "taught" their administrators to use their positions "profitably."

With the widespread presence of the parties in the various nerve centers of the public administration, *corruption becomes the rule*. As Luigi Carnevale, councillor of the former PCI and then PDS (Partito Democratico della Sinistra) for the Metropolitana Milanese, relates: "On entering the *Metropolitana* I found *an already tried and tested system* according to which, as a rule, virtually all contract winners paid a bribe of 3 percent. . . . The proceeds of these *tangenti* were divided among the parties according to preexistent agreements" (MPM:147, emphasis added). In a similar fashion, Mario Chiesa talked of an "environmental situation" favoring corruption: "My conduct in the PAT," the ex-administrator declared to the magistrates, "wasn't my own invention but the result of an existing *environmental situation* in the Milan health service (and in the public administration more generally), to which I adapted myself when, beginning my political activity from the bottom, I discovered it to be a source of finance for personal political advancement" (*Panorama* 1993, p. 27, emphasis added).

2.2. Reducing the Risks

Protected by their common membership in the party system, corrupt politicians can offer a series of reciprocal "services" that *reduce the risks* of participation in the corruption market (see Chapter 2). Besides acting as "notaries" for covert transactions, keeping note of rules and exchanges, the parties become efficient agencies of commercial intermediation, equipped with up-to-date databanks on the partners available for illegal operations. By exchanging confidential information corrupt politicians reduce the costs of identifying other parties on the illegal market. In this way, the magistrates have reconstructed what amount to nothing less than "handovers" between particular administrators, whether of the same or of different parties. A manager of the ICOMEC company, for example, revealed that when Ermidio Santi, Socialist ex-president of the IACP (a public housing body) of Genoa, was elected to parliament he "introduced" him to his successor with the phrase "Don't worry, everything's under control." In the illegal market of corruption these rituals were equivalent to formal investiture. The manager added in this connection, "I should specify that, for my part, I was convinced that my relations with Moro [the successor] were a continuation of connections with that body, which had always been presided over by men of the same party" (PRIM:125–26). The successive presence of members of the same party in running an institution thus facilitated corrupt transactions, reducing the risks that would have resulted from a renogotiation of the illegal agreements.

Exchanges of information however were not limited to members of a single party. In the judicial documents, in fact, we also find ritualized "handovers" between politicians of different parties, with the "presentation" of entrepreneurs already involved in corruption to successors in office. A Catania entrepreneur, a supplier to the USL 35 (a public health unit), recalls, for example: "I paid bribes to Prof. Platania [Republican party] until the summer of 1986, when he was elected regional deputy. Before leaving the Vittorio Emanuele Hospital, Platania instructed me that in the future the bribes I had to pay should be given personally to Attorney Giuseppe Strano, president [DC] of the USL" (ACA:104). The administrators who succeeded each other in posts in the various institutions "introduced" the "protected" businessmen, reducing the risk of a "first approach."

2.3. Guarantors of Illegal Business

The political parties' role as guarantor means that it is no longer necessary to trust one's partner in corrupt exchange personally (although both partners must of course be convinced of the protector's ability to enforce the agreement). According to Galeotti and Breton, political parties can be seen as guarantor of the performance of both representatives and citizens in the political-electoral exchange:

> Political parties are the loci of property rights through which the promises and expectations of citizens and of representatives are transformed into quasi or implicit contracts and through which these contractual arrangements are "enforced." Political parties can fulfill that function because they are networks of relationships based on trust. The links that constitute the networks and embody the trust can be strong or weak and can vary over time and as circumstances change. These bonds of trust are what support property rights and, therefore, permit exchange to take place. (1986:54)

The accumulation of trust within the political party permits the sanctioning of other trades that—like those between citizens and representatives—are not legally enforceable or self-enforcing: corrupt exchanges. As the currency issued by the state is guaranteed as the official medium of exchange, so the *trust* in the fulfillment of promises or the collection of credits, which is offered by political organizations, permits the reduction of otherwise very high transaction costs. Authority within parties becomes then a resource for the strengthening of beliefs or expectations that persons will honor their promises in the corruption market.

As we stressed in Chapter 2, the presence of an external guarantor is sometimes a necessary precondition to overcome the reciprocal distrust of contracting parties. The protection provided by the political parties appears important in settling the controversies that can emerge between the various actors in corrupt exchange, both at the central and at the local level. As for every scarce and valuable commodity, political guarantees can then be demanded and supplied in exchange for a bribe. Such a situation emerged over the contract for providing conveyor belts for the port of Manfredonia. The entrepreneur in question had to pay a bribe of 5 percent to Wladimiro Curatolo, a member of the DC. The latter was then to be responsible for dividing the money between the various parties involved. An argument broke out, however, among members of the PSI and the situation of the entrepreneur became critical. "Things were already agreed when Curatolo appeared saying, 'As of now I only represent the DC and PSDI. The Socialists are fighting among themselves and I don't want to have anything to do with it.' I protested but there was nothing to be done" (*La Repubblica*, 16 February 1993, p. 11). To overcome his problem the entrepreneur was obliged to contact the national administrative secretary of the PSI, Vincenzo Balzamo: "On hearing of the matter and the value of the contract, [the latter] told me that given the amount involved I should have gone directly to him and took the responsibility for dealing with the hot potato. When Balzamo contacted me he told me that he had been in touch with Manfredonia and the situation was a very difficult one. He then told me that he personally would contact the three PSI members involved" (CD, 8 February 1993, no. 202, p. 5). The three local PSI members were obliged to accept the arbitration of the party, and the situation, which was dangerous for the party as well, was resolved. The entrepreneur continued: "It was Balzamo himself who later told me that it had been hard with the three. . . . [T]hey were tough customers and untouchable. In the end though he was able to impose his point of view. In any case, after Balzamo's intervention I had the proof that things had gone well . . . because the work went better, without problems" (CD, 30 March 1993, no. 241, p. 5).

Moreover, the party presence in the public administration offers the various participants in covert transactions the possibility of apportioning sanctions to those who violate the rules, such as exclusion from the corrupt game: "[T]here is a network of political machines aimed at making widespread, continuous, and reciprocally protected corrupt exchanges" (Belligni 1995:178). In the circumstances of illegality associated with covert transactions, the political parties can be likened to a credit agency managing trust between the various parties involved (Pizzorno 1992:32–33). Given their widespread power of nominating the upper levels of public bodies, the parties can "sanction particular transactions thanks to their punitive power over political administrators and private individuals, guaranteeing the fulfillment of secret agreements and the overall functioning of the illegal market within distributive 'norms' created over time" (Vannucci 1993:85). In fact, these functions were "paid" by the allocation of a "supplementary" portion of the bribes to the parties, over and above that received by individual administrators involved in the decisions necessary for closing the secret deal. As Maurizio Prada, DC "treasurer" of Milan revealingly explains: "Even before 1987 I received contributions from certain companies and continued to do so after the end of my mandate as president of the ATM in 1990. . . . In other words, the companies paid me because I was one of the local treasurers of the *Democrazia Cristiana*" (TM:74).

3. PARTIES, CORRUPTION, AND PUBLIC POLICIES

Participation in covert transactions transforms the way in which the parties fulfill their traditional tasks, acting on their three main functions: the selection of personnel, the integration of the citizenry, and the formation of public policies.

3.1. Traditional Party Functions and Corruption

As far as the *selection of political personnel* is concerned, in a functioning democracy politicians must be capable of elaborating general programs, convincing citizens of their benefits, and putting them into practice. The rewards will be public: appreciation, power, and prestige should count for more than material advantage. With the development of political corruption, however, the characteristics of the political class are transformed. As we mentioned in the previous chapter, the parties begin to select those individuals most proficient in the organization of illegal financing. In a public structure where information circulates concerning the gains that can be made in certain positions from bribery, it is to be expected that certain agents will try to influence the internal decision-making process in order to occupy these positions, spending both their own resources and, where possible, those of the organization. In other words, as mentioned in the previous chapter, the institutional mechanisms for selecting political and bureaucratic personnel are altered in favor of individuals with fewer scruples, who are willing to "invest" in creating influence: "Thus many more teams will be formed to capture control of government, and each team will employ more factors of production in its political activities—more, that is, than if there were no corruption revenue expected from being the government" (Johnson 1975:54).[4] In this way political corruption leads to the proliferation of actors who do not properly belong either to the state or to the market and therefore "violate" the rules of functioning of both. As Pizzorno has noted, "[T]he sense of party membership is altered. One no longer joins to contribute voluntarily to the work of government, but in order to be admitted to the competition for positions of private interest. . . . The various filtering processes, then, will be designed to ascertain whether the future business politician is a person willing to participate in illicit practices or who, at the least, will behave 'responsibly' and pose no moral objections should he become aware of them " (Pizzorno 1992:27).

A second function of political parties is the legitimation of the political system through the *integration of the citizenry*. In a democracy, the parties are the principal actors in structuring the vote, creating electoral identifications that are frequently maintained over generations. The structuring of the vote takes place by the definition of programs that are then proposed to the electorate. The search for the highest number of votes should lead the various parties to represent the opinions and interests of particular groups of citizens. The diffusion of corruption would seem, however, to transform the structure of electoral preferences: rather than the vote of identification or opinion, the cliental use of the vote as an object of exchange prevails—vote in exchange for favor (see Chapter 2). Political corruption produces, in fact, a value system oriented to the fulfillment of individual objectives through interaction based on extrinsic or instrumental benefits at the same time as it discourages "ideological" types of relations based on intrinsic or expressive benefits. We can say, therefore, that political corruption, by encouraging the diffusion of a structure of preferences oriented to individual mobilization, erodes the effective capacity of the parties to integrate, select, and mediate citizens' interests. In Italy the use of corrupt practices has reduced the capacity of the parties to mobilize ideological resources and distribute participatory incentives. While political analyses, including those on the Italian case,[5] have normally underlined the negative consequences of the excessive use of ideological incentives by political parties, the recent investigations by the magistracy lead to an emphasis on the risks attached to the opposite condition: the excessive availability of material incentives.

A third function of political parties in a democracy is *the formation of public policy*: in a functioning democracy the parties have the job of defining the direction of public policy and controlling its implementation. Concentrating on the organization of corruption, the parties have privileged instead those decisions most "productive" in terms of *tangenti*; the tendency is to spend most in those sectors where controls are weakest.

3.2. Corruption, Parties, and the Definition of Public Demand

The definition of public demand is a pivotal moment in the democratic political process since it is here that the administrative system is confronted with the needs and demands of social groups. Political mediation is the filter through which interests are articulated and aggregated, and its task, as Pizzorno has pointed out, is "to identify and interpret the needs and desires of the population; select and generalize those which can be expressed in political terms; propose, justify, and criticize policies and measures to achieve these ends or, when necessary, to explain why they cannot be satisfied" (Pizzorno 1992:22). Corruption radically alters this function, privileging the satisfaction of so-called "internal demand" (Chevallier and Loschak 1982:113).

Our research indicates a fragmentation of public demand in order to satisfy particular interests while, at the same time, no wider vision of the problems develops among the various public officials involved. As the State Audit Court pointed out: "After long, involved preliminary planning and a difficult passage through parliament, wide-ranging measures designed to launch the process of rationalization and coordination of the country's major infrastructures were approved. These have failed to materialize, either remaining largely unimplemented . . . , suffering unexpected interruptions . . . or being seriously delayed" (CC, 1990, vol. II, I, p. 494).

When political corruption is systemic, the parties' discretional management of public spending often becomes—as the Catania case quoted at length at the beginning indicated—an objective *in itself*. The aim of administrators is to attract as large a quantity of resources as possible to the areas where they have power in order to pocket a fee for mediation in the form of a bribe and/or gain support as a result of the effects of public investment on employment (treated as a sphere for clientelistic exchange). Public spending is therefore diverted to those sectors where gains from corruption are greatest and in which the discretional nature of the procedures reduces the risks involved. In general, little attention is paid to whether the needs of the collectivity are served by these works or services.[6] It is not even necessary that they be completed or brought into use, as demonstrated by the countless projects never finished or never actually used. As the judges noted in the case of the Teardo Clan of Savona, the actions of corrupt administrators can "radically and seriously distort administrative activity, works being contracted exclusively as a function of exacting bribes more safely and easily and not on the basis of any actual technical requirement" (TRIS:155).[7] It suffices to notice that annual per capita consumption of cement in Italy was 800 kg, double that of the United States and triple that of Germany and Great Britain, at a cost of 33 thousand billion lira. According to one expert, "at bottom, at least 80 percent of these works are unnecessary; some of them are undoubtedly a disaster" (*Il Mondo*, 2–9 September 91, p. 25). And construction is a sector in which bribes proliferate with ease.

Predictably, the priority given to obtaining funding brings about scarce regard for the quality of the projects that are at the basis of public demand. Antonio Persico, an engineer and secretary of the CRTA, technical organ of the Puglia Region, recalled the changes in evaluating dossiers: "Previously, the CRTA functioned like clockwork. . . . Each dossier was examined thoroughly as it came up, as befits a body composed of (often high-level) technical staff. This practice was completely overturned by Councillor Di Giuseppe [later charged with corruption], who was only interested in an opinion on feasibility in order to obtain the funding and did not think it either necessary or expedient to slavishly investigate every aspect of a project" (CD, 23 February 93, no. 201 bis, p. 6).

Corruption also developed around public works that, either for their size or evocative power, had symbolic significance or a cathartic effect in relation to public dissatisfaction with the inefficiency of the state. The massive programs of special funding for events such as the Columbus Celebrations or the Soccer World Cup of 1990, for example, provided the cue for public works that later turned out to be unnecessary, exorbitant, or simply impossible to realize,[8] but that were lucrative in terms of bribes for the administrators involved in the decision-making. In this kind of project the politicians who are formulating public demand retain an interest in the final outcome of the work since the short-term symbolic satisfaction that comes from it can later be translated into valuable electoral support. Thus in the case of *Italia '90* it has been observed that "everywhere the decisions concerning the stadiums took on strongly 'personalistic' connotations. . . . The decision-making process became restricted to an exclusive circle, in an attempt to avoid the (public) political confrontation that normally characterizes local government" (Morisi 1991:18).

We can add that either real or artificially created emergencies constitute a further factor that can have an influence on the formation of public demand. Indeed, corrupt politicians often attempt to have the administrative activity in which they have an interest classified as "urgent," since the level of public spending and the degree of discretion in its management will be particularly high. Here the case of public hospitals provides a good example: an error, or deliberate "oversight," in ordering equipment or medicines immediately leads to an emergency situation. The magistracy, for example, had the following to say of the Catania local health board (USL 35): certain chief physicians "were in the habit of dishonestly certifying that products were needed urgently or were required for specialist reasons. These products were afterwards bought privately and on occasions were actually delivered before the purchase ordered had been considered." The USL administrators were thus enabled to pocket bribes from the suppliers whom they themselves had chosen (ACA:35).[9]

Public demand may remain unsatisfied in this context if the politicians involved do not find the amount offered by way of bribes sufficient. The ex-president of the Environmental Commission of the Lombardy Region, Luigi Martinelli, described the case of building authorization for a refuse treatment works at Casal Maggiore in the following terms: "An agreement by which Paonessa [the entrepreneur] would pay a sum equal to 2 percent of the construction costs [as a bribe] was proposed. I said to Moroni that the project would never get off the ground because the bribe proposed was too small. Moroni agreed with me that the smallness of the sum proposed by Paonessa would damage the 'market'" (CD, 27 July 92, no. 66, p. 7).

We can conclude, then, that in the 1980s the Italian political parties focused their action on those functions connected with illegal exchange. As Pizzorno has observed, when corruption spreads, "the activity of the parties tends to concentrate on the individuation of those demands identified as producing the greatest spending power. In fact, [it becomes] the interest of the parties to satisfy these demands, taking the full advantage (even when mediation costs are taken into account), rather than suspending the satisfaction of dispersed, single demands in order to organically aggregate, generalize, and make them uniform" (Pizzorno 1992:27). The parties' occupation of the public administration did not have the object of realizing political projects but that of accumulating funds. As far as their other functions are concerned, the presence of the parties was weakened. This explains the apparent paradox noticed in Italy of a strong party presence in society contemporaneously with the absence of credible party policies in many areas (Dente and Regonini 1987). The diffusion of corruption leads to the concentration of the parties on those activities most functional to illicit exchange, scarce interest being shown for those types of policy not immediately convertible into cash. Besides, political corruption imposes a short-term logic, with little attention being paid to the longer-term consequences of public policy. Focusing on an integration based on the exchange of favors, the parties have consequently abandoned the elaboration of political programs.

4. PARTY CONNIVANCE: CORRUPTION AND CONSOCIATION

The distribution of public power frequently means that it is impossible for a single agent to offer the service demanded by a corrupter. When corruption is practiced by a number of politicians in collaboration, centralized power management and a consensual division of the proceeds become necessary; power-sharing brings the risk of contention, reciprocal denunciations, and judicial investigation if disagreements arise (Harendra 1989:507). As long as those involved are all subject to a single center of power (a party secretariat to whom all owe their election or nomination, for example) disagreements can be reconciled at that level. However, many decisions involve individuals from different parties, party currents, or factions, who are not therefore subject to a single authority having the power to smooth over subterranean antagonisms and conflict. In such cases open conflict may well lead to disastrous consequences for all.[10] If the likelihood of success in what are extremely contentious questions is outweighed by the likely costs of failure, then the various power centers involved in corruption may seek an understanding based on (a) a consensual and jointly managed division of the proceeds of corruption, or (b) a long-term division of public power into spheres of influence, this division being cemented by mutual silence over their corruption.

In concrete terms, such agreements are sometimes based on a fixed distribution of public contracts among firms based on the "color" of their political protection (or to consortia whose composition reflects the relative weight of the various power centers[11]) or on distributing payoffs according to the electoral strength of the parties involved (TRIB:81). In others the agreement takes place at an earlier phase and regards the power distribution in the governing bodies employed in attracting bribes rather than the proceeds. The management board of ENEL, for example, was composed of eight directors appointed by the political parties. According to one, "each director was responsible for procuring his own party money. A tacit understanding was reached: each looked after his own back yard and stayed out of the others' business" (*Panorama* 14 February 1993, p. 46). The apportioning of offices among the various political parties therefore gave each political actor control over certain, defined areas of public activity, areas that were negotiated or arranged at a higher level. The former DC regional councillor Luigi Martinelli reconstructed the tacit division made in Lombardy between the regional secretaries of the DC and PSI, Gianstefano Frigerio and Sergio Moroni:

> I remember that Moroni got particularly annoyed about the Mozzate refuse disposal site. I told him, as Frigerio instructed, that there was no use getting angry because the regional DC was in credit with the PSI for the period in which [he] had been regional transport assessor [and] had not given anything from that to the DC. On this subject Moroni told me that he would happily have spoken to Frigerio about it . . . but that the DC, in turn, had given nothing from low-cost municipal housing. He likewise said that, in virtue of the last question, everything canceled out. (CD, 27 July 1992, no. 66, p. 7)

In this particular case, the balance arrived at was the result of an unspoken agreement. Other agreements, however, were more explicit. Luigi Manco, a former communal assessor in Naples, confessed: "In what I can confirm was the division of major public works among the parties, the construction of car parks was considered a sphere of influence of the Liberal party." When a subsequent round of payoffs was due, "De Lorenzo was not satisfied [with the 100 million]: he insisted that the Liberals should get a larger share because they controlled the assessorship with the greatest input as far as car parks were concerned" (CD, 28 May 1993, no. 386, pp. 4, 3).

There are also, of course, incentives for politicians to defect from such agreements: if backed by the leader of the current to which he belongs, for example, a politician may try to hang on to the bribes he has collected personally. The situations that can bring on a crisis are numerous: the extension of corruption to new areas, the emergence of *rampanti* and unscrupulous politicians demanding a bigger share for themselves, a hiatus between changes in the balance of forces brought about by elections and their recognition in the criteria for sharing out the proceeds of corruption. Any temporary attenuation in the flow of public resources, moreover, heightens internal conflict by calling established privileges into question.[12] In the absence of a "court of higher instance" with the power of maintaining discipline, the tenacity (or fragility) of the equilibrium depends on a number of factors, such as the frequency with which exchange takes place, and the easy detection of defection and the severity of punishment: "Enforcement of joint profit maximization in bribe collection is closely related to the problem of enforcing collusion in oligopoly" (Shleifer and Vishny 1993:609). During the construction of Milan's subway, for example, "the question of public contracts created tensions—the DC cashier Maurizio Prada, claimed—because the work could not be portioned out in such a way as to keep everybody happy. . . . A race to find the 'best political sponsorship' therefore took place through the intervention of the national secretariats, certainly that of the DC and, as far as I am concerned, that of the PSI as well" (*La Repubblica*, 12 February 1993, p. 10). In fact, where one enormous business transaction is concerned there is a strong risk that the successful company will recompense only its own political protectors and ignore the others. The absence of an agreement among the politicians encourages competition between entrepreneurs to secure the most effective political guarantees. When the opportunities for corruption are recurrent, on the other hand, it is more likely that the proceeds will be peaceably shared out among the politicians involved.

The emergence of spontaneous forms of cooperation is also favored by the prospect that the same political actors will stay in power over a prolonged period of time (Axelrod 1984). In the case being discussed, forms of coordination and communication did in fact develop between the various political actors, thus allowing rapid countermeasures to be taken when disagreements or defections threatened. According to Vincenzo D'Urso:

> the Right Hon. Balzamo [administrative secretary of the PSI] and Right Hon. Citaristi, administrative secretary of the DC, met frequently to define the best strategies for obtaining contributions from firms together. . . . I understand that lately Citaristi and Balzamo have been working on a common strategy for obtaining contributions from enterprises operating the "high speed [train]" business and those who would operate in the "light urban railway" business. (CD, 5 March 1993, no. 210, p. 10)

Insofar as there is full understanding between the various power centers, their action can be compared to that of a unitary organization, a sort of "superparty" coordinating the actions of corrupt administrators independent of their party affiliation. Giovanni Cavalli told the Milanese magistrates:

> Senator Severino Citaristi instructed him to keep an eye on what was happening in the environmental sector in order to ensure that a satisfactory equilibrium was maintained between companies "friendly" to the DC and companies "friendly" to the PSI and also in order to guarantee that there was a satisfactory division of the money coming from companies operating in the sector between the two parties. He proceeded by saying that he carried out this job in collaboration with Bartolomeo De Toma of the PSI. (CD, 5 March 1993, no. 210, p. 8)

In this way highly resistant, horizontal alliances form in certain areas or particular illegal transactions: "In Pescara—the entrepreneur Sergio Pelagatti claimed—what amounts to a business committee has operated since 1986 and still operates, cutting across party lines. It has decision-making power over all the activities of the commune and province . . . regardless of who is mayor or provincial president. Nothing happened, and nothing happens, without it being decided or approved by that committee" (CD, 6 May 1993, no. 330, p. 7).

In this situation, shared adhesion to the rules on payment minimizes the danger of mishaps or contestation, facilitating reciprocal control and the avoidance of controversy (see also Chapter 9). It is not by chance that the criteria for dividing bribery money between the different political parties or party factions were often regulated on a customary and agreed percentage basis. In the SEA (Society for the Airport of Milan), for example, considered a socialist fief, the party took half, the DC 35 percent, the Italian republican party (Partito Repubblicano Italiano, PRI) 10 percent, and the Social-Democrats 5 percent (TNM:46). According to the Socialist ex–board member of the National Electricity Board (*Ente nazionale per l'energia elettrica,* ENEL), Valerio Bitetto, management of tenders was shared with the DC, each party taking half of a bribe, which varied, according to the type of work, from 2 to 3 percent. In this way occasions for conflict between corrupt politicians are reduced because it is easier to verify that the sum expected is that actually handed over. A Codelfa employee specialized in speeding up the firm's requests for payment to different public bodies thus states: "Asked to specify the method of establishing the amount to be paid, I should make clear that all the firms who dealt with those buyers operated in the same way. There wasn't, therefore, a system for knowing how much it was opportune to pay: *there was a recognized custom*" (VICM:4, emphasis added).

The cashiers of the various parties coordinate the task of collection among themselves, reducing the amount of energy any one party needs to invest in covert exchange. The "municipal cashiers" in particular operated with each other in a coordinated way, taking turns demanding and collecting bribes for all the parties and thereafter redistributing them according to precise (but unwritten) rules (della Porta 1993). Within the across-class structures that existed for the collection and distribution of illegal funds, the various party representatives even alternated in fulfilling the functions of cashier and redistributor. In complete consociational agreement, the cashiers of one party would occasionally carry out their activities in the headquarters of another or would meet together in order to redistribute the proceeds of bribery. Thus the figure of the "collective cashier" emerged. The "national cashiers" also met in order "to work out in agreement between themselves the best strategies for obtaining contributions from enterprises, even where this is in violation of the law on political financing" (CD, 5 March 1993, no. 210, p. 10).

In the Italian party system, the concentration of the individual parties on gathering illegal income has favored the search for reciprocal connivance. On at least one point, the fierce clandestine battles over the division of these funds was accompanied by a secret nonbelligerence treaty: the nondenunciation of the system of corruption. In a democratic system, political competition—in particular between the governmental party and the opposition—should in fact help deter "bad behavior" by politicians in power, limiting the willingness of public agents to indulge in illegal activities: The competition between different parties and individuals aspiring to govern (in order to fulfill the targets defined by contending programs) should help those who are most honest or more willing to denounce the illegal actions of others. Defeated parties and politicians should have a definite interest in exposing the misappropriation of resources on the part of those in government. In this way, citizens can acquire the necessary information to inflict electoral retribution on parties indulging in illegal business at their expense.

The dynamics of the Italian political system, however, have powerfully limited this possibility. For over forty years, the absence of turnover in the national government of the country has represented the principal "anomaly" of Italian democracy (see, among others, Pasquino 1985, 1991). The very low expectation of change in the short term has made the discovery and denunciation of corruption more difficult. The strong ideological identifications of the electorate, moreover, have largely circumscribed its mobility, rendering voting behavior impervious to political scandals. The main opposition party, PCI, was strong enough to challenge the majority effectively, but not to take on direct responsibility for government. On the government side, the absence of turnover weakened the capacity for planning, favoring instead the immediate interest in dividing up and occupying public offices for clientelist ends (*lottizzazione*). In the management of the public and semipublic agencies and in the enterprises with public capital, members of those very parties that had nominated their protégés inside the administrative bodies were in charge of the institutional controls. As one of them explained, "In practice and beyond the bureaucratic procedures that were legally established, the names listed [for the nomination in the administrative body of the MM [Metropolitana Milanese] were those chosen by the party secretaries, that is, by those who are the final receivers of the bribes" (TM:36). Consociational agreements extended to those bodies that had control of the functioning of the public administration.

The opposition's strength could, however, not be ignored in either general or distributive political decisions precisely because of the weakness of the government coalitions and the splits within the parties. Continuous negotiation was necessary to avoid the danger of paralysis through obstructionism and head-on conflict. At the same time, the opposition (with no immediate prospect of winning power) found a way of "governing" from its minority position. Sharp verbal and public dissension was accompanied, in reality, by a practice of under-the-table negotiations and deals. This related in the first place to legislative activity[13] but, from a certain moment, included also the dividing up of minor government posts. A tenacious consociational equilibrium was thus created: formally opposed political forces became part of a hidden network of relationships. In most cases, the opposition exchanged its silence on corruption for political influence, while the various parties within the governmental actively shared bribes, developing therefore a connivance relating to their respective illicit activities. According to the actual results of the investigations, in a few cases—such as ENEL—the opposition also participated in the distribution of the bribes. The consociational agreements eliminated, even inside the elective organs, the normal controls between the majority and the opposition.

While in the *visible* political arena, in which various political groups seek to gain votes by distinguishing between themselves (Pizzorno 1993), corruption creates social costs by inducing an excessive expenditure of resources on political and electoral competition, in the *secret* political arena (including the market for corruption) there is a tendency toward inter-party collusion. The Italian party system can be likened to an oligopoly in which the consumer-citizen pays a rather high "price" for collusion between the parties as exemplified by the level of public intervention, designed to ensure large parasitic incomes for the political class. The major political parties demonstrate an underlying homogeneity in this regard, notwithstanding the different objectives they *declare* that they pursue through control of the state. Agreeing on this fundamental point, political conflict was prevalently about image, as between firms that collude in maintaining high prices but at the same time spare nothing in advertising in order to win a larger share of the market (della Porta and Vannucci 1994:Chapter XI).

5. POLITICAL PARTIES, THE COSTS OF POLITICS, AND CORRUPTION: COMPARATIVE REMARKS

Gathering the threads of what has been said so far, we can return to the initial question: Does corruption favor strong or weak political parties?

5.1. Partitocracies?

As we mentioned at the beginning of this chapter, the Italian (corrupt) party system has been described as a *partitocrazia*. The first element for defining *partitocrazia* is the presence of mass political parties, tightly controlled by their leadership.[14] According to Gianfranco Pasquino, *partitocrazia* is "the social and political presence and diffusion of mass parties. . . . Rather than party government, [*partitocrazia*] means their domination of, or ambition to dominate, the political system" (1990:774). In fact, in the years immediately after the Second World War the term *partitocrazia* was used in Italy to indicate—and attack—the growing power of the mass parties compared with the older parties of individual representation. Similar terms were used in other countries to refer to the same phenomenon. In particular, the large number of functionaries and professional politicians necessary for the functioning of mass parties has been considered as a main cause of an increase in the costs of politics, and therefore an incentive to corruption.[15] The *partitocrazia* has been linked to high political costs: "Political costs were always high in Italy, in part because of the length of political campaigns and the importance, until recent years, of competition between party lists for preference vote—a practice that not only increased the ferocity and expense of campaigns but also encourages personalized and often corrupt forms of campaigning and party organization" (Rhodes 1996:10; see also Chapter 1). Similarly, the low costs of electoral campaigns in Great Britain have been cited to explain the low level of corruption in that country (Adonis 1997).

Is political corruption favored by the presence of centralized, mass parties? As we have seen in our research, systemic political corruption in Italy had centrifugal effects on the political parties. The mass parties that emerged with the formation of the Italian Republic after the Second World War—either of an ideological or a clientelistic nature—gradually transformed themselves. A hidden structure emerged in the organization of corrupt exchanges, becoming more and more influential in determining party decisions. Moreover, the concurrence on the corruption market was reflected in internal fights between party factions, temporarily aggregated around business interests. When the scandals exploded in the nineties, the structure of the parties did not correspond to a model of *partitocrazia*. As Pizzorno noted:

> The term *partitocrazia* is not suitable for such a system. The very term "party" is a term of open political discourse. . . . Certainly it is too indistinct a term for the language of analysis. There are not many acts easily imputable to a party as such. The term *partitocrazia* comes from a period in which the parties acted as collective subjects, guided by powerful leaderships responsible, if not to the membership as such, at least to elite circles composed of members. The leaderships could answer for their members, parliamentary groups, and mass associations before other actors within the political system, represented for their part by other parties. Decisions regarding the selection of political personnel were taken by the party leaderships according to largely preestablished rules. (1993:304–5)

In fact, recent research has indicated the widespread presence of political corruption exactly where mass parties were not present. For instance, the Spanish party system is characterized by a low level of militancy and rootedness in society, a high degree of personalization, and pragmatism. Legalized in 1977, the political parties of the Spanish republic have always remained weak in organizational terms, with a very low 6 percent of party members within the total population. In fact, it has been observed that the Spanish parties developed from parties of notables at the beginning of the century to the contemporary parties of electors, skipping the phase of mass parties. Notwithstanding their small number of members, the Spanish parties have a large (and expansive) organizational structure, widespread throughout the country, which implies the need for many paid functionaries (Heywood 1997:73–76). Lacking a grass-roots base of supporters, the political parties have to rely on other sources: "The rate of public income in the treasury of Spanish political parties is probably the highest in Europe: 100 percent for the PSOE and 90 for the 'Partido Popular.' And . . . the income from membership is particularly low: 1 per mil for the PSOE and 15 percent for the second" (Pujas 1996:4). Similar conditions have been recalled to explain the development of corruption in the other

Southern European countries that began their transition to democracy in the midseventies: Portugal and Greece (Magone 1996:16). In an analysis of political scandals in Austria, Pelinka observed, "The political parties have lost much of their original ideological character. One of the consequences of this 'secularization process' has been the increase of various pragmatic 'machinations' and the quest for nonideological 'deals,' which not only have led to a deideologization of the parties but also to a concomitant proliferation and legitimation of individual careerism. Often linked to schemes of personal enrichment, the loss of ideology has upon occasion also led to an increase in the temptation toward criminal deeds" (1988:169).

The Japanese example illustrates very well the way in which corruption interacts with centrifugal tendencies in party life and the enormous costs for political activities. In Japan, where during the Liberal Democratic party's long reign (1955–1993) nine of its fifteen prime ministers have been implicated in political scandals, the cost of politics is particularly high—so much so that political corruption has been defined as a "redistribution system" (Bouissou 1997). An electoral system with preference votes for the individual candidates has made electoral campaigns enormously expensive, in particular those of conservative candidates who compete with each other in the same constituencies. If the candidates of the opposition usually rely upon the support of their party, conservative candidates instead have to conquer their votes one by one. The cost of an electoral campaign is in fact four times higher for a candidate of the government than for one of the opposition, because only the former has to face internal competition by other members of the party (ibid.). For an MP of the Conservative party, the clients are organized in *koenkai*, or support organizations, with an average of ten thousand to thirty thousand members: each of them consists of a network of small groups, built around particular social categories or recreational activities.[16] Because of internal competition, in order to avoid "losing" his *koenkai* in favor of a rival party-colleague, each candidate has to employ ten to fifteen secretaries, whose task is to organize specific groups, distributing gifts (in particular at marriages or funerals) or invitations to parties or trips (ibid.:136–38). During electoral campaigns, aspiring Conservative MPs offer, in fact, concrete rewards to their supporters: "Apart from campaign literature, he or his staff will usually hand over a cash-filled envelope ('for your trouble'—like posting his campaign poster on the wall of the [supporter's] residence) to his presumed supporters and voters during house calls in his district. Another must is regularly organized all-expenses-paid trips to Tokyo or wining and dining at regional spas for members of the thousands-strong local support organizations (*koenkai*), as well as any amount of charitable and individual donations" (Rothacher 1996:3).

Political corruption does not seem therefore to be an effect of ideological mass parties; instead, it seems to grow with the transformation of the political parties into "cartel parties," with fluid ideology and little grass-roots presence. Unable to mobilize a stable constituency, with no membership available to pay the party's expenses, and a political class that, lacking ideological motivation, sees enrichment as the only real incentive to politics, these political parties become more and more available to corrupt practices. "Political entrepreneurs face serious financial problems. Not only are there no party members to voluntarily help with their campaigns, there are no party members paying their dues either. The party has to buy services, but has no income, or projected income, with which to do it" (Hopkins 1996:15). Together with the decline in membership financing, an increase in the costs of campaigning has been observed: "The 'media revolution' has clearly exacerbated this problem by allowing previously prohibited private broadcasts, thereby driving up information, propaganda, and campaign costs. At the same time, the 'office revolution' caused by the spread of new technology (personal computers, photocopying and fax machines) required large investments to provide party headquarters and party-owned newspaper with new equipment. Finally, . . . salary expenditures reveal real increases in the major parties' official budgets" (Rhodes 1996:10).

5.2.   Party Power and Corruption

The Italian case can also help frame another definition of *partitocrazia* as the degeneration of a specific form of regulation of social conflict, counterposed to neocorporatist (organization of strong interests), pluralist (strong civil society), and policy network (strong technocracy) formulations: that is to say, *party government*.[17] The Italian system has been defined as a government by the parties, with the parties in a position to control pressure groups (whose influence in the political system depends upon their clientelistic relationship, with ideological proximity to a political party)[18] the technocrats (*lottizzati*, i.e., appointed in proportion to party strength), and civil society (social movements too being aligned around party actors). The power of the parties, therefore, is seen as having characterized both society and institutions. As Pasquino has observed:

> The party presence in Italian society, in the centers of decision-making, has been permitted by the expansion of the public sector, by the existence of municipal enterprises, by the number of positions subject to political nomination. . . . As regards the institutions, at the risk of providing too rudimentary an explanation, it is opportune to remember: firstly, that recruitment to administrative and political posts is largely the monopoly of the parties; secondly, that in the formal centers of decision-making the presence of

personnel of party extraction is not only dominant but frequently absolute. (1987:60)

In our research, we saw in fact that an overreaching presence of the political parties has been often stigmatized. However, as Alessandro Pizzorno (1971) argued many years ago, the "strength" or "weakness" of a party can be differently evaluated depending on whether one considers its power (1) to procure advantages for the representatives (the party apparatuses, in other words), or (2) to transmit the demands of its constituency.

The use of corrupt practices would seem to be negatively correlated with the second kind of party power, *reducing parties' ability to elaborate long-term programs, mobilize ideological resources, distribute participatory incentives, and gain the support of an electorate of opinion.* As revealed in the Italian case, by concentrating on the organization of corruption, the political parties privilege those decisions most productive in terms of bribes rather than those which might generate the greatest support among the electorate. In addition, corruption, by its very nature, leads to the dominance of hidden over visible politics, small-group logic over the search for wider participation. As in the case of the American political machine, "[T]he party organization did not play an important role in developing alternative courses of municipal governmental action. Indeed, since machine politicians drew their resources from the routine operation of government, they did not concern themselves with policy formulation" (Wolfinger 1973:104). The diffusion of corruption has been related to the weakness of political parties in such different contexts as Latin America— for instance, the fragmentation in Columbia, with 628 electoral lists in the 1994 elections (Zuluaga Nieto 1996; Njaim 1996)—as well as in France (Ruggiero 1996b). In the long term, the evident squandering of resources connected to misadministration impedes corrupt politicians from attracting an electorate of opinion by presenting themselves as the bearers of prosperity and progress. The pragmatism of under-the-counter deals substitutes for ideological appeals.

Political corruption interacted with *the parties' power to reinforce delegation.* With the alibi of the "political " nature of administrative decisions, the parties have invaded the managing boards of public bodies, using their power in ways not always directed to the collective welfare and not always lawful. More or less official mechanisms of political control over the nomination of certain public sector bureaucrats have led to the *partitizzazione* of the public administration, producing feuds that the parties and their representatives have used for patronage and corruption. The influence of the parties in areas beyond the public administration—from banks to newspapers—has led to an occupation of civil society, further lowering society's defenses against corruption and mismanagement. The political parties have occupied civil society not in order to realize long-term political programs but to facilitate the extraction of a parasitic rent. As we observed, the parties acquired an important function as organizers of political corruption. First of all, they diffused in the political system values that justified corruption as the "normal " way of doing politics. White-collar crime has been explained with reference to work-related subcultures:[19] "These work-related subcultures tend to isolate their members from the mainstream of social life and its construction of reality. . . . Because of this isolation, work-related subcultures are often able to maintain a definition of certain criminal activities as acceptable or even required behavior, when they are clearly condemned by society as a whole" (Coleman 1987:422–23). In the case of corruption, political parties facilitate corruption, reducing the moral barrier against illegal actions:

> Political party membership, and the experience of political life in general, also has secondary socializing effects that become constitutive of a person's identity and therefore of their moral principles. Someone belonging to a political association can receive recognition for: technical or cultural abilities; loyalty, or conformism, in ideological commitment; loyalty to a particular leader; astuteness, aggressiveness, or lack of scruples in "taking out" adversaries; capacity for forming links with the wider society and bringing in money for party funds or other kinds of contributions; or, naturally, some combination of these qualities. The "moral quality" of associated life will vary according to the prevailing criteria for recognition. The more an individual's activity and relations are restricted to the concerns of party life the more the identifications on which identity is modeled will reflect its "moral quality," and on this will depend the moral cost of corruption. The more corruption is diffuse the more political parties themselves function as agencies for socialization in illegality, reducing the moral cost paid by their members for participation in corrupt practices. (Pizzorno 1992:47)

In systems of extensive corruption the parties not only socialize into illicit practices, reducing the moral costs of corruption, they also secure a kind of continuity to the game of corruption through its diffusion in every geographical area, in the various public bodies, and in the different sectors of public administration: whoever respects the unlawful agreements can continue to do business with the public administration; anyone who opts out on a given occasion will be permanently excluded from the market for public works. Controlling the nominations to public bodies, the parties can generalize the *kickback*, transforming corruption from an exception into an established practice with accepted norms, at the same time guaranteeing the continuity of the system over time despite changes in the political personnel of the public administration. That is to say, the parties assume the *function of guarantors of the illegal bargain*, participating in those operations demanding a "certification of trust: in other words, the promises of others, requiring to be guaranteed in some way, are used to obtain a benefit" (ibid.:31). Moreover, reaching an agreement between them, majority and opposition reduce the material risks connected with identifying suitable parties and negotiating the bribes.

Italy is, of course, not the only case in which political parties seemed particularly involved in the organization of corruption. In France, for instance, various associations, often financed by the state, have developed with links to the political parties, allowing them to collect money and escape, at the same time, the rules for the public accounts. These associations provide salaries to members of the party they are associated with, finance in various way their campaigns, and pay party activities (Becquart-Leclercq 1993:9–10; Mény 1992). One of the scandals that pushed the Socialists out of power was related to the disclosure of the activities of Urba, a *bureau d'études* that collected illegal party financing for the Socialist party, distributing it, in the word of its director, "according to the principle 40-30-30 (40 percent for the functioning of Urba, 30 percent for the national headquarters of the party, 30 percent for the local elected politicians)" (*Le Monde*, 3 March 1995). Collecting bribes by local entrepreneurs (hidden as compensation for services that had not been provided), Urba paid the salary to functionaries of the central headquarter of the party, as well as various expenses for political campaigning at the local or the central level (ibid.).

Moreover, not only in Italy does a collusion between governmental and opposition parties seem to be a common practice as far as corruption is concerned. An extreme case is Japan, where the silence of the opposition seems to have been bought through significant sums of money paid from the Conservatives to their adversaries—sometimes behind the screen of a fake *mah-jong* game between politicians of the government and the opposition (Bouissou 1997:140–42). In general, cartel parties, characterized already by collusion with a massive use of public financing,[20] manifest their reciprocal solidarity when scandals related to party financing emerge.[21] In the French context, Becquart-Leclercq observed within the network of corruption a shared adherence to operational modes of implicit codes that include "the conspiracy of silence: it operates particularly between leaders of various political parties, despite their sometimes bitter and violent conflicts; to survive, all must respect the rules of the game and maintain silence about the rules themselves" (1989:205). In Germany, resilience to scandals was connected to

> the organizational oligopoly on which parties could build. The stability of this system rests, above all, on a strong interparty consensus about the basic rules of the game (including the legal/illegal ways of party financing), and on the commonly shared interest of the "established " parties to retain their de facto monopoly of public decision-making and to guard it against outside

forces. This common interest has in good part suspended the functioning of the checks and balances and the institutional mechanisms of control usually associated, at least in theory, with competitive party systems, replacing them with conventional patterns of tacit agreement and mutual privilege enhancement (Blankenburg et al. 1989:922)

If corruption has transformed the foundations of power within the parties and their functions, it can be added that, in the Italian case the influence of the parties in the operation of networks of corruption varies considerably from one geographical area to another. As the ex-mayor of Reggio Calabria, Agatino Licandro, observed:

The difference between *kickbacks* in the North and South is that [in the North] there is a centralized structure. A collection point controlled and run in a unitary fashion. The party collects the money and then divides it among the factions, after retaining what is required for the party itself. Here [in the South], on the other hand, it is exactly the reverse. If whoever collects is the head of the party at that moment, that's where the money finishes up. But it's a subterfuge. In reality, the party means one's own faction or corresponds to immediate group interests. It is not a small difference. The mechanism provokes tensions and dramatizes the whole of political life. Worse than that, everything else—alliances, decisions—is subordinated to bribery and money. (Licandro and Varano 1993:122–23)

As we are going to see in Chapter 8, in certain regions of Southern Italy in particular, organized crime partly substitutes for the political parties in the function of certifying trust between those involved in covert exchange and consequently receives a part of the bribes.

This observation leads to our final remark. If it is true that the parties function as guarantors of illegal exchange, they are not alone in doing so. Alongside them, in fact, range a series of aggregations—some of them formal, others not—all of which have in common a low level of visibility. Political corruption, being covert exchange, subtracts power from visible sites. The arenas of decision-making are therefore shifted from visible to hidden politics, where the parties are not necessarily the dominant actors. Weakened by the spread of corruption, the parties become supporting actors, behind the scenes of the cryptogovernment in which the real decisions concerning the public sphere are taken. To the latter, we will turn our attention in the next chapter.

NOTES

1.   In the 1960s, according to the classic studies conducted by the *Istituto Cattaneo* (Galli 1966; Alberoni 1967; Poggi 1968), the Italian mass parties had a number

of particular characteristics. As far as the DC is concerned, weak levels of activism and a circumscribed party machine were combined with the influential role of "notables," Catholic associational militancy, and, above all, the "occupation" of state institutions. The PCI, on the other hand, was characterized by a structure halfway between Leninist democratic centralism—the "cells" (i.e., an organizational form best suited to a "class" party with propaganda aimed at a homogeneous social group) maintaining an important role—and openness to recruitment through "ancillary" associations.

2. Similarly, about his nomination as a member of the ENEL board, Valerio Bitetto declared: "The PSI proposed me for that position and on the occasion I met with Hon. Craxi in person, who literally said to me, '[D]on't sit there keeping the seat warm': in other words, he told me that I had to use my position to get votes and money for the party" (*Panorama* 1993, p. 51).

3. Of his role in socializing other administrators in the system of corruption, the ex-mayor of Reggio Calabria has written: "Once, talking of people who accepted bribes, an entrepreneur reasoned: 'For politicians money is like taking drugs. After you take it once you can't do without it. It's difficult the first time. Then, it becomes like heroin and you go and demand it.' One of the people I initiated into taking *mazzette* [packages of cash] afterwards started to make small deals of his own, *gli assolo* [solos] as they're called in the jargon" (Licandro and Varano 1993:47–48).

4. When the priority of public agents is the (unproductive) search for gain rather than the raison d'être of the institution, a loss in organizational efficiency is to be expected. The *influence cost* of such activity is twofold: on the one hand, the distortion of the decisions taken (which would otherwise have been different); on the other, the investment of time and effort in appropriating revenue without creating any collective advantage. "Rent-seeking on the part of potential entrants in a setting where entry is either blocked or can at best reflect one-to-one substitutions must generate social waste. Resources . . . might be used to produce valued goods and services elsewhere in the economy, whereas nothing of net value is produced by rent-seeking" (Buchanan 1980:8). For a review of the literature on the social costs of rent-seeking activities, see Buchanan, Tollison, and Tullock (1980), Tullock (1984, 1989), and Rowley, Tollison, and Tullock (1987).

5. Italy has long been considered the paradigmatic case of polarized pluralism, characterized by a plurality of political parties, the existence of antisystem parties, a division into two hostile ideological camps, and a dynamic of centrifugal competition (Sartori 1982).

6. Mauro analyzes in a cross-country context the potential effects of corruption on the composition of government expenditure, showing how corrupt agents tend to collect bribes from some especially *vulnerable* components, thus influencing the allocation of resources. For instance, "government spending on education [a sector with few opportunities for corruption] as a ratio of GDP is negatively and significantly correlated with corruption" (1996:13, see also 1995).

7. More in general on this point, see Somogyi (1992:80).

8. According to the State Audit Court, the Commission of the Chamber of Deputies responsible provided "particularly broad guidelines . . . encouraging too 'elastic' an interpretation at the administrative level of the connection between the

functionality of the works to be realized and their presentation to the public, thus inflating both the number and the cost" (CC, 1992, vol. II, I, p. 510).

9.   Even in a real emergency, exceptional spending procedures can create an artificial increase in public demand. This was particularly evident in the case of reconstruction after the Irpinia earthquake. A Parliamentary Enquiry Commission revealed "the existence of building work greatly exceeding what was actually required. . . . There was much superfluous construction. This squandering of money was encouraged by the system of awarding contracts" (CPDT:647–48). As an entrepreneur involved in the reconstruction process noted: "In a field where the public administration had ample discretionary powers, paying the politicians was the only way to get the work. . . . Since the contracts were spread over time, the good offices of politicians had to be maintained over time also" (CD, 18 May 93, no. 365, p. 6).

10.   Besides the increase in the risks of reciprocal denunciation, there is an effect on the amount of the bribes that can be collected. As Shleifer and Vishny have shown, in political contexts where corrupt officials act independently and it is not clear who needs to be bribed and for how much, they can hurt each other, by reducing their global bribe revenues (1993:606).

11.   According to Paolo Pizzarotto, an entrepreneur, any consortium wishing to compete for public contracts needed to include firms that "from their geographical presence and influence could show that they were also the most 'complete' politically vis-à-vis the purchaser" (SDM:13).

12.   This point also introduces a crisis factor *endogenous* to the system of corruption: the inclusion of new actors—indispensable for ensuring their silence—tends to reduce the size of individual shares in the proceeds of corruption and, at the same time, encourages and reinforces competitors in the open political struggle. Corrupt politicians therefore see their sources of finance and hold on positions of power being undermined, aggravating dissension and conflict.

13.   In the first five legislatures of the postwar period, the average vote in favor of laws passed in parliamentary commissions was 91 percent. The vote in favor in the chamber itself was not unanimous, but nevertheless high at 76.5 percent (Di Palma 1978:85–89). The difference between commissions and chamber is to be explained by the greater publicity of voting in the latter, which makes clear prearranged agreements difficult to justify before the electorate. On consociationalism and Italian politics, see Pizzorno (1993). On the prevalence of "micropolicies," see Cotta and Isernia (1996),

14.   On the concept of partitocracy, see also de Winter, della Porta, and Deschouwer (1996).

15.   In Italy, the elected political personnel reaches 160,000, the second highest number in Europe (after France). The number of people with an income mainly related to political activities is about 2 million (Bettin and Magnier 1991; *Panorama*, 19 July 1992, p. 44).

16.   In Japan, in fact, "The incredibly high cost of political campaigning and the blatant illegality of many campaign practices discourages voters from working actively in elections, thereby impelling Japanese political candidates to develop their personal support association, known as *koenkai*, which are manned by politi-

cal pros, while providing services to mass constituencies much in the manner of traditional American urban machine politics" (Macdougall 1988:205).

17. According to the classic definition (Katz 1986:43), for there to be *party government* at least three conditions are necessary: "Firstly, all major governmental decisions must be taken by people chosen in elections conducted along party lines, or by individuals appointed by and responsible to such people. . . . Secondly, policy must be decided within the governing party, when there is a 'monocolor' government, or by negotiation among parties when there is a coalition. . . . Thirdly, the highest officials (e.g., cabinet ministers and especially the prime minister) must be selected within their parties and be responsible to the people through their parties" (ibid.:43).

18. See the classic study of LaPalombara (1964).

19. Work-related subcultures are "epistemic communities that provide the locus for specialized reality construction in society on the basis of work concerns or ideological commitments" (Holzner 1972:95).

20. In Italy, after a big scandal related to illegal party financing, Law 195/74 was passed in 1974 in order to regulate the field by introducing public financing and rules for private financing (Rhodes 1996:8–9). After the first law had been abrogated by referendum in April 1993, new laws substituted the subventions to parties with the reimbursement of campaign spending to candidates (law 515/93) and regulated political financing through tax payments (law 2/1997). A strong relation between irregular campaign financing and political corruption was found also in Brazil (Fleisher 1997). On cartel parties, see Katz and Mair (1995).

21. For example, see Frognier (1986) on Belgium; Roth (1989) and Seibel (1997) on Germany; Jiménez Sanchez (1995, 1996a, 1996b) on Spain.

5

Political Corruption, Bureaucratic Corruption, and the Judiciary

Between the mid-1970s and the end of the following decade a system of corruption existed within the ATM, Milan's public transport company, so extensive and well-rooted (the magistrates were able to document over two thousand illegal transactions) that not a single denunciation or internal controversy disturbed its functioning. A double division of roles seems to have operated among the corrupt ATM functionaries, partly based on office held, partly on internal agreements. One division was between organizers and "cashiers," the other between material participants and those who simply turned a blind eye (and were paid for so doing). The head of the purchasing department would appear to have specialized in making contacts with businessmen and bringing the practice of illegality to their attention: "[B]y then he had become quite able in adopting this or that tone, persuasive and kind or arrogant and imperious, according to the cultural and social characteristics of the person with whom he was talking. Sometimes he would be courteous, sometimes threatening, whichever appeared most likely to be productive in view of the personality of the other party." On different occasions, to different entrepreneurs he had "stated things clearly, demanding the sum owed," "said he was obliged to give something to the party," "put the alternative: either pay the money or find it impossible to get on with the work in peace," "did not ask openly but made it understood that it would be opportune . . . ," "asked that he be able to see to expenses and gifts," "suggested going along with what the other companies did already," "imposed his conditions with the threat of receiving no more contracts," "made it understood that it would be opportune to look good in the eyes of those who had appointed him," "merely asked his commission," and "made it clear that it was necessary to give money to the parties" (TAM:44). Another functionary was responsible for collecting small-scale bribes, a task that would have distracted the chief "cashier" from his other duties. Before distribution, the illegal proceeds of corruption were held in a common fund, indicative of the very high levels of trust among those involved. Another of the functionaries admitted that his task within the division of labor was the distribution of information to firms, in particular giving "favored competitors a list of the other firms competing so that they could contact each other and agree on the price to be submitted to the purchaser" (TAM:44).

As one of these functionaries told the magistrates, such activities were "something [he] considered to be normal practice" (TAM:44). It appears to have been precisely this transformation of illegal activities into "normal practice" that guaranteed the continuation of corrupt exchange over time. For fifteen years, functionary fol-

lowed functionary as individuals were transferred or retired; the entrepreneurs involved alternated or were replaced by newcomers. Yet throughout this time the system of covert exchange with its iron laws of distribution survived unchanged. Each commodity area had fixed percentage payoffs based on the profit margins of supplying firms. The bribe to be paid was calculated automatically by taking a percentage of the value of the order. The image of a well-entrenched system is confirmed by the existence of rules for dividing the proceeds on the basis of fixed percentages ("the percentage going to each person was always fixed. . . . The calculations were ridiculously precise, even a handful of lira being shared out") and by the extremely detailed accounts kept of covert exchange (TAM:96–97).

The presence of established internal rules of corruption minimized the risk of being exposed and kept down transactions costs on the percentages to go to any particular individual. At the same it increased confidence that promises would be maintained and debts paid. As one functionary involved in the system commented, "I found myself in a mechanism with a life of its own, which sucked you in, and I didn't know how to get out" (ibid.:94). The belief that bribery was "everyday practice" also led entrepreneurs to go along with activities that were presented as "normal." This process of degeneration produced a perverse equilibrium of generalized corruption: "Money illegally demanded, offered, and consigned was flying in all directions. Every desk had its lists of corrupt and corrupter, every pocket an envelope destined for oneself or someone else. Every product sector in which the accused were concerned seems to have possessed an archive of company information worthy of aspiring industrial spies" (TAM:84).

In the ATM as in other bodies where corruption is rife, frequent repetition of exchange favored the emergence of a form of conditioned cooperation. Under pain of permanent exclusion from the system of distributing the proceeds of corruption, fulfillment of his respective obligations appeared the best strategy for each agent to adopt. The presence of codified rules of conduct contributed to the consolidation of reputations for "honesty" in illegal activities. The costs of negotiation and exchange were reduced by the dissemination of information on the modalities of bribery and, as the system of corruption expanded, residual moral restraints on illegal behavior tended to dissolve. Political corruption also spread from one sector to another. The frequent promotion of corrupt functionaries became an opportunity to "export" illegal procedures from one office to another. The magistrates noted that one bureaucrat accused of corruption "was able to continue his criminal conduct in spite of continual transfers. . . . Indeed his illegal activities always emerged reinvigorated and reinforced, widening the sphere of corrupt and corrupters on the one hand and the necessary circle of complicity on the other" (TAM:171).

The protection offered by certain politicians was an important resource for corrupt bureaucrats. The explicit political affiliations of career bureaucrats suggest that a complex system of exchange relations involved the political parties as well. The corruption administered by ATM functionaries and the covert market controlled by the politicians managing the company do not appear closed and separate systems. A symmetry of political affiliations appears to have existed between political administrators and the bureaucrats involved in corruption (the works manager, a Socialist, and the head of purchasing, a Christian Democrat, in particular, both of whom had enjoyed rapid promotion and brilliant careers). Also, numerous scandals had *emerged in the past concerning falsification of competition results regarding the hiring of ATM personnel and the company was considered a Christian Democrat fiefdom. Moreover, the original gang of corrupt ATM bureaucrats all belonged to the Loreto section of the DC and the bonds of trust and friendship between them stemmed from their shared political affiliation. Explicit reference was made to "party requirements " in demands for bribes and an influential behind-the-scenes political presence was alluded to by at least one corrupt functionary, when he stated that "there were others behind him directing the operation and enjoying the fruits" (TAM:175). As the later investigations would reveal, exchanges between functionaries and politicians went well beyond mere complicity and reciprocal noninterference in illegal activities. Functionaries handed over money to politicians in the public sector hierarchy and to party organs (the price they paid for political protection of their illegal activities and their careers). They also abstained from entering into competition with or hindering the larger affairs of the political hierarchy. In exchange, functionaries were allowed to take bribes on tenders under 100 million lira, assisted in promotions within the company, permitted arbitrary decisions, covered up illegal activities, and were unsanctioned for inefficiency. The politicians also acted as guarantors of the internal agreements governing corruption.*

Until now, we have focused our attention on the corrupt politicians. As this illustration indicates, however, political corruption is often linked to bureaucratic corruption. Bureaucratic corruption, in fact, reduces the risks for corrupt politicians by reducing the efficacy of controls. Incentives to corruption grow, as they do for any other illegal activity, the less the probability of being discovered and punished, that is, the less efficient control mechanism are.[1] *External* types of control, such as the mass media or the public opinion, present problems because of the "public good" character of their results: the incentives for citizens to combat illegal behavior may prove insufficient (Benson and Baden 1985:401).[2] For this reason, bureaucratic and legal controls, *internal* to the state apparatus, are very relevant for reducing corruption. In general, an incorrupt bureaucracy represents an essential watchdog on and counterweight to the activities of politicians. Civil servants are often in a position to denounce the illegitimate actions of politicians, or they can refuse to carry out the measures desired by the latter. For their part, the politicians define the essential lines of the public administration's activity, influencing both the opportunities and risks of bureaucratic corruption. Internal controls suffer, however, from a congenital weakness: *the vulnerability to collusion between controllers and controlled,* to the detriment of the public (Elster 1989a; Tirole 1986). The same principle is also valid for the control politicians should exercise over bureaucrats: political corruption also facilitates bureaucratic corruption insofar as politicians would seek to collude instead of denouncing illegal behaviors in the public administration. As we are going to see in Section 1 of this chapter, in the Italian case, political corruption was intertwined with bureaucratic corruption. Not only did the illegality of the politicians dispose them to tolerate that of the bureaucrats, moreover, the corruption of the bureaucracy reduced the risks for corrupt politicians.

When reciprocal controls between elected and career public administrators do not work, given that corrupt exchanges are breaches of the criminal law, the "natural" adversary of corrupters and the corrupt is the magistracy. The latter performs, in fact, a decisive function in the control of corruption: any eventual punishment of corrupted politicians in political terms is tightly bound up with the existence and visibility of criminal prosecution. The efficiency of the magistracy marks the degree to which indulging in political corruption is dangerous. As far as political crimes are concerned, the efficacy of the magistracy is, to a large extent, determined by its degree of independence from political authority. If at the formal level the magistracy is a separate power, with a neutral attitude toward politics, in practice most democracies have tried to produce mechanisms of political interference in the activities of the magistrates (Guarnieri 1992). This interference may be oriented in two directions: repression of the political opposition, and tolerance of administrative misconduct. In the Italian case, two apparently contradictory peculiarities emerge in the relationship between the judges and the political sphere: on the one hand, a very high formal degree of independence; on the other, a high level of "politicization" of the judges. As we will indicate in Section 2, these peculiarities had a differential effect on the attitudes and behavior of the judiciary toward the crimes of the political class. In Section 3, we attempt some cross-national comparison and some generalizations on the interactions between political and bureaucratic corruption.

1. POLITICAL CORRUPTION AND BUREAUCRATIC CORRUPTION

1.1. Veto Power and Fast Lane

In Italy, political corruption was often accompanied by bureaucratic corruption of two kinds. First of all, bureaucrats invested their (limited) autonomous power in *petty corruption*. As a Milanese entrepreneur explained, the corruption market was structured on two levels: "Two were the categories to which I made the payment. On the one side, there were the bureaucrats, who systematically blocked the process and produced sluggishness in many ways. This kind of resistance could, of course, be overcome by paying what was demanded. On the other side, there was the category of the politicians who governed over the aforementioned functionaries, and they also had to be satisfied in the same way" (CD, 22 March 1993, no. 234, p. 5).

Bureaucratic corruption reflected the characteristics of the resources available for the public bureaucrats. Traditionally, the Italian bureaucracy has been characterized by a limited capacity for initiative, combined with a strong veto power, exercised through omissions and delays in the application of the law (Mortara 1974). The behavior diffused in the public administration has been defined as "oriented to let it be, postpone to the next day, wait until the others will demand, ready to bargain. Therefore, the antithesis of a Weberian model of administration. A type of administration founded not on the legal-rational power, but on the contractual-conventional one" (Cassese 1994:17). A limited specialization was combined with the structural exclusion of the administrative leadership from the ruling class, which produced a vicious circle: "a) the high bureaucrats, excluded from the circles of those who take the decisions, take a defensive stance, looking only at increasing their status; b) the 'political class,' in an attempt to counter the resulting situation, adopt inefficient and counterproductive remedies; c) the high bureaucrats, in turn, seek a refuge in legalism, using it against the 'intrusion' of politicians; d) the political class multiplies the laws in an attempt to lead the administration . . . ; e) at the end of the circle, the result is an increase in the viscosity of the procedures and administrative inefficiency" (Cassese 1983:64).

Bureaucratic *veto power* was in fact used on several occasion by corrupt bureaucrats in order to impose bribes in exchange for a "faster" response to the needs of the entrepreneurs. As the judges noted, "In a city administration like that of Milan, composed of thousands of sections and offices, no politician, including the mayor or the alderman, has enough influence to impose a positive, fast, and secure processing of a dossier, without the collaboration of those functionaries in control of the neurological ganglia of the administration a dossier has to pass through" (TRDM:677). One of the main resources for a corrupted bureaucrat is the "signature" necessary to forward a dossier from one office to the next, until the final payment. For instance, a functionary of the regional administration in Treviso decelerated or accelerated a dossier, according to the kickbacks he received: "Never mind, if you want to release the dossier, you have to pay," he used to tell the entrepreneurs (PROM:277). As one of them explained, two functionaries of the office responsible for public works in Milan refused to issue to the entrepreneur certifications stating that the various steps to advance the work had been taken, certifications that were necessary for the entrepreneur to receive advanced payment. Payments started only after the entrepreneur agreed to negotiate a fixed-percentage bribe with the corrupt bureaucrats (ibid.:317). As for the signature on a payment bill, the administrators were so aware of their different blackmail power in different situations that they calculated the bribes according to how fast entrepreneurs needed a procedure. So, the managers of Milan's *Provveditorato alle Opere Pubbliche* demanded 1 percent of a contract as a bribe to an entrepreneur who had a solid financial position (and could therefore afford the "wait") and 2.5 percent to another entrepreneur who instead was in chronic deficit, and for whom each delay in the payment meant high interest payments to his bank (PROM:277, 317).

Corruption can in fact be seen as a way to create a "fast lane" to administrative decisions for those who are willing to pay bribes. The procedures governing the bureaucracy in Italy often ignore the human, time, and organizational constraints of the public administration. Agents therefore have more work than they are capable of performing, and thus have the opportunity to decide which dossiers take preferential paths or how certain resources are administered. A certain decision can be taken or not; it can be taken immediately or left indefinitely under consideration; one private concern can be chosen as opposed to another; a larger or smaller amount of public money can be spent. A price must be paid in return. Three corrupt functionaries in the urban development department of the Milan city council, for example, played a decisive role in the allocation of work in the Ronchetto area: "The head of this department had a notable influence in speeding up the said dossier. . . . It received a particularly favorable treatment from the assignment office. The first thing that strikes the eye is the extreme rapidity with which it was dealt by the office in question" (PRDM:655). The bribes paid were proportional to the time saved.

Bureaucrats may use their power to decide how much time and effort to dedicate to their official duties in order to raise bribes for working or for working less, depending on their preference. When long delays become the rule, a functionary can ask for a bribe simply to do his job within the regulation time, given that this has become an unexpected "service." In the Catania public health board (USL 35), for example, "[corrupt] functionaries had no need to threaten problems since the bureaucratic machine itself was the problem. Private suppliers [paid] to elude the delays that were the rule" (ACA:57). According to Fabrizio Garampelli, an entrepreneur, "[I]t is difficult to say whether a delay is intentional or not. In any case, certain situations are best avoided" ("Un giorno in Pretura," RAI 3, 22 February 93). As they become increasingly common, long procedural delays represent a plausible threat inducing private parties to find an "arrangement." One Sicilian entrepreneur stated: "[I]t was frequently necessary to pay those politicians having the influence and prestige to eliminate the problems that arise before and after the awarding of a public contract, to avoid antagonizing them" (CD, 24 June 1993, no. 450, p. 2). Moreover, corrupt politicians find in administrative inefficiency a justification for a wide range of their activities. The judges investigating political corruption in Bari noted, for example, that "immunity for [corrupt politicians] is derived from that involution of the bureaucratic process that provides a post hoc explanation for delays" (TRIB:267).

Where mechanisms limiting access to public benefits (official or otherwise) are absent, the possibility of gain can create "overcrowding" among aspiring beneficiaries. The resulting bottleneck in claims on the public administration generates further delay and malfunctioning, and increases the incentives to resort to corruption. The State Audit Court, for example, described contracting by ANAS in the following terms:

> A further characteristic is . . . the participation of a large number of firms (tenders frequently exceeding 200). . . . These large numbers create problems. . . . The intensity of competition leads to extremely low bids . . . , forcing the ANAS into long and involved exchanges with firms in order to identify and exclude anomalous proposals. On the one hand this state of affairs led to significant alterations in tendering procedures, on the other to a notable increase in conflict. (CC, 1987, II, 290)

Judicial inquiries have shown that this critical situation for ANAS's functioning resulted from a vast and hidden market of corruption. Alberto Zamorani, a public manager, asserted that "with the ANAS both the management of the firm and the political parties must be bought off. This system [of bribes] has been in place for at least twenty years" (MPM:173). Initially entry into the public market was "checked" by the existence of a cartel of firms (benefiting from political protection) that determined the necessary "rotation." However, "in more recent times," Zamorani continued, "the firms continued to pay but the politicians were unable to help them. A nefarious and unproductive cycle developed in which everybody, big or small, was on an equal footing and one would pay more than the other in order to get ahead. The amount of money available steadily diminished while the number of aspirants for it steadily grew" (*L'Espresso*, 23 August 92, p. 21). Such heated competition between corrupters in the private sector has a *directly* negative effect on the public administration, while at the same time it causes a greater flow of illegal income into the public sector, increasing the cost of influencing decisions.

Besides, when preferential treatment can be bought through corruption, the rest of the public is increasingly subjected to the negative effects of inefficiency through bureaucratic holdups and hindrance. For instance, since the time and effort of functionaries represents a limited resource that (beyond a certain level) is subtracted from one task in order to perform another, then a firm that receives payment more rapidly through bribery slows down payment to others. As one entrepreneur put it:

> Making use of personal acquaintances in the public administration is the norm. Particular functionaries have to be approached because the system is deficient. The lack of competence and technical means in the bureaucratic apparatus has to be compensated by following cases personally. . . . The absence of an authentic structure, capable of responding to the needs of busi-

nessmen and acting as a filter between them and politicians, forced me to approach the politicians directly. (Scaccioni and Marradi 1994:37)

In the circumstances considered above, the agent may have to neglect equally deserving cases to the advantage of the person using corruption; the speeding up of one dossier slows another down. The functionary in charge of payments for the Catania local health board (USL 35), later found guilty of corruption, "left a great many invoices lying unattended with the excuse that he could not sort out the dossier, while he was quick in approving others, disregarding chronological order" (ACA:58–59).

Besides accelerating a dossier, corrupt functionaries may also disregard a technical control. Since bribes are taken from political rent, illegally earned by an enterprise (see Chapters 1 and 7), corruption often involves fraud against the public administration. In order to save money, low-quality products are often supplied. With the complicity of the bureaucrats responsible for them, account controls and technical tests can be faked, resulting in high illegal gains for the supplier. Vice versa, a dogmatic implementation of controls can produce serious problems for those who refuse to pay bribes.

As well as the corrupt politicians and the private brokers, the corrupt bureaucrats have still another important resource to invest in illegal exchange: *secret information*. For instance, the firm Codemi paid the not insignificant sum of 150 million lira to Giovanni Sommazzi, a functionary of the technical bureau of Milan city administration for a series of "insider information"—according to the owner of Codemi, kickbacks were offered "for small consultations referring to the work he did in the city administration, . . . whenever there was the necessity to know where a dossier had ended up, or which kind of praxis I had to follow in order to bring a dossier to a successful conclusion, I asked Sommazzi, and then naturally I felt obliged for his intervention" (PROM:713). Bureaucrats therefore used information collected during their activities in public administration for a sort of insider trading in the illegal market.

1.2. The Exchanges between Corrupt Bureaucrats and Corrupt Politicians

Petty bureaucratic corruption is usually related to political "grand" corruption insofar as politicians and bureaucrats reciprocally connive on their illegal business: "The aldermen, who are politically nominated, deal with big business; and, on purpose, they leave to the top bureaucrats the smaller business *so that each of them can work without troubles in his own field*" (Federazione Italiana Pubblici Esercenti [FIPE] 1992:13–14, emphasis added]). In some public bodies, therefore, entrepreneurs were asked to pay two different bribes. For instance, a bureaucrat of the city administration in Rome asked an entrepreneur to pay a kickback for the approval of a building project, specifying that "it would be used just for the technicians, while for the politicians it was necessary to follow other ways" (CD, 22 February 1993, no. 200, p. 2).

Besides autonomous petty corruption, however, the bureaucrats often had the chance to enter into complex—and economically rewarding—negotiations with the politicians. As the case of Milan's ATM, presented at the beginning of this chapter (see also Chapter 2), indicates, the first resource politicians can use to gain the connivance of bureaucrats is a clientelistic distribution of favors. While the security of a career formally based upon seniority—and therefore automatic (Ferraresi 1980)—did not allow efficiency and loyalty to the institution to be rewarded, political affiliation became a precondition for enjoying a series of privileges. The intervention of the political parties in the public bureaucracy did not take the form of a visible "spoils system" based on ideological congruence—which should help policy implementation—but rather that of a very pragmatic party allocation of public positions: "[O]n the one side, the bureaucracy accepted a 'low profile' and a scant external visibility. There is a kind of 'yes, minister' bureaucratic Italian style. But, different from the English model, the Italian administration accepted a diminution of its own role. Instead then of administering the country, it ended up administering itself" (Cassese 1994:14). The relationship between bureaucratic and political elites is based upon a clientelistic exchange: the contact between them "in most cases refers not to policy elaboration, but instead to administrative decisions of a limited range, sponsored by politicians for clientelistic, or at least particularistic reasons" (Guarnieri 1989:227).

To understand to what extent the public administration formed a privileged field for clientelistic practices, it suffices to recall that, in the seventies and the eighties, entering the field through temporary contracts and securing a permanent position by so-called *titolarizzazione* (that is, assignment of a tenured position, without regular competition) involved 60 percent of all public employees (Cassese 1994:15). Personnel expansion, accompanied by the brazen use of any and every law allowing the requirement of impartiality in hiring to be circumvented,[3] permitted business politicians to create entourages of faithful vassals. Not by chance, the public bodies in which corruption was most widespread were also those in which clientelist hiring practices were most common, often in favor of party activists (see Chapter 3, Section 3).

An intermediary class of *bureaucrat-politicians*, whose first loyalty lay with the political parties that promoted their careers, thus developed and expanded. These bureaucrat-politicians generated a dense exchange network with leading political figures in the public administration, which extended to collaboration in the "grand corruption" market. In order to obtain easier career advancement or greater decision-making power, or to collect bribes and other private advantages, bureaucrats require the protection, or at least the abstention from supervision, of their political superiors. In return, they can offer the services of their office to particular private actors or divide the proceeds of illegal activities with their political protector.[4]

In the organization of systemic corruption, the collusion of the bureaucracy serves to increase the *immunity* of the politician. For this reason, political influence has been extremely evident on those organs—such as the Regional Control Committees (*CORECO*)—responsible for administrative control of local administrations. Their members, the majority of whom are nominated by political organs, have frequently revealed a greater propensity to collude with the politicians to whom they owe their nomination than to control them. As the prefect of Milan, Carmelo Mancuso, noted, "[T]he negative experiences of CORECO, which are heavily conditioned by politics, and the extreme fragmentation of procedures and decisional centers created a thousand occasions for corruption and diluted, and even dispersed, the attribution of responsibility" (*L'Espresso*, 14 October 1990, p. 10). The former mayor of Reggio Calabria, Agatino Licandro, condemned for corruption, provides some illustration of these mechanisms: "Somebody at CORECO prepared and manufactured the legislation for the entrepreneurs-corrupters, then passed them to this or that town councillor, so that they could be approved by the city council. . . . Corruption is the norm . . . eventually the political bosses arranged things in order to send to CORECO people who could play their game" (Licandro and Varano 1993:68). As former minister Sabino Cassese observed: "The situation has deteriorated since politically appointed, nonprofessional individuals have been placed alongside the three professional controlling bodies (the province, the public accounts department, and the State Audit Court). This has produced terrible results: the law used for illegal purposes; every decision the occasion for demanding money; efficiency considered as a threat" (Cassese 1993:16).

In the corruption market, the public bureaucrat is moreover a necessary ally for the corrupt politician because his help is often necessary for the *implementation* of the political decisions that have been paid through bribes. According to the trial records of the *mani pulite* investigations, the politicians acknowledged "the need to have 'reliable' administrative managers who can implement the political desires of those who have the majority in the Administrative Committee" (TNM:52). Although the party leaders decide upon the handing out of public contracts, they still need the administrative structures in order to implement their decisions. In particular, by reducing or abolishing the internal controls altogether, the corrupted bureaucrats allow for the formation of the political rents from which the bribes are drawn.

Besides that, thanks to the stability of his position, the bureaucrat can offer to the politicians additional favors, *reducing the risks* of the illegal exchange by taking care of the contacts with the entrepreneurs as well as of the "coordination" of the distribution of the bribes to the various public actors. To take just an example, an employee of the local administration in Bari, Paolo Bellomo, efficiently worked as broker between the entrepreneurs, other bureaucrats, and the politicians of different parties and positions. Bellomo's first task was *to arrange the tendering* in such a way that the firms already chosen would win. As the judges noted, "he decided which firms would be invited to tender, or indeed requested participation to divert attention and then ensured the decision went in favor of the firms chosen beforehand" (TRIB:504). The rule that only Bellomo was *licensed to collect bribes* served to reduce the risks of denunciation. According to the testimony of a provincial councillor of the DC, "[N]o councillor was supposed to have direct contacts with entrepreneurs. It was legitimate on the other hand to collect payments through Bellomo, as instructed by the provincial secretary, this being a service for the party" (TRIB:84). Bellomo was also responsible for the *accountancy* connected with corruption since "he always remembered with absolute precision what was owed by this or that entrepreneur and his participation in any activity connected with requests for, and the subsequent destination of, bribes was therefore absolutely essential" (UIB:17). Bellomo, moreover, *distributed the proceeds of corruption* to the parties: the politicians had come to an agreement on the division of bribery money based on the size of their groups in the provincial council. Fifty percent went to the DC, 16 percent to the PSDI, and 34 percent to the PSI: "[I]n the absence of specific instructions from a firm about who should receive it, he simply passed the packets or envelopes to the first council group leader he bumped into" (TRIB:69). Finally, Bellomo, because he was trusted by the various political parties involved, acted to *guarantee* that the set division of proceeds among them was respected, furnishing information to the party secretaries on the exact amounts of illegal funds they should receive.

2. CORRUPTION AND THE MAGISTRACY

When the system of internal control between politicians and bureaucrats does not work to prevent corruption, the judiciary is the main institution that has to intervene in order to discover administrative illegalities and repress them. In fact, political scandals not only call into question the legitimacy of the political class; they also have an impact on the legitimacy of those who have to investigate them: the magistracy. In some cases, in fact, the discovery of widespread illegality brings about criticism of the judiciary system as having been inadequate in the fight against corruption. In other cases, however, the judges who investigate the failures of the political class are acclaimed by public opinion as heroes. If recent events in Belgium are a clear example of the former reaction, the evolution of the Italian *mani pulite* investigation well illustrates the latter.

If we try to abstract from the socially constructed images developed during the evolution of the scandals, even in Italy the relationship between judges and politicians appears more complex. Alessandro Pizzorno has identified five distinct positions taken within the Italian magistracy with regard to political corruption:

1. *Class collusion*, "typical of traditional magistrates, who are led to assume certain ideological positions and certain interpretations of the facts to be judged simply because their class perception does not allow them to consider, or more exactly to see, any alternatives."

2. *Interest collusion*, where "the conduct of the magistrates (normally belonging to the higher ranks of the judiciary) is influenced above all by their belonging to the same social environment (sometimes the very same circles and associations) as businessmen (political or otherwise)."

3. *Ideological identification*, given that "although they cannot actively participate in politics, many judges have more or less precise political views."

4. *Role substitution*, where magistrates, faced with the evident collusion of the political system, consider it necessary for "another institution to fill the void and restore the threat of punishment for those indulging in corrupt practices."

5. *Institutional impartiality*, as demanded by the law (Pizzorno 1992:62–63).

The significance of these five positions has varied over time.

In the fifties, the magistracy aligned with the government. A sort of class collusion pushed the judges, who were mainly drawn from the upper class, to sympathize with conservative positions. Not only, in fact, did most of the "requests for permission to proceed" presented in parliament refer to the opposition (Cazzola 1988:130), but they were oriented more against "opinion crimes" than "appropriation crimes" (Cazzola and Morisi 1995:87; see also Cazzola and Morisi 1996). Occupying the top hierarchical positions, the senior judges, socialized during the fascist regime, had the power to punish any deviation from their standards. In fact, until the 1960s, the activity of the magistracy seems to have followed prevalently the interests of the political forces in government.

Only in the sixties, did the implementation of the Consiglio Superiore della Magistratura (CSM), the self-governing body of the magistracy, reduce the power of the high hierarchy, paving the way for the political splits of the seventies. From the very beginning, the formation of the CSM created tensions between the superior and inferior grades of the magistracy in the National Association of Magistrates (ANM), particularly over career issues. The former eventually abandoned the ANM to form their own organization, leaving the ANM to represent magistrates on the lower rungs of the career ladder (Canosa and Federico 1974:171ff., 224ff.). Disagreements over issues internal to the judiciary led to the formation of increasingly well-organized and ideologically rigid currents (Freddi 1978:121ff.).[5] Also in this period, however, the few political scandals that emerged were not a result of judicial investigation but rather of the diffusion of compromising information (sometimes originating from the secret services) on the part of politicians with something to gain from implicating others. In a scandal that erupted in 1961 over irregularities in the construction of Rome's Fiumicino Airport, for example, "not even the Minister of the Interior escaped attempts at blackmail, carried out by the secret services using their dossiers and inspired by other Christian-Democrat leaders" (Galli 1983:90–91).

The situation started to change in the seventies. In a climate that had been polarized by a wave of social and political conflict, the judges also became polarized on different ideological position. Some of them openly supported right-wing positions, contributing—according to their critics— to blocking the trials against the illegal behavior of politicians and secret service agents. The word *insabbiamento* (literally, covering with sand) came to indicate the several cases in which delicate investigations—among others, investigation into the 243 billion lira illegally paid by the public enterprise IRI to political parties, politicians, and newspapers—were taken away from their natural judges, and were heard by the Tribunal of Rome (known for a long periods as "foggy harbor"), resulting in the acquittal of all defendants (Galli 1991:255).

In the seventies and the eighties, however, the left-wing component became stronger and more and more audible. A different type of judge entered the magistracy. As mass education also opened the way into the university to the lower classes, the protest cycle of the late sixties influenced the political attitudes of a generation. In the judiciary system, the so-called *pretori d'assalto* ("attack judges," i.e, judges who took a proactive stance, using the law to reduce social injustice) often took antigovernmental stances on labor and environmental issues. At the same time, especially in the fight against terrorism and the Mafia, the magistracy exercised a proactive power, which became a surrogate for a weak political power. The courage of many judges, who often paid with their lives for their defense of Italian democracy, was contrasted with the collusion of a divided political class, and the magistracy won a sort of direct legitimacy by public opinion. In the late eighties and the nineties, there was also a weakening in the attitude of complicity of some judges with the political forces that had partly hindered the activity of the magistracy. A new generation of so-called *giudici ragazzini* (little-boy judges), lacking any sense of deference toward the political power (and conscious instead of the levels of collusion between politicians and the organized crime), began a series of investigations into administrative and political misconduct. The frequency and magnitude of the scandals through which political corruption has been brought to light has dramatically increased in the past few years, culminating in the recent political upheavals caused by the *mani pulite* investigations of corruption, meaningfully defined as a "revolution by the judges."[6] In the dynamic of the Italian political scandals, "the role of the judiciary was not limited to the unveiling and repression of corruption: public prosecutors and judges took on a much larger symbolic function, that of representative of public morality" (Giglioli 1996:388).

It should be borne in mind, however, that recent research on covert exchange has demonstrated that the long tradition of collusion between (often highly placed) judges and corrupt politicians has continued to thrive. The Italian republic's history has seen a "strong tendency toward the development of contacts and connections between the magistracy and the political world, the judiciary and the political world; between judges and political parties and between factions of the judiciary and political parties or party factions" (Guarnieri 1991:25–26). The favors of certain magistrates had long been "bought" through well-remunerated consultancies or illegal benefits, when not directly by a share of the proceeds of corruption.

Recent investigations have revealed that in the course of the 1980s and 1990s part of the judiciary protected corrupt exchange and, in certain cases, actively and systematically participated in the division of bribery money. Corrupt politicians are aware of how to use their power to recruit allies among the judiciary. First of all, they offer a wide range of "favors." One corrupt Sicilian politician, for example, "invited judges or their wives to teach courses in specialist schools, offered consultancies to important members of the profession, attaching himself to the professional and entrepreneurial circles of Catania and elevating corruption to a rule" (Interview CT1). According to Leonardo Messina, a member of the Mafia who turned state's witness, when a new magistrate arrived "an entrepreneur [close to the Mafia] would always see to finding him a house, see to the garden [usually with the mediation of a local politician] . . . and then wait. . . . Some do, some don't, some die" (MPU:72). In some cases, common participation in secret masonic lodges cemented collusive relationships between judges, politicians, and entrepreneurs (Canosa 1996:113–20).

As we mentioned, corrupt politicians and entrepreneurs could offer judges high fees for private arbitrations. Indeed, with civil tribunals overloaded and consequently slow, there was an increasing demand for extrajudicial arbitration, a service for which career judges were handsomely paid. Judges' favors could therefore be obtained legally, through their nomination as an arbitrator, with the fees being paid by a friendly businessman or public body. The case of reconstruction in Irpinia after the earthquake of 1980 demonstrates the way in which the magistracy's role in scrutinizing public decisions is subverted by involvement in the distribution of public and private resources: "Presidents of the Tribunal, the Court of Appeal and the Regional Administrative Courts (TAR), State Prosecutors and magistrates of the Audit Court were all appointed as inspectors on the very public works whose pharaonic developments they should have been regulating" (Barbagallo 1997:87). Although the CSM refused authorization for magistrates to accept such commissions, the Campania Regional Administrative Court (a judge who had himself received a grand total of twenty-two such appointments presiding) decreed the CSM's authorization irrelevant. The compensation for each inspection was around 100 million lira and "busily involved in this intricate business, the noble judges failed to notice the acts of corruption and embezzlement on which rested these wonderful works (many of which were, in truth, falling to pieces)" (ibid.:89).

Corrupt politicians may also support the careers of some judges, both inside and outside the judiciary system. The existence of organic relations of mutual support between corrupt politicians and certain judges has often been noted. The former DC deputy Raffaele Russo, for example, remarked on the influence of Antonio Gava [former budget, post office, and interior minister investigated for corruption and Camorra (the name of the criminal organization in Naples and its region) involvement] on the appointment of leading magistrates: "No long-term position in either the magistracy or other institutional sectors could be acquired without the consent or at least nonopposition of Gava. This went for the heads of executive judicial offices and police chiefs" (ibid.). According to the boss of the Rome DC, Vittorio Sbardella, the career of Claudio Vitalone, ex-magistrate, senator, and DC minister closely associated with Andreotti, resulted from a transaction between the two men: "Since Vitalone had no electoral or political support of his own he got Andreotti's support by performing miracles in order to get him politically advantageous results by judicial means. What I mean is you can do something that will gain the appreciation of a politician either by judicial favors for their friends and supporters or, on the other hand, damaging political personalities who might inconvenience your friend judicially" (PP:153). Claudio Martelli, justice minister in Andreotti's final government, stated: "Claudio Vitalone was a man very close to Andreotti who had, at the same time, considerable influence in Roman judicial circles; not just in the Roman Public Prosecutor's office but also among judging magistrates and the Court of Cassation. You could say that Vitalone was the 'long arm' of Andreotti in judicial circles" (PP:225–26). According to evidence presented in the trial of Giulio

Andreotti, seven times prime minister, the connivance of certain highly placed judges with corrupt politicians and Mafia members was obtained through the special relationships the judges maintained with leading national politicians, the latter intervening to promote special treatment for those they protected. According to Leonardo Messina, "[T]here are magistrates very close to Cosa Nostra. In my own province I have never heard of any magistrates who actually belong to Cosa Nostra, but there are magistrates who are very close to it" (MPU:56).

The active sharing of bribes was not unknown in the Italian judiciary. In the document ordering the preventive arrest of a leading Roman judge, the charge of corruption was motivated by his having had "the object of committing an unknown number of acts contrary to the duties of his office, *being regularly paid* to put his public functions at the service of the donors' interests . . . in all the cases and other activities requested" (*Avvenimenti*, 27 March 1993, p. 13, emphasis added).

Collusion of this kind has long obstructed investigations of political corruption. In exchange for the resources they received from the various actors of the corrupt exchange, unscrupulous judges could offer various services. First of all, they may of course reduce the risk of committing crimes, by providing "assistance" in the various phases of the judicial proceedings. According to the Palermo public prosecutor's office, the Mafia bosses received a directive in prison: "[S]tay calm, have faith in the DC, and in the end everything will be resolved in Cassation through the good offices of the Right Hon. Lima and the Right Hon. Andreotti, the latter having a special, personal relationship with Dr. Corrado Carnevale" (DAP:35).

Moreover, they could help develop various strategies of intimidation to stop those magistrates who pierced the circle of political illegality: pressure by superiors more sensitive to "political needs," marginalization, or transferral. Inquiries were removed as quickly as possible from the magistrates responsible for the initiative and transferred to judicial seats more inclined to suppress the matter. For instance, the judge who indicted, in 1983, the socialist "boss" Alberto Teardo was invited by other judges, in higher hierarchical positions, to abandon the case, and was marginalized when he did not (Del Gaudio 1992). Another judge, Carlo Palermo, who had mentioned in his investigation the involvement in the illegal trafficking in firearms by then prime minister Bettino Craxi, had a similar destiny:

> Those, such as Judge Carlo Palermo, who initiated investigations which brought them too close to centrally organized plots involving networks of politicians, masons and organized criminals met fierce resistance; the case would be taken from their hands to be given to a colleague or taken over by another court. Just as in the fight against 'Organized Crime,' troublesome judges could find themselves moved by disciplinary proceedings to other parts of Italy (and the policemen working with them could be transferred

even more easily at the will of their respective Ministries); they became targets for defamation or even assassination (Nelken 1996a:198).

The work of the hardened pool of anti-Mafia magistrates in Palermo and other southern courts was frequently undone by the decisions of 1st Section of Court of Cassation, led by the judge Corrado Carnevale, which regularly annulled sentences against Mafia members and their protectors.

Regardless of its immediate, material consequences on particular investigations, the uncertainty of judicial action against "the entrenched powers" also had more general effects. Particularly in areas where organized crime was most strongly entrenched, the widespread conviction that there existed collusion between leading judges and corrupt politicians further strengthened the impunity enjoyed by the latter.[7]

In "visible" politics, part of the political class—in particular, the Socialist party—reacted with several attempts at reducing the independence of the judges (Neppi Modona 1993:15). These attacks, which increased the tensions between the executive power and the judiciary power, probably strengthened the internal cohesion of the magistracy. In this period in fact, we note, at the same time, both a weakening of the politicization of the magistracy as far as deference toward the politicians is concerned, and an increasing intervention of the judges in the political process, with the development of an autonomous strategy of communication with the citizens (Righettini 1995).

Only with the development of the *mani pulite* investigations, the fight against political corruption became a primary task for many judges and, not without internal resistance, judges who had been considered "troublesome" by the governmental parties were appointed to lead the most important public procurators' offices. The investigations of these judges went as far as exposing the activities of their corrupted colleagues, who in a few cases have already received administrative and penal punishments. Especially after the election of 1994, the conflict between the magistracy and part of the political class—in particular, Forza Italia, whose leader, the media tycoon Silvio Berlusconi, is currently under investigation—escalated. The politicians involved attempted to delegitimize the magistracy, by denouncing an alleged "ideological stance" of the investigating judges. They also tried to attack the judges politically, by claiming the "superiority" of the political power over the judiciary power, and the lack of electoral legitimization of the judiciary.

3. CORRUPTION AND CONTROLS: COMPARATIVE REMARKS

As we have observed in this chapter, "grand" political corruption is intertwined with bureaucratic corruption. First of all, the presence of political corruption reduces the risks and costs for the bureaucrats who want to engage in petty corruption. The normal reciprocal control between the political class and the bureaucracy is hampered in fact when both parties connive to cover their own wrongdoings. If the politicians are corrupted, bureaucrats almost certainly will not dare to denounce the corruption of the functionaries, because of the risk of retaliation.

Moreover, the very diffusion of corruption reduces its moral costs. The corruption of the political leaders makes it easier for the bureaucrat to justify his own corrupt behavior as adhesion to an unwritten procedural code. If the recognized moral criteria of the public organization to which the individual belongs are analogous to those of the public authority, the potential *exposure* consequent on involvement in corruption will appear particularly costly. Vice versa, the moral costs of taking part in illegal activities diminish when an institution functions according to alternative norms. The internalization of norms depends on so-called *pride in position* and the prestige of public service: the more public roles are sought and socially rewarded, the less desirable will appear the violation of group norms. In the Italian case, the diffusion of corruption in the bureaucracy may have been facilitated by the traditionally low status of the public bureaucracy.[8] In fact, compared with the German, British, or French public administrations, which have traditionally shown a strong *esprit de corp*, the Italian bureaucracy is characterized by a generalized lack of the sense of the state, related to the importance of political protection (or, in the best of cases, seniority) in career development. From a comparative perspective, the Italian bureaucrats emerged as "legalist, illiberal, elitist, hostile to the uses and practices of pluralistic politics, fundamentally nondemocratic" (Putnam 1973; see also Aberbach, Putnam, and Rockman 1981:2). Similarly, in the Russian transition to democracy, a major risk has been singled out: the extreme weakness of the public bureaucracy, which is interested more in private enrichment than in providing services to citizens, incompetent and antidemocratic, capable of protecting friends but unable to take responsibility for the pubic good (Mendras 1997:126–28).

In Italy, low status for the public bureaucracy came together with a growing dependency on the political class for various clientelistic favors. The Italian bureaucracy is, in fact, characterized by a process of *political fragmentation*: "The lack of alternation and the lengthy permanence in power of the same political personnel has led to forms of vertical alliances between politicians and bureaucrats that transcend the traditional separation between political personnel on the one hand and civil servants on the other. Here too, the cement has been provided by corruption, or at least by the use of public resources for private or partial ends" (Pizzorno 1992:59). The vertical alliances developed in the direction of a formation of hybrid figures: "In the local structures, there was the development and consolidation of an intermediary class, a mix of political-bureaucrats, of bureaucrats loyal to a politician, of unionists-politicians-public administrators, etc. that do politics, govern, and administer: that is, a class that exercises three powers that should be kept separate. . . . [I]t is not clear any more where politics ends, and where administration starts " (Cassese 1992). These pathological links between politicians and bureaucrats were used in the corruption market, where the connivance of the bureaucrats was bought via favors or money. In corrupt exchanges, the bureaucrat may offer to the politicians not only his collaboration in the implementations of the corrupt decisions and his complicity, but also some "extra service" that reduces the "identification costs." In particular, because of his longer permanence in an administration, the bureaucrat accumulates information on possible partners for illegal business, as well as loyalty links with the corrupt entrepreneurs.

Research in other national cases indicated that, once again, the dynamics that link bureaucratic corruption to political corruption in Italy are not unique. In the Japanese case, it was observed that corruption is particularly widespread where senior policy specialists of the governmental party are particularly powerful exactly because of their increasing influence on "key personnel decisions at senior level (promotions, early retirement, etc.)" (Rothacher 1996:3). In Japan, in fact, since the beginning of the century, corruption and the permeation of the political leadership and the bureaucratic elite have gone together (Bouissou 1997:135). Traditionally, in the Spanish case, "despite the reforms of the nineteenth century, the political parties continued to look upon the bureaucracy as an instrument whose control had to be ensured through the ideological fidelity of their personnel" (Heywood 1997:77). A sort of spoils system developed in the contemporaneous presence of two bureaucracies: one in power and one (waiting for its turn) in the opposition. In Spain as well as in Russia, bureaucratic corruption has been explained by a long tradition of premodern arrangements, when public functionaries were allowed to ask citizens for private compensation for their services (Heywood 1997; Mendras 1997). As for France, Cartier-Bresson noted that "grand corruption is possible because of the politicization of public administration (vassalage as the key variable for career advancement) and a 'functionarization' of politics (with politicians coming from the public function)" (1996:121).

Also collusion between corrupt politicians and judges in the Italian case was the effect of a certain degree of informal political influence on the magistracy. First of all, the very composition of the self-governing body, the CSM, with a minority—albeit large—presence of "political" members, elected by the parliament, led to electoral lists of judges that reflected the ideological positions of the parties:[9] Several matters, such as the nomination of the general prosecutors in the most important cities, the distribution of scarce resources, and the punishment of politically "rebellious" judges, became highly political issues on which the judges and lay representatives split along a left-right cleavage. The same kind of alliances were then maintained even for decisions involving the careers of individual judges, who therefore had an incentive to align with one party or the other. An additional factor that made the judges more sensitive to external pressure was the availability of (rich) economic compensation for "extra-judicial" arbitrations, which were used to settle conflicts among entrepreneurs or between entrepreneurs and the public administration, a mechanism that often replaced the inefficient system of the civil courts.

This informal influence was, however, counterbalanced by a peculiarly high level of (at least formal) independence of the judiciary from the political power (Guarnieri 1992), due first of all to the implementation of constitutional principles to prevent the magistracy from again becoming, as it had during the fascist regime, a "long arm of the government." In particular, since 1959, the CSM has taken over several tasks that once had been assigned to the bureaucratic elite, in particular career and disciplinary decisions. A system of promotion based mainly on years of service reduced the possibility of blackmailing the most "troublesome" judges. On many occasions, the CSM worked as a corporatist actor to defend and increase the autonomy, status, and wages of the judges. Since both judges and prosecutors are part of the same profession, and may freely interchange roles, the latter enjoy the same degree of autonomy from the government as the former. Another principle that limited political interference was the formal rule of compulsory prosecution for all reported offenses. Since the law requires that Italian judges prosecute any crime, "the doctrine of compulsory prosecution prevented the government from raising consideration of public interest even when the investigations came to involve leading government figures and the Minister of Justice himself" (Nelken 1996a:196). Differently than in common-law countries, recruitment to the magistracy—based on competitive examinations open to all those who have a university degree in law—also increases the autonomy of the judges. This institutional level of independence was certainly a very relevant resource for those judges who carried out the investigations against the corrupt politicians.

If in Italy the political class has attempted to reduce this autonomy, asking for a "normalization" of the Italian situation with reference to other democracies, sociological research in other countries indicates that political control over the judiciary hampered judicial inquiries in the field of corruption. In France, for example, "a number of articles of the penal code allow the executive to deprive judges conducting sensitive investigations of their power to investigate" (Ruggiero 1996b:119). A law of 1974, which remained in force until 1993, stated that prosecutors could not investigate mayors, who were entitled to a special judge nominated by the Court of Cassation from among the magistrates of the High Court of Justice, and that any investigation of public administrators had to be transferred to the higher levels of the judicial hierarchy (ibid.:119ff.). As the case of Jean-Pierre Thierry, forced to leave the magistracy after investigating a scandal linked to illegal funding of the French Socialist party, indicates, the dependence of junior magistrates on those above them in terms of promotion and salary can easily become an effective means of blackmail. It continues to be the case in France that obstacles to the investigation of corruption come from the power exercised over prosecutors by the Ministry of Justice, to which they must answer, particularly where more delicate investigations are concerned (ibid.:122). Only following a wave of political scandals at the beginning of the 1990s did the French magistracy succeed in gaining greater autonomy, *privilège de juridiction* being abolished and a series of matters relating to careers and salaries transferred to the French equivalent of the CSM. In Japan's case, the discretionary element in penal actions—"a prosecutor may abandon any legal proceeding on the grounds of the 'context surrounding the offender' or 'circumstances subsequent to the offence'" (Bouissou 1997:140–41)—has led some to talk of a "domesticated "justice system. Judicial action against political corruption has been considered particularly weak because judges are reconfirmed in office every ten years and their careers are in the hands of the Supreme Court, nominated by the executive and accused of faithfully serving the interests of the governing party, "relegating the independently minded to minor posts in distant provinces" (ibid.:141). In Belgium a series of failures in sensitive investigations has been blamed on the "party politicization" of the magistracy, nominated (usually after extensive negotiations) by the political parties (van Outrive 1996:376). The surfacing of corruption in Belgium has led to projects for reform based on the Italian model, introducing an autonomous council for the magistracy and recruitment through state examination (ibid.:380ff.). As far as the Anglo-Saxon model is concerned, commentary on the Italian *mani pulite* investigations has revealed a "puzzlement in seeing judges turning on their own government [which] may only reflect the English ethno-centric assumption that the judiciary consists of a small groups of middle-aged and middle-minded members of the establishment" (Nelken 1996b:99).

The development of political and bureaucratic corruption appear to be influenced by the nature of the restraints and controls on political and administrative activity. Systems of *civil law*, such as the Italian one, are characterized by a strong suspicion of discretionary power, which is harshly limited by a series of intersecting *procedural controls*, that is to say, by a rigid and extensive predisposition of norms for putting into practice and verifying each individual action. These controls are mainly formal ones, addressing the respect for procedural rules, while there is a lack of substantial controls on the costs and quality of the product: "Preventive controls . . . are suffocating, formalistic, and to a good extent insufficient to insure a 'good administration'" (D'Auria 1993:233; see also Guccione 1993:28).[10] Legislative proliferation (and confusion) is a further factor reducing the possibility of effective controls. As one businessman put it: "[L]ots of laws and minilaws simply increase the power of functionaries to blackmail entrepreneurs. Even if the latter are convinced that they are respecting the law they cannot be sure and therefore prefer to pay [bribes]" (Benassi and Sganga 1994:42). Many such norms are clearly inefficient because, through an unclear definition of individual cases, they encourage contravention or because the rules are too many and overly imprecise.[11] The unsatisfactory performance of the public administration associated with these delays and deficiencies offsets or negates the collective interest supposedly served by such norms: "The procedure becomes longer and more complicated. . . . Waiting time becomes more important than working time" (Cassese 1983:284). In any case, "institutions and their functionaries are not held responsible for remaining inactive, for taking no decision at all. . . . It soon becomes clear that it is more dangerous to decide (a decision involving the possibility of error and punishment) than not to decide" (Freddi 1992:226).

As we saw, these formal controls produced a large veto power for the bureaucracy, which could collect bribes by simply threatening to slow the overcomplicated procedures. Moreover, the existence of a complex system of prescriptions for and constraints on the behavior of public agents, and the resulting uncertainty on the norms to be applied, often end up by aggravating inefficiencies and delays, favoring the factual reintroduction of discretionary power.[12] The existing regulations foresee a multiplicity of controls ex ante, with a merely formal character, that enormously increase the time of the procedures, justifying a recourse to discretionary, "emergency" mechanisms, which in their turn hamper substantial controls and facilitate corruption. Pizzorno, in fact, has described the Italian situation in terms of a *vicious circle of guarantees*:

> Worry about distortions and injustice in access to the services of the public administration (resulting from a distrust of the individual functionary left to his own devices) leads to particularly strict rules concerning discretionary powers. The slowness and inefficiency that result cause problems for those using these services. Functionaries will inevitably be left to take decisions on their own discretion in order to obviate these delays. Because it is not explicitly recognized, the discretionality reintroduced in this way is more vulnerable to corruption. (Pizzorno 1992:55)

"Exceptional" procedures are thus normatively recognized or legitimated by dissatisfaction with public administrative action, impeding further the activity of control and increasing the gains to be made from corruption. In this way, inefficiency increases administrative discretionality in each stage, leading to "bought" decisions, whether it be the artificial creation of demand, the distortion of decision-making, or the slackening of controls. Furthermore, the inadequacy of the system of controls allows public agents to be indifferent about their work while facing no threat of censure. "The principle of inefficiency underlies administrative controls in Italy. Internal controls are virtually nonexistent. . . . External controls are conducted by a series of unconnected bodies not all of which are neutral or politically and administratively independent" (D'Auria 1993:233). Lengthy delays weighing on citizens using public services end up by legitimating ex post a greater discretionary power of public agents. In this area of decision-making, opportunities for illegalities are greater because *extraordinary* discretionary power, not foreseen by the regulations, is more difficult to control. Even where the bureaucracy has a long tradition of professionalism and esprit de corps,[13] as in France, the development of political corruption has been related with a basic mistrust toward the citizens that multiplied procedural ex-post controls, which usually produce delays in the administrative process (Mény 1997:17). The bureaucracy acquires therefore a veto power that can be exchanged on the bribe market.

NOTES

1. According to the economic theory of crime, besides the probability of being discovered, the decision to undertake a given illegal activity depends on the severity of punishment expected and other variables, such as income to be derived, expectations of gain in other illegal activities, and the propensity to unlawful action (Becker 1968:169).

2. The presence of a collective principal poses, in fact, not only the problem of the definition of that principal's will, but also problems related to the possibility of exiting and free-rider behaviors. As Banfield noticed, unlike a shareholder, a citizen cannot easily quit a corrupt country. Moreover, he/she does not have any incentive to invest in the fight against corruption, since a corruption-free market is a public good that, as such, also benefits the free-riders (Banfield 1975:598).

3. For a systematic analysis of the mechanisms that allow for patronage appointments, see Golden (1995).

4. In fact, the Italian bureaucracy has traditionally demonstrated a conspicuous permeability to interest and pressure groups where these have close links with the governing political parties (LaPalombara and Poggi 1975).

5. Third Power concentrated on salary and jurisdictional issues. On the right, Independent Magistracy (formed by judges of the Court of Cassation who had rejoined the ANM) reiterated an image of the judicial system as "nonpolitical." On the left, Democratic Magistracy, founded in 1964, proposed democratic reform of the judicial function.

6. Official statistics, which nonetheless only provide a partial picture of the phenomenon, show a gradual increase in the number of offenses against the public administration (such as corruption, extortion, embezzlement, and abuse of office): 466 in 1970, 557 in 1980, 1,111 in 1985, and 1,198 in 1990 (CENSIS 1992:102). The investigations on political corruption enormously increased in number and relevance in 1992. See also Chapter 1.

7. One person interviewed in the course of research on political corruption in Catania, for example, explained the absence of denunciations or moralizing campaigns on "atavistic distrust of the magistracy, strengthened by the fact that no one was punished" (della Porta 1992:248). It is perhaps not surprising that the leading magistrates of the city, including the attorney general of the Republic, were removed under the charge of collusion with corrupt politicians.

8. A low social status is often sanctioned by low wages. Van Rijckeghem and Weder (1997) show how the empirical evidence points to a negative relationship between corruption and wages across developing countries.

9. The CSM is a body composed two-thirds of representatives elected by the judges and one-third of politically appointed representatives.

10. At the same time, successive administrative controls have all but fallen into disuse because "they were contrary to the interests of the politicians who should have been leading the administration but who instead were using it to their own advantage" (Cassese 1992).

11. "A great deal has been written concerning the Byzantine nature, tortuous progress, and long delays associated with administrative procedures. Another aspect has perhaps not been sufficiently analyzed: that of a public administration whose writ remains a 'dead letter' because it is impossible to verify respect by private subjects or even, on many occasions, compliance on the part of the administration itself" (Cassese 1989:72).

12. As the former Italian Premier Giuliano Amato observed, "The procedures that govern public behaviors remained based on the alternative between a formalist warranty and a derogatory discretionality, two faces of the same coin" (Amato 1980:95).

13. Bureaucratic corruption seems however to be relatively high in France, although not as high as in the Italian case. According to the German magazine *Der Spiegel* (9 August 1993, p. 73), 50 percent of the French managers and 90 percent of the Italian ones think that functionaries are corrupted (against a much lower 17 percent in Great Britain and 28 percent in Germany).

6

Brokers and Occult Power

The activities of the broker Adriano Zampini were exposed in 1983 when Diego No-
velli, mayor of Turin, advised an American firm's commercial director to make an offi-
cial complaint regarding the pressure and intimidation he had been subjected to by
Zampini. Zampini's contacts in the city administration were two brothers, Giovanni
and Enzo Biffi Gentile, both members of the Socialist party and at the time, respec-
tively, provincial administrative secretary and deputy mayor. Zampini initiated con-
tacts between entrepreneurs and political administrators, retaining a "mediation fee"
for himself and then handed on the rest of what he received in bribes. Giusi La Ganga,
Socialist party spokesman on local government, various Christian Democrat politi-
cians, and a number of functionaries were also implicated in the affair.

Adriano Zampini was born into a peasant family and a life that consisted of "lit-
tle money and a lot of hard work," in Valpolicella, northern Italy on March 14, 1949.
His ambition was to become a chemist but his family's financial circumstances ruled
out attending university and he was obliged to take a manual job in a safe-making
factory (Zampini 1985:18). After winning the factory owner's trust he was put in
charge of maintaining customer contacts and finally, in 1972, moved to Turin in
search of his fortune. There he met a real broker for the first time, the provincial sec-
retary of the neofascist MSI (Movimento Sociale Italiano), who introduced him to
the art of business mediation (ibid.:23). Still on the lookout for a "real" job, Zampini
began helping his protector (the owner of a furniture business) bribe public admin-
istrators to supply information on contracts and protection. "When I came to Turin,
to work as a salesman for a Genoa-based company," he declared, "I learned the mean-
ing of the word bribe immediately. The owner boasted that he had paid lots of
them. . . . After he had me act directly. The first time I accompanied him when he
went to pay the bursar of a Turin girls' school. Afterwards I followed the tender for
furnishing some regional offices. Finally I decided to set up on my own, to earn more
and make the best of what I had learned. I never had any ethical problems; nothing
like that ever crossed my mind. Watching my first boss in action I realized that pay-
ing bribes was the simplest thing in the world; just the same as giving money to a
mediator, to a business advisor" (L'Espresso, 18 November 1984, pp. 39–40).

Zampini thus developed his contacts among politicians of the city's ruling party
(the DC) and among entrepreneurs. Later he would use these contacts to accumu-
late classified information, which could be employed to enhance his reputation as a
successful broker. Having been schooled in the techniques—the whos and hows—of
corruption, Zampini parted company with his employer to found his own enterprise,
which he pompously named Iuppiter. *When the local elections of 1975 brought the*
Left to power in Turin, Zampini had to rebuild his contact network within the pub-

lic administration. Very quickly, however, he succeeded in becoming the right-hand man of Socialist deputy mayor Enzo Biffi Gentile. By his own admission he was a means of facilitating transactions between different bodies, institutions, and individuals: "Let's just say that I was a conduit for politicians of different parties and currents. A group had been formed that cut across the political spectrum from the Communist party to the Italian Social Movement [MSI]. A strategy was put together with Enzo Biffi Gentile and big profits were envisaged. How they would be divided was agreed in general terms with Enzo. He was more interested in the political design; he wanted to draw everybody in, like a spider drawing in flies" (L'Espresso, *18 November 1984, p. 43).*

Management of the channels of communication between the private and public sectors was one of the resources Zampini employed in order to extract his mediation fee. By devolving the job of contacting firms to an intermediary he could trust, the deputy mayor reduced the personal risks he was taking. As a result, however, the ordinary contacts and official relationships between entrepreneurs and politicians were removed from the public arena, becoming an informal practice ungoverned by official responsibility or duty. Zampini thus became a hidden go-between without whom approaching the decision-makers was impossible, a go-between who could open up or shut down those channels of communication at will. One entrepreneur later recalled how Zampini gradually imposed his exclusive control over the channels of communication between private and public actors: "I realized that Zampini was on good terms with the deputy mayor. In fact, it became increasingly difficult for me to contact the deputy mayor personally. Instead, Zampini took the initiative in making contacts, presenting himself as the person who acted as intermediary for the public administration. The only person who was granted an audience with the deputy mayor was Adriano Zampini. Adapting themselves to the situation firms began negotiating with him" (QGT:372).

Zampini cultivated relationships with the key bureaucrats in public bodies as well as contacts with politicians. As the magistrates noted, "Zampini had been hanging around the regional administration offices since 1973 and created an entire network of functionaries with whom he swapped favors, picking up gossip and information among other things" (QGT:381). *In consequence the information he supplied interested entrepreneurs on public works schedules was frequently more up to date than that in the possession of the assessor responsible himself. "Good relations" with bureaucrats were also a resource that could be employed in transactions with politicians. Thanks to his contacts Zampini could furnish politicians with information, not simply about entrepreneurs who were willing to take part in covert exchange but also about bureaucrats who could be trusted: "I therefore became indispensable to a lot of politicians as well. . . . A politician who takes up an administrative position of a certain importance, an assessorship, for example, needs to surround himself with people he can trust, with whom he can work and from whom, naturally, he expects to get some personal advantage in exchange. So, as soon as a new assessor is appointed you have to go and offer your services. If you don't someone else will and then there won't be any room left for you"* (L'Espresso, *18 November 1984, p. 42). Finally, Zampini also supplied politicians with information on individuals who failed to respect illegal agreements. In one case, for example, the deputy mayor "had* been the object of rumors in relation to a putative bribe for realizing a computer system." Zampini, who demonstrated himself well informed concerning these indiscretions, conducted a small personal "investigation" among the representatives of supplying firms in order to find out who had been responsible (QGT:359).

Zampini's networking was also furthered through his organization of "foreign junkets," an innovation for which he claims authorship: "These trips were the real cement of the superparty and the real idea allowing me to form close relationships with a lot of different people. It was my own idea and it proved a very profitable one. Travel abroad was offered by companies who wanted to supply particular kinds of machinery. I had recognized a weakness of politicians. Although they might have a lot of money of their own they almost always refrain from showing it. The trips I organized combined business and pleasure." At a certain moment mere awareness of the existence of illegalities became collusion: "The money flowed briskly. Once on the plane, Concorde I think, I spent 3 million [lira] for presents for everybody. I remember I asked Giuseppe Gatti [leader of the DC group on the city council] to draw up the bill and he was astonished by the amount. But he didn't say anything and as far as I was concerned, from then on, he was 'done,' compromised, prepared to come in on the game" (L'Espresso, 18 November 1984, p. 45). The first objective of these "trips," then, was to strengthen relationships, making it more difficult to end or interrupt them: "To succeed in moving in a short time from the kind of friendship that exists between people who do business together to the far more solid friendship that comes from going swimming together, getting drunk together, telling each other jokes, and other things of that kind. All this was deliberate, studied, on my part" (ibid.:47).

Organizing junkets also served Zampini in creating a reputation for reliability, and reinforcing it by ostentatious display of his privileged relationships with public decision-makers. By organizing junkets he "earned the good will of the public administrators, who appreciated his organizational skills and were at the same time indebted to him." Above all, however, "to firms Zampini appeared as a person in close contact with the public administration, with the people who decided on contracts worth billions [of lira]" (QGT:369). By showing himself a friend (a "crony") of politicians Zampini automatically became a desirable contact for anyone wishing to establish relations with them. This required clear signals that he really possessed the necessary power and from the trial records it does appear that the deputy mayor of Turin on more than one occasion indicated that the job of managing contacts with the firms supplying the city council had been delegated to Zampini.

Zampini's success depended on his pragmatic conception of alliances and view of the public administration as a private patrimony. This value system derived, he stated, from a long process of socialization in "the practice of corruption." Day-to-day experience reinforced a value system that could be seen to work: "Having chosen a path you follow it through to the end, right or wrong. On mine I found people willing to be corrupted. Indeed it quickly taught me that if you did not learn how to corrupt others you would never be anybody, you would never be able to do business. One day when I have to explain to my son why his father went to jail that's exactly what I'll tell him, and I'll also explain that 90 percent of the people he will find in front of him during any negotiation can be bribed" (L'Espresso, 18 November 1984, p. 38).

The story of Adriano Zampini, who was arrested on 2 March 1983 and later charged (along with a numerous group of Turin politicians and entrepreneurs) with corruption is a perfect illustration of the activities of the broker, a crucial figure in the world of corrupt exchange and the subject of the present chapter. Together with political parties, other actors in fact mediate between politicians and entrepreneurs who take part in corrupt exchanges. Their task is to facilitate the contacts, by providing secret information and to help implement the illegal contracts. In the course of our study the figure of the broker (or *faccendiere*, in the Italian familiar term) emerged, with the function of easing interactions and reducing the risks in the negotiations between the two or more parties interested in the corrupt deal, as well as acting as go-between for the arrangement and receipt of payoffs. Second, associations such as the freemasonry offered resources of loyalty to the corrupt exchanges, strengthening the ties among the different actors of illegal transactions.

1.   BROKERS IN THE ILLEGAL MARKETS

The presence of mediators is common to several human activities. From the "lonely hearts" agencies to the real estate agencies, the role of the mediators is to facilitate exchanges by reducing the costs of missing information and reciprocal mistrust. In the illegal market the function of the brokers is all the more important, since they take upon themselves part of the high risks of the exchanges: in fact, "they have the task to substitute for the lack of trust between the exchange holders, thus making possible transactions that are in the interest of the contractors, but impossible to realize without the intervention of a third party" (Arlacchi 1988:427). In this context, the middleman "lets it be known that he is willing to dirty his hands: not only is he experienced (knows the subtle hints, knows the techniques of passing money), but making use of him also allows the briber to distance himself from the transaction. . . . His services are necessary, he asserts, because he has special knowledge of the procedures, access to officials, time to spend, and dirty hands" (Oldenburg 1987:527).

A most important resource for the mediators is *contacts*, what Zampini defined as "the confidence of many people." Building up a network of friendship ties is essential for brokers. The organization of pleasure time—such as so-called business trips—is a technique scientifically developed by the brokers in order to build personal relationships, which can then be exploited for illegal exchanges: "You do not always talk business; to the contrary, almost never, but you build up those kinds of links that are typical for those who go together for a sauna, nude as worms. Formality is broken. And, once back home, that familiarity remains" (Zampini 1993:121).

In fact, the function of the intermediaries appears to be essential when the relationships between private entrepreneurs and the public administration are sporadic or fragmentary, but also when they are complicated because of the involvement of large networks of different actors. When illegal exchanges are not frequent, to pay for the services of specialized mediators seems more rational then investing in order to build links directly with politicians or administrators. In two corruption cases in Florence, for example, where the contacts between the public administrators and the owners of some buildings bought by the city council were not systematic, middlemen emerged with the political contacts necessary for corruption and, on many occasions, for covering up the payment of bribes.[1] The mediator, therefore, create the contacts between the actors potentially interested in entering business relationships with each other. As a politician involved in a corruption case in Florence explained:

> *Somebody needs a favor and does not have a direct contact. Well, there are individuals who place themselves on the market with their stock of personal connections. Some do it professionally.* In general they are squalid individuals. The broker, or *faccendiere*, is a braggart operating above all on a personal level, with the councillors. They are not usually in contact with the party directly, but live in the political undergrowth, offering themselves as go-betweens. Generally they call themselves consultants, but they have no precise position. (Interview F18, emphasis added)

As the story of Zampini illustrated, the broker meets his task by collecting and transmitting *privileged information*. The information is necessary to win the *confidence* of those who want to participate in the illegal exchange: to spread trust, and push the people to collaborate with each other. Showing that they have privileged information about public procedures or the economic situation of the enterprises, the mediators strengthen their reputation of reliability. In passing over information, however, the brokers also *reduce transaction costs*—in particular, the risks of being denounced. Confidentiality is in fact a central problem for corrupters and the corrupted. If compromising information about their wrongdoing circulates, the risk of being denounced or blackmailed increases. Since "an increase in the number of employees involved in a decisional process will increase the number of those who may wish to share the bribes, or to denounce them" (Gardiner and Lyman 1978:148), the middleman role is to avoid any unnecessary (and potentially dangerous) spread of confidential information. As the then-vice-president of the Campania region explained to the judges: "Keep in mind that . . . in these situations you have to be very tactful; since it was clear that it was something not really regular, nobody said more than it was strictly necessary to say" (CD, 24 June 1993, no. 443, p. 6). His privileged relationships with politicians and bureaucrats provided Zampini with exclusive control of a very important resource: confidential information. As he put it himself: "I had reached the point where I had people inside the public administration who could provide me with a lot of details about public contracts, enterprises willing to pay bribes, and so on" (*L'Espresso*, 18 November 1984, p. 42). In one case, an entrepreneur told investigating magistrates that Zampini had appeared "profoundly knowledgeable on every aspect of the tender, even showing them the conditions for the contract and naming the other firms interested"; another he "showed a list of the works he might be interested in" (QGT:337, 381). Zampini himself has stated that it was "thanks to confidences from a lot of people that I was able to create a contact network. I told one person what another had told me, I knew everything there was to know about everybody, I even went to the length of inventing information in order to get the trust of people I needed. But I did all this with a great deal of circumspection, judging the right information to give at the right moment. A corrupter who talks too much has a short career" (*L'Espresso*, 18 November 1984, p. 42).

In order to build the necessary bonds of trust between participants to a corrupt exchange, the brokers may even *assume the risks* of illegal transactions. An illustration may be found in the case of the Lockheed scandal, when bribes were paid to the Italian minister Mario Tanassi in exchange for a contract to the U.S. enterprise Lockheed. According to the judicial investigations: "There was for Ovidio [Lefevbre, the broker] a problem that was difficult to solve because, while the firms wanted to pay [the bribe] only after the emission of the letter [with the commitment for the payment], the minister conditioned the emission of the letter to the payment. Ovidio, then, found the solution, predisposing the anticipation of the payment in Italian liras, without touching the dollars of the Lockheed" (CCR:2256). Like any financial broker, Lefevbre anticipated the money; confident of being reimbursed, he took upon himself the risks of a fraud.

Moreover, mediators reduce the exposure of the leading politicians in the illegal business. As the Venice magistrates observed, "In the Veneto Region the figures of two men who assumed relevant institutional positions are dominant: Senator Carlo Bernini and *Onorevole* Gianni De Michelis. They make use of two trusted and loyal collaborators: Franco Alberto Ferlin and Giorgio Casadei, who minutely maintain their contacts with the local political forces, administrators of their own and of other parties, and the entrepreneurs" (APV:15). Both "loyal collaborators" derive their power from their reputation as "operative alter ego" of the two parliamentarians, a reputation that is enforced by the fact that "they had their offices inside the ministries led by *Onorevole* Gianni De Michelis and Sen. Carlo Bernini, notwithstanding the fact that they do not possess any official position there" (ibid.:19). In other cases, lawyers as well as public managers assumed the risks of materially collecting the bribes destined for politicians.

Brokers also help *solving problems of coordination* that may arise between the central authorities allocating resources and those at the local level who must manage them. This is all the more important in the Italian case, where the lack of financial autonomy has made it essential for local administrators to create more or less "official" and visible transaction networks, generally characterized by relations of kinship or political protection, with the central authorities (Amato, Cassese, Coen, and Galli della Loggia 1983:7).[2] In such a situation, specialized intermediaries, usually consultants or planners with political connections to a party, assume the crucial function of developing informal contacts between the bodies that allocate funds and those responsible for the framing of public demand. De facto, they are delegated the task of identifying the projects to be realized, with the aim of reconciling the interests of the politicians and firms involved in corrupt exchange. In practice this means presenting local authorities with the possibility of funding tied to "take it or leave it" projects for public tendering, projects that they will then direct and oversee, while holding out the prospect of gains to the different political actors involved in the game. As regards the construction of the stadiums for *Italia '90*, for example, the figure of the "consultant" was particularly important: "developing and promoting policy choices of his own or acting as guarantor and promoter vis-à-vis the other political actors. It was he who identified or delineated the ways and means to mediate politically between the various participants, safeguarding the integrity and success of the 'good cause,' the project with his signature at the bottom" (Morisi 1991:41). The management of public tendering would thus appear to be characterized by a dense web of subterranean exchanges. This is confirmed by the ex-mayor of Baucina, a small commune near Palermo: "I was supposed to nominate as director of works the person favored by the head of the regional assessorate, which would be providing the funds. The above would then give part of the money he earned to the councillors and functionaries of the assessorate" (*L'Espresso*, 23 December 90, p. 31). This intermediary was "all but indispensable to obtain funding for public works in Baucina and the surrounding area. He took care of distributing contracts fairly among the other participating firms. . . . He would contact them and the bids would be agreed on in such a way that the designated firm got the contract" (PRP:20). These brokers also play a decisive role in gathering information on projects that will be most rewarding in terms of bribery and should therefore be given priority. Concerning the three-year plan for the improvement of the environment, the broker De Toma testified:

I remember that a lot of local bodies (communes, consortia etc.) presented projects, asking for funding. . . . However the funds available could not meet all the requests. At this point, Cavalli and I intervened for the DC and the PSI, with the aim of identifying and selecting those projects that would be undertaken by reliable firms; reliable in all senses, both from a technical point of view and that of contribution for the political parties. (CD, 5 March 93, no. 210, p. 12)

As well as "self-employed" brokers, intermediaries working for state-owned (or partially state-owned) companies also appeared. "In practice," the ex-Mayor of Reggio Calabria, Agatino Licandro, claimed, "there are brokers linked to 'companies' who come to the commune and explain: 'We have the right connections to get you this funding. Without our help you won't see a penny. The ministry responsible for it is one of ours.' . . . If the commune, the province, or the mountain community didn't agree, no problem. The 'company' and the funding moved to greener fields" (Licandro and Varano 1993:21).

Coordination problems in bribe collection may also arise within public enterprises between top managers, who are politically appointed, and the political elite. According to Silvano Larini, personal trustee of Bettino Craxi, the broker Pierfrancesco Pacini Battaglia had a pivotal role both in foreign and internal bribe compensations in the import-export transaction of ENI (Ente Nazionale Idrocarburi). Pacini Battaglia was the manager of a Swiss merchant bank, Karfinko, which was used by top managers in ENI's international affairs: "Pacini Battaglia was the middleman for such international dealings, from which he tried to get back some money that, after he retained his brokerage fee, went to the party system" (SLM:3). Pacini Battaglia was a personal friend of ENI's leading administrators, whose careers he intentionally protected through his corrupting activities:

He was the political parties' trustee in ENI's illicit dealings. Pacini Battaglia had a strong discretional power, since there was no control on the amount of money he could get from ENI's foreign contracts. He regularly paid government parties that could change the ENI top management, since his middle-man's role was informally and covertly delegated by them. Sometimes Pacini paid with his money bribes to parties, because he had a strong interest in maintaining the key roles within ENI administrators who recognized him as a friend. (ibid.:4–5)

Trust, "friendship," and professional skills in financial brokerage are the qualities that made Pacini Battaglia's activity particularly appreciated by political parties: "The flow of money from ENI to political parties became more substantial and regular. . . . Pacini being a banker, he often anticipated sums needed by parties, and then recovered his credit through funds coming from firms owned by ENI. He could arrange these dealings because he was linked by personal trust relationships with the management of ENI companies. Pacini was a devoted friend of several administrators of ENI firms, who could guarantee him back the money he advanced" (ibid.:6).

While the brokers, in general, carry no party card, their careers are nonetheless of a "party" type, dependent on privileged contacts with particular politicians. A member of the Catania professions recalled, for example:

> I worked for a company offering services to the public administration. In most cases when I contacted administrators they asked me, "What's in it for me?" At first I didn't understand and explained the nature of the service again, but their reply remained the same. In the end it was decided to put an advertisement in the newspaper: "Organization working in connection with public institutions seeks administrators and individuals with contacts in public bodies to present their product." Town councillors and canvassers responded to the advertisement, people who already did the same kind of thing for other firms. The job of the broker was to make contact with public administrators and negotiate the business. The firm had a contract with the broker, or with someone acting as a front for him, containing an article in which it was pledged that legal principles would be strictly followed. Officially, the broker received a percentage from the company according to sales, and the payoff came out of the percentage without the firm knowing anything about it. Speaking to one of these people, I was told that it is frequently the political boss who decides who can and who cannot be a broker. (Interview CT7)

When the contacts with an actor are particularly frequent, he becomes a sort of affectionate client of the mediation services: this may be true for a politician, but also for an enterprise, a party, or a public agency. While some mediators resemble autonomous entrepreneurs, others are, in a more or less subordinate fashion, members of an organization. We can therefore distinguish between different types of mediators, according to their privileged relationships with some participants in the corrupt exchanges:[3]

1. Some mediators have a *single political "referent,"* in the name of and for whom they take care of the contacts with the private actors. These kinds of figures have been particularly relevant in the recent scandals, but their presence is, at least in Italy, a tradition more than a century old: "Many members of parliament have a personal secretary, normally with a law degree, who is charged to act in all the lucrative affairs that are proposed to them, but that they 'honestly' refuse, indicating, however, the

person who could, maybe, take care of them. In short, the member of parliament does not reject reality, but keeps up appearances, accrediting an accomplice with whom he shares the honorarium" (Colajanni 1888, 141). These mediators—usually referred to as *portaborse* [flunkey, or gofer]— have a strong fiduciary tie with their bosses, to whom they have to be grateful for all their good fortunes. The link of gratitude—and sometimes of friendship—makes them particularly reliable as a sort of filter for any kind of questions. In fact, they have all possible incentives to be loyal to the interest of the politician, whose protection they need, especially when they lack any other professional skill. Let us take as an example the relationship between the former minister Pietro Longo and the mediator Felice Fulchignoni. According to the judges: "Any business done by him [the mediator] was conducted together with Longo. The operations they have done regarded, almost exclusively, public contracts and negotiations with public agencies" (PRIM:99–100). Together, they founded and acquired firms active in brokering between foreign enterprises and Italian public agencies (ibid.). In fact, according to the trial records, Pietro Longo, who had been the secretary of the Social Democratic party (PSDI), signaled which enterprises he protected to various public administrations; while Fulchignoni collected the bribes. Sometimes, the former had to formally intervene in order to "accredit" the latter. According to an entrepreneur:

> In the beginning, ICOMEC [his enterprise] aimed just at being able to participate at the competition for public contracts at ENEL [the public electric company]. When we realized that in order to win the contracts additional "promotional work" was needed, we gave Fulchignoni a first payment. He had told us that his channel at ENEL was Hon. Pietro Longo, so we decided, in order to check his credibility, to get in contact with Longo himself. (TRIM:34–35)

2.   In other cases, the mediator establishes an *organic relationship with a political party*, smoothing the way for the business of the party leaders.[4] To refer to an illustrative case, the mediator Ilio Mungai was presented to the leaders of the Socialist party in Lucca as "a comrade who takes care of the interests of the party in the economic sphere, and who was accredited from the national and the regional party directive bodies" (TPI:71). In the corrupt exchanges related to the construction of Local Magistrate's Court in Viareggio, he thus approached the entrepreneur Luigi Rota:

> He told me that he was well known in the political milieu and that, if I agreed to pay certain sums, he would be able to help me and I would have better chances of obtaining public contracts . . . , I would be among the trusted (or at least "reliable") enterprises, and I would preestablish the possibility of obtaining other contracts in the future, and in any case many opportunities would be open to me. Instead, if I did not pay, he told me that I would be

inscribed in the "black book," and I would have no other possibility of working in that field. (VPI-40)

The proposal of the mediator appeared all the more convincing, since he demonstrated that he had privileged information on all the procedures (VPI-18).

3.   Other mediators tend to establish, *in the name of and for a private entrepreneur,* his relationships with a number of public bodies. For instance, an employee of the enterprise Codelfa, active in the construction sector, was specialized in "following the dossiers," trying to accelerate the payments coming from several public bodies: CASMEZ (a public body for the development of the South), the Ministry for Public Work, the Ministry of Defense, ANAS (highways), IACP (housing) of Rome, and the City Council of Rome. As the judged reconstructed it, this employee went from office to office, carrying with him all the documents needed to speed up the procedures for a dossier. To accomplish this, he was in charge of paying bribes to various employees, from porters to high functionaries. In this way, instead of the average six months, he was able to obtain payment in forty-five to sixty days (VICM:3).[5]

4. Still another type of mediator operates as a *private broker,* cultivating privileged links with many politicians, parties, and enterprises, offering his services to all those who demand them. Zampini is an example of this kind. As he himself explained, in order to start a career as a private broker, one needs to frequent the places where politicians and entrepreneurs meet, and to make contact with this milieu, he needs to become friends with someone who is already known, who can function as a *passe-partout*, or a go-between: "With the *passe-partout* one has to build an intimate relationship. . . . With some information and a *passe-partout* it is very easy to enter the political network. Then, you always find a way to enter Lions, Rotary, and a good masonic lodge" (Zampini 1993:112).

These different types of brokers share some characteristics in common: their knowledge of what Zampini called the rules of the "good broker" in the corruption market. The first rule is reliability: "Above all, if you want to have a minimum of credit as a corrupter it is necessary to honor commitments and be as precise as a Swiss watch. If 10 million must be paid at 10 o'clock on the 10th of November, you have to be there five minutes early with not a sixpence less than the sum agreed. " Reciprocity is a second, related rule: "If you want to build a good relationship with a person to whom you have presented a project, you just need a small sign of agreement after you have been the first to do something concrete for him. Favors, reciprocity, and coherence with that first engagement would permit a future development of that relationship. . . . Being coherent means relying upon rational bases and this builds up trust and security. Never think, not even jokingly, to manipulate the other; the possible exposure would end up in your losing the relationship" (ibid.:113). Discretion is a third rule: it "should be an essential characteristic of the corrupter. You should avoid showing a friendship relation in public with your business partner." The broker should also be specialized in his own competence: "In your interaction with your interlocutor you have to show a kind of psychological subjection: you have to remain a step behind him, especially when he is talking of things in his specific competence. You, corrupter, should instead show yourself ready and very well informed on those issues about which he knows nothing, you have to be available to solve any kind of problem, regarding banking, finance, furniture, cars, or even women" (*L'Espresso*, 18 November 1984, p. 40).

For all the different type of brokers, mediation is a lucrative activity. In exchange for their services, they receive in fact a compensation that goes from gifts once in a while to lavish salaries. A Tuscan middleman recalls, "I discovered that, thanks to my connections I was able to provide favors to friends in need. . . . Naturally, the friends I helped gave me a gift, which could also be a conspicuous sum of money. So I also started to provide mediations at a very high level, becoming a professional" (VPI:74). Moreover, because of their privileged relationships with politicians and entrepreneurs, the mediators may become partners of their more powerful friends in legitimate business. Taking a cut of what he negotiated for himself, Zampini became rich through his activities as an illegal intermediary. He managed a series of companies that secured extremely lucrative contracts from the public administration, making a profit by subcontracting work his own companies did not actually carry out. His companies were "empty boxes" and since he "employed neither experts nor technicians the entire potential of his businesses rested on his own position coordinating the various computer firms and as an intermediary between them and the political class" (QGT:369).

In fact, he obtained valuable contracts for computer systems and cartographic services from the Turin council and Piedmont region despite the fact that his company had neither the equipment nor the expertise to fulfill them: "The way in which Zampini spun his web, using his usual tactics to insinuate himself between the companies supplying the equipment and the Region in order to personally gain control of the recovery and maintenance of the machines, emerged clearly from the [intercepted] telephone calls" (QGT:359). Zampini bought material from a number of private firms, being careful to keep all of them happy, then resold it to the public administration. Naturally, he kept a mediation fee, which he divided with the public administrators involved. The following example demonstrates the way in which Zampini's business enjoyed the protection of the public administrators. In order to ensure that the Turin council acquired a turnkey computer system from Zampini's firm, the corrupt administrators had a "friendly" external consultant appointed to work alongside and influence the decision of the council working groups that had already been set up. A number of subtle forms of pressure were brought to bear to ensure that the consultant's work would reflect Zampini's wishes: "Iuppiter [the firm owned by Zampini] contacted me by telephone and Zampini in person invited me to come to Turin to meet the deputy mayor" and discuss the proposed consultancy (QGT:370).

Besides earning himself a debt of gratitude for having masterminded the conferral of a prestigious position, Zampini (on instructions from the deputy mayor) also "rounded out" the consultant's salary, paying him additional millions of lira as an advance on the expenses that would be incurred. At the same time, the public administrators involved had been indicating Zampini as the certain winner of the contract and the future supplier, even to other entrepreneurs. In the future, it was he who should be contacted concerning any business. As his partnership with the deputy mayor and his brother in one firm illustrates, Zampini's business interests would expand even further in the future thanks to his common interests with public administrators.

2. THE DOMAIN OF COVERT POWER

Entrepreneurs, professional people, middlemen, business politicians, and bureaucrats, variously implicated in corrupt exchanges, may feel the need to meet each other in a secure environment, where they can come to know each other, learn about their reciprocal availability, negotiate, and exchange promises and payments. By participating in the formal or informal associations (across class lines and secretive) in which the affairs of their city are customarily decided, they can also acquire the information necessary to identify occasions for corruption and corruptible people. A point that frequently emerged in the course of our research is that political corruption requires *specific sites of interest mediation and business administration*, alternative to those offered by public institutions. It is not a coincidence that a characteristic common to corrupt administrators—as we mentioned in Chapters 3 and 4—is contempt for representative institutions. One of the conditions facilitating corrupt exchange is in fact the removal of decisions from institutional sites, where opposition forces exercise a function of control. Alongside elected assemblies, which have neither the time nor capacity to control an increasingly complex system of government, secretive forms of associationism among the local elites— political or otherwise—propagate. Networks of power, whose official ends range from charity to the promotion of culture, serve for illicit lobbying and the negotiation of more or less lawful business. In these sites different

interests meet, and illegal pacts are negotiated. In order to fulfill this function as a clearinghouse for particular interests, meeting places of the local
elite must possess specific features: they must be "protected" from indis-
creet attention or, in other words, have selective membership procedures;
they must favor the development of solidarity/complicity among members; and they must bring together, across class lines, the various actors
interested in or necessary for the exchange.

In fact, systemic corruption appears intertwined with the creation (or
reinforcement) of (semi)*covert aggregations* in which the real decisions are
made, safe from prying eyes. As already mentioned in Chapter 2, business
politicians often found various types of associations. For instance, Alberto
Teardo—former president of the Liguria regional government, involved in
a case of corruption—founded the Centro di Azione Democratica (CAD,
later CAD2), whose function was, according to the judges, "to offer a meeting point to the leaders of the [criminal] organization in order to discuss
the programs of the group, address the most important decisions in which
only the most influential members are admitted, receive the clients"
(UIS:148). Moreover, the Knights of Malta, the Club des Anysettiers, and
the Knights of the Holy Sepulchre are more or less exclusive societies mentioned in Italian political scandals (della Porta 1992). Most important, corrupt administrators displayed a marked propensity to participation in
freemasonry, and particularly "concealed" or "semiconcealed" lodges. In
the case of Savona, infiltration of freemasonry appears to have been a tried
and trusted strategy, with both concentration in certain lodges—referred
to as "socialist" lodges—and a dispersed presence in others. In the case
studies of the three cities we analyzed in detail, the presence and power
of freemasonry has been considered "abnormal," i.e., higher than the
national average, particularly in the construction and health sectors; complaints have even been raised from within freemasonry itself about such
degeneration of the freemasonry into an association for dirty business. The
presence of numerous masons among those administrators and entrepreneurs involved in cases of corruption confirms the utility of masonic membership in hidden exchange (*Corriere della Sera*, 4 November 1992, p. 15).[6]
In the case of one secret Sicilian lodge, whose members included
various public functionaries, local and national politicians, entrepreneurs,
bankers, and *mafiosi*, the magistrates noted that "the affiliates of this
Masonic brotherhood interfered in public affairs, intervening in the
awarding of public contracts and in the procuring of votes during elections, attempting to maneuver judicial proceedings and corrupt friends in
the forces of order" (CPMF:15).

Besides secrecy, the developed sense of *solidarity among members* facilitates the conducting of illegal business in masonic lodges or similar associations. In freemasonry the selective nature of membership, coupled with

particular ritual forms, reinforces loyalty to the organization. In such cases the organization presents itself as a "second identity," a strong source of loyalty sometimes counterpoised to that of the state. In a system of widespread corruption, such associations therefore seem functional to the creation of the bonds of reciprocal trust and protection necessary for corrupt exchange. In particular, freemasonry presents characteristics that strongly reinforce the bonds of loyalty among members, reducing the risks involved in illegal transactions. According to the former grand master Lino Salvini, the members of the freemasonry have to demonstrate "affection" for each other, and help, comfort, and defend each other in case of necessity (CP2-ter/1:373). Various archaic and apparently irrational rituals contribute to the formation of the sense of common identity. For example, in the masonic lodges in Trapani, Sicily, "some initiation ceremonies had a strange ritual, consisting in the incision of the wrists of the initiator and the initiated, which were then placed on each other, and ended with a kiss on the lips. This ritual recalls Mafia initiations" (PRT:10). Being a member provides a "certificate of trust," and failure to respect agreements has not only a direct economic cost (the exclusion from future opportunities, for exchange) but also the symbolic cost of isolation from and stigmatization by the other affiliates.[7]

Finally, sites of covert power offer the possibility of *across-class connections*. In this context a "modernization" of particular masonic lodges has been reported. First, a change in the nature of membership is said to have taken place in the 1970s, affiliates becoming chiefly doctors, engineers, lawyers, accountants, businessmen, architects, politicians from all political parties (with the exception of the Communist party and of the neofascist MSI), and public functionaries. This changed social complexion corresponded with the new role of "centers of business" taken on by these lodges which functioned as negotiating arenas for many political and administrative decisions or "centers of paraprofessional activity, patronage, protection, mediation, and negotiation of business" (Botta 1983). Their activity "aimed at intervention in and control of various sectors, such as local public enterprises, banks and other economic and social organs, the press, state institutions, etc., etc." (GFS:30).

As the grand master of the Grande Oriente Scozzese d'Italia (the so-called Scottish rite) observed, the lodges offer specialized mediation services: "As always, they are not able, they are not willing to make an open, unscrupulous discourse, because they are always afraid that the other may talk . . . so they look for somebody who can conduct this mediation activity. And this is our capacity, our possibility of intervention. . . . [T]hey know that we are, by hook or by crook, pimps" (from a telephone interception, in *La Repubblica*, Florence supplement, 24 September 1993, p. III). For this reason, adhesion is usually instrumental. As an entrepreneur

involved in a corruption case in Milan explained, "I joined the freemasonry for idealistic reasons. . . . But I naturally also knew very well that
joining the freemasonry I was going to develop relationships such that I
could obtain and offer favors, have some points of reference" (TRDM:731).
The Mafia collaborator Leonardo Messina recalled, in fact, "Many *uomini
d'onore*, in particular those who succeed in becoming Mafia bosses, belong
to the freemasonry . . . because it is in the freemasonry that they can have
total relationships with the entrepreneurs and with the Institutions"
(MPU:54).

The relationships between political corruption and covert powers
emerge with particular relevance in the vicissitudes of the masonic lodge
Propaganda 2, or P2. The affair of the secret P2 masonic lodge came to light
on March 17, 1981, when the Milan magistracy confiscated important documents in a villa belonging to its grand master, Licio Gelli. Gelli's activities were geared toward *elite* covert proselytizing on a national scale. The
lodge membership roll—a list of 962 affiliates discovered during the
sequestration—was not deposited with the secretariat of the Grand Orient,
the main Italian masonic order. The lodge did not hold meetings or elect
its officials. Secrecy inside the lodge was carried to an extreme through its
tentaclelike structure. Members included three government ministers,
thirty members of parliament, more than fifty generals (including the
highest ranks of the secret services), high-level functionaries, diplomats,
journalists, financiers, and industrialists. At the center of the web stood
Gelli, who maintained the contacts between the various members, thus
ensuring his exclusive power as a mediator: "Able to capitalize on tenta-
cles that linked bankers skillful at illegal financial dealings, virtually the
entire top echelon of the country's secret services, the conspirators behind
the right-wing 'strategy of tension,' and the world of organized crime,
Gelli and P2 had become—or were on the verge of becoming—the center
of the system of 'covert power' that constitutes the dark underside of Italian democracy" (Chubb and Vannicelli 1988:126; see also Colombo 1996;
Magnolfi 1996).

P2 offered a confidential arena in which entrepreneurs, members of the
liberal professions, intermediaries, functionaries, and politicians could
meet, get to know each other, propose business deals, negotiate, and work
out agreements and guarantees. Indeed, secret masonic lodges generally
represent a *market* for individuals disposed to and interested in making
clandestine contacts, legal or otherwise. An essential resource for Gelli was
the control of *confidential information*. By way of General Allavena, former
chief of the disbanded Italian secret services SIFAR, he received its confidential files, which enormously increased his stock of compromising material on representatives of the political, economic, and financial worlds.
Moreover, at the moment they joined, Gelli demanded a "fee" from would-

be adepts in the form of information regarding "eventual injustices, abuses, persons responsible" (CP2:53). The information in his possession steadily accumulated. In this way Gelli was able to create a monopoly of blackmailing power on a range of individuals and, thanks to that power, obtain access to further resources—in particular, through Roberto Calvi, the president of Italy's largest private bank, the Banco Ambrosiano:[8] "Sindona [the financier] in particular provided Gelli with the documentation that could have definitively exposed Roberto Calvi. From that moment, Gelli's power multiplied because, with Calvi and the *Banco Ambrosiano* at his disposition, the Grand Master could conceive financial operations on a grand scale" (Galli 1983:207). The Banco Ambrosiano became the financial arm of the covert lodge, acting as an intermediary in diverse transactions.[9] The bank was used to extend the lodge's influence into the world of the media through the acquisition of the Rizzoli group and the placing of P2 affiliates in prominent positions in Italy's leading daily newspaper, the *Corriere della Sera* (CP2:121). As the case of the faked kidnapping of the bankrupt financier Michele Sindona demonstrates, a number of channels of communication with the Mafia created the possibility of exercising *violent* sanctions (CPMF:16; see Chapter 9).

Gelli used this mix of blackmail, corruption, and coercion to expand the network of connections created in the economic and political realms (CP2:109). P2 thus came to resemble a "state within the state," with the power to influence prominent sectors in both institutional and economic life (Teodori 1986). The lodge operated in a plurality of—at times illegal— markets: national and international finance, publishing, corruption, arms trafficking. In fact, P2's grand master offered "an extralegal system of handling rather murky dealings" (CP2-bis/1:43). As a result of the resources at his disposition, Gelli frequently appeared as *guarantor* of deals he helped arrange, operating on a scale that transcended the confines of Italy itself.[10] As Gelli himself recalled, "A judge in Switzerland asked me why and how I had accumulated so much money. I told him that I am a banker without a license. In the sense that, if Egypt needs 500 million dollars, they call me and charge me with finding it. This is not an easy enterprise, believe me. . . . It is a mediation brokerage that is based on trust. Naturally, when I collected the money, I received a commission" (*La Repubblica* 28 December 1993, p. 2).

The financing of political parties increased Gelli's power as a guarantor of illegal transactions; for instance, as the grand master himself explained: "The *Banco Ambrosiano* financed the political parties, who more or less covered their debts. All except the PSI. At the beginning of 1980 the PSI owed Calvi 15 billion. He wanted to get it back and I [Gelli], being a guarantee of good faith for all concerned, suggested a viable transaction" (*La Repubblica*, 19 February 1993, p. 8). The state company for hydrocarbon, ENI, would deposit 50 billion dollars in the foreign account of the Banco Ambrosiano and the *tangente* due to the PSI for the operation would go to cover the debt. Not only the president of the Banco Ambrosiano, Calvi, but also the president and vice-president of ENI, Giorgio Mazzanti and Leonardo Di Donna, belonged to P2.

The notable presence of representatives of the military hierarchy in the ranks of P2 can be explained in a like fashion. Appointment to senior posts in the military apparatus depends on discretionary political decisions and thus permanence in the job is rendered uncertain. As a result, it may become necessary to safeguard or advance career prospects by political means, as happened in the case of the appointment of General Giudice, P2 member and protagonist in the "Second Oil Scandal,"[11] as Commander-General of the *Guardia di Finanza*.

The presence within the lodge of an authority in a position to punish anyone failing to honor agreements or to keep quiet helped maintain this complex edifice of covert transactions in equilibrium. The return on the "services" offered by Gelli was not always immediate. Gelli's activities contributed to the production of the resources (compromising information, the web of reciprocal obligations between various centers of economic, political, financial, and military power), which in turn permitted him to offer his services on an ever-expanding scale. Whoever advanced in their careers or dealings in the public or private sector thanks to P2 affiliation in turn favored, through the filter of Gelli, the success of other members. Thus, the overall influence of the secret organization in the economic and political fields was extended.[12]

3.   HIDDEN POWERS AND CORRUPTION: SOME CONCLUDING REMARKS

We defined political corruption as a hidden and illegal exchange. As we saw in this chapter, these two characteristics had a relevant impact on the nature of corrupt transactions, and the networks of people involved in them. First of all, corrupt exchanges require particular skills, which are not always directly controlled by the corrupted administrators or entrepreneurs. Both may instead buy these resources from a particular category of broker, who possesses "illegal skills." As Pizzorno observed,

> Since corruption is punishable by law and the relative transactions must of necessity remain secret, this kind of intermediary must possess certain abilities, which can be generically termed *skills in illegality*. They must be able to act under the threat of sanction, find those paths least open to scrutiny, cover and protect themselves and, even more importantly, have as wide and direct

a knowledge as possible of both the individuals willing to participate in illegal transactions and those who, while not wishing to be involved, occupy positions of authority in the areas where such opportunities are most frequent. This specific kind of mediating capacity is frequently offered by mediators referred to in the interviews conducted by the suggestive title *faccendieri*. The latter do not participate directly in politics, or only in minor roles. On occasion they do not even belong to a political party. Frequently they also act as intermediaries outside the political sphere (estate agency, public relations, advertising and the like). (Pizzorno 1992:23)

In the market of corruption, illegal brokers fulfill similar functions to those which have been singled out in the legal market. To use Coleman's (1990:180–85) classification, they sometimes work as *consultants*, limiting their role to introducing to each other the actors who may be interested in building a relationship based on trust, investing their credibility in the process; at other times, they function as *warrantors* instead, investing other (mainly material) resources that they risk losing if there is a violation of trust; eventually, they act as *mediator-entrepreneurs* who create the contacts between numerous actors, offering them reciprocal compensation for the resources used in the exchange.

Illegal brokers trade mainly privileged information on the occasions for illegal exchange and, above all, on the possible partners. They facilitate contacts between the potential actors of a corrupt contract; facilitate the agreements by using their own reputation to "certify" the "honesty" of the various actors; and often materially carry around the "payments" for the illicit transactions. They use their own resources—their reputation but sometimes also their own money—to build bonds of trust, or to prevent mistrust from jeopardizing the agreements. Moreover, they reduce the risk of the illegal transactions by carrying out the dangerous tasks of collecting and distributing bribes. As Susan Rose Ackerman noticed, "[A] firm . . . may purchase the services of independent entrepreneurs to do the firm's dirty work rather than hiring them as employers. The outsider provides specialized contacts with decision makers or expedited service through a government bureaucracy, and the seller asks no questions about how the service is performed. The use of agents illustrates the role of market transactions in *reducing* information flow. . . . Officials who demand high bribes can be told by the middlemen that they will bring no further business if concessions are not forthcoming, and a bureaucrat who threatens to report a corrupt offer can be deterred by the professional's threat to expose the official's previous indiscretions" (1978:192–93).

Misadministration and illegal brokerage are linked to each other in a vicious circle. While the lack of transparency and efficiency in public administration creates clients for the illegal brokers, their work increases inefficiency and renders public administration less and less accessible to the citizens who do not enjoy special protection. The mediators tend in fact to reproduce the conditions for an increase in their own power. Not only do they reduce the high risks involved in the corrupt exchange, they also contribute to spreading expectations about the unavoidableness of corruption, and that therefore the private actors need a protector. By presenting public decisions as the reign of arbitrary power, a middleman increases the number of demands for protection, since "he has the clearest interest in maximizing the belief that corruption is pervasive" (Oldenburg 1987:526). At the same time, by their very presence, they produce more and more arbitrary decisions, therefore confirming the pessimistic expectations of the entrepreneurs, and pushing them to look for privileged, protected access to the political power.

Illegal brokers, corrupt politicians, and their clients often meet each other in hidden places. In fact, we noticed that, in illegal transactions, secret associations are especially important in producing bonds of trust: "The importance of skills in illegality helps to account for the political function that actors otherwise very different from each other such as the secret services, secret or semisecret societies (freemasonry, for example, or rather its covert sectors), and organized crime tend to acquire in the evolution of such systems (at differing levels, naturally). They are able to offer precisely these capacities, and the deeper traditional political actors are drawn into illicit business networks the greater the demand for their intervention in political affairs" (Pizzorno 1992:23). The function of power networks in stabilizing contacts between the criminal world and the legitimate power have also been discussed in relation to other forms of crime. Characteristic of these networks is that they aggregate around "voluntary associations with very varied, completely legal, declared goals (the sharing of acquaintances and contacts, charity, legitimate lobbying, the promotion of cultural and religious values, etc.), but that accentuate the reserved, semisecret character of their membership's identities and activities" (Arlacchi 1988:420). Freemason lodges create special bonds of loyalty, which can be used to implement corrupt exchanges. In the Italian case, the importance of these "secret places" in the making of political decisions has been often mentioned. Not only in Italy, "businessmen's clubs" provide the space for the development of personal links between the participants to corrupt exchange [for an example in the U.S. case, see Chambliss (1978:Chapter 4); on Japan, see Reed (1996)]. Most actors involved in a recent French corruption scandal were members of the freemasons (Mogiliansky 1995:2). Within these more or less formal associations, the respect for corruption agreements is secured by the network's ability to discipline its own members: "[T]he enforcement of bribes is made possible by the exploitation of punishment opportunities within a nonsecret network" (Mogiliansky 1995:3).

Deviant secret services emerged often in the history of the Italian Republic, mixing private and political goals, and the search for money and power. According to Pizzorno, "the concealed, or hidden, level" began to lay solid roots in the Italian political system with the terrorist threat in the 1970s, "converging—perhaps with the intent of provoking, perhaps of controlling, these tensions—with secret activities whose inspiration lay within the state or its organs. Accompanying activities . . . that aimed at controlling parasitic income were operations whose referents lay in illegal international markets rather than in the country itself. The resulting parallels between the concealed activities of the political class and those of organized crime are striking" (Pizzorno 1993:298–99). Concluding, we can single out another vicious circle: The diffusion of a "cryptogovernment" (Bobbio 1980), where public decisions are taken outside the democratic institutions, offers important resources (privileged information, covert bonds, etc.) for the development of political corruption; political corruption, in turn, augments the number and importance of these hidden places. Both reduce the confidence of the citizens in democratic institutions.

Research on political corruption in other countries indicates that the role of private, professional middlemen in the development of political corruption is not an Italian peculiarity. For instance, in the North Sea oil industry, "much of the corruption . . . is taking place by some private agents buying bid information from employers in the oil company and selling it illegally to one or several suppliers" (Andvig 1995:299). Usually, information brokers buy their information about the bid from the oil company, and sell it to the lowest bidder, who will increase his price, remaining just below the second-lowest bidder. As the North Sea case indicates, the price of brokerage increases with the quality of the service offered:

> [T]he most lucrative manipulation of the bid—Jens Andvig notes—is when they are able to deliberately keep some reasonable specification of tasks outside the bid. Then it become possible for the bidder to go lower and increase his chances of winning the bid. Then, if he wins, he is paid for these omitted tasks, as they now have to be classified as change-of-order work. This is, of course, a rather demanding form for information manipulation, and it is better paid: 10–15% for this kind of variation in order manipulation, against a 2–3% commission, is said to be normal rate. (ibid.:306)

Also in this case, the role of the information broker is to reduce the "search costs," that is, the costs related to the search for the right contacts to obtain privileged information: "With a broker, the employee of the oil company need not do the costly and risky process of reaching the relevant employee of the relevant supplier himself. Seen from the point of view of a supplier, the advantage with an information broker is that he usually has established a network of contacts in different oil companies and in different parts of the same company. He may therefore save the costs of an extensive network of agents. It is clearly advantageous for a firm to relate to an information broker with a large network since it may then relate to a single broker for many different assignments" (ibid.:309). Also in the North Sea the mechanisms to build trust seem to be quite similar to those described by Adriano Zampini: "With regard to methods of recruiting insiders, both agents and broker seem to follow similar procedures—to create an atmosphere of friendship within a setting of parties, dinners, and alcohol" (ibid.).

In line with our research, other national cases also demonstrate that, although "private" professionals, middlemen are helped by their visible ties with (corrupt) politicians. If Zampini made a display of his relationship with Turin's vice-mayor, in Spain, one of the first scandals that started to erode the power of the Socialist prime minister Felipe Gonzales was related to the brokerage activities of Juan Guerra, the brother of the deputy prime minister Alfonso Guerra. Socialist himself and personal secretary of his brother in their home town Seville, Juan Guerra, who once received unemployment benefits, rapidly became rich thanks to his brokerage activities, linking entrepreneurs with the public administrators of many socialist-led Spanish cities. It is significant that, although he did not have any official position, Juan Guerra used governmental buildings for his activities, so stressing his proximity to those who took public decisions. In Brazil, the scandal that led to the impeachment of President Collor brought to the fore the role of the president's alter ego P. C. Farías (Grau and Gonzaga de Melo Belluzzo 1996). Many similarities emerge if we look at the career of the British broker John Polson, involved in serious scandals that brought about two parliamentary inquiries into political corruption: Polson has been described as "an architect who exploited contacts from every area in public life—contacts made through his involvement in politics, business dealings, masonic activities, and accidental meeting—to obtain contracts. He used any resource of his architectural firm to provide both rewards and incentives; by this means he managed to persuade himself and the recipients that he was not giving them a bribe" (Doig 1996:43). His success was helped by his partnership with a former city councillor of Newcastle-upon-Tyne, who had resigned and founded a public relations firm.

The role of brokers seems to have increased with the growing sophistication of modern corruption. With the diffusion of "grand corruption" in the global trade, trust has become an even scarcer commodity among partners who are physically distant, have only sporadic transactions, and do not possess reliable information concerning reciprocal reputation. In the context of such a "globalized" economy of corruption, "The official remuneration of 'brokers' or the use of local subcontracted companies to carry out the 'dirty job' are among the simplest, most cunning ways of achieving the objectives sought without committing a statutory offence. . . . [T]he corruption takes place via middlemen, brokers, and technical engineering and financing and banking agencies at the interface of the corrupter and the corrupted. The intervention of a go-between body is official, as is its remuneration. Only the service is fictitious or overvalued, the trading of favors masquerading as the anodyne provision of services" (Mény 1996:318).

NOTES

1. The Florentine judges, for example, described one of the accused in a local scandal as a man of a thousand trades, ex-restaurant owner, unlicensed estate agent, broker (QGF:24), officially unemployed but with millions in the bank and in bonds. Another, they described as a *segnalatore di pratiche* [literally, someone who signals, or indicates, dossiers].

2. In Italy, in the nineties, the fiscal revenues of the state constitute more than 92 percent of the total fiscal revenues in the public administration, while 52 percent of the state's current expenses (net from interests) are formed by the transfers to all other public agencies (state-controlled bodies, regions, provinces, and communes). Centralized credits and decentralized expenditure decisions remove fiscal responsibility from the decentralized bodies, which decide on most of the public expenditure (Cassese 1994:16).

3. See Oldenburg (1987:531) for a schematic reconstruction of middleman roles in corruption exchanges, with special reference to less developed countries.

4. This type of mediator is similar to the party-cashier, described in Chapter 2. The role of the party-cashier is, however, a more ambitious one.

5. Since interest rates were at the time higher than 20 percent, the "quick" payment of about 100 billion [lira] of credits thanks to the work of the mediator-employee saved his employers about 7 billion (VICM:2).

6. In 1992, there were 597 official lodges of the Grand Orient of Italy, the most important masonic order (Gran Loggia di Piazza del Gesù, originating from a schism in 1908, also exists). Florence had the highest number of lodges (47), followed by Rome (45), Turin (39, and Palermo (29) (*Corriere della Sera*, 2 November 1992, p. 3). According to the grand master, in 1992 there were 18,000 masons "all at the top of their professions" (Mola 1992:873).

7. Freemasonry as an organization tends to display a high degree of goal congruence among members, obtained through rituals and socialization processes. Furthermore, there is often a certain degree of ambiguity in the evaluation or measurement of affiliates' "performance" and a traditional legitimation of authority within the organization. Ouchi describes a mechanism for mediating transactions similar to that of a *clan*, an organization in which "common values and beliefs provide the harmony of interests that erase the possibility of opportunistic behavior," reducing transaction costs within it (1980:138).

8. After the bankruptcy of his financial empire, which had been a channel of reinvestment abroad for Mafia as well as Vatican capital (through the Vatican's

bank, Istituto Opere Religiose), he was found dead in London, probably killed, on 18 June 1982 (see Cornwell 1983).

    9.   As Letizia Paoli (1995) noticed, the Banco Ambrosiano case points at the often underestimated relationships between organized and economic crime.

    10.   As honorary consul to Argentina, Gelli was one of the few Italians invited to the swearing-in ceremonies of presidents Carter in 1977 and Reagan in 1981 (CP2:2-ter/1, 754).

    11.   A number of oil businessmen, some of them belonging to P2, were illegally importing oil from Saudi Arabia without paying the necessary duties. Politicians and elements in the *Guardia di Finanza*, also belonging to P2, received payoffs in return.

    12.   P2 would go on to elaborate a political project of a conservative-authoritarian stamp: the "Plan for Democratic Rebirth," a sort of political program for covert intervention to produce an authoritarian and conservative regime.

7

The Market for Corruption and the
Economic System

Paradoxically, the business career of Elio Graziano began when he was granted a disability pension by the State Railway Company (Ferrovie dello Stato, FS), where he had worked as technical director of first the Florence and then the Bologna workshop. Graziano's case demonstrates how corruption subverts the laws of the legal market—as a company that did not even possess the capacity to produce the goods demanded by the state was able to triumph over the competition. All the time remaining on a state disability pension, at the height of his career as a businessman Graziano employed 700 people in three plants and produced an annual turnover of 700 billion lira (L'Espresso, 8 May 1988, p. 24).

IDAFF, the company owned by Graziano, began life producing detergents and other commonly used chemical products, which it sold to the Italian railways. In April/May 1979 the breakthrough took place. Graziani returned from Rome and informed one of his employees that they "should get ready to supply paper sheets for the Italian Railways. He [the employee] did not fail to express his perplexity to Graziano since the necessary equipment and expertise was completely lacking but the latter reassured him that he would take care of it" (PR:77). In October 1979 the railways' tendering competition was suspended in order to allow Graziano's as yet nonexistent venture to participate. A preliminary site visit by railway functionaries would be necessary to this end: "Graziano himself made the suggestion that a length of paper toweling be run from a machine for producing detergent and laid out along a table. On the basis of the specifications set out in the railways' tender a 90-cm-wide roll had been purchased from a competing firm and this was wound onto a beam, exactly like a roll of toilet paper" (PR:78). The surrounding area was cleaned of all traces of detergent and cordoned off with a sign MACHINERY STOPPED FOR MAINTENANCE. The functionaries' visit lasted ten minutes and ended in a local restaurant. Graziano's firm was judged suitable to tender a bid and won the contract at 838 lira per piece, the maximum price to be paid having been "confidentially" set at 840 (40 percent higher than the price that had previously been paid for a superior product). At first Graziano supplied the railways a good-quality product purchased from other firms operating as a mere broker. Two years into the contract he began his own production of inferior-quality paper sheets. The whole operation had to have been founded "from the very beginning on the obvious presupposition that all ulterior controls—on the company but above all on the product—would be a pure formality and therefore fictitious" (PR:85).

When the contract came up for renewal in 1982, half of the order was placed directly with Graziano, the other half being awarded through an open tender whose conditions quickly "revealed themselves a perfect ambush for the competition, upon whom the criteria would inexorably be applied, while to Graziano they merely served to justify a further increase in the price" (PR:98). Graziano won the order with an offer of 1,698 lira, the "undisclosed" ceiling having been set at 1,700. The total value of the contract was 50 billion lira. When the contract was renewed for the period 1987 to 1992, half again went directly to Graziano, the other half to open tender. Formally twenty-two firms were invited to tender, none of them specialized in the product line requested (indeed some of them were road contracting firms) but seventeen never actually received the invitation. Graziano's company presented the only bid and unsurprisingly won the contract at a total price of 150 billion lira. The market value of the goods to be supplied did not exceed 15 billion (L'Espresso, 8 May 1988, p. 24). Due to the inefficiency of his firm, Graziano was never actually in a position to satisfy the contracts completely and in the end only about half the goods were actually supplied. The real demand for the product had been exaggerated to such an extent, however, that the Italian railways still managed to accumulate surpluses.

Anything else the railways might "require" Graziano was only too willing to supply. In September 1985 he suggested increasing the size of the sheets (and therefore the price he received for them). The suggestion was immediately taken up by the functionaries responsible, citing the "AIDS psychosis" and the necessity of avoiding passenger contact with a potential source of infection in the form of the woolen blankets used on their trains. It is clear, then, that "Graziano had in effect become the sole arbiter of decisions he himself suggested to the company and the cost of which he dictated" (PR:101). When it was decided that disposable blankets should be used, the examining commission (largely composed of functionaries secretly on Graziano's payroll) recommended that they should be attached to the sheets. In this way "orders for 9.7 billion [lira] were placed with Graziano without the completion of even a single formality" (PR:113). The Italian railways requiring disposal of the used sheets, Graziano set up a company specifically to recycle them and got the contract. However, the quality of the sheets supplied fell even further as a result: "A down was visible on the surface and the material was . . . adherent, leaving fibers sticking to the faces and clothes of passengers" (PR:200). When the railways needed their carriages stripped of carcinogenic asbestos, the work (worth more than 30 billion lira) was once more awarded to Graziano without any tendering operation (PR:235). The work was badly done and substantial quantities of asbestos remained in the "stripped" carriages.

Graziano made systematic use of bribery to obtain contracts from the Italian railways. All the functionaries involved in either the initial decisions or the subsequent inspection process were on his payroll. A tariff existed, which ranged from 100 million for the risks involved in illegitimately suspending the tendering operation down to 40 million for a "walk-on part" in false inspections. The flow of payoffs reached all the way to the top of the company bureaucracy, including the managing director, the company president, and the undersecretary for transport. When the company lost its autonomous status in 1985 and became a state agency, its administration fell to party appointees and the latter too began to receive personal bribes from Graziano (ranging from 350 to 500 million lira). One of them, the Liberal (PLI) Francesco Baf-

figi, was paid at the party's national headquarters: "The rendezvous took place in the courtyard of the building and the money was handed over on the first flight of steps because there were always police there and I was scared of being stopped and checked. The first time I gave him a leather bag in which I had put the bundles of cash and he gave it to the man accompanying him, telling him to take it upstairs. I then left, without even getting the bag back. The handover took place in the same way the second time with the exception that this time I put the money in a plastic bag" (PR:162–63).

In a number of cases payoffs took place in installments, taking on something of the character of a hidden salary paid to railway functionaries and administrators. For example, Giovanni Coletti, the managing director, was paid 50 million lira a month over two years (PR:159). Besides cash, Graziano was also in the habit of giving Christmas and Easter gifts as well, "some of them extremely valuable: watches, jewelry, silverware, electrical appliances, video recorders" as well as huge quantities of canned tomatoes and detergent (PR:71). Employment for relatives was a further means of winning the gratitude of public functionaries. Graziano took on the sons of the two functionaries responsible for verifying that the goods ordered from him were actually delivered, for example. Each of them was also given a new car, as an "incentive." Enrico, the twenty-three-year-old son of the president of the company, Ludovico Ligato, complained to Graziano that the money he received from his father was not sufficient to meet his family's needs: "I asked him how much he would need, suggesting 10 million a month. His only reply was that you couldn't even 'get laid' for that. I told him that was what I could [pay] and he eventually accepted" (PR:182). Through his employment of corruption, Graziano's influence on the decisions of the company became such that one functionary was induced to ask for intercession to help his career rather than money, Graziano being "in a position to pilot the new setup in whatever direction suited him best" (PR:210)

The laws of the market (as well as those of the state) were completely subverted by corruption. Graziano's success resulted not from his talents as an entrepreneur but from his stock of contacts and covert relations within every level of the publicly owned company. Every railway employee of any importance was on his payroll. He decided success or failure in the careers of functionaries. He decided which products the railways would purchase, in what quantities, and at what price. And he was able to force the company into accepting inferior goods. Thanks to the use of corruption he had no need to try and beat the competition by offering the products required by the railways at a lower price. He merely had to create covert exchange relations with anyone who could influence the decision in his favor. According to the magistrates, Graziano paid more than 8.7 billion in bribes for supplying paper sheets alone, receiving in exchange orders worth 260 billion lira.

When a political scandal emerges, usually mass media and public opinion are ready to stigmatize corrupt politicians' behavior, while the participation of entrepreneurs or other corrupters in the illegal transaction often remains within the shadows. What does this common attitude reflect? First of all, we should notice that, in the case of a public agent, corruption involves the violation of the rules that protect the public interest. The corrupt public agent is a bad example for his peers, since he is supposed to act according to those rules. To the contrary, the task of the entrepreneur consists, by definition, in making profits: if in order to reach this goal he has to pay bribes, his choice may seem more than justified. This asymmetry in the moral condemnation of corruption reflects the belief that a more rigorous respect for the law is demanded of state representatives than of the common citizen. Moreover, it is asserted, bribery is often not an exchange, but an extortion from the public administrators, who have the power to impose their orders and the conditions needed to intimidate economic partners.[1]

Are similar considerations realistic? As shown by Graziano's tale, entrepreneurs' role in corruption practices may not be so passive: in fact, he became the real engine and main actor of a corrupt network that extended to the entire political and bureaucratic structure of the *Ferrovie*. Although at first glance he seemed to be deprived of entrepreneurial capacity, Graziano had accumulated large fortunes by selling low-quality products at high prices to a public body. His case is assuredly not an isolated one. Top managers from Italy's leading firms, such as Cesare Romiti (FIAT), Silvio Berlusconi (Mediaset), Carlo De Benedetti (Olivetti), Raoul Gardini (Montedison, who committed suicide because of the scandal)—men certainly not intimidated even in front of top politicians—have been variously involved, sometimes even for the payment of small bribes to low-level functionaries. Along with them there is a vast undergrowth of small- and medium-sized firms, specialized in meeting public sector demand by exploiting political contacts.

In this chapter we will concentrate on public contracting procedures, each phase of which can create occasions for corruption, orienting competition between firms toward a dimension of hidden exchange with politicians and bureaucrats. This process undermines the conditions of *market competition*, which, through the mechanism of public tendering, should guarantee *productive efficiency* in the provision of goods and services to the public administration. In Section 1, we will show how political corruption facilitates the construction of cartels. In Section 2, we will examine the relation between political protection and extortion. In Section 3, a typology of the varying forms of organization of relations between firms and centers of political power will be presented. As we will see, these relations can be placed on a scale of greater or lesser "integration" between the economic and the political sphere. In Section 4, the factors that lessen the "moral costs" of engaging in corruption on the part of entrepreneurs will be analyzed. In Sections 5 and 6, we will study some of the perverse consequences of corruption on the "demand side" of the market of corruption, particularly referring to the adverse selection of firms and the higher prices paid by public entities. Finally, in Section 7, an attempt will be made to clarify the strategic dimension of the interaction between corrupters.

1. CARTELS AND BRIBES

Private actors competing to satisfy public demand can use corruption to create (or augment) requests for the products or services they produce.[2] When the nature and amount of public spending have been determined, however, the purchasing procedures are often characterized by the principles of *competition* and *equal treatment* for all participants. It can therefore be expected that the cost of corrupting those who formulate public demand will be met by:

1.   An enterprise with a monopoly in the private market and thus certain of being the only possible supplier of the good demanded by the state. Similar cases are generally rare, since the law usually allows state legal monopolies (thus eliminating the need for a public demand of that commodity) and forbids others with antitrust regulations.

2.   A single or a small clique of firms that have the certainty, or a very high probability, of winning the tender thanks to the protection of politicians or bureaucrats previously corrupted. In any case, protected firms will seek to direct public demand toward the particular characteristics of their own products or to ensure that successive stages allow them to make profitable use of their privileged relationships with politicians. Such a case is described by Vittorio Caporale, a Ministry of Transport consultant who coordinated the preparation of legislation on high-speed transport:

> The two firms [Ansaldo and FIAT Impresit] wanted to introduce a kind of exclusive right for their own products. . . . In substance, Ansaldo and FIAT wanted the technology employed to be "tried and tested," thus excluding foreign technology. It was only as the legislature approached its close that the law's passage through Parliament accelerated sharply. It was clear, a posteriori, that parliamentarians would have appreciated a reward to help finance the imminent 1992 election campaign. (CD, 21 June 93, no. 435, p. 5)

The public decisions will therefore privilege those enterprises willing to pay bribes.[3] As we will see in the next paragraph, protected enterprises can obtain several public benefits, included the possibility either of suggesting or of deciding, de facto, the nature and amount of demand created by the public administration.

3.   A "cartel" of all the firms involved in tendering, which are thus able to redistribute the rent derived.[4] Collusive agreement may actually appear

even at a later stage of the contracting procedure. In fact, firms that participate in public auctions can collude successfully by coordinating their
bids, thus ensuring ample profit margins. Firms F_1, F_2, and F_3, for example,
can decide that F_1 will present a lower bid than its competitors and win the
contract. In exchange, firms F_2 and F_3 will receive monetary compensation
("side-payments") or the promise that the favor will be returned in the
future.[5] A Milan entrepreneur described the functioning of the market
there in the following terms:

> When tenders for contracts are issued, the interested firms meet on the rec-
> ommendation of those of us who are most directly interested in the problem
> in order to find an agreement for a fair distribution of the contracts. . . . I was
> contacted and the contract that I could hope to get was decided. In conse-
> quence, the other firms would not undercut me and present a lower bid. At
> the same time, in relation to the contracts that other firms were supposed to
> win, I was pledged not to get in their way. (TM:45)

Different criteria existed for the division of contracts between the cartel
firms: by turns, territory, demanding institution, market sector. Alberto
Zamorani, a public sector manager, described the "scientific" precision
with which work for the National Road Authority (ANAS) was distributed: "For many years a cartel of about 200 firms has existed. They meet
periodically, look at the list of works that have or will be presented to the
Board of Directors and decide on the order of who wins. The choice is
made by lot. The names of the firms are written on pieces of paper and
then extracted at random. The first group of firms extracted gets the first
contract and so on" (MPM, pp. 172–73). This system is certainly not confined to the area of major infrastructure. In the health sector, for example,
"there are groups of firms divided by product sector and business capacity that have created a de facto . . . cartel for distributing work in the hospital sector, and thus in the different departments the firms delegated to
win the contracts are already known" (TNM:27).

Similar cartel agreements are illegal. Thus, they cannot be regulated by
an official contract. How, then, can firms trust one another? Firm F_1, for
example, might decide not to compensate the others or not to desist from
future tenders. If agreement between the firms is for one contract only, the
probability of the cartel failing to work is higher.[6] If, however, a limited
number of firms stay in business over a long period, the probability of successful collusion improves. The repetition of the game, in fact, creates a
sanction available to be imposed against violators. Any cheating behavior
can then be punished by exclusion from the long-term gains of collusion:
higher profits deriving from the elimination of competition.[7] Raffaele San-
toro, president of the publicly owned Italian General Petrol Company
(AGIP), confirmed that a solid and restricted cartel regulated the division
of work for the company's major projects: "Over the years, I was able to

note that Snam Progetti, TPL, CTIP, and Technit frequently operated a cartel, a pact of nonbelligerence for dividing up the major projects. One company makes a bid to win the contracts while the others make covering bids and a 'parachute' is agreed (the winner pays the other firms a sum proportional to the value of the contract)" (*La Repubblica*, 6 May 1993, p. 11). Indeed, corruption may become superfluous, since the cartel acquires the power to decide autonomously on the attribution to its firms of property rights to political rents.

It is possible, however, that purchasing certain services from politicians and bureaucrats will augment cohesion of the cartel. Corruption again becomes indispensable if one wishes to avoid procedural holdups, acquire restricted information, which facilitates collusion, limit the number of firms invited to tender, or ensure that the flow of money is not interrupted: in short, to create conditions that make public contracts easy to share. According to one entrepreneur, for example, "an agreement among entrepreneurs for subdividing the market without having to accept the trouble of competition" had taken root in relation to tendering by Milan's public bodies: "Naturally . . . after each of us had won the contract they wanted we were contacted and informed that the 'system' required money in return. Each of us made a one-time payment proportional to the contract . . . destined to thank those exponents of the political-institutional system who guaranteed the awarding of contracts independently of the preexisting cartels of 'nonbelligerence' we formed" (TM:46). Corrupt administrators thus reenter the game through the sale of various resources, information on future works and above all on the (confidential) range within which bids must fall to be valid, as well as the power to block the entry of outside firms.[8] Thus one Sicilian entrepreneur claimed that "another important role of the functionaries of the contracting body is to provide the entrepreneur with a list of the other firms invited to tender. He will then have the time to contact them and ask them to adopt a noncompetitive conduct (either by not taking part in the tender or by making a 'supporting' bid agreed upon before hand)" (CD, 11 June 1993, no. 417, p. 4). Organizing contemporaneously many tenders—already shared by the cartel—avoids the risk of someone later forgetting to pay for the favor received: "At the provincial administration of Milan," Mario Chiesa recalled, "the same entrepreneurs decided among themselves who had to win. In order to avoid conflicts . . . all the tenders were attributed on the same day" (Andreoli 1993:49).

When an external center of power directly guarantees respect for the collusive agreement, the solidity of the cartel is further reinforced. Firms F_1, F_2, F_3 (and so on) then give up a part of the rent gained to a guarantor who can punish defection and discourage rivals. Higher profits for the firms involved thus create greater opportunities for enrichment for the corrupt politicians, since they can be bribed with part of the rent derived from the absence of competition.[9] As Ades and Di Tella observe: "[T]he lack of product market competition can not only benefit the firms in the industry, but can potentially also benefit tax inspectors, regulators, suppliers and other agents with some control rights over those firms. The reason is that as competition decreases, the value of their control rights increases, so it becomes more profitable to exchange them for bribes" (1997b:94). The protection provided is often impalpable: firms can count on the willingness of politicians to intervene, but the corrupt politicians limit themselves to accepting the bribes offered them by the cartel as long as things "run smoothly." Marco Bosca, representative of the PSI, stated:

> When I became president of the ACEA [the public agency for water supply in Rome] I noted that a cartel also operated in the water services sector, subdividing maintenance work, supplies, and operations. These firms too had a "referent," with whom I even spoke and agreed that the cartel would pay 5 percent of the value of contracts. I also spoke with both the politicians responsible . . . and the members of the board and everyone was agreed that I would receive the money and then distribute it in the same proportions. (CD, 13 April 1993, no. 263, pp. 6–7)

Normally the firm coordinating the cartel communicates the names of those failing to keep the agreement to the politicians, who resolve the problem by imposing penalties such as exclusion from tenders under their jurisdiction. A Sicilian entrepreneur testified that "[w]hen a firm contacted does not agree to 'pass' as requested [i.e., does not agree to collude], the interested firm turns to a more important one that, because of its economic influence and political contacts, has the function of regulating and resolving disputes within a particular area" (CD, 11 June 1993, no. 417, p. 4). If there is effective political protection against competitors, a decision to participate in "forbidden" tenders, make a bid different to that agreed upon, or refrain from paying one's part of a bribe—depending on the content of the collusive agreement—loses much of its attractiveness. Effective protection, therefore, may be aimed more at *preventing* challenges to the cartel than at *punishing* them.

It can be expected that, where cartels are present, the firms involved correspond to the coalition of politicians guaranteeing the continuity of business in terms of their market influence and political orientation. Thus in Bari "an agreement had been reached between all the biggest firms of the city and the politicians" in relation to tenders for schools, and "a precise coupling between company X and party X had been created in order that each party was assured a bribe of 5 percent of the gross value of the works tendered" (TRIB:66). At times the collusive agreement between the political parties predates and causes an identical division in the economic field. Thus in relation to many public contracting procedures in the Veneto area "the agreement between the parties (DC and PSI) on the distribution of bribes came first, and afterwards the enterprises were chosen according to their importance . . . , political coloring, trustworthiness for the system, and recommendations from those who count" (APV:II). The market for public works is thus founded on a two-way collusion: the agreement on bribery among politicians favors collusion among participants in tendering and vice versa.[10]

2. THE POLITICAL PROTECTION OF ENTREPRENEURS

The boundaries between protection and extortion are sometimes blurred. As Charles Tilly noticed:

> Which image the word "protection" brings to mind depends mainly on our assessment of the reality and externality of the threat. Someone who produces both the danger and, at a price, the shield against it is a racketeer. Someone who provides a needed shield but has little control over the damage's appearance qualifies as a legitimate protector, especially if his price is no higher than his competitors'. (Tilly 1985:170–71)

These considerations provide a starting point for a discussion of why "extortive corruption" is presumably less relevant than "transactional" corruption in democratic regimes.[11] In fact, we believe that extorsive corruption is marginal in the democratic systems, where public agents cannot employ physical violence in order to impose compliance with arbitrary requests (with the possible exception, as we will see in Chapter 8, of connections between politicians and organized crime), and several institutional and impartial control mechanisms do exist. Dissatisfied private actors can free themselves from extortion by denouncing the perpetrator or having him arrested if they consider it inconvenient or ethically wrong to pay a bribe. A democratic system guarantees the presence of a plurality of independent actors and institutions—the magistracy, hierarchical superiors, political adversaries, the mass media, citizens—to be turned to in order to punish corruption by politicians or bureaucrats. If threatened by extortion, economic actors involved in contractual relationships with the state can withdraw and concentrate on the private market or on noncorrupt public buyers. A private actor can only be forced to accept extortive corruption if there are unfavorable "environmental conditions," that is, if withdrawing or bringing charges is precluded by the risk that the actions of other corrupt agents will nonetheless lead to a heavy cost being paid. But this means, to use Tilly's definition, that the demand for a bribe rests on the threat of harm or loss over which the corrupt agent has little control. What counts is that the agent is effectively in a position to spare the private actor this loss, in which case the service he provides is more similar to protection than racketeering. If, on the other hand, he is not in a position to do so, he is more akin to a conman than a extortionist.

There is not necessarily extortion even when bribes seems to be paid in exchange for nothing more than the performance of a duty. As we have seen in Chapter 2 and will examine here from the entrepreneur's perspective, bribes can be directed to *political patrons* or *guarantors*. Those engaging in corruption, in fact, may be seeking to obtain a generic protection for their entrepreneurial activities and for their exchange relations with the public administration and its corrupt agents. For example, when a supplier pays a bribe in order to avoid administrative inefficiencies and delays, there may be a voluntary, not extorsive transaction if those unfavorable conditions are not under control of the corrupt agent, who can nevertheless eliminate or at least attenuate—performing his duty—their costly consequences. By paying such bribes the entrepreneur purchases the right to continue working in a protected market, which, like the public sector, offers the possibility of substantial gains. This is not to say that there is no extortion at all in the corruption market, but rather that in democratic systems it is extremely circumscribed. As a result of high levels of corruption, we may add, a form of extortion concerns primarily entrepreneurs who do *not* pay bribes and taxpayers who are forced to finance such illegal practices. In a similar context, in fact, "honest" entrepreneurs are obliged to suffer a cost from the corruption of others, coming up against an insurmountable barrier to entering the public market, while the fiscal charge of common citizens grows in correspondence with the appropriation of political rents by corrupt agents and protected entrepreneurs.

A firm "twinning" with a center of power generally hopes to obtain protection in its dealings with public institutions, discourage competition, and protect itself from the dangers of being cheated in corrupt exchanges. According to the ex-president of INADEL, Nevol Querci, hidden exchange sometimes take place on a one-time basis (with immediate payment) while in other cases protection is based on a long-term "contract": "All acquisitions were from entrepreneurs for whom the party had given me the go-ahead. In some cases the entrepreneur paid directly to the national secretariats of the parties, and afterwards I would be given the green light. In others, they paid the money directly to me" (TNM:76). The activity of *protection-seeking* thus becomes essential for understanding the behavior of entrepreneurs specialized in the public sector. The magistrate Piercamillo Davigo has noted that "the enterprises implicated in the system of corruption give the impression that entrepreneurs are the last to believe in the market, whatever they may say. They are scared to stand on their own two feet, preferring to seek protection and will do anything to remove even the possibility of competition" (1993:9). From this point of view, seemingly bizarre phenomena can be explained: take, for example, the marked tendency for firms, notwithstanding the legal dangers, to create and openly display political relations, up to the point of being "internalized" (to use an economic term) by the centers of political power to which they entrust part of their entrepreneurial initiatives. Actually, "contracts of protection," by which political guarantee is exchanged for bribes, are more effective when they are long term. This is the description offered by the former mayor of Reggio Calabria, Licandro:

> [A surveyor of the Lodigiani firm] explained to me that they gave 4.5 percent of the value of the work contracted. Three percent was for local politicians, including the big names: faction leaders or others important for some reason. The rest was for Rome. But for that they paid in a regular way, not in relation to each individual contract. Permanent relationships are preferred by the firms that pay bribes for public contracts, and all of them do. The relationship consolidates; it's less risky like that. There's no need to start over again every time, having to intercept the right person and running the risk of being cheated. (Licandro and Varano 1993:83)

This ambiguous nature of protection is not lost on those who trade in it. Where firms maintain enduring relations with public organizations, short-term, intermittent protective services present serious inconveniences for both protector and protected. As for the protector, it may become difficult for a politician to prevent previously protected firms from being helped even when they are not regular with payments,[12] or that they turn to someone else in an "extracontractual" period. Intruders without backing or even swindlers can taken advantage of such interruptions. For instance, in a secretly recorded meeting, Bruno Lucari, ex-regional assessor of the Lazio Region, vividly displayed his surprise and annoyance on discovering that he had been backing a firm without protection:

> Assessor: "You mean you did fuck-all till now?"
> Entrepreneur: "No, fortunately not, I told you."
> Assessor: "What assholes!!! . . . I sign everything . . . face up to everything. . . . You saw the continuation and enlargement of the works I got. . . . I did that. . . . I don't know who you are. I thought you people knew somebody. Get the idea?" (*La Repubblica*, 15 November 1991, p. 7).

As for the protected, a precise political mark simplifies dangerous activities, as the experience of a middleman in Bari reveals: "It was well known that such and such a firm was connected with such and such a party. Thus when the person to whom the envelopes or packets of money should be paid was not specifically stated, he already knew precisely to whom the consignment should be made" (TRIB:271). On the other hand, with short-term protection contracts, the protected enterprise risks having to operate in an insecure environment, facing bureaucratic obstruction or being put under pressure even when up to date with bribery payments. Both parties, therefore, have a common interest in creating a relationship of indefinite duration; in these cases, as it has been observed for the Italian Mafia, "protection works better through prevention rather than repression. . . . Thus, protection is a potentially infinite sequence of acts that cannot be identified or distinguished from one another" (Gambetta 1993:56).

3. A TYPOLOGY OF PROTECTED ENTERPRISES

If the actors of corruption realize that their relationship is unlikely to arise again in the future, their interests will converge only for the positive conclusion of the transaction at hand. When, instead, such a relationship has a wider expected duration, with a sufficient frequency of contacts, *ties of greater density* may be profitable between certain political actors and their "clients." A number of entrepreneurs—specialized in satisfying public sector demand—have shown an interest in establishing an (only thinly disguised) *long-lasting relationship* with centers of political power. In their turn, the latter press for a long-term contractual relationship whose object is a wide-ranging protection of the firm in its dealings with the public administration. As Pizzorno observed:

> [W]e could say that the party system in Italy was not a *participation* system anymore, having become a *protection* system. Joining a party was not aimed at participation to public activity, but at being favored, backed up, *protected* in one's own private activity. A good politician, especially at the local level, was mainly a good protection supplier. . . . A firm could find it profitable to belong to a political area—which did not mean necessarily a party's area, but even a fraction's area, or even an area close to a certain political actor. . . . It could then obtain public contracts, privileged information, absence of controls, and so on. Sometimes there were no specific benefits, but the firm could simply be admitted to the "inner circle," to acquire a privileged and protected citizenship that opened, by paying the price, a "window of opportunities." (1996:269)

It is thus possible to construct a typology of protected enterprises depending on the scale of their political protection and the particular public bodies in which their interests were concentrated.

1. Excluded and Extorted Enterprises. As we indicated in Chapter 2, Section 3, efficient protection presupposes the existence of *excluded* enterprises.[13] The guarantee that an extra cost will be imposed to new entrants in a market can be in itself a good reason to buy protection:

> Whether we are dealing with extortion or genuine protection depends on whether we are the new entrant or the protected dealer. In essence the two

are equivalent, as it is impossible to protect someone against competition without damaging competitors at the same time. The same applies to lobbies, governments, and the mafia. (Gambette 1993:32)

In reality, some entrepreneurs are excluded or left at the margin of the corruption market, or are subject to extortion. We may take, for instance, the case of a Savona entrepreneur, "who was well aware of the conditions that would have allowed him to win the tenders he wished, who was willing to accept those conditions but nonetheless remained excluded from both bribery and contracts of a certain value, having to make do with the crumbs " (TRIS:146). Depending on the particular preferences of a political protector, such criteria of exclusion affect those of the "wrong" political label, who arrive too late in the game, who do not inspire sympathy, or who are not considered trustworthy, as—for instance—the entrepreneur Luigi Agostinelli. He stated:

> Prandini, the minister of public works, gave contracts to whoever he liked. Local administrations gave contracts to whoever they liked. So what is someone who doesn't have, or doesn't want, political protection supposed to do? Go out of business? . . . It was explained to me that Prandini had a man for every district and that there was quick and continuous turnover. Private offices where it was possible to negotiate were mentioned. I was told that things would get better. But I never found anybody to introduce me in those offices. I had been put on the blacklist. In short, I wasn't trusted. (*Panorama*, 14 February 1993:pp. 57–58)

Examples of corruption more closely resembling extortion do exist and the demanding of bribes is, ultimately, based on the threat of a greater loss than that due to "normal" inefficiency. One supplier of the PAT recalled:

> In retaliation Mario Chiesa was in the habit of delaying payments for months. . . . He threatened, moreover, to find fault with the activities of my company. Normally the PAT paid suppliers after four to five months. Because of Chiesa's capriciousness, or rather because it was in his interest to do so, the PAT managed to take as much as seven, eight, even eleven months to pay me. (MPM, p. 91)

A number of factors influence a corrupt politician's propensity to extortion. First, such attitudes should be linked to the politician's interest in creating a "bad reputation" (see Chapter 2), arrogance being one of the resources favoring success in the careers of corrupt politicians. In addition, uncertainty as to the length of their career might induce corrupt politicians to charge extremely highly for their services or to resort to extortion in order to make as much money as possible in as short a time as possible. If, on the other hand, their career prospects are sufficiently long-term, they may prefer to have "satisfied" customers, conceding them a wider profit margin and refraining from the use of threats in order to have their demands met.

2. Sporadically Protected Enterprises. If an entrepreneur's relations with the public administration are sufficiently infrequent and unimportant financially, they do not need to enter long-term contractual relationships with centers of political power, limiting themselves to paying bribes when necessary. In other cases, it is the politicians who refuse the advances of the businessmen because, though willing to engage in occasional exchange, they are not interested in offering protection on a continuous basis (often because they have preexisting commitments with others). When the entrepreneur De Mico sought to obtain fixed protection from the management of the state railways, one of the secretaries of the managing director, Ligato, informed him there was no point insisting: "Ligato was not the least bit interested in his firm. All he wanted was money, 100 million, to unblock the situation." The entrepreneur made subsequent attempts to meet Ligato in order to "present [his] company's profile" but never got past the waiting room (PROM:757).

3. Enterprises with Exclusive Protection. This type of firm presents itself as a privileged supplier to a given public body, often helping to promote that body's demand for goods and services. This is the case of IDAFF, the company belonging to Elio Graziano: as we saw in the introduction, Graziano's firm had no single political referent or protector. Rather, the company created a web of privileged relations at every level of that public structure, taking advantage of the complex and fragmented nature of decision-making procedures. The offer of protection tending to require a long-term contract, the public servants in this case were *internalized* within the protected firm as hidden employees, many of them being bribed in the form of (undeclared) monthly salaries.[14] According to the judges, the "evident frauds and irregularities committed in this way by the functionaries of the FS in agreement with Graziano, were so obvious and crude that they must have had the approval of all levels of the organization's hierarchy" (PR:85–86). The bribes paid by Graziano caused the public purchase of an exorbitant amount of material, in a process "aimed more at covering the investments made in the meantime by the furnisher than defending the company's interests" (PR:98).

4. Party Public Enterprises. In certain cases political control over firms is achieved through publicly financed companies, filtered by the representative bodies to which they formally respond. Such companies, "initially created to work alongside public bodies to guarantee greater efficiency by recourse to the free market, have frequently ended up . . . ensuring 'mediated returns' to the power groups who set them up" (Di Pietro 1991:11). One such example is the *Lombardia Informatica* (L.I.) firm, of which the magistrates state: "It is not only its institutional shareholders (the Lombardia Regional Council and the CCIA) who decide how and by whom Lombardia Informatica is to be run, nor do its legal representatives take orders only from them. Rather, *certain party secretariats act as filter and go-between for every decision and it is they, in the final analysis, who decide concerning the company*" (PRLIM:105, emphasis added). These "party public enterprises " are used as an instrument for secret fund gathering and for clientelistic placement of personnel.[15] Protection from competition is within their "genetic code," since they offer their services to the public administration in a regime of legal monopoly. Besides illegal funding, these firms can guarantee employment and support to the parties with which they are linked. An advertising brochure for the firm T. Service S.R.L. (subcontractor from Lombardia Informatica) publicized quite openly its clientelist function, Christian Democrat in this case: "It should also be underlined that hiring policy was entirely directed to young people . . . whose political (and familial) reliability within the party, and particularly in the main area of common interest, had been verified (and guaranteed by those who presented them)" (PRLIM:117–18). The brochure also noted that this Christian Democrat enterprise was a response to analogous Socialist and Communist firms, until then alone in providing work for young people in the area. The success of the initiative was manifested by the continual and pressing attention of "important members of the ecclesiastical world and also parliamentarians, complete with recommendations in writing or by telephone." The demand on party-controlled public bodies is a natural consequence of these premises: "To obtain new, direct supply contracts by any means possible, in order to increment opportunities for providing jobs" (PRLIM:120).

5. Party Enterprises. Numerous corrupting firms were distinguished by a *party label*. In return for the informal use of this "trademark"—which ensured a stable and prolonged influence on public decision-making—party enterprises provided lasting finance for that particular center of power. Romano Tronci claimed, for example: "In our field we're known to be 'friendly' with the PCI. . . . There is a continuous and organic relationship of contribution and support between our group and the PCI in the sense that we consider ourselves integrated in the system of the party and as such part of our proceeds go to it." The "trademark of protection" must be identifiable so that local administrators have a firm idea of an enterprise's position and do not create problems. For this reason the contributions made to the party (3 billion lire over eight years) were paid by "participating at *L'Unità* [the party's daily paper] festivals throughout Italy, by sponsoring the Party Almanac. . . . What Assessor, knowing our serious and organic links with the party, would demand a bribe?" (*L'Espresso*, 4 April 1993, p. 59). With these political ties firms can plan future investment and activities with greater certainty, without having to overcome "political" obstacles. The Milan cashier of the Socialist party, Sergio Radaelli, recounted that he had been approached by an entrepreneur who was looking for protection: "He gave me a white envelope filled with money. . . . He simply said: 'I have a good relationship with the party, but I am not able to meet the mayor" (TM:59). The *personal* component that characterizes many illegal relations becomes less important in such cases. As already noted (see Chapter 3), a collector for bribes (the administrative secretary, or someone else trusted by the party leadership) is secretly selected within the party and firms then deal with that person, regardless of the individual delegated at any particular moment. A fixed annual sum given to the cashier of the party with whom relations are maintained, as a sort of tax, appears the standard form of payment. Augusto Rezzonico, a member of the DC, recalls: "Many entrepreneurs came with money asking to be introduced within institutional organs. . . . The Right Hon. Citaristi [party administrative secretary] was the person who managed relations between the enterprises and public bodies in order to establish a privileged channel of access to public contracts" (*Panorama*, 6 December 1992, p. 47).

On their side, the politicians nominated or elected in the governing bodies of public enterprises—who need the support of their party for their career—have all the interest in actively favoring party-protected enterprises. Pierfranco Paletti, nominated by the Republican party in the governing body of ENEL, stated: "The firm Fochi from Bologna, which has received contracts from ENEL, is considered as a 'friend' of the PRI. As such, I acted in order to protect it for public tenders" (CD, 30 March 1993, no. 246, p. 7). Firms will have an incentive to follow the advice of their political protector who, pocketing a sum proportional to the political rents, will seek to direct them toward the most fruitful opportunities.[16] Salvatore Ligresti has stated, for example: "The Socialist secretariat had a general disposition in favor of my group, also because of the periodic contributions we paid. As far as I know it was not us who pressed for the success of this or that initiative. The politicians decided autonomously, case by case, which of our initiatives to sponsor" (*L'Espresso*, 6 December 1992, p. 58). According to Roberto Buzio, collaborator of the PSDI's secretary Cariglia, from an agreement between the latter and Minister of Public Works Prandini "the PSDI had the right to single out three 'friend'-enterprises to whom ANAS would have given tenders and from whom we could autonomously receive the money we wanted. I singled out three enterprises, and named them to Prandini" (CD, 24 June 1993, no. 443, p. 4).

A high degree of *identification* thus develops between firm and political protector; a congruity of interests and objectives cemented on occasion by active political involvement on the part of the entrepreneur. However, by tying its fortunes to those of a particular center of political decision-making, a firm exposes itself to the natural turbulence of party competition: mobility of particular leaders; shifting coalitions; internal political conflict; electoral uncertainty.

6. *Personal Protection.* An entrepreneur may seek the protection of individual politicians at the local or central level, depending on his scale of activity and areas of interests.[17] As Vincenzo Lodigiani explained: "A direct relationship was formed between the various firms and particular political parties or their representatives. Some entrepreneurs favored direct links with a local or national politician, depending on the kind of tender or orders they sought to protect. Others chose what could be called an 'institutional path,' creating direct contacts with the party secretariats" (TNM:42). Camillo Zuccoli, assistant to the ex-minister Gianni Prandini, described the approach made by one entrepreneur as follows: "Angelo Simontacchi expressed his desire to become a follower of Prandini, extolling the minister's qualities and offering to finance the grouping; 500 million lira drawn from individual ANAS contracts" (*La Repubblica*, 10 April 1993, p. 6). Mario Chiesa also recalled that "there was what amounted to a competition between entrepreneurs in presenting themselves as the friend of this or that politician, supporting him in everything. 'I share your ideas, I share in your success.' It was a vortex of complicity" (Andreoli 1993:114). For example, according to the judges, the Firouzabadi firm received special protection from the president of the Serenissima public motorway, the only company for whom they worked (RPV1:2–4). They won tenders with such startling regularity that "the other firms slowly stopped participating in tendering for the motorway, probably because they had little chance of being awarded the contracts" (ibid.:27). This *invisible but impenetrable barrier to competition* represents a most effective form of protection. It had a *preventive* more than a *repressive*, character, discouraging possible challengers: the reputation to be supported by important people allow an enterprise to win over competitors, even without having to openly violate rules. Nevertheless, protection contracts are not easy to broker: the entrepreneur must evaluate both the career prospects of his potential political protector and the context in which he intends to carry on his economic activity before deciding which "horse" to bet on.[18]

7. *Politician-Entrepreneurs.* In certain cases this mixing of political and economic interests is also sanctioned at the level of formal *property rights* in the firm. An emissary of the clan of corrupt politicians gathered

around the Liguria boss Alberto Teardo, for example, knowing that a Savona entrepreneur intended to extend his activities in the tar macadam sector, "told him that if he wanted to work [in that area] he would have to form a company and take 'one of their people' as a partner" (TRIS:174) The new company included Teardo's nephew, who did not, however, pay anything into it. This hidden "political participation" in a firm ensures prompt obedience to corrupt politicians' demands and a mean of collecting invisible bribes, through the distribution of dividends to shareholders. In fact, close kinship between the heads of businesses and politicians is an ideal shield, avoiding legal obstacles but allowing the underlying mark of protection to filter through: this explains the proliferation of entrepreneurial activities owned by the wives, children, nephews, cousins, brothers, or sisters of Italian political bosses (of varying degrees of importance) in recent years. Michele De Mita, entrepreneur and brother of Ciriaco, former prime minister, found himself in a privileged position during the postearthquake reconstruction in Irpinia. According to a fellow entrepreneur, "[H]e was known to be someone who did as he liked in the area. . . . He was able to foresee the flow and timing of funding, something that would have appeared to an outsider as exclusively the business of the highest political and administrative levels" (*Panorama*, 28 March 1993, p. 51). Also Ludovico Ligato, a leader of the Calabria DC and former president of the FS, during his career had founded—directly or registered under his son Enrico's name—as many as twenty-seven firms active in real estate, construction advice, and the production of building materials. In the world of business, he invested the resources of information and trust accumulated during his political activities: "He asked, collected information, wanted to know the situation of several commercial enterprises. To this end, he exploited the political network and friendship ties he maintained with local leaders of his own party" (Ciconte 1994:144).

In relation to Sicily, Michele Pantaleoni has noted that "it is significant that of eighteen entrepreneurs in public works . . . two are the direct relations of parliamentarians . . . , three married to the children of national-level party leaders, one the son of the director of a regional assessorate, another the son of the president of a public body" (Pantaleoni 1984:184). Matteo Litrico, entrepreneur and ex-communal assessor of Catania states: "To confirm my business relations with the Right Hon. Salvatore Grillo it may help to recall the formation of the company 'Rododendro,' in which Grillo placed his wife, Alì Maria Carmela. To be honest, I don't remember what business that company was involved in. I can only say that it was Grillo who asked me to set it up" (CD, 22 December 1992, no. 145, p. 7). As emerged in an earlier investigation of corruption, it is common that "political career and economic activities, particularly those rendered more 'profitable' precisely through control of public power, become intertwined. . . . Such positions not only allow the rounding out of earnings coming from political activity but also act as a counterweight to the swings of fortune that occur in elected office" (della Porta 1992:308). Another function of politicians' participation in entrepreneurial activity is to cover up the payment of bribes. The ex-administrative secretary of the Tuscany PSI, Giovanni Signori, arrested for corruption, was manager of five firms and also controlled 90 percent of the majority shareholding in Unione Ltd., the PSI estate agency in Tuscany, from which more than twenty national companies operating in the region had purchased "services of representation" (*Il Manifesto* 25 May 1984, p. 4).[19]

In a democratic system, every blurring of the line of demarcation between political and economic power is a worrying sign. Integration between actors in politics and in the market nullifies reciprocal control, producing an overlap of roles and interests that renders corruption ambiguous, and therefore more threatening. If the identity of corrupter and corrupted coincide, in fact, it is no longer possible to speak of an illegal exchange, such as the payment of bribes, nor will there be any identifiable signs of corruption, although the nature of the act itself remains unchanged. In addition, a politician participating in business can present each act aimed at personal enrichment as the pursuit of a "general interest", redefined to suit the occasion.

4. THE "MORAL COSTS" FOR THE CORRUPTER

The initial impulse for the *mani pulite* investigation came from ILVA, a small cleaning firm belonging to Luca Magni. Rather than pay a bribe of 7 million lira to Mario Chiesa, president of the Pio Albergo Trivulzio, the municipally run old people's home in Milan, Magni notified the magistracy. However, there is no sign of moral indignation or civic revolt in this seemingly "heroic" deed. Magni himself stated the economic reasons behind his decision: "I found myself in a particularly bad moment. The firm was going through a difficult period and besides my sister was unwell. . . . It was an economic problem for me. Ten percent was too much" given that "Chiesa wanted the money immediately, as soon as the contract was awarded, while many months passed before we were paid" (*Il Mondo*, 13–20 July 1992, p. 42). Thus dissatisfaction with the "price" of the exchange, caused by a temporary problem of liquidity, was the decisive motivation to exit from the corrupt game: "I tried to justify the delay of the bribe payment to Chiesa, explaining my problems, but he did not react" (*Panorama*, 19 July 1992, p. 48).

As we observed in Chapter 1, however, the decision to pay or not a bribe (or to inform or otherwise the authorities)—besides the economic (dis)advantage that may be obtained—also depends on the entrepreneur's "moral propensity" to illegal behavior. The condition of illegality may cause in fact a kind of "emotional suffering," which can influence that choice, even considering it as the result of rational calculation. To explain his final rebellion, an entrepreneur from Bari who had paid bribes for fifteen years declared: "I couldn't look at myself in the mirror any more. I felt completely shitty. It seemed wrong, humiliating" (*L'Espresso*, 18 November 1984, p. 34). When examining corruption choices, therefore, we have to consider the associated "moral cost," that is, that loss of utility connected to the very illegality of the act, reflecting both the degree of "civic spirit" among the public functionaries and the propensity of citizens and entrepreneurs to illegal behavior.

Moreover, the degree of aversion to corruption can change with time following variations in the diffusion of illegal practices. Such a process of informal "codification" of corrupt practices has an intrinsic solidity. In Italy the corruption market has developed its particular "rules," certainly capable of guaranteeing stability, continuity, and even a certain air of "legitimacy" to illicit and socially deplored activities (see Chapter 2 and Chapter 9). The simple expectation that corruption is inevitable or that others might profit from it provides then a powerful incentive for seeking privileged channels. Remo Marinelli, an entrepreneur, described his involvement in the market thus: "I've been paying and paying since I began to work. For 13 or 14 years now if I want a contract from the Province . . . I have to come up with millions and millions. . . . My colleagues also told me that that was the way things worked, that everyone did it and at bottom there was nothing strange about it" (*L'Espresso*, 18 November 1984, p. 41). Another entrepreneur, Paolo Pizzarotti, accounted for the 400–500 million he paid annually to the national administrative secretaries of the PSI and DC in similar terms: "It was a sort of custom. There wasn't any precise reason. Having heard that someone else did it, I decided to follow the same procedure because I would get an advantage in terms of the financing of the works and more generally. . . . Since that was the system, more or less, I preferred to be part of the system" (*Panorama*, 14 February 1993, p. 61).

In addition, according to the entrepreneur Vincenzo Lodigiani, the moral costs of breaking the law are attenuated by the "ethic of responsibility an entrepreneur has toward his firm and employees" (*L'Espresso*, 21 June 1992, p. 31). Olivetti's general manager Carlo De Benedetti justified having paid bribes in similar terms: "On some occasions I resigned myself to giving bribes, but only when it was necessary for the company's survival, in the interests of the thousands of employees and shareholders to whom I felt I owed paramount responsibility" (*La Repubblica*, 18 May 1993, p. 5). When a conflict arises, individual responsibility toward the organization-firm (whose economic success must be sought) takes precedence over that toward the organization-state (which demands respect for its norms). Thus, a manager of the Icomec firm stated: "Although aware that it was unorthodox, I decided to accede to bribery demands because I was responsible for keeping a firm with a thousand employees going and it was clear that without paying there would be no work. I heard from other firms that it was necessary to accept the practice and had no alternative" (PRIM:15).

The organization of larger firms, by fragmenting individual responsibilities within an articulated decision-making process, may facilitate the removal of moral barriers in the name of its "superior interests," just as politicians have on occasion evoked "superior party interests." As Rose Ackerman notices: "A firm's internal organization may reflect the desire to facilitate low-level corruption. Executives may delegate responsibility and avoid close monitoring in order to create an environment hospitable to corruption" (1978:191).[20] Moreover, mechanisms exist inside firms for a progressive and "painless " inclusion in the "rituals" and informal conventions of corruption. Enso Papi recalled that, when he was nominated manager of Cogefar, a company controlled by FIAT, he was given "a notebook recording the various 'obligations' and the dates they should be paid. A list of names and sums; an inheritance that had to be respected to the letter. *Illegality was so regularized that I didn't feel I was committing a criminal act*" (*Panorama*, 16 April 1994, p. 86, emphasis added). Thus each manager ends up considering his individual contribution to the complex operation underlying an act of corruption—establishing contacts with politicians, negotiating the sums to be paid, creating hidden funds from which the money can be drawn and effecting payment—as part of a decision-making process that lies outside his personal responsibility. Similarly, skills and knowledge in corruption practices are passed on, in numerous family-run businesses, directly from father to son: "I paid my first bribe in 1966, when I inherited this enterprise from my daddy. We paid for forty-five years, since when the Republican Army was founded" stated an entrepreneur who had been arrested regarding supplies to the army (*La Repubblica*, 25 October 1995, p. 9).

Moreover, there is a generally tolerant (or at least not hostile) attitude within the work environment to illegal actions whose aim is the success of the firm. Like other "white-collar crimes," corruption is an illegal act closely connected to activities that are both legal and considered socially positive (Solivetti 1987:71).[21] This is all the more true when the firms involved in corruption—as often happened in the Italian case—were specialized in satisfying public demand, thus reducing their opportunities of working in the private sector. The particular location of their plant, the specific skills they had developed in a learning-by-doing fashion, or the discrete investments that are made at the behest of the public customer rendered them particularly susceptible to bribery demands (Williamson 1989:143).[22] One of the Pio Albergo Trivulzio's contractors stated: "Giving these people money wasn't a result of free choice. Having equipped the firm with sophisticated and expensive machinery and taken on a large number of highly specialized employees, the firm's survival depends on getting contracts" (TM:30).

In a society that presents widespread opportunities for gain in unproductive fields (such as rent-seeking in corruption activities), it can be expected that many entrepreneurs will converge on those areas where the structure of remuneration is most favorable (Baumol 1990:894). The *allocation of talent* will then favor parasitic activities: the more talented and highly educated (with more valuable human capital) will be more inclined to engage in corruption activities than in productive works, with adverse effects on the country's opportunities for economic growth (Murphy, Shleifer, and Vishny 1991). Risk-taking has been traditionally presented as the most specific of entrepreneurial resources (Knight 1921): in the presence of favorable opportunities for illegal gain, a greater propensity to sustain the risks of illegality will also favor the economic success of entrepreneurs. This factor may cause an adverse selection of competing firms, which reduces the average level of "moral costs" in the entrepreneurial class and provides incentives for an even wider recourse to corrupt exchanges.

5. THE ADVERSE-SELECTION OF FIRMS

Preferential deployment of resources in rent-seeking activities rather than in economic investment may lead to a progressive loss of efficiency of firms specialized in supplying public demand.[23] Public contracting procedures should tend to reward firms with lower costs, which can therefore bid lower than their rivals. On the other hand, when decisions are discretionary or privileged information may influence them, other "informal" criteria may underlie the selection of a firm. As we have seen, friendship, kin relations, blackmailing power, or common political orientation often become determining factors in the choice of public agents, thus reducing the likelihood of being cheated in corrupt exchange. Selection can also be simply on the basis of the corruptor's willingness to pay: in that case the real competition (between bribe offers) takes place in the hidden market of corruption.[24] Whatever the case, not only will productive efficiency—the ability to perform the task requested better, more quickly, and with a lower outlay of productive factors—be rewarded but also the capacity to build relationships of friendship and trust with corrupt agents, for example, or an absence of moral scruples.

Through corruption a firm can defeat competitors independently of its technical skills. As a director of ENEL, Valerio Bitetto, recalled concerning a tender to furnish turbines for its power stations: "Ansaldo [Nuovo Pignone] began to propose innovative technology, more powerful turbines that produced less pollution. . . . In the name and on behalf of FIAT Avio, Engineer Bertini met with me and pointed out that they were willing to make a contribution to the party system (DC and PSI) on condition that the Ministries for Industry and the Environment maintained their present technological position" (*L'Espresso*, 2 May 93, p. 60). In exchange for 2.5 billion the technologically more advanced proposal was not taken into consideration. The ability to offer higher quality products at lower cost is therefore but one (and often not even the most important) of the factors that increase the probability of winning a public contracting procedure in a system where corruption dominates. On the contrary, more efficient firms may be unsuccessful precisely because their competitors, marginalized in the private market, are willing to pay higher bribes in order to maintain a share of the public sector market, which has become vital for their survival. As alternative sources of profit arise in the private sector (or abroad), some of the most productive firms will then exit from the public sector and be replaced by less efficient ones.[25] In any case, given that the return on investment in privileged contacts with politicians frequently turns out to be greater than in the research and development of new technology, the incentive to follow the latter course diminishes for every firm in the public sector: "Almost all industrialists only think about making money, so if it's easier to do so in the lobbies of important hotels in Rome and ministry offices than by racking one's brains to better satisfy the requirements of customers and reduce production costs, it's natural that they prefer the hotel lobbies to their factories" (Rossi 1993:98).

The potential exclusion of most efficient (or most law-abiding) firms from the public sector,[26] and the smaller advantage of investment in research and development, with progressive loss of competitiveness, have an important consequence: firms that work regularly with the public administration may come to form a *separate, productively inefficient clique*. Further, in a system where better opportunities for gain are offered by influence activities on the political and bureaucratic power, it can be expected that the energy and inventiveness of economic operators will concentrate on the field of corrupt practices (Baumol 1990:893).[27] Unscrupulousness and skills in influencing public spending power will be rewarded, rather than entrepreneurial ability and innovation, attracting to economic activities individuals who possess similar qualities. As a further example, a company (COPIM) was formed by an entrepreneur and a mediator who, thanks to his political connections, was in a position to guarantee the awarding of a 2 billion lira tender for the San Carlo Theatre in Naples. In other words, the pair put into the firm the different kinds of "capital" they possessed: "I put my technical skills into the COPIM, the broker his political connections" (TN:13).

In a corrupt system, the *isolation of the public market*, surrounded by impalpable "entry barriers," *tends to increase over time*. First, an intentional intervention by the corrupt agent is possible, who will prefer reliable and "tested" partners, consequently influencing public decisions. Since the efficiency of firms that work prevalently in the public sector tends to deteriorate, he will therefore raise increasingly robust barriers to the entry of outside firms.[28] Furthermore, protected firms are compelled to maintain over time corrupt relations with the public administration precisely because their greater inefficiency would condemn them to a marginal role in the private market. Bribery requires also a specific-assets investment in the creation of hidden channels of communication, learning, and exchange with the most influential public decision-makers. This capital of information, personal connections and trust, shared by the corrupted and corrupters, reduces the transaction costs involved in new contacts. An interruption of these relations would thus imply a loss for both: "Faceless contracting is thereby supplanted by contracting in which the pairwise identity of the parties matters. Not only is would the supplier be unable to realize equivalent value were the specialized assets to be redeployed to other uses, but the buyer would have to induce potential suppliers to make similar specialized investments were he to seek least-cost supply from an outsider" (Williamson 1989:145).[29] As the Milan magistracy noted: "The illicit channels for obtaining and managing public tenders through corruption constitute a sort of 'commercial start-up' for the company and its individual administrators. If the company fails, that start-up is nullified. But for the individual administrators it represents a residual value that they seek to safeguard at all costs in the hope of recycling themselves in the sector" (PRIM:45). We may add that possession of compromising information concerning a politician's earlier illegal activities can be used by entrepreneurs to obtain work through blackmail. In fact, firms favored for similar reasons were in possession of neither the technical capacity nor the finances required to fulfill the contract. The president of the Padua Savings Bank, for example, informed magistrates:

> [T]he commune had decided on the concession system for the construction of the new Court of Justice partly, perhaps primarily, in order to favor GE.CO.FER, the firm belonging to the Ferraro brothers (from Padua), which was on the point of going bankrupt. In the event of their not being 'rescued' they threatened to "publicly accuse those local politicians for whom they had (up to then and over a long period) done numerous favors." The witness specified that "at the time GE.CO.FER was already in such serious financial difficulties as to be unable to carry out the work given them," a fact "well known in Paduan political circles." (CD, 4 September 92, no. 96, p. 3)

Such technical and financial inefficiencies caused a great deal of expense to the public administration—in terms of delays and increased cost—but provided corrupt politicians with ulterior opportunities for raising income. Paying a bribe, another firm entered the consortium holding the concession (ibidem).

To conclude, less efficient firms—often already specialized in supplying the public market—are more likely to acquiesce to the demands of corrupt functionaries, having less remunerative alternatives in the private sector. Of course, this process tends to reduce their bargaining power in the corruption agreements and makes them even more vulnerable to extortion. Indeed, time after time exiting from the public sector and recourse to the private-sector market may become virtually impossible. This is the case described by the entrepreneur Fabrizio Garampelli:

> I took over the business from my father, who had always, and almost exclusively, worked with public bodies . . . so that was the world of work I inherited. I would have liked to change, to escape a certain kind of logic. But it wasn't easy, and still isn't today. *Having to stay in the ambit of public works, therefore, I couldn't lose my "certificate of trustworthiness" by refusing to pay, refusing the request, because without it I wouldn't have worked anymore. Within six months I would have gone out of business.* (recording of "Un giorno in Pretura," RAI 3, 22 February 93, emphasis added)

As they become less competitive, firms depend even more on political rents to cover their growing inefficiency and obtain substantial income. Entrepreneurs themselves are clearly aware of this, as emerges in a confidential letter addressed to the president of the Builders' Association, confiscated during the *mani pulite* investigation, confirms:

> A number of battles need to be won, the first of which is to enter into one or another grouping [of firms]. Today, however, it is not enough to have a healthy firm that works well, has an efficient operational structure, possesses commercial ability and notable power of market penetration. Infamously, "political clout" [is also required], allied to a "specific" disposable income. . . . Associations of firms no longer aim to lower costs by arduously seeking the best technical solutions but to increase their gains by the methods of which we are all aware. (TM:47–9).

In this perspective, the arbitrariness and opacity of public decision-making tend to grow over time because corrupt public agents are interested in maintaining privileged relations with the firms that bribe them. The diffusion of corruption adds impulse to this process of "adverse selection," the end results of which are delays in completion (connected with the difficulties less efficient firms have in respecting contractual obligations); inflated final costs; poor quality work; more frequent noncompletion or faulty completion of work that, in order to be remedied, can create further opportunities for corruption.

6.   THE ELEVATION OF COSTS

The incentive for firms to conscientiously fulfill their contractual obligations with the state is undermined by corruption. The latter therefore aggravates problems that can appear even in the absence of hidden agreements. Often, in fact, the public administration assumes de facto all contractual risks without, however, being able to effectively control the operations of the firm executing the work. Our research confirmed that an "uncontrollable increase in costs" is produced, "as a result of unreliable planning methods, systematic alterations of the original project during the course of work, and automatic revision of prices" (Mastragostino 1993:9). The contractor, therefore, has no incentive to perform efficiently, nor to present credible estimates at the tendering stage.[30]

Numerous cases demonstrate that corruption increases the cost of public works. Both corrupter and corrupted share an interest in having the costs of bribery accredited to the public purse, in order to widen their margin of rent. By the end of the process it is impossible, as the Catania magistrates have observed, to "distinguish between who is leading the dance and who following: the illegal demands of functionaries may have led suppliers to augment prices further while the former, accustomed to receiving a percentage compensation, not only had no interest in enforcing the official price list but if anything had quite the opposite interest" (ACA:60–61). Procedural obstacles are removed through discretionary awarding of contracts, continual revision of prices, and modification of the services contracted. Corruption may even produce an alteration of the public demand, the latter being formulated mainly in order to acquire bribes, without any interest in the public utility of goods or services acquired. As the Savona judges remarked, the corrupt activities of the president of the regional government Teardo "had brought about a serious distortion in public activity, since the work to be contracted was chosen with reference not to the technical need, but to an easier collection of bribes" (TRIS:155)[31]

The uncovering of cases of corruption normally coincides with the discovery that the public administration is paying too much for goods and services that not infrequently turn out to be of poor quality. A few examples from the many available will suffice. The contract for the prison of Pontedecimo was awarded to the CODEMI company (in exchange for bribes to prison service heads) despite the fact that the estimated cost was 374 million lira per inmate compared with an average, at the time, of 150 million. The reinforced concrete for the prison was calculated at 500,000 lira per cubic meter compared to a market price of 300,000. Other materials were estimated from 30 to 400 percent higher than the current market prices (*L'Espresso*, 13 March 88, p. 8). The State Audit Court investigation of the prison-building program revealed cases where the final cost was twenty times that originally estimated or in which the works had taken twenty years (*L'Espresso*, 13 March 88, p. 11). Of twenty projects decided in 1972 only four were complete on 31 December 1987. The variation in cost per inmate was extraordinary, ranging from 27 million lire for Bergamo to 320 million for Florence. Years of delay took place simply waiting for the final inspection after the termination of the works (three and one-half years in the case of Salerno). Changes to projects after work was already underway led to buildings already completed being demolished, as happened at Ascoli Piceno. Years have passed with works suspended or deferred: 1,019 days at Ivrea, for example, or 1,135 at Vercelli. In addition, more than 40 percent of the projects for new penal institutions have since been abandoned because it was later discovered that the land for building was not available (CC, 1988, vol. III, p. 28). These examples of extremely overpaid and delayed works significantly overlap with a scandal that, in 1988, revealed a vast bribery ring, the entrepreneurs who were awarded contracts having paid functionaries, local politicians, and government ministers.

Lombardia Informatica (L.I.), the already quoted public capital company, subcontracted works entrusted to it "because it did not possess the technical structures to fulfill the contract. Doing nothing more than this mediation, it simply caused an increase in the costs but in this way public money could be managed 'privately,' without the requisite controls" (Di Pietro 1991:12). In the case of putting prescription information into the regional computer system, for example, L.I. subcontracted five firms who, in their turn, subcontracted to others. This serial subcontracting could take place as many as five times, in each case representing nothing other than an increase in the cost. These firms "were all related in some way to political parties or business associations" (PRLIM:165). When a normal tender for private bids was finally held in 1990, the successful firm's prices were 40 percent below those paid previously (PRLIM:403). The elevation of costs reaches particular extremes where extraordinary public works (frequently connected with real or presumed "emergencies") are concerned. The State Audit Court had the following to say, for example, concerning Italia '90 and the Columbus Celebrations:

> The inflated costs associated with "Italia '90" can be traced to serious lacunae in the planning and control phases. The infrastructures for this event, which swallowed up 27,000 billion lire instead of the 11,000 billion originally

foreseen, turned out to be an extended episode in approximation. . . . The works for the so-called *Colombiane* also revealed inefficiencies in the execution of the projects. The costs rose from 3,000 billion in the original plan to 5,600 billion in 1991, when the works should have been completed. On the contrary, only 60 percent had been finished and a further 3,500 billion has been set aside for the completion of the program (CCL, 1991, vol. I, pp. 629–30).

In comparisons with other countries, the partial information available indicates that there is a certain specificity to the Italian case. Concerning public works in Milan, for which judicial investigation has determined the amount paid in bribes, it has been noted that "[t]he Milanese rail loop is costing 100 billion per kilometer and will take 12 years to complete; for Zurich, 50 billion and 7 years. The *Piccolo Teatro* has so far cost 75 billion and should be ready in 9 years; in the UK, Leeds's new theater cost 28 billion and was completed in 2 years and 3 months. The restructuring of San Siro stadium cost 140 billion, Barcelona Olympic stadium 45 billion. The number 3 line of the Milan metropolitan railway cost 129 billion per kilometer; the Hamburg underground 45 billion" (Barbacetto 1992:70). After the *mani pulite* scandal, public contracts in many sectors were awarded with bids almost 50 percent less than those of the preceding years (*Corriere della Sera*, 21 January 1997, p. 5). Taking such recent values of contracts as normal prices in a competitive system without (or with less) corruption, and calculating that bribes had previously varied from 2 to 20 percent of the contract value, then with corruption the firms derived a political rent from corruption varying from 30 to 48 percent of the contract value. The politicians benefited from this as well but, surprisingly, they took as a bribe the smaller share of the political rent. These data give some idea of the enormous amount of money drawn from the public coffers for the benefit of corrupters and corrupted.

Thus, corruption has a *redistributive effect* in favor of the beneficiaries of covert exchange: "A corrupt system of government services has the distributional disadvantage of benefiting unscrupulous people at the expense of law-abiding citizens who would be willing to purchase the services legally" (Rose Ackerman 1978:8). In other words, corruption generates *distributive inefficiency* by assigning property rights on political rents to actors who violate the criterion of public interest represented by respect for the law, correspondingly increasing the fiscal burden on the collectivity.

7.   THE BRIBER'S DILEMMA

In the Italian context, the best strategy for entrepreneurs has for many years appeared to be a "painless" adaptation to the rules of corruption, thus contributing to the further weakening of restraints on illegal practices. An understandable fear of being marginalized and bankrupted in the event of an *individual* exit—through denunciation or confession—from the corruption game has thus been reinforced among the numerous firms specialized in meeting public sector demand.[32] Leaving the illegal market thus becomes impracticable. The case of one firm, which suffered a sort of tacit reprisal following the confession of the head of the firm in 1990, provides an example: "I think my testifying in this trial has had certain effects. For example, I am not invited for the tenders I ask to participate in and which I think I would have a right to. . . . I am not called although I meet the requirements. They don't even reply" (DPI-19). However, if individually the costs are too high, corruption could effectively be combated by cooperation between a number of entrepreneurs.

In Italy, both before and after the *mani pulite* investigations, there have been few collective efforts to combat corruption, even where bribery has become a sort of *entry fee* for the system of distributing public resources, "controlling and regulating the entry of new associates" (Sapelli 1994:41). As a result of the very diffusion of bribes, the system has begun in fact to show signs of strain. Competition between aspiring corrupters has led to an increase in the bribe-price that has to be paid for entry and permanence in the "system." Alberto Zamorani, a public manager, noted that "in recent times [political sponsorship] was no longer effective. That was the difference. The firms continued to pay but the politicians were unable to help them. A nefarious and unproductive cycle developed in which everybody, big or small, was on an equal footing and one would pay more than the other in order to get ahead. The amount of money available steadily diminished while the number of aspirants for it steadily grew" (*L'Espresso*, 23 August 92, p. 21). In other words, the growing number of corrupt politicians competing to guarantee access to the *restricted circle* of protected firms undermined the real service bribes were paid for: limitation of competition. In such a context an individually rational choice by entrepreneurs leads to an unsatisfactory outcome for all.[33] The space would therefore seem to exist for joint initiatives against corruption. A reciprocal and binding pact of honesty would allow entrepreneurs to obtain an outcome preferable to that of generalized corruption. Why is this result difficult to obtain, even in a context of systemic corruption like in Italy?

In the first place, an unbridgeable gap remains between the collective objective—the elimination of corruption—and calculations of individual convenience, which suggest a more cautious strategy. In a corrupt organization, Banfield remarks, the individual "will have no incentive to invest in its reduction because it [corruption], or rather the absence of it, is a 'public good' the benefits of which will accrue as much to 'free riders' as to others" (1975:598). The entrepreneur Carlo De Benedetti has described vividly the individuals' inability to escape the dilemma. Where the others pay bribes, the best strategy is to pay as well: "Every action should be judged in its historical context. Therefore I want to make it clear that if I found myself in the situation they put me in again, a situation that I did not choose, I would be forced [to pay]." In fact, according to De Benedetti, mistrust concerning the intentions of the other corrupters inhibited individual denunciation: "Nobody would have believed it. . . . And no other entrepreneur would have associated himself with the denunciation. " A collective denunciation, the only way out, was made impossible by the lack of reciprocal confidence among entrepreneurs. Asked by the interviewer whether the big business groups could not have reacted against corruption, De Benedetti replied: "A major force? If there was cohesion, yes. But there never has been. Each group has always looked solely after its own interests and exulted when the others were unsuccessful" (*L'Espresso*, 30 May 1993, pp. 39–40).

If contacts between entrepreneurs are not episodic, then the best strategy may become not to pay bribes, *on condition that others do not pay them.* But this "conditional honesty" strategy would require that the actions of others could be verified, in order to punish eventual defections. This kind of mutual control, however, is all but impossible in the corruption market, where, by definition, exchanges take place secretly.[34] Some kind of institutional mechanism for communication and for guaranteeing reciprocal honesty is thus indispensable. An explicit agreement for overturning the ruinous equilibrium of corruption would appear the way out of the dilemma. According to the description given by a Catania shopkeeper, a situation similar to that described above had developed in that city: "The representatives of the supermarkets were told: it was you who invented the system of bribes to corrupt the commune. Do we want to put an end to it? Everybody agreed that yes, they wanted to put an end to it, because the cost had become too high. Evidently everybody was paying" (FIPE 1992:54). The problem of verifying that no one defects and secretly pays bribes without the others knowing (thus acquiring a valuable competitive advantage) remains unresolved, however. In this way, each shopkeeper could be tempted to resume paying. In the absence of a bond that is *verifiable and effectively binding* the agreement described above may turn out to be precarious.

Joint denunciation to the magistracy represents instead a credible commitment for a verifiable exit from the market for corrupt exchange.[35] An example is the so-called "shopkeepers' revolt," which took place in Ostia. The initial situation was one of an equilibrium of generalized corruption: bribes were required for virtually every public decision. A local shopkeeper stated: "A crescendo of complaints came from the shopkeepers. Everything had to be paid for. We even reconstructed the amount of bribes, from the 500,000 lira for permission to display a neon sign up to the 30 million for a stall on the market" (*Panorama*, 15 December 1992, p. 51). How could this impasse be broken and a credible strategy of reciprocal honesty created? The local Shopkeepers' Association chose to start an antibribery hotline for denunciations of corruption and abuses. This system of coordination proved successful, spreading information concerning reciprocal willingness to denounce corrupt officials. Although not all shopkeepers and entrepreneurs adhered to the initiative, the information received was sufficient to break the wall of silence and increase denunciations to the authorities. A series of arrests of communal assessors, ward councillors, functionaries, and judicial officials followed. The development of a "cooperative" strategy in this case was facilitated by the fact that most of the private parties were not in direct competition with each other, by the small dimensions of the group involved, and by the local context. It is an exception, however.

Besides the lack of mutual trust, a second explanation for the failure of a common strategy against corruption to develop among entrepreneurs also exists, however. The model of corruption as a "dilemma, " leading to outcomes unsatisfactory for corrupters themselves, does not always appear convincing. It presupposes, among other things, that in reality no entry barriers to the corruption market exist; that any entrepreneur who seeks to corrupt a public functionary will be successful in doing so. But, as we showed (in this chapter and in Chapter 2), open access to the market of political protection would be contrary to the interests of both corrupters and corrupted, even if sometimes the functioning of the market is not completely satisfactory. For this reason, as soon as firms perceive an invisible barrier to contacts with a public structure they attempt, if they are still in time, to acquire protection. The above cited Carlo De Benedetti described the attitude of the PSI's administrative secretary in the following terms: "Balzamo claimed that it was extremely difficult for him to overcome the well-known aversion of the PSI and its leader toward me. In short, the absurdity was reached that Balzamo claimed to be doing us a favor by asking for bribes because if it was up to his boss we would not even have been allowed to give the money" (*La Repubblica*, 18 May 1993, p. 4). Where there is exclusion, better occasions to acquire rents emerge for corrupters: a situation of generalized corruption may then be preferable for them to one of shared honesty.[36] We noted, moreover, that there are a number of reasons to believe that the political rents pocketed by protected businesses were extremely high, particularly in relation to public contracting. De Benedetti himself recalled that once Olivetti began paying bribes, the value of its supplies to the Post Office Ministry increased from 2 billion to 202 billion in the single year between 1987 and 1988 (*L'Espresso*, 30 May 1993, p. 32). As the behavior of the hundreds of Italian entrepreneurs implicated in judicial inquiries reveals, moral cost is in any case a relative value, which can be sacrificed for a high enough return, even when this involves payment of bribes.

8. THE CORRUPTION MARKET: CONCLUDING REMARKS

In this chapter, we analyzed the relationship between politics and the market, when both systems are permeated by political corruption. Some observations about the involvement of the private actors in corrupt exchange emerged:

1. The universe of corruption is immersed in a dimension of voluntary exchange. In the great majority of cases, illegal practices are not a simple extortion of private capital by politicians and functionaries. Rather a voluntary exchange takes place in which, *together*, public agents and entrepreneurs appropriate political rents created by public intervention.

2. The foregoing point is confirmed by the fact that corruption is frequently associated with the extensive presence of cartel agreements for dividing up public contracts between firms. Through corruption these cartels can then acquire protection from potential outsiders, thus maintaining levels of profit that would be eroded by real competition.

3. Since they provoke, adhere voluntarily to, or benefit from the payment of bribes, corrupters are at least as responsible as public agents for the consequent violation of the legal rules. Furthermore, corrupt acts of economic managers represent a violation both of general rules posed for the general interest—as for public agents—and of contractual rules safeguarding the interests of stockholders.

4. Corruption induced by the entrepreneurs has serious negative effects not only on the political but also on the economic sphere. These negative effects damage those enterprises that are excluded from the corrupt market, and, more generally, the citizen-taxpayers.

We can observe that the links between entrepreneurs and corrupt politicians are multiple and intense. This seems to demonstrate that corruption does not advantage the poor or the weak. As Wolfinger noticed about the American political machine,

"There is no reason why the advantages of political influence appeal only to the poor. Where the political culture supports expectations that official discretion will be exercised in accordance with political consideration, the constituency for machine politics extends across the socioeconomic spectrums. . . . Certain kinds of business and professional men are more likely to have interests requiring repeated and complicated relations with public agencies, and thus are potentially a stronger constituency than the working classes" (Wolfinger 1973:112).

We have seen that, when corruption is widespread, firms develop an interest in creating organic relations with political patrons, in order to enjoy a general protection in their (legal and illegal) interaction with the state. We distinguished, in fact, different levels of political protection, depending on economic and institutional conditions that favored more or less binding contractual agreements. The logic of political corruption pushes these firms to build up politically heterogeneous cartels, in order to control public sector demand. In a similar context, a system of values may develop that reduce the adversion to participation in illegal action. New moral conventions spread among entrepreneurs justifying corruption on the basis of the necessity of defending the "supreme" value of the survival of the enterprise in a system where "everybody does it." The emergent norms reduce the moral costs of participation in illegal exchanges, since corruption is considered "inevitable." This situation produces negative consequences ranging from technical inefficiencies in the enterprises involved in the system of corruption to the growing costs and bad quality of public services suffered by the citizen-taxpayers. Often if private entrepreneurs agree to pay bribes it is not so much because they are not able to develop those links of mutual trust necessary to resist corrupt politicians, but much more because by paying bribes, they obtain privileged access to property rights in political rents.

Some of the things that facilitate political corruption, as well as that favor the emergence of cartels, are the restricted nature of Italian markets, their lack of openness to international competition, and the stability of power-holding within firms operating in high public demand sectors. The willingness of entrepreneurs to engage in illegality, in fact, increases in line with the importance of public demand for their goods or services. Technological development and alternative private sector applications for productive resources, on the other hand, offset any impulse to collusion with political power (at least as far as extortive demands are concerned).

Market structures *less open to competition* also facilitate the formation of niches of political protection. In Italian medium- and large-scale industry the state and family models of control have prevailed. Effective barriers to the abuse of patrimonial property rights have thus been absent (Barca 1994:183) and the formation of slush funds (from which the money for corruption, among other things, was drawn) has been made easier. The familial nature of property in the leading private economic groups has also encouraged recourse to unmediated forms of personal influence given the weakness of sectoral and category organization among enterprises (Pizzorno 1993:309). Rare and ineffective internal controls and entrenched concentration of property in restricted groups on one side has been mirrored by the permanence in power of the political elite on the other. This has favored the creation of sustained relations of trust between public administrators and entrepreneurs, the foundation of the system of covert transactions whose consummation was guaranteed by the expectation that the process would be repeated indefinitely. It has even been suggested, in this connection, that the Italian entrepreneurial class has suffered from "political anomie": "As in Japan, in fact, the traditional values of deference are entangled with a modernizing radicalization: the orientation is toward *parental homogeneity* and corporatist connivance rather than competitive risk" (Sapelli 1994:84).

In economic systems where *private demand* is of relatively greater importance, on the other hand, entrepreneurs can oppose unwelcome demands for payoffs with fewer consequences. Effective antitrust legislation, such as that of the United States, can also curtail the amount of market resources available for buying the services of public decision-makers: "[C]orruption develops more easily in monopoly situations where the inefficiency of market regulations leads to public regulation and therefore a greater frequency of contact between politicians and entrepreneurs" (Chiesi 1995:129).

In addition, by increasing the probability that those excluded by corruption will take official steps concerning such practices, the opening of markets to *international competition* and an absence of customs barriers check the creation of relations of political protection. Protection from international competition also generates rents, a share of which may be converted into bribes by local entrepreneurs. As Rose Ackerman observes: "A multinational firm is vulnerable to corrupt demands from a country's officials if it is earning 'country-specific' rents that exceed its profits elsewhere" (1996:368). Country-specific rent depends on a country's location in the world market, and the characteristics of its labor force, public regulation, transportation, and raw materials. Countries closer to world markets are under stronger competitive pressure and are less corrupt, since in a country with low country-specific rents an enterprise that pays bribes risks its profits. Ades and Di Tella show a significant negative correlation between the degree of openness of the economy (on the basis of the sum of imports and exports as a share of the GDP) and levels of corruption in over fifty countries. More generally, cross-section and time-series evidence support the hypothesis that the diffusion of corruption is higher in countries with economies dominated by a small number of firms, where antitrust regulations are not effective, or in which domestic firm are protected from foreign competition by political barriers to trade (Ades and Di Tella 1995).[37]

Also the degree of *institutionalization of the enterprises' structure* influences corruption. Anonymous property models with effective external control reduce the possibility to form the extrabudget reserves needed to pay kickbacks. At the same time, the dispersion of property among many shareholders and the turnover of enterprises' managers thwart the possibility to build those long-term trust relationships with politicians that facilitate corrupt exchanges.

NOTES

1.   This position is illustrated by the words of the leader of Forza Italia party, Silvio Berlusconi, when as prime minister he received a communication that he was being investigated for having previously, as an entrepreneur, corrupted public functionaries: "I am the victim of a big injustice, because the facts I'm accused of represent an extortion [on the side of the public officers]. Those who suffer this accusation are victims twice: for having been forced to pay bribes, like hundreds of thousands of entrepreneurs who just wanted to keep on working, and then for the groundlessness of the accusation" (*La Stampa*, 24 November 1994, p. 3).

2.   This is a case of "supply creating demand," which is common to many markets. In the corruption market, however, it has certain distinctive features: first, *public demand* is not defined by the final consumers of the goods or services, but by their political representatives; second, it usually involves illegal acts.

3.   This is, for instance, the case with the Augusta scandals in Belgium. Corruption in this case here related to contracts for the substitution of the Belgian army's military helicopters with heavy aircraft. This choice limited the selection to only three firms: "All three of them were ready to assign 'compensative' contracts to enterprises located in the socialist strongholds in the Vallony" (Bouckaert 1995:41).

4.   A cartel can be distinguished from a tacit agreement because participants meet to communicate and select coordinated strategies. As with any collusive agreement, the group of independent firms involved joins forces to make price or output decisions. They must ensure (through repetition of the "game," selective use of sanctions, etc.) that none of the participants defect from the deal. If so, anyone can become a free-rider, benefiting from the growth of public demand in his market without having to pay a share of the cost of corruption. For an analysis of the economic factors that facilitate or hinder collusion and of the types and extent of horizontal collusion, see Jacquemin and Slade (1989).

5.   The first rule of compensation should reduce the risk of defection, since such payments can be contextual or given in pawn until the awarding of the contract. On the other hand, as Gambetta and Reuter observed, "because of illegality, there is a strong inclination to avoid rules which require 'side-payments' among members that could provide valuable evidence for a prosecutor. More generally, illegal agreements are likely to minimize the number of transactions necessary for their effective execution" (1995:118).

6.   Robinson (1985) shows that there is no cartel equilibrium if there is a lower-bids contracting procedure with *secret* offers, while *open* bids permit defection to be immediately discovered and punished, thus increasing the stability of the cartel. Jones and Menezes (1995) examine the opportunity of corruption offered by first-price sealed-bid auctions; oral and second-price sealed-bid auctions are demonstrated to be corruption proof.

7.   According to the theory of repeated games, in a similar context cooperation can emerge when there are frequent interactions between a limited number of individuals, and the discount rate of future payments and the probability of ending the relation are low enough (Axelrod 1984; Taylor 1987).

8.   According to the judicial inquiries, the collusive sharing of public con-

tracts in exchange for bribes to public administrators had become a rule in Grenoble, involving groups of companies as Buygues Cge, Lionnaise des Aux, Alcatel (*La Repubblica*, 27 January 1995, p. 18). Examples of informal market-sharing arrangements between corrupt firms have been often observed even in the United States, such as in the awarding of engineering contracts in Maryland (Amick 1976:43). Between 1977 and 1982, the U.S. Department of Justice filed more than two hundred indictments against highway contractors on charges of collusion: incentives to collusion in fact are stronger when through bidding activities there are opportunities to increase the cartel's profits by passing misinformation to the public purchaser (Feinstein, Block, and Nold 1985).

9.   In general, the effects of restriction on competition are higher prices, smaller firms, and diminished firm efficiency, the latter having no incentive to improve productive techniques in order to lower costs since existing customers are allocated (Reuter 1987:7). In each dimension, the effect is likely to be greater for a cartel specialized in satisfying the demand of public institutions, which are typically more careless about quality and price than private consumers. Victims of cartels in public auctions are then citizen-taxpayers, low-quality products being purchased for higher prices by the state, and potential competitors, since entry into the public market becomes virtually impossible.

10.   The lower the competition in either the political or economic arena (between a number of corrupt politicians or corrupting enterprises), the more robust would be collusive agreement in the other. In fact, a corrupt politician in search of clients may persuade an entrepreneur to defect from the cartel in exchange for a special advantage. Similarly, a particularly enterprising entrepreneur might be able to convince a politician not to divide bribes with others, thus obtaining exclusive protection. This is not to suggest that the presence of a cartel on one side of the market automatically brings it about on the other also, but simply that when a "bilateral monopoly" is realized, the probability that the resulting equilibrium is stable increases.

11.   For the distinction between *transactional* and *extorsive* corruption, which entails some form of compulsion, usually to avoid a harm or an arbitrary cost being inflicted on the donor by the public agent, see Alatas (1990). On the difference between economic transactions and interactions brought about by coercion (extortion and crime), see Liebermann and Syrquin (1983).

12.   Hall (1996), in a study on private taxi service in Hong Kong, explains how police officers elaborated a complex but efficient system to protect the circulation of taxi-drivers, who systematically corrupted them: in order to distinguish those they protected from the others, special badges were provided to those who paid the bribes. The form and color of these badges changed every week, with every payment.

13.   If this does not happen, those entrepreneurs who pay the bribes in order to be protected from their competitors feel betrayed, and therefore the risks of denunciation increase. According to a public manager, the entrepreneur Paolo Pizzarotti "told me of the system of ANAS, that it did not offer warranty. He complained that the administrative secretaries of the political parties had a long queue [of entrepreneurs ready to pay a bribe] in front of their doors, and they said yes to

any enterprise whatsoever, wherever it came from, and whatever contracts it was interested in" (*Panorama*, 18 October 1992, p. 49).

14.   With this particular form of payment, the public agent who does not comply with the corrupt agreement, may be immediately punished by the corrupter, who can stop the payments. The new general director of the FS, Lorenzo Necci, was arrested in 1996. He was accused of secretly receiving 20 million lira per month from the financier-middleman Francesco Pacini Battaglia (*La Repubblica*, 21 September 1996, p. 1).

15.   In the case of these publicly financed companies, the loosening of the restraints connected with public procedures determines a shift of corruption from the *public* to the *private* sphere, rendering the gathering of proof concerning illegal activities more difficult because their management is characterized by wide discretion. In addition, the status of the managers of this kind of company as "public officials" is juridically uncertain, thus placing in doubt whether they can be pursued for corruption and extortion. It has been noted that "L.I. was turned into a purchasing department, a *brokerage center*, by the regional leadership, absolving the regional administration from the necessity of public tendering and making the activities of administrators increasingly opaque and unfathomable" (PRLIM, pp. 374–75).

16.   On occasion, the symbiosis between political organization and firm is such that the party leaders can act as if they were proprietors. In such cases they exercise a sort of *patrimonial power* that, according to Weber, considers public power and economic rights as private assets (Weber [1922] 1981:232).

17.   These coalitions of politicians-entrepreneurs, observed in many countries, are often organized from above. For instance, according to the "company-based" election campaign invented by the Japanese political leader Tanaka during the election of 1974, firms were assigned a candidate of the Liberal party whom they had to support (Reed 1996).

18.   Agostino Licandro, ex-mayor of Reggio Calabria, confessed that he received regular financing from the Lodigiani firm precisely because he had brilliant career prospects. One of the firm's managers "was certain he was making a good investment because they had told him I was a politician who was moving up, who had an assured future. But obviously Lodigiani would never have given me money had they not already had interests in Reggio. . . . I could rise and become powerful thanks to their money as well, and they reckoned I would be grateful" (Licandro and Varano 1993:83–84).

19.   A similar situation has been observed in France, where consulting societies, linked to the Socialist party, collected bribes paid under the form of honoraria for nonexistent services (Mény 1992:256–61). See also Chapter 3.

20.   In general, white-collar crimes often have a collusive nature, and require the participation of a number of actors, playing different roles. Under this aspect, they are similar to organized crime (Sutherland 1983).

21.   According to Sutherland (1983), the ideal businessman, like the professional thief, often engages in crimes and violations that are not stigmatized in his peer group. Unlike the professional thief, however, the businessman defines himself as an "honest man." On those aspects of firm organization favoring lawbreak-

ing on the part of businessmen and other "white-collars" crimes, see Leonard and Weber (1978).

22. In these cases the enterprises have carried out specific-assets investments that make pursuing the contractual relation with the public entities convenient. As Williamson observes: "(1) asset specificity refers to durable investments that are undertaken in support of particular transactions. . . . (2) the specific identity of the parties to a transaction plainly matters in these circumstances, which is to say that continuity of the relationship is valued, whence (3) contractual and organizational safeguards arise in support of transactions of this kind" (Williamson 1985:55). In this perspective, paying bribes may be conceived as a particular—illegal—contract of protection between the corrupter and the corrupted, that sustain the—legal—contract between the corrupter and the public entity.

23. Therefore, corruption can be a source of *dynamic inefficiency* (Majone 1988), since the allocation of resources to networking with politicians rather than to productive investment undermines the potential for economic development of a country. This process imposes significant social costs even in the long term.

24. The allocative equivalence between a lower bid auction and corruption has been asserted by Beck and Maher (1986), since the lower cost firm can also offer the higher bribe. This result no longer holds when the corrupt official's choice is determined by considerations other than the amount of the bribe (Lien 1990), or when the moral costs of corrupters differ (Alam 1990). Furthermore, in the real world, information concerning other firms' bribe offers is not easy to achieve, since its diffusion increases the risks of corruption, and consequently more efficient firms are not certain to win the "corruption auction."

25. A possible limitation to this process has been described by Magatti (1996): when firms operate—through corruption—both in the private and in the public sector, they may use the additional rents derived from bribery to acquire a competitive advantage on their competitors in the private market. Even in this case, however, political rents introduce heavy distortions in the market process, since the additional resources to invest are not derived from the satisfaction of consumers' demand, while productive investments become comparatively less profit-bearing.

26. Thus the "harm suffered by entrepreneurs who refused to accept the rule of bribery and have therefore been excluded from public tendering" (TRIS:434) must be considered a consequence of corruption, as well as the increased burden on the public budget.

27. Mauro's (1995) cross-country analysis provides empirical evidence that corruption lowers investment and economic growth with considerable intensity.

28. In particular, the complexity of Italian bureaucratic procedures and the low planning competence of the public administration lengthened completion times for public works, legitimating the use of arbitrary decisions in the awarding of contracts (Vannucci 1997c).

29. Since this capital would be lost if the relationship were to be interrupted, continuity of the corrupt transaction in time acquires an economic value. The importance of those networks of power able to sanction the exchange increases accordingly (Williamson 1991:241).

30. The purchasing administrator cannot know with precision either the commitment effectively made by the contractor to the work or the extent of difficulties

he may have encountered. When the public structure offers absolute guarantees against eventual cost increases, the latter will be encouraged to put in little effort, attributing the higher cost to circumstances beyond his control (Balassone 1991:662). Controls on carrying out the work are in any case weakened by political collusion, while for the firms involved increasing the cost and prolonging the work indefinitely offer the best possibility of recovering the outlay in bribes or for widening their profit margin.

31. The preliminary findings of the Ministry of Public Works Commission on Uncompleted Works provide an astonishing survey of poor execution of public contracts. Among other cases: a 450 billion lire industrial estate in Lamezia Terme, which has never been used; a hospital in Catania under construction since 1962 and in 1991 not yet opened (maintenance costs alone amounting to 40 billion lira); a viaduct left unfinished in Val di Sangro because the two ends did not meet; a port in construction for twenty years at Sibari at a cost of 121 billion lire; an ENEL power station at Gioia Tauro begun in 1975 at an estimated cost of 75 billion lira, which has so far cost 1,000 billion lira; a 2 billion lira Olympic swimming pool in Nuoro, soon abandoned as impracticable (*Il Mondo*, 2–9 December 91, p. 19).

32. On the importance of similar "countervailing actions" against corruption—comparable to Hirschman's (1970) voice and exit options—see Alam (1995).

33. In game-theoretical terms this is a "prisoner's dilemma" situation: a divergence occurs between the individually rational choice and the collectively desirable outcome (unobtainable unless individuals stipulate a binding agreement). Each entrepreneur must decide whether or not to pay a bribe. If only one entrepreneur pays, he will obtain a particularly advantageous position. If everybody pays, he will avoid being excluded completely from the public sector market. Whatever the others are doing, there is then an incentive to engage in corruption. However, the final result when everybody pays is analogous to that when nobody pays, but each entrepreneur will have to sustain the additional cost of paying bribes (MacRae 1982; Massarenti 1996).

34. Strategies forming an equilibrium require cooperation (the decision not to engage in corruption) conditional on the cooperation of others: be honest as long as others are honest too; when others begin paying bribes, then pay bribes also. Taylor has extended this analysis to situations with more than two actors, demonstrating that "cooperation between a large number of players is less probable than cooperation in a small group." The reason is that conditional cooperation requires that individuals can observe defections. "Clearly, such control becomes progressively more difficult as the dimensions of the group grow" (Taylor 1987:105).

35. Actually, after his overt denunciation of corruption, it seems very implausible that an entrepreneur could be trusted and involved again in corrupt exchanges.

36. Alam observed that "corruption is a contest between two parties: those who gain and others who lose" (1995:432). Generally, protected entrepreneurs gain from corruption, while "others who lose" are out of the game, excluded from the hidden exchanges (or unaware of them): "[C]orruption is a form of agreement among a minority with the aim of appropriating the goods belonging to the majority of the population, considered as the whole of consumers and citizen-electors" (CSPC:3).

37.   With a similar approach, Ades and Di Tella (1997a) find a strong positive correlation between active industrial policy and corruption. As corruption reduces investment, this negative effect must be taken into account when considering the policy initiatives aimed at increasing internal spending on research and development.

8

Politics, the Mafia, and the Corruption Market

On 27 March 1993, a group of magistrates from the Palermo public prosecutor's office headed by chief prosecutor Giancarlo Caselli requested authorization from the Senate of the Republic to proceed against Giulio Andreotti, one of the most powerful politicians in Italy, for association with Mafia activities. Andreotti, a leading Christian Democrat, had been a major political figure since 1946. He had been present in almost every postwar government, holding a variety of ministerial posts (foreign affairs, finance, the budget) and had been prime minister on seven occasions, the first in 1972 and the last between 1989 and 1992. In 1991 he was made a senator for life. According to the magistrates, Andreotti had "participated in the maintenance, reinforcement, and expansion of the Mafia, putting at its disposal the influence and power derived from his position as the leader of a political current as well as the relations he had fostered in the course of his activities" (PP:100). In Italy and elsewhere, subterranean links between the Mafia and certain politicians have frequently been suspected and occasionally brought to light. However, there has been no more striking a case of interaction between politics and organized crime in any Western democracy. Regardless of the final outcome of the criminal prosecution against Andreotti, the investigations of the Palermo public prosecutor's office, aided by the numerous mafiosi who turned state's witness, give an astonishing glimpse into the continuous influence exercised by the Sicilian Mafia—in a complex world of favors, protection, and promises exchanged—on Italian politics in general and the Andreotti current within the Christian Democrats in particular.

Before being murdered by Mafia killers in 1992, the leader of the Andreotti current in Sicily, Salvo Lima, had been mayor of Palermo and a member of the Italian and European parliaments. He and his followers joined Andreotti's current in 1968 and Lima brought with him "his existing, organic relations with some of the most important figures in the Mafia, Stefano Bontate, Gaetano Badalamenti, Antonio and Ignazio Salvo (men of honor of Salemi) among them" (PP:884). According to a number of mafiosi collaborating with the authorities, "Andreotti was precisely the person to whom Lima constantly turned concerning decisions to be taken in Rome involving the interests of Cosa Nostra" (PP:13). The Salvo cousins, Antonino and Ignazio, holders of tax franchises, "were used by leading members of Cosa Nostra for political contacts in Rome" and according to mafioso turned state's witness Tommaso Buscetta had "an even closer relationship with Andreotti than Lima. . . . They called Andreotti 'the uncle'" (PP:112, 114). Members of the Mafia who headed an economic empire grounded in tax collection contracts in Sicily, the Salvos were, according to the Christian Democrat Mario Fasino, "an economic and political

217

presence with the power to influence between half and two-thirds of the entire Chris-
tian Democrat representation on the regional council. . . . For a long time they pro-
vided crucial support for the electoral success and expansion of Andreotti's group in
Sicily" (PP, p.163). Mafia boss Giovanni Brusca recalled: "[D]uring the 'Mafia
wars' Nino Salvo told me to tell Totò Riina [another leading Mafia boss] that
Andreotti wanted us to stay calm and not kill too many people, otherwise he would
be forced to intervene with special laws. . . . Riina replied that Andreotti should be
advised that we had been at his disposal for votes and other matters, now he should
let us work in peace. We voted DC on the advice of Lima and Andreotti" (La Repub-
blica, 15 April 1997, p. 19).

With the most powerful party current in the Christian Democrat stronghold of
Sicily behind Andreotti, an alliance with him was decisive for being elected national
secretary of the party. Thus Andreotti had immense bargaining power when it came
to the division of offices at the political-institutional level, as the various govern-
mental positions he held demonstrate. The Mafia obtained a twofold advantage from
this exchange: on the one hand, an authoritative political figure who could be turned
to for specific interventions (particularly in relation to the judiciary); on the other,
access to an articulated political structure (the Andreotti current within the DC)
that could "satisfy the many-sided interests of the Mafia in political and adminis-
trative life" (PP:884). Sicilian political life was heavily conditioned by the "men of
honor." This was the case, for example, in the political ascent of Salvo Lima, "decided
by Cosa Nostra, with public meetings of politicians and 'men of honor' in Mon-
reale. . . . Already mayor of Palermo, Salvo Lima was personally accompanied to
these meetings by the most noted and authoritative members of the Mafia" (PP:829).
The overlap between politics and organized crime was such that, as Tommaso
Buscetta commented, "[T]here were internal wrangles within the DC and each boss
of a district [a territorial subdivision of Cosa Nostra] participated in the commission
on behalf of his political 'vassal,' saying 'let's kill one of those and spare one of these.'
The conflicts within the commission of Cosa Nostra exactly mirrored the political
divisions within the DC" (PP:115).

On a number of occasions it is believed that Andreotti intervened in person to
promote and favor the success of Mafia-backed individuals within his own current.
All the leading members of the Andreotti current in the Enna province were arrested
between 1992 and 1993, the "entire current [being] run by men of honor or person-
alities linked to local Mafia families" (PP:887). Another member of the DC testified
that these men "made no mystery of the fact that they took no notice of the advice or
decisions of the party's provincial organs, having the unconditional backing of the
Right Hon. Salvo Lima and the leadership of the Andreotti current" (PP:889). Dur-
ing the 1991 regional elections in the province of Trapani, Andreotti participated, in
the role of prime minister, in the closing election rally of Giuseppe Gianmarinaro, a
local member of his current. Gianmarinaro had been accused of serious crimes on a
number of occasions and the local police "had made enquiries into his notorious con-
nection with members of the Mafia, proposed preventive measures against him, and
refused him a firearms license for these reasons" (PP:891). He was elected on a mas-
sive vote (more than 46 percent of the votes cast for his party), one reason—accord-
ing to Rosario Spataro, a mafioso *turned state's witness—being that "in the course*
of his political career he had always carried on his activities on behalf of Cosa Nos-

tra . . . , nor could he have done otherwise since he owed his office to the electoral support of Cosa Nostra" (PP:894). The leading member of Andreotti's current in Catania was Antonino Drago, former mayor of the city and an ex-parliamentary deputy who was eventually arrested for taking bribes on public contracts. Drago was publicly slapped in 1987 by Mafia boss Agatino Ferlito for minimizing the role of Cosa Nostra in his election. The local leader of the Andreotti current in Caltanisetta, Raimondo Maira, "had been indicated by the Caltanisetta Mafia as Cosa Nostra's candidate as early as the 1991 regional elections" (PP:897).

A number of Mafia state's witnesses have claimed that Andreotti participated in three meetings of the Cosa Nostra leadership. The first two seem to have taken place between 1979 and 1980 when Piersanti Mattarella, the president of the Sicily region, was murdered by the Mafia, which was opposed to his policy of reconstruction, thus throwing the established relationship between the Mafia and the DC into crisis. According to another Mafia collaborator with justice, Marino Mannoia, Andreotti came to the second meeting seeking "clarifications on the murder of Mattarella. Bontate (the Mafia boss, Stefano) told him: 'We're in charge in Sicily, and unless you want the whole of the DC canceled out you do as we say'" (PP:737). The third encounter also took place in a moment of difficulty, following the opening of the "supertrial" of Cosa Nostra's leaders in 1987. The bosses were unhappy over the DC's passivity in the face of approval of a law blocking the release of imprisoned Mafia members: "Only Andreotti, their most important political referent, could give explanations and renegotiate the relationship with Cosa Nostra, taking on future obligations and offering guarantees" (PP:758). Baldassare di Maggio, collaborating with the authorities, has claimed that on meeting Andreotti the Mafia boss Salvatore (Totò) Riina (a fugitive from justice at the time) greeted him with a ritual kiss on the cheeks, "demonstrating that Cosa Nostra was subaltern to no one, not even this man, the symbol and incarnation of power, who had come from Rome especially to reaffirm that he 'was always at the organization's disposal'" (PP:767–68).

The leadership of Cosa Nostra counted on Andreotti's relationship with Corrado Carnevale, president of the 1st Section of the Court of Cassation and famous for setting free many dangerous Mafia figures by annulling their sentences, to overturn the guilty sentences at the supertrial. Collaborator with justice Salvatore Cancemi stated that "the Salvo cousins, Salvo Lima, Andreotti, and Corrado Carnevale all knew each other and had close ties. They were the right circle to fix the supertrial in the Court of Cassation" (La Repubblica, 14 March 1997, p. 25). According to fellow collaborator Gaspare Mutolo, "everything was quiet because Cosa Nostra had a mathematical certainty that the supertrial would end favorably. But this favorable prospect suddenly reversed, the first inklings of it coming in November 1991." The guilty sentences passed on the Mafia bosses were confirmed in January 1992 after a college of the Court of Cassation that could not be "maneuvered" by Carnevale was unexpectedly nominated to hear the case. The Mafia boss Totò Riina is supposed to have commented: "Even that sod Lima has double-crossed us" (La Repubblica, 22 October 1992, p. 3). The murder of Salvo Lima on 12 March 1992 and the later killing of Ignazio Salvo marked the beginnings of the Mafia's reprisals, striking at "the symbol of the political grouping that had used Cosa Nostra and failed to deliver on its promises. . . . The murder was both a punishment for Andreotti (since it was very damaging politically) and a warning concerning his future actions" (DAP:32).

Claudio Martelli, a minister in Andreotti's government at the time, has stated that following Lima's murder Andreotti "was scared, either because he did not understand or because he did" (PP:786–87).

As is evident from this reconstruction of the Andreotti case, when trying to understand the role of the Mafia in the corruption market it is important to consider not simply the local political situation in Sicily or another regions of southern Italy but the whole national political scene. Also the report of the Parliamentary Anti-Mafia Committee[1] on relationships between Cosa Nostra and politics, of April 1993, made the following assessment:

> Consideration of Mafia connections should not focus only on the "lower branches" of politics. It is unthinkable that the vast phenomenon of collusion with the Mafia in communities of the South could have developed as it has without some sort of participation of political actors at a higher level. This collusion tends to spread beyond local circles because Mafia heads, who control votes and direct them toward local politicians, are also willing to support regional and national candidates, who in turn are linked to local politicians by party loyalties or, more often, faction or group loyalties. (CPMF:2)

Many illuminating revelations have recently emerged as a result of judicial investigations into organized crime and corruption in southern Italy, investigations that have relied on the testimony of more than three hundred collaborators with justice.

In this chapter we analyze the corruption market of southern Italy, addressing several questions: Have the investigations into political corruption revealed—as many southern politicians would like to think—that "it's the same all over the world" (*tutto il mondo è paese*)? Or have the investigations instead established that substantial differences still distinguish the regions of Italy? Do politicians become corrupted in the same way in Milan as in Palermo? Or do the characteristics of political corruption vary according to the relationships existing between the political class and organized crime? The evidence that we present below indicates that the traditional divide separating (at least) two Italies has been reflected in the development of (at least) two kinds of *corruption markets*. Whereas in the North, in fact, parties and other political subjects seem to have exerted a certain degree of control over hidden exchange and over the illicit gains that flowed from it, in the South the parties have had to share power and money with an increasingly prominent actor: large-scale organized crime. The meeting ground between politicians and *mafiosi* may be visualized as a hidden market within which the operators trade many different commodities: protection, public measures, classified information, use of violence, and intimidation. In fact, according to the detailed reconstruction of the magistrates, in the *Mezzogiorno* (as the South of Italy is known) the Mafia, the Camorra, the 'Ndrangheta, and the Sacra Corona Unita[2] have actively participated in organizing the market for corruption, building complex networks of exchange with politicians (Section 1), with businessmen (Section 2), and with both (Section 3).

1. THE CORRUPT POLITICIAN AND ORGANIZED CRIME

Where organized crime is deep-rooted, corruption finds a particularly fertile soil. As one of the better known of the former *mafiosi* who decided to collaborate with the judges, Tommaso Buscetta, stated:

> It is not the Cosa Nostra that contacts the politician; instead a member of the Cosa Nostra says: that president is *mine* (*è cosa mia*), and if you need a favor, you must go through me. In other words, the Cosa Nostra figure maintains a sort of monopoly on that politician. Every family head in the Mafia selects a man whose characteristics already make him look approachable. Forget the idea that some pact is reached first. On the contrary, one goes to that candidate and says, "*Onorevole*, I can do this and that for you now, and we hope that when you are elected you will remember us." That candidate wins and he has to pay something back. You tell him, "We need this, will you do it or not?" The politician understands immediately and acts always. (*La Repubblica*, 8 November 1992, p. 2)

This quotation vividly portrays the hidden exchanges that link politicians and organized crime. The Mafia and the politicians invest different types of resources in these exchanges. And each side derives numerous advantages from them.

1.1. Violence, Private Protection, and a Reputation for Dangerousness

The first resource that organized crime can offer politicians is physical violence: the elimination of adversaries in extreme cases, but also, and more often, attacks upon property rights or threats against political opponents or personal enemies. Investigations into political corruption have revealed episodes of violence against people who refused to pay kickbacks and bribes or who attempted to negotiate the amount to be paid, as well as against potential witnesses in criminal trials. If occasional relationships between politicians and organized crime have been documented in other regions of Italy (della Porta 1992), the investigations into political corruption in the South have uncovered generalized mutual protection linking some politicians and important organized crime bosses. In this situation the politician's "flaunting" of his privileged relationship with a Mafia boss is intended to create a reputation for dangerousness. As the Naples judges observed, referring to the former minister Paolo Cirino Pomicino: "There are elements . . . that indicate that . . . the Hon. Pomicino . . . has used Engineer Greco as his technical instrument . . . and Carmine Alfieri as his reference point in the Camorra capable of assuring him every type of coverage, assistance, and protection in the areas he controls and in all sectors with which he might interact: political factions different from his own, aggressive groups in the Camorra, timid or enterprising city officials, or whoever might not recognize his power" (APN:20).

Organized crime in the South has at its disposal an enormous potential for intimidation, for it can credibly threaten the use of force. In the words of Antonio Calderone, a Mafia figure turned state's witness: "Any *mafioso* understands perfectly, when all is said and done, what the source of his power is. People are afraid of being physically attacked and no one wants to run even a minimal risk of being killed. The *mafioso* instead is not afraid to take risks and so he puts the lives of others at risk" (Arlacchi 1992:200). But, in order to understand how the Mafia interferes in corruption activities, we must first look at the "specific nature" of Mafia activity: *dispute settlement* (Reuter 1983). According to Gambetta: "*Mafiosi* are first and foremost entrepreneurs in one particular commodity—protection—and this is what distinguishes them from simple criminals, simple entrepreneurs, or criminal entrepreneurs" (Gambetta 1993:19). Protection must be chiefly intended as a resolution of quarrels, the defense of agreements and property rights, and sanctions on the breach of private contracts. Instead of being offered by the state as a "public good," protection is sold arbitrarily and selectively by the Mafia. The system of property rights is thus determined by individuals' willingness to pay. As in a modern Hobbesian "state of nature," the guarantee of criminal activities can be interpreted as a perverse affirmation of the gangsters' property rights.[3]

In this perspective, violence constitutes a resource that can be used to settle or override controversies in those markets in which transactions are dominated by mutual distrust and uncertainty—and especially in those contexts in which the protection elsewhere supplied by the state as a public good is either unavailable or ineffective.[4] *Mafiosi* operate typically in markets and social relations in which trust between individuals is fragile, or less than required by a society regulated by normal negotiation strategies. This is the case, for example, in black and illegal markets (Gambetta 1993).[5] The Mafia state's witness Antonino Calderone fully confirms this situation: "The reputation that we, the Mafia, had was that we were impartial, that we were above suburban criminal groups that trusted us and accepted our intervention in their controversies" (Arlacchi 1992:153). Even though an ability to use force is indispensable when providing credible protection, the two resources do not coincide: violence is not the core Mafia activity, but a necessary means to offer reliable protection. As an input in a costly production process, violence, whenever possible, will be used only to the extent necessary and, when possible, it will be "economized on." As judge Giovanni Falcone observed, "In these organizations violence and cruelty are never gratuitous but instead represent the last resort, to be used when all other methods of intimidation have failed or when the gravity of the behavior requiring Mafia 'correction' is such that it must be punished by death" (Falcone 1991:28).[6]

For the Mafia, violence is tied to another resource, *reputation*, which with time can become a substitute for violence, allowing drastic savings on the "production costs" of protection. If individuals expect that the *mafioso* is capable of deploying effective and violent instruments of dissuasion, his need to turn to actual violence declines: "A reputation for credible protection and protection itself tend to be one and the same thing. The more robust the reputation of a protection firm, the less the need to have recourse to the resources that support that reputation" (Gambetta 1993:44).[7]

The resources of violence—or the reputation of being able to use violence—help politicians in their careers in several ways. The reputation that a politician enjoys the protection of organized crime, which is often reinforced by using bodyguards with a clear Mafia stamp, generally offers an advantage in electoral terms. As the Parliamentary Anti-Mafia Committee reported, "Support from the Cosa Nostra can also involve supplying a constant 'supervision' of the candidate, who, as he makes his rounds in his electoral constituency together with members of the [Mafia] family, is not only protected in terms of personal safety, but shows voters that he is backed by 'men who count' " (CPMF:16). Second, these resources of violence can be activated in attacks against political adversaries, so as to put them out of the running or "soften" their positions. Third, in the market for bribes, access to resources of violence strengthens the position of the politician expecting payment and discourages any attempt to avoid paying him. According to the Tribunal of Palermo, for example, the career of Christian Democrat Vito Ciancimino—former major of Palermo—was repeatedly favored by the support of several Mafia families. Thanks to the forces of intimidation marshalled by his Mafia allies, "not only could one never fail to consider Ciancimino's requests, but he never needed the least bit of documentation to claim his money, since it was unimaginable that anyone could have betrayed his trust." (TRP:194).

1.2. Protection of Political Exchanges

Mafiosi can also offer their services of violent protection in the more general area of political agreements and exchanges. Before the new municipal electoral laws were approved in March 1993, city-level government and administration almost always required the formation of coalitions among multiple parties, each of which was subdivided into factions in harsh competition against each other. Often, especially in the South, these political coalitions were extremely precarious and unstable and thus blocked the distribution of key positions and the division of public resources. The progressive extension of spheres of competence and of power given to local authorities has increased the strategic importance of these agreements, from which an increasing share of money and consent could be derived. At the same time, the incentives became stronger for those political actors who could alter the precarious balance of government in exchange for the promise of a bigger share of power. The role of *mafiosi*, in some cases, has been to ensure the stability of political coalitions and of agreements in the allocation of positions (and the bribes deriving therefrom), or to induce a change of the subsequently agreed distribution of political resources for the advantage of their protégés. For instance, the Camorra state's witness Pasquale Galasso says that after the election of the town council in Poggiomarina (near Naples) "I was asked to intervene with a reluctant councillor to tell him, with all the weight of my Camorra fame, to ally himself with Antonio Gava [DC political boss], who had promised him the position of mayor." An agreement emerged between the two main DC representatives in the local government. This agreement became stable only thanks to the presence of the *camorrista*: "For the duration of that government," Galasso continues, "I was the tongue, convincing the one, who didn't want to renounce his position as Mayor, and the other, who wanted to occupy it, to remain united" (Barbagallo 1997:149–50). In exchange, the *mafiosi* obtained money, or influence over the political power to whose stability they had contributed.

The protection of Mafia bosses thus serves to restore the stability of political exchanges behind the managing boards of municipal agencies. Frightening their enemies and avoiding political crisis, *mafiosi* ensure a (more or less) peaceful and continuing division of public funds. One example of a Mafia guarantee of a municipal coalition was described during the investigations into the murder of Ludovico Ligato, a powerful DC boss in Reggio Calabria. According to a state's witness from the local Mafia, "The two parties, DC and PSI, competed against each other to divide up between them all the positions of power and all the economic interests in the city of Reggio. But Ligato, who was determined to take up, from the top, the management of local politics himself, found all doors closed to him. At this point he chose the strategy of threats. This was the overall situation that resulted in Ligato's physical elimination" (*Panorama*, 13 December 1993, pp. 52). The state's witness observed: "The problem became most dramatic once several thousand billions of lira were about to arrive in Reggio (through the so-called Reggio decree), because it was clear that whoever held political power in the city would also control these funds" (Galasso 1993:198). Around these public investments, a "political argument, with very unclear boundaries" had developed, related among other things, to the distribution of an expected 35 billion lira bribe. According to the state's witness, the assassination "should be framed as a moment of the conflict inside Reggio's business committee," given the fact that Ligato, with his political power and his contacts with a rival Mafia band, "interfered in the political life of Reggio" (Ciconte 1994:168). The murder had the effect of consolidating the nascent political coalition in Reggio: "After the assassination, or, better, because of it, the game was made and the new agreements were implemented thanks to a series of very important decisions, which previously would have been discussed for months in the city council" (ibid.). Any element that might have disrupted the coalition and its plans for sharing out public resources was thus eliminated through the use of violence and intimidation. Thanks to this forced "pacification," the corruption market could expand undisturbed and benefit Reggio's "illicit, Mafia-type structure, which was called the 'business committee'" and was composed of "prominent figures in the dominant political class, who were able to influence the choices of local and central public agencies, [of] 'favored' national companies that routinely received public contracts, [and of] local entrepreneurs who acted in symbiosis with local organized crime and were thus the actual executors of the work" (CD, 1993, no. 256, p. 2).[8]

In a similar way, Vito Ciancimino, a leader of the DC in Palermo, thanks to the exclusive protection of the Mafia family of the Corleonesi—according to the former mayor Elda Pucci— "acquired power beyond that which he should have had from his party role" (UIP:247). The possibility of using violence therefore stabilized, independently from his institutional position—his "rights" to the management of public resources. Even when he ceased to be on the town council, "no mayor could keep his position without his agreement" (UIP:17). In fact, according to the former mayor Insalaco (killed by the Mafia in 1988), Ciancimino "played an essential role. . . . He has continued to manage events in Palermo not because he had any official position, but because of his very strong group of allies who backed him and whom he represented" (PRP:249–50). According to state's witness Buscetta: "As I learned from Stefano Bontate, Martellucci [then Mayor of Palermo], thanks to the mediation of the Salvos, had accepted that Ciancimino manage the slum-clearance of Palermo [a business worth many billions]" (TRP:57).

1.3. The Vote of Exchange

Along with physical protection—which, as just observed, can by itself strengthen the electoral position of a candidate—corrupt politicians may also demand bundles of votes from organized crime. As a mafioso told the judges: "I do not solicit politicians. They solicit me at election time. They need me, I don't need them" (APN:8). Electoral exchanges between politicians and the Mafia, forbidden by Italian law, seem to have assumed especially noteworthy proportions in Campania, Calabria, and Sicily. In general, the hidden market for votes, given its characteristics, has a particular need for outside guarantees in the exchange between sellers (voters) and buyers (politicians).[9] Mafia groups are well equipped to supply such protection: "A more ideal setting for the Mafia can scarcely be imagined. Although the market for votes exists in areas of Italy where there is no Mafia, in Sicily it appears to be larger and more efficient" (Gambetta 1993:184). The Parliamentary Anti-Mafia Committee has learned that organized crime has several ways of controlling bundles of votes:

> The Mafia makes it known in the environment in which it operates that it is able to control the vote and it thus makes voters fear reprisals. Intimidation of this type is rather widespread and so also is the surveillance of polling places. In various cases elections have been rigged. More often no outright intimidation is needed. Advice is sufficient. The absence of political energy and passion, the notion that a vote serves only to mark one's adherence to a clientele group and not to indicate a choice of ideas, and the leveling of political traditions among the different parties all lead [voters] almost naturally, without any forcing, to respect the "marching orders" [given by the Mafia] (CPMF:16).

Mafia groups can also organize the consensus of their affiliates, relatives, and friends. The block of voters that *mafiosi* are able to mobilize directly is indeed impressive in both size and discipline. For example, according to former Mafia affiliate Antonio Calderone:

> The family of Santa Maria del Gesù is the most numerous and has about 200 members. . . . We are talking about a terrifying, massive force, if you keep in mind that every *uomo di onore*, between friends and relatives, can count on at least forty to fifty people who will blindly follow his directives. . . . If we think that in Palermo, in my time, there were at least eighteen administrative districts, and that each of these areas included not less than two or three [Mafia] families, we can readily understand the significance of Mafia support in electoral competition (DAP:39).[10]

Raimondo Maira, candidate at the regional elections of 1991, in return for a payment of 25 million lira, had obtained from the local Mafia family "control and protection for its electoral office and leafletting. Even if no violence was deployed, it was understood that those who did not respect the vote suggestion of the family could suffer consequences" (PP:897).

It should be noted, finally, that the electoral strategies of organized crime reflect quite pragmatic considerations: "It is natural for the Cosa Nostra to influence votes. Its influence results not from an ideological choice but instead from a search for advantage, from exploiting fully its roots in the society and territory" (CPMF:16). Organized crime directs the votes it commands toward the candidates that it maintains are both useful (in resources controlled and expected permanence in power) and reliable (in respecting illegal agreements). As one state's witness has revealed, "It is important to know which political figures receive electoral support from the Cosa Nostra, because, if that is the case, it is possible to turn to them for favors in compensation for the electoral backing already given" (DAP:39).

In exchange for protection and electoral support, organized crime asks politicians for what one state's witness has called "small favors"—that is, above all, protection from judicial investigation. According to the repentant *camorrista* Galasso, the boss Alfieri told him "that he would have engaged all his authority to have Mastrantuono [former Socialist Member of Parliament] who had promised to help him with the judicial proceedings against him, including a triple assassination" (Barbagallo 1997:169). The bundles of votes become than a possible means of revenge when the agreements are not respected. According to state's witness Di Maggio, during a meeting of the Cosa Nostra Committee, "Riina complained that the DC did not help the organization with the supertrial. The meeting ended with the decision to vote for the PSI . . . to slap the DC. It was permitted, however . . . to continue to vote for single DC candidates, provided that they were 'friends' and were ready to continue to help those families with whom they were in contact" (DAP:50). We now turn to this issue.

1.4. Impunity

Mafiosi sometimes directly corrupt public agents. To pay politicians, officials, and magistrates, or to corrupt police agents so that they close their eyes to illegal trafficking, is often a necessary condition to reduce the risks of those activities and to crush competition: "*Organized crime* almost always involves corruption" (Maltz 1985:24). Since the costs regulators can impose on illegal operators are particularly high, "corruption has a centrality for illegal markets that it does not have for legal markets generally" (Reuter 1983:123). The profits coming from illicit markets give organized crime opportunities for corruption: gaining exemption from application of the law or acquiring a "rigid" application of the law against competitors, thereby gaining a monopolistic position in the criminal activity (Benson 1988:75; Van Duyne 1997).[11]

Impunity for crimes committed is a resource of prime importance for *mafiosi*, who live in a situation of illegality, often as fugitives or in jail. According to several judicial documents, the relationships between Mafia and Camorra members, on the one hand, and political figures of national prominence, on the other, were in fact primarily directed toward obtaining protection in investigations and acquittals in trials; these ends were achieved as political "patrons" pressured the forces of order and magistrates. As another state's witness—Gaspare Mutolo—recalled: "The unanimous belief was that one could usefully influence the action of the courts through politicians and that, further, the function of Sicilian politicians was critical for 'Roman politics' [or national-level political decisions] with regard to Sicilian matters involving the Cosa Nostra" (DAP:24).

The cases range from the politician who sees that house arrest is arranged, to the politician who works to hinder investigations of people improperly certified to receive disability payments, to the politician— Salvo Lima—who negotiates the transfer of particularly disagreeable public officials (PP:38). According to state's witness Carmine Schiavone, the nonintervention of the police during several summits of the Camorra clan Nuvoletta, which involved "tens and tens of armed fugitives" followed from "the political protection that the Nuvolettas had thanks to the support they offered to Hon. Gava [DC boss and former minister of the Budget, Justice, and Home Affairs] and other politicians" (Barbagallo 1997:37). In some cases, the *mafiosi* looked for contacts in the judiciary. For instance, according to state's witness Salvatore Cancemi, the Mafia paid 600 million lira to a freemason lawyer in Palermo, who had offered "his intervention with President Carnevale with regard to a trial in the Court of Cassation," which had ended up with the annulment of the penalties against the defendants (PP:253; see also Chapter 5).

For *mafiosi*, impunity not only has an instrumental value but is also particularly important in a symbolic sense. As the Parliamentary Anti-Mafia Committee has asserted,

> Impunity for the Cosa Nostra has a relevance far greater than the natural hope of criminals that they may escape punishment for crimes committed. Beyond its effect on individuals, immunity from punishment confirms the overall power of the criminal organization, legitimizes the organization in the eyes of citizens, and mocks the function of the state. Thus, impunity is a structural necessity for the organization that confers the aura of "de facto legality" on its operations. Impunity is the principal concern of the Cosa Nostra. (CPMF:9)

Along with the concrete advantage of sparing the *mafioso* from legal penalties, immunity from judicial action has a crucial demonstrative effect that enhances his reputation for force and power.

2. ORGANIZED CRIME AND BUSINESS

In addition to its relationships with politicians, the Mafia maintains a dense web of interactions with several business sectors. In what follows, we focus on how the Mafia supports illicit business cartels through threatened or actual violence, receiving in exchange money or brokering services.

2.1. Violent Sanctions and Privileged Information

As we showed in Chapter 7, the formation of collusive agreements allows businessmen who should compete for public contracts or subcontracts to realize high profits. Concealing the coordination of their respective bids, these entrepreneurs are able to fix in advance both who will win the competition and how much the public body will pay. The company awarded the contract can then compensate the others with a share of its profits, or let another company take its turn in the future. However, firms participating in this hidden cartel have to resolve the problem of potential defection, since their hidden agreement cannot be sanctioned by the state: we have seen that cooperation based on reciprocity, especially when there is a repetition of the game, and guarantees offered by corrupt administrators are possible ways of escape from this dilemma.

In the South several factors have contributed to the success of such collusive agreements. Local businesses are few and they depend almost entirely on demand from the public sector, given the scarcity of opportunities in the private sector. The prospect of frequent and prolonged interaction with other companies fosters stability in cartel agreements. But it is above all the presence of Mafia-type organizations that makes such cartels so strong and durable: "The suppression of competition is a nearly universal dream of established entrepreneurs. The Mafia is one of the few nongovernmental institutions that can help accomplish this goal" (Gambetta and Reuter 1995:133). In this context, too, organized crime offers the service of preventing or resolving controversies within the monopolizing cartel.[12] The agreement is upheld or revised under the threat or use of force. Any businessman who defects from the collusive agreement or refuses to take part in it exposes himself to violent retaliation from a Mafia protector. In this context, racketeers, "by promising to take illegal but effective action against any member who tries to break the rules of the conspiracy, provide potential members with credible assurance that it is likely to be of lasting benefit. . . . They can bring members together for the initial discussion, provide them with greater assurance that the conspiracy will last, and make it last by enforcing the rules" (Reuter 1985:60). Naturally similar cartels are not limited to the sector of public contracts. In many other markets, conditions may be such that a forced regulation of competition is highly desirable. Mafia protection allows a firm to keep dangerous rivals at a distance or acquire other competitive advantages.[13] According to state's witness Baldassare di Maggio:

> We started out by helping the various businesses involved come to agreement, in the sense that we formulated bids so that the contract would be awarded with a minimal "discount" that allowed for the payment of a kickback of the proper amount. The person who acted to assure coordination

among the various companies was Siino [entrepreneur nicknamed Cosa Nostra's "Minister of Public Works"]; and I remember that in this first phase those of us from the Cosa Nostra had the task of accrediting him with individual firms and with the *uomini di onore* in the areas in which he was operating. (in *Panorama*, 11 April 1993, p. 61)

Also another Mafia state's witness Antonio Calderone has confirmed that:

Almost all Sicilian firms of a certain size and importance turned to the Mafia so as to be able to work undisturbed and to keep firms from the North out of their market. . . . Having the Mafia on your side meant that you could work undisturbed and make a lot of money without the risk of seeing your machinery damaged, without the fear that strikes might stop your job halfway through, without the requests for payments that even the least important *mafioso* thinks he has the right to demand from anyone who makes an investment in his territory. (Arlacchi 1992:195, 189)[14]

The successful method for dividing up the market was the following:

After a request for bids is announced, the cartel's allies in the agency contracting out the work reveal to Mafia personnel the list of companies that have officially communicated their intent to bid. The firms on the list are then contacted and (with a mixture of veiled threats and promises of future benefits) are invariably persuaded not to present bids or to present their bids in a way that assures that the contract is awarded to whatever company the [Mafia] organization has selected. (PRP:7)

Once firms have effectively established collusive agreements, they can in some cases do without attempts to corrupt politicians and public officials. Access to privileged information—such as the identity of companies invited to bid for contracts—can suffice for collusion to work. The firms in the cartel can receive this confidential information from the *mafiosi*, who in turn can obtain it from their "reference points" among politicians and bureaucrats in public agencies.

Palermo magistrates stated that at the end of this process, when the cartel protected by *mafiosi* has consolidated its operations and reputation, every local businessman finds himself forced to choose among the following alternatives: "(1) accept the rules of the game and thus enter into an arena in which each player will eventually be awarded the contracts assigned to him under the discretionary rule of the Mafia organization; (2) reject those rules but still compete for contracts, which means meeting retaliation from the [Mafia] organization; (3) abandon the Sicilian market" (PRP:8). We would also identify a fourth course of action that is surely the most dangerous of all: denounce the facts publicly or to investigating authorities. The presence of Mafia groups, which can sell their intimidation power to sanction collusive agreements, tends to make cartels more stable; this in turn makes the first and third [which is, in Hirschman's (1970) terms, *exit*] options more attractive, and the second and fourth (*voice*) alternatives, more risky.[15]

It should be noted that businessmen are not always passive victims of the *mafiosi* who foster the success of these agreements. As the Palermo judges discovered, in some instances, "after the businessman is contacted by the [Mafia] organization and accepts its rules, he gradually begins to participate actively in manipulating competition for contracts, deriving repeated benefits from doing so" (PRP:9). Investigations in Palermo further indicate that "the entrepreneurs involved do not seem to require intimidation any longer. This explains why crimes against property and persons are much rarer than the number of illicit agreements in effect. . . . Those who operate in the sector have no need to be explicitly reminded of the rules of the game. A tacit and clear understanding of these rules is in place" (LCC:123–24). By rotating access to contracts over time, all participating companies share the gains of collusion and carry out a perverse sort of "distributive justice." Some entrepreneurs can thus find it individually advantageous to build ties with *mafiosi* in order to give power and pervasiveness to the cartels set up to subdivide the market. By delivering a portion of their earnings to the Mafia, firms receive from the Mafia the guarantee that collusive commitments will be binding for all and that politicians will not obstruct the cartel.

2.2. Bribery and Intermediation

In return for their services, *mafiosi* receive different types of resources from businessmen. First, as might well be imagined, they get money. The Mafia's bribe (*pizzo*) is often just that, a percentage of the value of the contract that parallels the "cut" paid to corrupt politicians, as discussed below. The Parliamentary Anti-Mafia Committee has observed that:

> in Sicily a committee for managing contract competitions exists, a sort of executive board composed of businessmen—the most important Sicilian entrepreneurs and a few of national stature—who decide a priori (and regardless of the choices that might be made by public bodies) how the contracts will be awarded to firms. This committee can operate only with the Cosa Nostra guarantee behind it: This [Mafia] presence explains why Sicilian businessmen remain silent about corruption. The Mafia does not intervene to settle which company should win the contract, unless it happens to have a special interest in some company or unless it must use threats to demand that the criteria for allocating benefits be respected. Whatever company wins, the Mafia's share of the gains is assured. (CPMF:18)

Another resource that businessmen can use in their exchanges with organized crime is the acceptance or instead the boycotting of companies protected by the Mafia or, within some markets, of Mafia-owned companies.[16] Not even belonging to the Cosa Nostra or enjoying the protection of a *mafioso* permits a businessman to dictate to his competitors. One Sicilian manager describes the local market as follows:

> You need to keep your word, but other than that things work here the same as in other places. Along with ordinary business risk you have to add the risk of reprisals against property and people. Suppose a businessman is also a *mafioso*; this is not necessarily an advantage for him. He too must uphold agreements, he cannot win all the contracts he would like, he will not always find a public official or politician ready to cover him, and if he breaks an agreement, he could find himself facing thirty or forty companies united in a pricing war against him. (*Panorama*, 23 May 1993, p. 55)

No statement more clearly conveys the nature of the exchange between *mafiosi* and businessmen. Like anyone else, the *mafiosi* are constrained by the commitments they make. Businessmen retain some capacity to oppose the Mafia or to discourage defection even without turning to violence. If they were to abandon or boycott a collusive agreement, they would damage the *mafiosi* and those with Mafia protection.

As already noted, a crucial asset for *mafiosi* is *protection from measures taken by investigative bodies and the magistracy*. A company that has already established hidden contacts to secure corrupt favors can, at rather limited cost, pay the same public officials to extend the benefit of protection to *mafiosi*.[17] Thus, as a further means of compensating the Mafia, an entrepreneur can serve as an intermediary between the Mafia and the political authorities to be corrupted. Mafia repentant Calderone recalls:

> We were well protected and well informed. We protected the biggest businessmen from being disturbed by petty criminals and by non-Catania Mafia families, and they in turn protected us from any trouble we might have had with the forces of order or the magistracy. The Costanzo company had a lot of magistrates in hand. Costanzo cultivated them for his own reasons, because he had constant problems with the courts. Any large company has some complication in court practically every day: a fine, an accident on the job site, a dispute with another company. And since Costanzo had these contacts, he used them to help us with trials and other things. (Arlacchi 1992:28)

3. CORRUPTION, THE MAFIA, AND PUBLIC CONTRACTS

Along with those resources analyzed in Section 1, control of public contracts is another resource that corrupt politicians can furnish to organized crime and "protected" businessmen. As the judge Giovanni Falcone observed:

> On the subject of Mafia earnings, we should not forget contracts and sub-contracts. Indeed I wonder if this might be the most lucrative business of the Cosa Nostra. The control of competition for contracts dates back many decades, but today it has reached impressive dimensions. It doesn't matter whether the company awarded the contract is Sicilian, Calabrian, French, or German: Whatever its origins, the company that wants business in Sicily must submit to certain conditions, submit to Mafia control of the territory. (1991:142)

In general, the influence the corrupt politicians exert on local public agencies allows those politicians to administer at their discretion a range of public resources, such as contracts, licenses, permits, and jobs in the public sector. For example, the sentence of the Court of Palermo in the case of Vito Ciancimino cites a long series of favors given by the Sicilian politician to various associates of Mafia families: assigning subsidized housing to people not eligible for it, issuing permits to build on land set aside for public parks and gardens, granting construction licenses as a result of illegal pressure (TRP:88 and 151). As the Palermo judges observe, "Access to a political contact capable of decisively shaping the life and policy choices of municipal government in Palermo has done much to strengthen Mafia control of economic activity and to strengthen the Mafia itself" (TRP:202).

In this hidden market for contracts, triangular exchange relationships often form that bring together politicians, businessmen, and members of organized crime: "Cosa Nostra controls contracts in Sicily. It has the function of guaranteeing that agreements are respected and fulfilled, to intervene where 'disfunctions' occur, to damage the businesses that refuse to submit and, if necessary, to kill recalcitrant entrepreneurs" (CPMF:18). The supply of Mafia protection in corrupt transactions allows politicians to expand the market of bribery, reducing the risks of being cheated in illegal agreements and forcing individuals toward an obstinate conspiracy of silence.[18] As one repentant *mafioso* remarks, "There is an agreement between politicians and businessmen, then between businessmen and the Cosa Nostra, and finally between politicians and the Cosa Nostra. The function of the Cosa Nostra is to control everything, every step of the ray" (CPMF:70).[19] As noted above, in the South the system of public contracts offers particularly attractive economic opportunities, given both the magnitude of public expenditure and the weakness of private demand.

As the judges investigating collusion between criminals and politicians in Naples recently found, the availability of funds from illicit sources makes firms protected by the Mafia especially competitive and allows them to influence "a political-administrative apparatus that is by now . . . permeated by widespread illegality and is thus, in many instances, quite sensitive to the call of money or simply open to blackmail." Beyond vast funds, businesses with Mafia protection "also have an enormous capacity for intimidation, which they do not hesitate to display brutally whenever they encounter any resistance from 'honest folk' or, worse, from institutional or business actors believed to be infiltrated by rival [criminal] organizations" (APN:7). The support of a criminal boss able to guarantee that promises will be upheld and that bribes paid will elicit the behavior desired often represents a crucial advantage for businesses. The consequence is a "conquest of the market achieved through corruption or intimidation as well as economic assets that beat the competition (in the realm of prices, for example, or in the duration of deferrals of payment)" (ibid.).

The extension of Mafia protection on public contracts tends to stabilize relationships among crime, politics, and business, producing alliances among individual Mafia bosses, politicians, and entrepreneurs. The supply of Mafia guarantees can find interested customers even among corrupted politicians, who in this way receive certification of the reliability of corrupting businesses. The turning point in the relationship between the Mafia and politics may be located at the end of the 1950s when the Mafia of the countryside turned into the Mafia of the city and developed new ties to politics in the process. During the years of the so-called "sack of Palermo" [uncontrolled urban expansion] with Lima as mayor and Ciancimino as assessor to public works, "a pact was forged among the Mafia, the municipal administration, and construction companies that became a model for crime in many areas of the South " (APN:15). Particularly, Ciancimino "did not stop acting in a general way to promote the interests of private speculators, but in a more specific way was successful in favoring Mafia figures close to him" (TRP:86).

These tripartite agreements are cemented by the expectation that, if internal disputes or external obstacles arise, the criminal component will see to a prompt resolution of the problem. In this way the Mafia contributes decisively to the vertical expansion of the market for corruption. The Palermo judges assert:

> The criminal organizations making up the Cosa Nostra attempt to gain full control of public contracts in four phases: (1) intruding into the selection of public works to be financed, via technicians (planners, engineers, professionals, "meddlers") who act as illicit mediators among the public agencies financing the contract, the companies competing for the contract, and the public agencies receiving funds under the contract . . . ; (2) completely manipulating the bidding competition, through 'combination' techniques that are forced on participating companies with intimidation when needed; (3) managing subcontracts, which in the new system of Mafia control no longer constitutes simple parasitic interference, as in the past, but rather serves as a strategy for balancing the involvement of local Mafia groups; and

(4) expecting 'courtesies' and allowing 'mistakes' during the execution of work and during the final inspection stage. (PRP:5-6)

As observed above, companies that strike cartel agreements are able to eliminate all competition in the assignment of public contracts. Politicians, who would be cut out of the market if they did not act, have different ways of reentering the game. Under Mafia supervision they can provide "accessory services" (such as confidential information about the bidding competition or "steered" invitations to bid) that favor the cartel. Or they can get leverage by exploiting their power to solicit public financing, by adopting criteria for choice that leave great discretion to decision-makers (and are thus more difficult to "maneuver" from the outside), or by carrying out especially close checks on the contracting process.[20]

In some regions of Italy then, aggregates of interests from the political, business, and criminal worlds have solidified around public contracts. According to the Camorra repentant Pasquale Galasso, a complex division of roles and functions has been established among the actors of a politico-criminal cartel, which guarantees the respect of secret exchanges. Every Camorra clan has a "prime political sponsor" and in common agreement politicians and criminal bosses choose who should be elected to the principal political positions, which works should be planned and financed, which firms should stipulate public contracts, which sites should be earmarked for construction:

> The politician who directs the financing of the contract, and thus its assignment or concession, acts as a mediator between the company (which is almost always from the North or Center and is quite large) and the Camorra. This mediation occurs by forcing the company to pay a kickback to the politician or his direct representatives, and to accept that subcontracts be assigned to [local] companies directly controlled by the Camorra. The relationship becomes more complicated since the local companies flank the principal company as equal partners in the job: In this case an overall management of the operation emerges that involves politicians, businessmen, and *camorristi*, in complete fusion. (APN:9)

Even though both the Mafia and politicians supply "protection" to businesses in the market for corrupt contracts, it seems that the power of the politician tends to decline progressively as the relationship among the actors evolves.[21] This is evident, for example, in the distribution of payments for protection, that is, bribes. The Palermo judges write:

> Until the early 1980s, the politicians decided to whom they would assign a contract and pocketed as much as 50 percent of the kickbacks. This all changed when the Cosa Nostra changed. The bosses of Cosa Nostra conducted their business directly through their emissaries, with ministers, with

big entrepreneurs, with bureaucrats. . . . In recent years, the largest share ended up with the heads of the Cupola [the Mafia's multifamily committee, the apex of the organization], then came the local "family" directly involved in the contract, and the politicians were last. (*La Repubblica*, 27 May 1993, p. 8).[22]

4. CONCLUSION: ORGANIZED CRIME AND POLITICS

It is difficult for a politician to become a "man of honor." There is a strong sense of mistrust in Cosa Nostra toward politicians because they are treacherous, they do not keep promises, and they are sly. They are people who break their words and are without principles. (Arlacchi 1992:208)

This statement by the mafioso state's witness Antonino Calderone, unintentionally sarcastic, touches a very important aspect. Contrary to a common belief, the Mafia and corruption are completely separate phenomena when considered analytically. The Mafia and corruption can be considered as discrete "businesses," dealing essentially in different commodities: private protection on the one hand, property rights on political rents on the other. This explain the obsession of the *mafiosi*, as arbitrators in controversies, for respecting the given word, which is connected with a distorted principle of "honor." The unscrupulous attitude of politicians on this point cannot but arouse contempt. There is only a limited ground for potential interaction, a common market where both Mafia and political protection can be offered simultaneously.

The most recent judicial investigations into organized crime and political corruption have revealed, for southern Italy, continuous and systematic exchanges between organized crime, entrepreneurs, and members of the political class. As judges in Naples have observed, "It must be emphasized in the strongest terms possible that a constant relationship of functional interchange exists . . . between the political-electoral system, on the one hand, and the system of criminal interests, on the other, each aggregated around representative and charismatic individuals, interacting among themselves both directly and through their respective representatives" (APN:7). This "iron triangle" permitted triangular exchanges (see Figure 8.1) in which, according to the Naples judges, each subject obtained specific advantages:

The entrepreneur obtains from the politician work and the possibility of making profit, from the *camorrista* . . . "social peace" and "credit" in the relationships with the local administration: the *camorrista* obtains money from the entrepreneur, judicial "protection" from the politician, and social legitimation from both. . . . The politician receives electoral force and the capacity of an illicit influence on the public functions, added to relevant economical resources. (Barbagallo 1997:163)

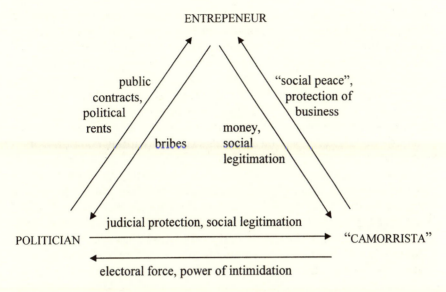

ENTREPENEUR

public
contracts,
political
rents

bribes

money,
social
legitimation

"social peace",
protection of
business

judicial protection, social legitimation

POLITICIAN "CAMORRISTA"

electoral force, power of intimidation

Figure 8.1. Triangular relationship between entrepreneurs, organized crime, and corrupt politicians.

In this situation a series of vicious circles seems to have been activated, in which political corruption and organized crime have reinforced each other and weakened the market, the state, and civil society. Organized crime has strengthened corrupt politicians with its bundles of votes and resources of violence, and in turn corrupt politicians have used their power to enhance the power of the organized crime families supporting them. Through the guarantee of impunity and the control of territory assured through manipulation of public contracts, corrupt politicians have further buttressed the underworld. The same argument has been made for the U.S. context: "The gangster depends upon political protection for his criminal and illicit activities. He, therefore, has a vital business interest in the success of certain candidates whom he believes will be favorably disposed to him" (Landesco 1968:183). There are several examples of organized criminal involvement in U.S. election campaign financing (Dorman 1972; Alexander 1985). Sometimes contributions were made by organized criminals to candidates for various political levels, or even to both major political parties, as "gangsters operate on both sides of the street" (Alexander 1985:93, reporting the U.S. Senate Committee Report known as the Kefauver Report).

The ties between organized crime and corrupt politicians have been favored by the presence of incompetent local government and have in turn helped to undermine governmental performance. Given *misadministration,* the dependence of citizens on organized crime has increased, since the

Mafia bosses, thanks to their connections with public administrators, have been able to offer favors of different types. The vast spread of governmental and administrative inefficiency, encouraged by political corruption, has led citizens to distrust public procedures and decisions.[23] These negative expectations apply also to the ability of the state to provide authentic and impartial protection to the public. Some citizens have thus turned to providers of a "surrogate" for public protection, boosting the demand for services of private protection supplied by *mafiosi*, whose power is thus strengthened.[24] Moreover, the agreements that corruption entails are often backed by Mafia groups, which are able to "persuade" the actors to maintain their commitments. By reducing the risks inherent in secret dealings, the Cosa Nostra has contributed to the expansion of the market for bribes. At the same time, a strong conspiracy of silence covers such activities, causing obstacles for investigations. Thus public inefficiencies, the Mafia, and political corruption feed each other, since the coexistence of corruption and Mafia within the same territory, reducing their "production and transaction costs," can increase the illegal supply of both private protection and political rents.

As we compare the *market for corrupt exchanges* of the South and corruption as practiced in the Center and North of Italy, we find that the search for protection in illicit exchange and in relations with public agencies has produced partially different patterns. In the Center and North, several centers of power have often supplied political protection, and citizens and businesses have turned to those centers to defend themselves against possible instances of nonfulfillment on the part of the public administration or partners in corrupt exchanges. As already mentioned, in many of the cases of corruption that have come to light in north-central Italy, it has been discovered that organizations of corrupt politicians coordinated and managed illicit transactions. These organizations handled the important task of guaranteeing respect for secret agreements in the system of corruption. In fact, these organizations assured repetitively playing the game: "It is advantageous for the actors who enter into such transactions to foresee a certain regularity in their ties. The collective actor that is created out of them will be more able than isolated individuals to both inflict punishment (or better, when obligations are accepted, to transmit credible warnings of punishment) and assure continuity, creating expectations that the game will be reiterated" (Pizzorno 1992:30).

In contrast, in the episodes of corruption that have emerged to date in the South, groups of corrupted politicians have been much smaller in size and the role of political parties in the subdivision of bribes more limited. Even though we must await the further evolution of judicial investigations to have a more detailed understanding, we can now advance the hypothesis that these geographic differences in corruption reflect different structures of the market for protection. Where organized crime provided effective private protection, the formation of informal groups of politicians aiming to endorse and sustain hidden exchange would have been super-fluous. Each individual corrupt politician could, in fact, obtain the desired guarantees of compliance and reliability—even in the more complex exchanges—simply by giving up and handing over to the Mafia a cut of the bribe.

Similar considerations apply even from a comparative perspective. If the "trademark" Cosa Nostra is owned by criminal organizations only in Sicily and in the United States (Reuter 1983; Gambetta 1993:127–55), in a few other (more or less) democratic countries similar suppliers of private protection exist. We may refer, for instance, to the Russian Mafia (Serio 1992; Varese 1994; Fituni 1996), where "all that undermines the legitimacy of the new, fragile Eastern democracies to the advantage of the criminal organizations who attempt to seize the functions of control and conflict resolution proper to the state through intimidation, violence, and extor-tion" (Rose Ackerman 1994:65). The functioning of the Yakuza in Japan is similar (Iwai 1986), where the role of organized crime in the protection of corrupt business emerged during the Lockheed scandal in the figure of Kodama Yoshio—a suspected war criminal and broker between politi-cians, gangsters, and right-wing extremists—who received an annual salary as consultant to the Lockheed Aircraft Corporation. In the Colom-bian case, the boss of the narcotrafficking Pablo Escobar, told a journalist that in his airplanes "flew, and not for a short flight but throughout the country for weeks and weeks, candidates for the presidency of the repub-lic, former presidents, senators, deputies, generals of the police and the army, an archbishop, a patriarch of our society, entrepreneurs" (Zuluaga Nieto 1996:159). In the same country, narcotraffickers contributed several billion dollars for the electoral campaign of President Ernesto Samper (ibid.:148). Drug and corruption money have similar effects on criminal-ization of the economy since, because of the very illegality of its origins, it cannot be invested in legal markets (Kopp 1996:80). In these contexts, the corruption market may expand thanks to the availability of effective pro-tective services to corrupt politicians and entrepreneurs who look for pri-vate advantage in the exercise of public power. At the same time, criminal organizations may find in this illegal market specific resources (such as money or impunity) that can favor their consolidation.

In the Organized Crime Task Force (OCTF 1988) report, for instance, we can find significant similarities between the construction industry in New York City and the public contracting activities in southern Italy described here.[25] New York has by far the largest number of Cosa Nostra members and associates in the United States, with five active families. The OCTF report found that "corruption in New York's construction industry is so pervasive and open that it inevitably contributes to a general impression that 'the only crime is getting caught'" (OCTF 1988:40).[26] In the construction industry, specifically, Cosa Nostra "can and act as a 'rationalizing body,'" since "its presence and power provide simplification and coordination. It can solve labor problems and assure that supplies are delivered and competition reduced. . . . It can assure that extortion will not exceed predictable and 'reasonable' levels and be the guarantor of the quid pro quo for illegal payments" (ibid.:70, 73). Furthermore, Cosa Nostra has a role "in establishing and policing cartels or 'clubs.' Cosa Nostra dictates who can participate in certain subindustries, who can obtain which contracts, and what price will be charged, " in exchange "for payments from the cartel members for the benefits that club membership provides: protection from competitors, inflated profit-margins" (ibid.:82).[27]

A similar regulating function in the market for corruption was played by organized crime in the operation of the International Longshoremen's Association and the U.S. shipping industry. According to the report made on March 27, 1984, by the Permanent Subcommittee on Investigations of the United States Senate, the competitive struggle of shipping firms in ports was riddled with kickbacks and illegal payoffs to union officials and organized crime was found to have a great influence on such transactions: "Witnesses testified that payoffs were a part of virtually every aspect of the commercial life of a port. Payoffs insured the award of work contracts and continued contracts already awarded. Payoffs were made to insure labor peace and allow management to avoid future strikes. Payoffs were made to control a racket in workmen's compensation claims" (Block 1991b:145). As we have seen in this chapter, where a *mafiosi* family or another organized crime supplier can meet the demand for protection that emerges from corrupt and collusive deals, partners are reassured that the illegal services they have paid for will be delivered, that no one will denounce them, that "things will run smoothly." As in this case, the extensive diffusion of similar practices is the predictable outcome.

NOTES

1. For a wide selection of parliamentary documents on the Mafia, see Tranfaglia (1992).

2. In Italy the terms Mafia and Cosa Nostra, in the narrow sense, refer to Sicilian families engaged in organized crime. Both terms are also used more loosely as labels for organized crime in general. The Camorra, the 'Ndrangheta, and the Sacra Corona Unita are more specific terms, referring to organized crime in the regions of Campania, Calabria, and Apulia, respectively.

3. The commodity "protection" has some "public good" aspects: once it is offered to some individuals, others also benefit from it. To transform protection services into a commodity to exchange, the Mafia has nourished mistrust and uncertainty concerning property rights, protecting criminal activities as well, and has promoted "energetically" its purchase in a general way. Moreover, when there

is a supply of private protection, mistrust and uncertainty spontaneously increase: "Distrust, in other words, becomes *endogenous* and need no longer to be thought of as a precondition external to the Mafia protection market" (Gambetta 1993:27).

4. According to Max Weber, payments to the Mafia are similar to those given to political groups in exchange for "extorted services": "These services are initially intermittent, but in practice they become 'periodic payments' in exchange for a guarantee of security. This is the observation of a Neapolitan builder as given to me 20 years ago, in reply to doubts on the efficiency of the Camorra with respect to his business: 'Sir, the Camorra charges me X lire each month, but guarantees security—the state takes ten times as much, but does not guarantee anything'" (Weber [1922] 1981:195).

5. In illegal transactions the threat of law enforcement agencies, the fear of deception, the absence of means of contract enforcement, the uncertainty of property rights, and the imperfect flow of information, contribute to making demand for protection significantly higher than in ordinary competitive markets.

6. The potential for violence is mutually exclusive; it cannot be shared, and must be continuously visible to reinforce reputation. Mafia structure can then be characterized as a set of local monopolies of private violence, which may ignore, cooperate with, or fight each other (Gambetta 1993).

7. The huge variety of Mafia symbols and initiation rituals can be explained by the nature of the commodity protection, whose quality is very difficult to ascertain. Everything that can convey information, expectations, emotions, beliefs about the quality of protective services then becomes very valuable. *Mafiosi* can take advantage in many ways of legends, novels, and movies, to reinforce their reputation of suppliers of authentic protection. Even "Mafia" or "Cosa Nostra" can be seen as successful trademarks of the main protection industry in Sicily. It is an asset that is the common property of different families who often fight each other in order to increase their market share (Gambetta 1993:155).

8. We further discuss this sort of tripartite alliance in Section 3.

9. In the market for votes, the fulfillment of similar "contracts" is not easily verifiable (hence a problem of trust), there is a question of scale (it is difficult to negotiate each single vote), and the exchange is illegal (Gambetta 1993:184). On the Italian anti-Mafia legislation of the 1990s, forbidding such activities, see CPMF:2.

10. The term *uomo di onore* (man of honor) refers to a member of the Mafia.

11. Corruption therefore can favor the development of dominant positions in illegal markets. Organized crime requires long-term corrupt exchanges with the public agents who have the power to sanction them; these relations "can be undertaken only by a fairly large firm that has reason to expect that it can enjoy most of the market and get a satisfactory return on the investment" (Schelling 1967:66). In fact, "this expectation of mutually profitable contracts between repetitive violators and enforcers . . . explains the development of organized crime: an organization is engaged more continually in violations than its individual members are, and can, therefore, make arrangements with judges or police that would not be feasible for these members" (Becker and Stigler 1974:4).

12. Why should racketeers not confer monopoly power on a particular firm, in exchange for a percentage of the returns deriving from the protection from and intimidation of competition? As Reuter remarks, instigation of a cartel "is an alter-

native method that reduces risks and may yield similar benefits." A first advantage of a cartel is that it is less noticeable. Moreover, by inducing entrepreneurs to enter into the collusive agreement there is little need for forceful intimidation: "Firms must be persuaded to join the conspiracy, it is true, and that may involve the use of coercion. But coercion whose objective is to persuade an entrepreneur to join with colleagues in an arrangement that may, at least in the short run, increase its income, is likely to be less disturbing than coercion whose objective is the elimination of an enterprise" (Reuter 1985:59).

13.   The Mafia-owned company described by Arlacchi with reference to Calabria combines three elements that give it a privileged position in the market: discouragement of competitors through intimidation, lower salaries and evasion of social security and insurance contributions, and greater financial solidity and flexibility given access to funds from illegal activities (1983:108–25).

14.   According to Mafia repentant Leonardo Messina, "[T]here are businessmen who pay a monthly stipend to the Cosa Nostra. Not only for protection. We also intervene to give them advantages in the market" (MPU:79).

15.   The power of the Mafia to deter and intimidate is tremendous. In Palermo alone thirty-four entrepreneurs and seventy-eight shopkeepers were assassinated by the Mafia between 1978 and 1987 (Santino and La Fiura 1990:413).

16.   Some *uomini di onore* also are engaged in legitimate business activities. Mafia repentant Calderone has recalled, for example, that "there have always been merchants, shopkeepers, and agricultural exporters in the Cosa Nostra, as well as an infinite number of contractors and builders" (Arlacchi 1992:28).

17.   The corrupting firm may then enjoy the "increasing returns" of corrupt activities aimed to obtain nonenforcement by police officials or judges. For instance, "an official bribed to ignore gambling will be more easily bribed to ignore prostitution as well" (Rubin 1973:156).

18.   The degree of stratification of corrupt transactions in Sicily seems to confirm the "efficiency" of the services of the Mafia. The system required strong trust: complex exchanges between local and regional politicians, mediators, bureaucrats, and firms were based on delegation of decisions (from regional councilors to intermediaries) and anticipation of payments (the companies selected to win the bidding paid a bribe equal to the 25 percent of the cost even before the contracting procedure began) (PRP:10–12).

19.   The often invisible Mafia presence sometimes becomes clearly perceptible. It is the case described by Michele Pantaleone, a specialist in this area, as the way to solve a "normal" controversy in corruption: "The firm made a commitment to pay the 'patron saint' a bribe of 10%. . . . Unfortunately the influential politician has died and the firm has lost its protection, with the entailing need to find a new 'patron saint.' The dead man's heirs insist on claiming the right that was acquired with the inheritance and demand continued payment of the bribe. There has already been one death and in the building yard there were two dynamite attacks" (Pantaleoni 1984:184).

20.   Before getting involved in the turbulent sector of public contracts, even the Mafia bosses expressed some doubts. According to the repentant Di Maggio: "Angelo Siino told me that he could receive the lists of public contracts before they became public and that, if Cosa Nostra succeeded in coordinating the bids of the

various entrepreneurs it would have large margins of gains. I talked about it with Riina who expressed some perplexity: 'This Siino wants to end up like Ciancimino?' However, Riina said that, if Siino took the risk, it was fine with him. And we started this activity" (*La Repubblica*, 7 July 1993:17).

21.   In a similar context, a competition may emerge (or a collusive agreement) between suppliers of political and Mafia protection (Vannucci 1997d:57). In case of conflict, however: "The relationship between Cosa Nostra and politicians is one of dominance of the first over the second; the availability of coercive methods gives Cosa Nostra infinite possibilities for demand and persuasion" (CPMF:16).

22.   In other contexts in southern Italy, the power relationships between politicians and organized crime are more balanced: "[I]n Calabria and Campania, . . . the acceptance of a diffuse and invincible illegality seems to have induced the representatives of the two separate worlds [politicians and organized crime] to meet in a stable way, forming a decision-making body where both components are represented" (Tranfaglia 1994:24). This is reflected in the division of bribes. According to the entrepreneur Bruno Brancaccio: "[T]he rule that I experienced is that, on the amount of the work, those who received a contract paid 3 percent to the politicians and, in the areas controlled by the *camorra*, 3 percent also to them" (Barbagallo 1997:134).

23.   Goldstock (1993) emphasizes the perverse effect of widespread interaction between corruption and organized crime in terms of higher consumer costs, lower quality of life, and ineffective law enforcement. Moreover, it affects the public's belief in the integrity and legitimacy of government.

24.   In the description of the repentant Antonino Calderone, the activity of a successful *mafioso* is to a certain extent similar to that of a normal political "patron": "We do not have to forget that the *mafioso* is a sort of authority, a person everybody addresses to ask a favor, solve problems. . . . When we, the Calderones, enjoyed great favor there was a procession in my office, people who asked for the most disparate things. . . . One looked for a job, another had participated in a selection for a position, and wanted to win it, another offered products for an enterprise" (Arlacchi 1992:149–50).

25.   On the similarities between the role of the Mafia in legitimate industries both in Sicily and the United States, see Gambetta and Reuter (1995).

26.   In the U.S. solid and toxic waste disposal industry, too, there is a wide-ranging presence of organized crime, which neutralizes enforcement efforts and protects waste firms, which often have to corrupt public officials (as, for instance, in the case of bribes paid to the New Jersey Public Utilities Commission; see Block 1991a:97).

27.   Other case studies seem to confirm the relation between Mafia, restrictive agreements among firms, and corrupt influences in the United States (Reuter 1987, 1993).

9

The Dynamics of Political Corruption:
A Conclusion

In June 1983 in Savona, the magistrates arrested Alberto Teardo, former president of the regional council, leader of the Socialist party in Liguria, and candidate for an MP's seat in the political elections that were to be held a few days later. Teardo will be put on trial together with more than forty public administrators and entrepreneurs from Savona and surroundings—city councillors, assessors, majors, presidents and councillors of banks and public bodies—most of them belonging to the Socialist party. Many of them were charged not only with corruption and extortion crimes, but also with participation in Mafia-style organized crime, due to the "intimidating force, the subjection of external individuals, and the conspiracy of silence" that characterized their corruptive activity. Teardo, in prison for charges of committing more than 360 corruption acts during eight years of political activity, garnered nevertheless more than 5,000 votes in the 1983 balloting. Although he did not win the seat, he almost maintained the electoral support he had obtained in previous elections.

The functioning of this illegal organization—which was called "Teardo's clan" —was reconstructed in great detail by the magistrates who two years later sentenced Teardo to more than twelve years of jail (reduced to seven in the third stage of the judicial proceeding). In Savona's administrative structures, corruption had in fact become systemic, regulated by an articulated network of rules of behavior that defined the roles of different individuals belonging to the clan, their connivance relationships with politicians and bureaucrats not directly involved in corruption, and the mechanisms of bribe exchanges with entrepreneurs interested in public benefits.

Several local entrepreneurs admitted that they had paid bribes at a fixed rate, 10 percent of the total sum, for all the public contracting procedures under the "control" of Teardo's clan. This is some of their testimony: "We all resigned ourselves and paid. Without a bribe you could obtain absolutely nothing." "I have received so many requests for the payment of bribes, too; in fact, I was one of the most harassed, since to my bad luck the premises of my firm were very close to the Socialist party's old headquarters and to Bar Rossello. It was really impossible to go into that bar, since you were immediately chased" (UIS:360–61). Fear of retaliation, in the form of exclusion from profitable public contracts, pushed the entrepreneurs to spontaneously conform to prevailing "codes" of behavior, which dictated bribery as the most effective way to obtain access to public structures. An entrepreneur says: "If we had not paid, no public work would have been financed in our area, since they would have preferred other places." And according to other testimony: "Not paying bribes I would have been excluded from public contracts, since nobody would have invited me." "I was obliged to pay bribes; everybody did it, I was told by Dossetti [Teardo's clan cashier] that I had no choice " (UIS:3370–71). In fact, "It was universally known that those who refused to pay bribes were excluded from public contracting procedures" (TRIS:145). The picture that emerges from this testimony shows that corruption was not a circumscribed pathology, but had finally become in many of Savona's public bodies a pervasive "normative" system. The actors involved in these illegal dealings—politicians, bureaucrats, entrepreneurs—converged in considering corrupt behavior unavoidable, and this in turn increased the economic advantage of adhering to the informal "rules" of corruption, undermining at the same time the moral barriers to illegal behavior. This "strategic equilibrium" of corruption, based on mutual expectations, was revealed to be very strong.

An informal but well-constructed organizational structure emerged within the clan of corrupt administrators. The hierarchical distribution of roles was determined partly by institutional positions held by the various members within the public administration and the political parties, and partly by the power resources connected with illegal activities (blackmail power or illegal skills). As the judges observed, members were connected to each other by "a set of ties due to common political memberships, friendship, masonic brotherhood, or simple interested cooperation, which constituted the foundation on which their illegal activity was built" (UIS:122). Alberto Teardo was the boss: he occupied the top in both the institutional structures and in the informal hierarchy of the illegal organization, planning the long-term political and economic goals of the clan, coordinating legal and illegal activities of its members, guaranteeing the fulfillment of agreements. In fact, "he took all main decisions and informed his 'lieutenants' with 'memos' specifying for each public contract or illicit dealing how much money should be required from the entrepreneurs, the conditions of payment, the identity of those who would collect bribes, and the shares of subdivision among associates to the clan" (UIS:433). Other public administrators were appointed as direct representatives of the boss at the top of several public bodies: with a limited autonomous power, they signaled and realized occasions of corruption, assuming the corresponding political deliberations. On a lower level some gregarious followers operated, selected by Teardo on the basis of trust: in fact, they had the delicate task of establishing and maintaining contacts with entrepreneurs, collecting and distributing bribes.

On its "visible," not corrupt, side the activity of Teardo and his clan often resulted in success from a political and electoral perspective. Actually, Teardo's public image was that of a dynamic and resolute decision-maker, updating the "old" and traditional politics of the Socialist party. A pragmatic attitude in political alliances and coalitions in local administrations, both within the internal factions of PSI and with other parties, and the pivotal position of his party could guarantee Teardo and his followers a wide placement in positions of power. According to a local Communist politician, "[H]e was very dependable. He always kept his word, both with the PCI and with the DC. Thus, he became a firm point of reference. Giving these guarantees to the parties, he obtained the possibility of doing what he wanted in exchange" (SV3, emphasis added). The circle of connivance and collusion with public administrators not personally involved in corruption became wider and wider: Teardo and his followers could then minimize the risk of being denounced. In several cases they used their "blackmail power" to tie together within the network of corrupt transactions politicians of different parties who occupied strategic roles in public decision procedures. A clientelistic management of their power was decisive to expand the electoral support of the boss and of the whole Socialist party on a local level. For instance, Teardo distributed benefits to supporters of the local football team, gifts to small communities of immigrants, and specific privileges in public housing assignation (TRIS:332).

Teardo's career—he was almost sure to become an MP and deputy minister in the national government—was interrupted by an unforeseeable accident from the "outside." The judicial inquiry that brought him to jail in fact started fortuitously with a denunciation of suspect financing to the Savona soccer team. The inquiry was conducted with obstinacy by two young public prosecutors, in spite of the requests to drop the prosecution coming from their superiors (Del Gaudio 1992). Ten years later, with the beginning of the mani pulite *inquiry, the internal stability of corruption equilibrium in Italy, as well as its vulnerability to the actions of independent magistrates, would be strongly confirmed. In spite of the potential friction in the sharing of the bribes, special benefits, and power positions among its members or clients, no serious internal crisis involved Teardo's clan during the almost ten years of wideranging corruption. Common knowledge of the informal "rules" of behavior sanctioned by the boss Teardo and the fear of retaliation—sometimes delegated to local criminals, as in the case of the bombing of some firms' courtyards—discouraged defection from corruption agreements and denunciations to the magistracy.*

The effects of corruption on local administrations in Savona and surroundings were extremely unfavorable: rising costs of public contracts, poor execution of work, heavy delays, extracontractual renegotiations. In this way, protected by corrupt administrators, entrepreneurs could richly compensate themselves for the bribes they had to pay (TRIS:434). In all the sectors monopolized by members of Teardo's clan, according to the magistrates, the conspiracy of silence created a perverse alteration of normal administrative activity. The main and only scope of administrative decisions had become a wider and very favorable collection of money, which only incidentally— as a sort of by-product of corruption—generated "normal" policies (UIS:329).

In the introduction to this volume, we stated that we were going to analyze the Italian *Tangentopoli* ("Bribe City") as an example of systematic corruption, that is, of a situation where corruption is so widespread that the illicit is the "real" norm, while those who follow the "old" norms are punished (Caiden and Caiden 1977:306). Teardo's clan story is an illuminating example of systemic corruption, the evolution of which was interrupted fortuitously a decade before the beginning of the *mani pulite* investigations. In this concluding chapter, we summarize the results of our research on corrupt exchanges, the actors involved in them, and the resources they used, singling out the dynamics of political corruption.

As mentioned, individual propensity to participate in corruption grows with those institutional conditions that increase corruption's material rewards and reduce its potential (material) costs. At a macro level, the first variable we found related to corruption is the *intervention of the state* in the organization of economic life: the proliferation of laws and regulations, the increasing dimension of the public sector, and the expansion of the welfare system enlarge in fact the opportunities for corruption. Given a certain degree of state intervention, the opportunities for political corruption increase also with the weakening of those checks and balances that should prevent the discretionary power of the public administration from becoming abusive—in particular with laws or practices that reduce the functioning of the internal system of controls inside the bureaucracy and between the bureaucracy and the political power. Corruption implies, in fact, a deviation from the main principles that should govern public bureaucracies—rationality, anonymity, and universalism among them. It potentially increases when careers in the administration are based on party affiliation; the legal system is overcomplex and the laws are unclear and contradictory; the bureaucracy has weak internal capacity of initiative.

Moreover, in democracies, corruption tends to grow with the *costs of political mediation*, that is, with the competition among politicians in the political arena, especially when the politicians acquire their votes (or a good percentage of them) through personalized exchanges with the voters. We can therefore say that there is an inverse correlation between generalized support—or the legitimacy of the institutions—and the costs of political mediation. Corruption itself intervenes then in the political class, creating dense exchange networks. In parallel and unofficial hierarchies, the power and prestige of a series of protagonists managing a public power subject neither to democratic investiture nor bureaucratic controls grow: "public service bosses," who found their careers on party appointment in public administration; "party treasurers," who coordinate the expenditure of the various institutions and the illegal revenue of the administrators involved in them; *portaborse,* who organize illegal activities in the public administration as emissaries of the more influential politicians; "protected professionals," such as architects, engineers, lawyers, or managers having contacts in politics and administration, placed by their parties as men of trust on the various commissions responsible for allocating and controlling public contracts; "party-card bureaucrats," that is to say, employees or managers of the public administration strongly loyal to their political patrons. For these "business politicians" the rewards are secret and economic in nature; their principal function is the organization of the hidden exchanges, the creation of contacts, and the favoring of negotiations between the two or more parts interested in corrupt transaction; and their principal resources are personal connections and the "confidential" information collected and exchanged on illegal markets. The power of these political brokers increased with the lack of transparency and certainty in administrative procedures.

To the institutional and political preconditions for the development of corruption, we should add normative ones. Also *normative conflicts* are likely to lead to corruption, insofar as loyalty to other primary or secondary groups interferes with loyalty to the state and loyalty to other groups, thus widening the gap between codified laws and accepted procedures. In particular, corruption spreads when social relationships based on traditional exchanges penetrate into other domains, where relationships should be based upon different kinds of social interactions. If corruption develops with the confusion of the borders between state and society and with value conflicts, it can be expected to grow during phases of transition, in particular during modernization processes, as well as when political elites are suddenly penetrated by *homines novi*, greedy for money and power, and with a weak sense of the state.

Establishing links between corruption and modernization might lead to the conclusion that corruption would tend to disappear in modern, democratic societies. This expectation, however, seems to be an illusion. Not only has corruption not disappeared but it shows a high propensity to spread along different lines. The very diffusion of corruption reduces its costs, increasing the general connivance as well as the opportunities for finding a partner for illegal exchanges. As emerged in our research, in fact, the very diffusion of corruption reduces its moral costs by creating what in the next section we shall describe as an emergent normative system. If new norms facilitate the intensification of corrupt exchanges, the diffusion of corruption interacts with the presence, in the political system, of other "pathologies." In particular, as we are going to see in Section 2, corruption, misadministration, clientelism, and organized crime establish vicious circles in which each phenomenon creates the preconditions for the diffusion of the others. However, this dynamic, as shown in Section 3, may be at least interrupted, if not reversed, as happened in the Italian case at the beginning of this decade. Although the problem is far from being solved, a reflection on the breakdown of the corrupt system in Italy may help in the search for strategies to curb corruption and improve the functioning of democracy.

1. CORRUPTION AS AN EMERGENT NORMATIVE SYSTEM

Many of those implicated in the *mani pulite* investigations claim to have had no choice when paying or receiving bribes; to have been nothing more than *victims* of a "system" that imposed its "will" upon them. A Milanese functionary found guilty of corruption claimed: "I found myself in a mechanism that had a life of its own, drawing you in, and I didn't know how to get out of it" (TAM:94). In order to understand how corrupt exchanges work, it is in fact necessary to analyze the system of *informal norms* that regulate relations between corrupter and corrupted. These norms do indeed "have a life of their own" insofar as they have not been purposely created, or, if they have been, are respected independently of this fact. This set of rules and conventions represents the "context" influencing, often in a determining way, successive individual choices.

Essentially, a "social norm" exists where a group of individuals adopt in a stable manner a line of conduct permitting those who comprise the group to coordinate their actions independently of the presence of a controlling and sanctioning central authority. In the bribery market a number of norms ensure that, given the expectations concerning what others will do, briber and corrupt official choose the most advantageous course of action for them. The resulting situation, confirming these expectations, also sanctions the behavior underlying it. In other words, a condition of *equilibrium* exists.[1] Thus if an entrepreneur expects his competitors to pay bribes it will generally be best for him to do so too, in order not to be disadvantaged. Where these expectations are shared, all the actors will spontaneously follow the norm that prescribes systematic recourse to corruption, regardless of whether any authority bothers to punish those who do not. As the previous chapters indicated, in fact, "Hidden norms regulate corruption. Systemic corruption is thus not anomie, but it does seem like it because the norms are parallel and implicit. These norms, however, are clear to those who are 'in' the game. They are the winners" (Becquart-Leclercq 1989:207).[2]

When the "rule" of corruption becomes an invisible guide to behavior, the relations between the actors in hidden exchange appear to follow a prepared script, reducing uncertainty and tension to a minimum. Mario Chiesa, the first victim of the *mani pulite* investigations, described the tranquil and unembarrassed atmosphere in which bribes circulated, even on the *first occasion* he consigned money to Carlo Tognoli, his political patron: "I handed him the envelope of money, casually, like offering a friend a coffee. He thanked me without asking anything. He knew there was money in the envelope but did not ask where it came from, which tender produced it, or the percentage of the payoff. Bribery has its etiquette. You accept and say thank you without displaying curiosity" (Andreoli 1993:61–62). There are no negotiations or demands; no suspicions or worries arise. To conclude the transaction successfully with a minimum of risk, it is sufficient to follow the *etiquette* of corruption.

How are the "rules of the game" in corruption created? In many of the cases described by protagonists in the *mani pulite* investigations, a process of progressive and reproduced adhesion to prevailing models of behavior can be observed. To borrow an expression from Hayek (1973), this can be considered an example of the "spontaneous evolution of rules of conduct." By obeying the illegal conventions, corrupters and corrupted obtain a desirable result, but not one intentionally sought: the *ordered* functioning of the market.[3] It is in everyone's interest to follow the rules precisely because the others have done so in the past and can be expected to do so in the future.[4] As one entrepreneur described it, the evolution of the rules is the fruit of the *actions* but not the *intentions* of those involved in the corruption market:

> We found ourselves in a perverse situation, overrun by events; the situation became insupportable. How did it start? It is not that one day someone said 'Well, now we should.' . . . Things evolved a little at a time and ended up in a situation like the one that has exploded. . . . There has been a enormous evolution in the last ten years, I would say. (*Un giorno in Pretura*, RAI 3, 22 February 1993)

For instance, according to politicians involved in episodes of corruption, the illegal financing of the political parties expands with their occupation of nonelected offices in the public administration. As stressed by Radaelli, the Socialist responsible for collecting bribes in Milan:

> This parallel system of party financing was not invented by me or by Prada [his colleague from the DC]. . . . Quite simply we conformed to a system that had existed since the 1950s, and when members of the parties were placed on the boards of the various public companies they had the task of continuing and perpetuating the system, asking for and receiving money from the enterprises. . . . Everyone knew how things stood and everyone acted their part. (*L'Espresso*, 21 June 1992, p. 27)

Above all, the bribery system appears to have spread with the reduced importance of ideology. According to Maurizio Prada, Radaelli's Christian Democrat counterpart, the system "grew by itself. . . . There was never any 'mastermind.' The development, growth, and rationalization of this system of financing came at the moment the traditional ideological confrontation between the parties declined" (PM:25), in other words, when its norms extended to opposition parties and the prospect of impunity was thus reinforced.

Since his intentions cannot be anticipated, an unknown entrepreneur winning a contract or a politician taking public office would represent a serious dilemma, if not a threat, for those already involved in corruption.[5] However, the existence of informal norms eases the entry of new actors into the market. In most cases there is little alternative to obedience for the newcomer who becomes aware of them, efforts at persuasion or intimidation thus being unnecessary. Spontaneous adaptation to the rules in force also allows a saving to be made on the costs of gathering information (Ullman-Marglitt 1977:86; Good 1989:51). The "cashier" of the Milan PLI, Giacomo Properzj, described this process:

I became president of the AEM in May 1987 and remained so until autumn 1990. As soon as I took on the position I was approached by Fiorentino Enrico, who told me that there was a group of firms . . . that normally contributed sums of money for the party system. I say this to make clear that the system of cash payments preceded my taking the post and I confined myself to the acceptance of what, according to Fiorentino, was an established practice. (CD, 22 March 1993, no. 231, p. 5)

In a situation of systemic corruption the payment of bribes is facilitated by the widespread conviction (emphasized by those seeking contributions) that it is *inevitable*. A small enterprise, after being awarded a 250 million lira order for the Fatebenefratelli hospital of Milan, was contacted by a Christian Democrat councillor: "He approached me in a perfectly normal way and asked for a 'contribution for the organization,' giving me the impression that it was an obligation and the usual practice. I considered it and decided to comply" (TM:83).

To propagate this idea of bribery's "inevitability," payment of a bribe should be necessary (at least potentially) for *any* public benefit. In recent years, according to Mario Chiesa, "[T]he tacit rule was that bribery extended to everything, from the biggest public works to the smallest provision of supplies. Bribery wasn't even brought up anymore" (*Panorama*, 13 December 1992, p. 45).[6] By paying bribes even before being asked, actors respond suitably to the actions of their competitors. A briber who waits for the opposite party to take the initiative risks being seen in a bad light, favoring a quicker and more unscrupulous competitor, or perhaps being faced with unexpected and exorbitant demands. If corruption is considered inevitable it is no longer worth engaging in the (embarrassing and dangerous) activity of finding out whether it is necessary to pay. As Elster observes, often social norms "are individually useful in that they help people to economize on decision costs. A simple mechanical decision rule may, on the whole and in the long run, have better consequences for the individual than the fine-tuned search for optimal decision" (1989b:106). When the whole of the political and bureaucratic class gains this kind of "bad reputation," entrepreneurs can no longer permit themselves to be overparticular. Expecting to have to pay in any case, distinguishing between the "honest " and the "corrupt" becomes increasingly problematic, given that a mistake or misunderstanding may lead to exclusion from the public sector market.[7] As observed by the former judge Di Pietro, when this norm has been consolidated, bribes are paid principally because everyone takes it for granted that this will happen:

There is an objective situation in which those who must pay no longer even wait to be asked. Knowing that in a given "environment" one pays a bribe or protection money they too promise to pay. In the same way, those receiving the money no longer need lower themselves to require or ask for it but

> simply wait, since they know that it will arrive eventually anyway. In short, hints on the part of the briber and threats and inducements on the part of the public official no longer take place. (1991:2)

One administrator of the firm ICOMEC claimed that "in the long term, payment is not connected to a specific cause, tending to become a kind of custom in relations with that public organization. This is demonstrated by the fact that in many cases payments continue even when the functionary changes, regardless of the physical person" (PRIM:62). In this way the "identification costs" of hidden exchange are reduced. Mario Chiesa states: "Garampelli proposed that I continue to work for the PAT [a municipal old people's home in Milan], guaranteeing the payment of a sum equal to five percent of the tenders. I suppose that things already worked that way because he proposed the payment as something quite natural" (TM:25). The president of the SEA, the Socialist Giovanni Manzi, also declared: "I couldn't say for what reason in particular the sums of money were given to me by entrepreneurs. They gave me it and I took it" (TNM:49).[8]

Where corruption is systemic, bribery not only extends to "everything" but precise rates of payment tend to emerge, reducing the risk of endless negotiation between corrupter and corrupted. In fact, in corrupt exchange the amount to be paid for the illegal services received, their *price*, must be fixed. Traditional economic models based on the laws of supply and demand in competitive markets have little bearing on the reality of illegal markets, made up above all of uncertainty, secrecy, and suspicion. The risks involved in corruption are such that privileged relations with a limited number of partners is to be preferred. Here, the end "price"—the bribe—does not emerge from the play of anonymous market forces, but usually as a result of negotiation based on contractual power and the relative abilities of the parties involved. Corrupter and corrupted would thus face a typical problem of *bargaining*: in trying to obtain a good price an individual will be more convincing the less interested he is in fixing the contract rapidly (instead waiting patiently for the position of the other party to soften)[9] and the more credibly he can hold out the prospect of dealing with someone else in the event of continued disagreement. Like any vendor and purchaser, at the moment of agreeing the price they have both conflicting interests (to obtain the most favorable conditions of sale) and interests in common. The inevitable divergence over the amount of the bribe to be paid notwithstanding, both have an interest in finding an acceptable agreement and in doing so as quickly as possible.

When corruption becomes systemic (and corrupt exchanges take place regularly and with a certain frequency), then once a "price" has been fixed in a specific case in some way—either by agreement after a bargaining process, by *diktat*, or by the application of a "tariff" valid in another context—those involved either may tacitly agree to replicate it in the future or attempt to attain better conditions. When a common conviction arises that a given "price" is known and agreed, then what amounts to a rule, the X *percent rule*, may emerge. In fact, where the probability of obtaining a more favorable price is outweighed by the risks and costs of renegotiation, the tacit repetition of the previously agreed price is the most convenient solution.[10] The entrepreneur De Mico recalled the "handover" between two Lombard superintendents of public works in the following terms: "When I had finished paying off Nigro with the last bribe I started paying Via on the same percentage basis. To all intents and purposes the latter substituted the former in his functions as superintendent and as bribe taker" (PROM:601). Precise tariffs applied to different kinds of services have been revealed. According to a Milan businessman "the tariffs paid to the parties were fixed: 5 percent on building contracts, 10 percent on cleaning services, and 15 percent on maintenance and refurbishment" (*La Repubblica*, 1 May 1992, p. 5).

A refined system of calculation for kickbacks developed in the revenue police (*Guardia di Finanza*) in Milan. According to the manager of Fininvest, Sciascia, "It was well known, as I learned from friends who were entrepreneurs, . . . talking with people of Falck, FIAT, Gemina, and so on, that when the *Guardia di Finanza* came, you had to pay. . . . [An official] at the beginning of the control operation told me that he had received the file with a pencil-written number on it, and that that was the amount that he had to take, in any case and independently from any notification of a fiscal nature, to . . . I think, the members to that power network who had the effective power on the *Guardia di finanza* in Milan" (MF:69). In fact, the official, who was a friend of Sciascia, told him that "if he had not brought them that amount of money, he would have to suffer serious retaliation, and be transferred to another city" (MF:70). In this case, the bribe was divided into a fixed part, which could not be negotiated, and another, calculated on the basis of the amount of violations discovered: "In relation to the fiscal verification at Mediolanum, Marshal Gilardino did not ask for money: he just told me 'you know very well how it works,' he was clearly referring to the 'entrance bribe.' One hundred million lira (with successive revaluation) represented the 'entrance bribe'; the additional money derived from a negotiation among the parties after the *Guardia di Finanza* had discovered fiscal irregularities (fake invoices, for instance)" (MF:70).

If it is expected that the other party will accept a given "price" and will not make concessions, any attempt to haggle becomes a waste of time. As we mentioned (see Chapter 4), shared adhesion to the rules on payment minimizes the danger of mishaps or contestation between politicians of different parties, facilitating reciprocal control and the avoidance of controversy. Not by chance, similar arrangements have also been discovered in other contexts. In some U.S. local governments, for instance, the "price" of corruption appeared to be significantly standardized: the kickback was 10 percent of the value of the contract (Amick 1976). In the Grenoble judicial inquiry that led to the indictment of former French minister Alain Carignon, all firms involved in the corruption system paid the same bribe percentage, as a sort of "fair price" for corruption in the awarding of public contracts (*La Repubblica*, 27 January 1995, p. 18). Even in Belgium calculation of the bribe as a fixed percentage of the public contract value was noted in several scandals (de Winter 1997).

In conclusion, in the situations described above, corruption tends to reproduce itself along with a system of norms and values that, while different from its legal counterpart, is far from being anomie. In this way, corruption can seep down from above—as "leaders, by definition, play an important role in directing public opinion and social behavior . . . the corruption of the leadership tends to reduce the confidence, loyalty and integrity of followers" (Werner 1983:150); but also from below—since "once the incentives for petty corruption have been created, it tends to extend upward through interest in complicity. This in its turn, by way of impunity, creates favorable conditions for the growth of corruption" (Cadot 1987:239). The constant movement of politicians from elective positions in representative bodies to posts distributed by the parties in public entities furthers the horizontal spread of corrupt practices from one institution to another. The diffusion of corruption in fact diminishes its costs, reducing both the sense of guilt and the risks of losing face, while increasing, on the other hand, the possibilities of finding dependable partners for corrupt transactions (Andvig 1991). In economic terms, the market for corruption presents a number of important "economies of scale": The costs of offering illicit services increase in a manner less than proportional to the overall level of diffusion of the phenomenon. Where corruption is widespread the risk of being accused is extremely low, given that the organs of control must distribute their resources over a much vaster area. Moreover, they meet increasing difficulties due to *omertà* between the corrupted or the greater ease of concealing evidence. In fact, since corrupt practices are usually closely bound up together, the number of people willing to testify or provide information becomes increasingly limited. The involvement and interests of leading politicians further discourages or obstructs controls and allegations. Given the absence of honest administrators to turn to, the incentives for entrepreneurs to pay bribes increase (Rose Ackerman 1978).

2. THE "VICIOUS CIRCLES" OF CORRUPTION

Systemic corruption is, therefore, a self-sustained phenomenon: corrupt exchanges facilitate the emergence of new norms, and these norms make corruption more and more attractive. Perverse mechanisms produce and reproduce the resources necessary for corruption. Honest politicians and honest entrepreneurs tend to be expelled from the government and from the public market. These mechanisms, which we observed "at work" in the Italian case, have undeniably favored the diffusion of corruption on a large scale. We can take a further step in understanding the evolutionary dynamics of this phenomenon if we go beyond its "internal" mechanisms, and look at the interaction between corruption and other phenomena—or pathologies—regularly mentioned in sociological and political studies of Italy. In fact, causal ties have often been noted between corruption and other pathological traits of the Italian system, in particular, misadministration, clientelism, and organized crime. These different pathologies have created a spiral of malfunctioning within the Italian political and administrative system.

2.1. The Vicious Circle between Misadministration and Corruption

A great deal of evidence has been found on the interdependence of *misadministration* and corruption (della Porta 1997:344). Bureaucratic inefficiencies and corruption appear to be intertwined. The correlation between the index of low corruption and the index of the efficiency of governance structure (average of low red tape and efficiency of the legal system) in sixty-seven countries, which resulted from standard questionnaires answered by Business International correspondents in 1980–1983, seems to confirm the complementarity of the two phenomena (Mauro 1995).

First of all, corruption generates "bad" governance. The system of corruption creates *social costs* and also burdens the public accounts. In other words, it is a *negative sum game* at the collective level. In a situation where procedures are inefficient or incapable of guaranteeing efficiency in every case to which they are applied, corruption could alter agents' behavior in ways conformable to the public interest.[11] For example, if the administration aims to provide a service to a particular category of individuals but the procedures do not ensure this result, then an act of corruption that allows the potential (but otherwise excluded) recipient of such a provision to benefit from it, then it would seem, at first sight, to enhance organizational efficiency. This would also be true of a bribe that improved the position of the corrupter by prompting an agent to act more quickly.[12] However, if the hypothesis that, in certain cases, corruption increases administrative efficiency cannot be dismissed a priori, a number of factors (which *always* tend to produce the opposite result) render it extremely improbable (Vannucci 1997c):

1.   As shown in Chapter 4, corruption may distort public demand, as well as any other decision-making processes, from the pursuit of the gen-

eral interest to the prevalence of those expenses and acts that produce bribes (Rashid 1981). In fact: "Corrupt politicians may be expected to spend more public resources on those items on which it is easier to exact large bribes and keep them secret—for example, items produced in markets where the degree of competition is low and items whose values is difficult to monitor. Corrupt politicians may therefore be inclined to spend more public resources on fighter aircraft and large-scale investment projects than on textbooks and teachers' salaries" (Mauro 1998:12).[13]

2. Decision-makers direct their energies toward personal rewards, activity that is likely to hamper organizational efficiency. As a consequence, influence costs within the public organization tend to increase, since corrupt agents will try to influence their career paths in order to gain access to the more bribe-lucrative roles at various levels of the hierarchical structure (Hillman and Katz 1987).

3. Corruption usually increases the costs the state pays for works and services, since bribes are taken from a "political rent." Moreover, corruption tends to reduce state revenues as far as taxation is concerned; in fact, "it pushes firms underground (outside the formal sector), undercuts the state's ability to raise revenues, and leads to even higher tax rates being levied on fewer and fewer taxpayers. This, in turn, undermines the state's ability to provide essential public good, including the rule of the law" (Gray and Kaufmann 1998:8).

4. Corruption that appears "beneficial" for all actors involved in the exchange has nevertheless "external effects" that damage others: "speed money" practices bring about a delay of procedures involving actors who do not pay bribes and will then be forced to wait.

5. Corruption entails high transaction costs, as time and energies are spent by all the parties involved in keeping the exchange secret, while negotiating, controlling, and protecting their property rights in the corruption contract (Paul and Wilhite 1994). On the side of the firms,

> Available empirical evidence refutes the grease and 'speed money' arguments by showing a positive relationship between the extent of bribery and the amount of time that enterprises managers spend with public officials. Responses from more than three thousand firms in fifty-nine countries surveyed by the World Economic Forum's Global Competitiveness Survey for 1997 indicate that enterprises reporting a greater incidence of bribes—even after taking firm and country characteristics into account—spend a greater share of management time with bureaucrats and public officials negotiating licenses, permits, necessary signatures, and taxes. And the evidence also suggests that the cost of capital for firms tends to be higher where bribery is more prevalent. (Gray and Kaufmann 1998:8)

Moreover, resources are wasted by the state in uncovering and sanctioning these illegal transactions.

6.   Corruption brings about an "adverse selection" of less honest public administrators and inefficient enterprises: efficient ones, which are able
to face private competition, can more easily exit from the public market,
while the corrupting firms have a smaller incentive in investing in technology and innovation (see Chapter 7).

7.   Since administrative inefficiency creates greater opportunities, corrupt administrators have a definite interest in deliberately slackening controls, increasing public spending, and fostering the conditions of procedural delay, viscosity, and unpredictability that widen the margins for
corruption (Kurer 1993). As the interests of corrupt administrators influence the organizational structure, we may have a multiplication of irrational and twisted procedures. In the end the pessimistic expectations of
the public concerning administrative efficiency and impartiality are "self-
fulfilling."

Majone (1988) has distinguished between different forms of (in)effi-
ciency on the basis of the kind of problem the public administration has to
deal with: allocative efficiency (which goods or services are to be produced
and in what quantities); technical efficiency (how such goods and services
are to be produced); distributive efficiency (how these goods and services
should be distributed); dynamic efficiency (how to improve the quality
and increase the volume of goods and services over time). As the present
research shows, corruption creates inefficiency in all four of these areas: in
allocation, resources are directed toward the areas most profitable for those
involved (thus distorting public demand); the *production* of goods and services is entrusted to the least efficient firms; their *distribution* is to the
advantage of those with illegal skills possessing a privileged exchange
position with the public authorities;[14] finally, an *increase in the volume of
resources available* over time is obstructed by the waste associated with illegal activity.

On the other hand, misadministration, eroding the citizens' trust in a
just state, facilitates corruption. The poor functioning of the public administration generates widespread skepticism among citizens and entrepreneurs concerning the efficiency and impartiality of the procedures that
regulate access to the state; in other words, in the possibility of enjoying
those rights sanctioned by the law. As one Sicilian politician observed:
"Administrative paralysis transforms any right into a favor. If you need a
certificate or a building permit and have to wait about two years to receive
it, then you end up asking (and paying) for it as a favor" (*La Repubblica*, 17
October 91). Corrupt politicians and civil servants have an interest in presenting the functioning of the public administration as inefficient and
unpredictable because then they can selectively offer *protection* from such
inconveniences. In exchange for bribes they are willing to guarantee
speedier consideration of particular cases, favorable interpretation of the

regulations, simpler procedures, or a positive outcome in clashes with the public administration.[15] As a Milan businessman complained: "Since it is the best way to keep everyone over the coals, a lot of dossiers remain open under consideration" (FIPE 1992:54). Where corruption reaches those centers of power that influence the rules agents must follow, irrational and contorted procedures will multiply as the organizational structure comes to reflect the interests of those who are corrupt. In other words, the "external effect" even of apparently "beneficial" corruption is a change in the rules and practices of the public administration that leads to a greater overall inefficiency of the system as in the already-noted case of Apulia's CRTA (see Chapter 4). Judicial inquiries have since revealed that much of this financing was accompanied by the payment of bribes, among which 4 billion for the contract for conveyor belts in the port at Manfredonia of which Di Giuseppe was one of the beneficiaries (ibid.).

Thus the successful conclusion of a particular case comes to depend on the *personalization* of relations with the public bureaucracy. This encourages the creation of privileged channels of communication with the public administration—regarding services, contracts, or jobs—in order to obtain profits, reduce waiting times, or forestall other potential corrupters. A Milan shopkeeper described the public administration thus:

> If someone had to comply with all the legislation as well as the local regulations before opening commercial premises they would be in a tight spot because of the speed the bureaucracy moves at. . . . Obviously they are directly in the power of the bureaucrats, who can decide whether to follow things closely or not; to make an inspection or not; to apply the regulations to the letter or not apply them at all (FIPE 1992:64–65).

The "demand" for corruption that is created in these ways produces *selective inclusion* of private actors on the basis of their willingness to pay bribes. For example, the owner of premises in Florence was clearly told by an intermediary close to the local administration that "in the event that he did not agree to pay, the value of the premises would be irremediably depreciated because it would be sucked into an inextricable administrative maze." In short, "if you pay the bribe you can sell it for a good price; otherwise, an endless torment against which the private citizen has, to all intents and purposes, no defense other than a court case, which as is well known will take many years" (TFI:338, 342). Growing corruption creates increasing pessimism concerning the arbitrariness of administrative action. Dissatisfaction with the functioning of the public administration and the incentives to obtain protection through bribery thus increase among those initially excluded from the market of corruption.[16]

Awareness that corruption is widespread and that others can take advantage of it (or even the simple expectation that this is so) is a strong incentive for seeking privileged links with political power. The ex-presi-

dent of ENI justified his predecessor Enrico Mattei's "free-and-easy" attitude thus:

> Mattei was not a born corrupter. When he was a small businessman he never
> bribed anyone; at the most he might have 'tipped' a traffic warden. But when
> he was forced to work in a particular environment, well. . . . I once saw him
> so happy that he went down the stairs three at a time. He had finally man-
> aged to persuade the Socialist party to accept 50 million. Before that they had
> been receiving funding only from others. (*L'Espresso*, 22 November 91, p. 41)

On occasion it is the politicians themselves who stimulate competition
between those bribing them. One of the ICOMEC company's managers
recalled: "Moro [President of the Genoa council housing authority (IACP)]
pointed out that two other firms were very interested in taking on the tendered work and asked me whether, if ICOMEC got the contract, they
would be willing to contribute finance as in the past and in the same measure. I said yes, because the work would allow us to cover it" (PRIM:125).

Precisely through attempts to get around it by bribery, however, belief
in the dishonesty of public agents is destined to proliferate autonomously,
by a kind of chain reaction. In the first place, someone who engages successfully in bribery receives a confirmation of their pessimistic expectations. As the often-mentioned broker Zampini said: "As I went on I
became more sure of myself because I realized that no one turned down
the offer of a bribe. Indeed, in my long career as a broker the money was
refused only once. I sent a box of chocolates containing 2 million [lira] in
cash, simply to keep him on friendly terms. He kept the chocolates but sent
back the money" (*L'Espresso*, 18 November 1984, p. 42). At the same time,
mistrust spreads among those who *do not pay* and therefore find, for no
other apparent reason, that they are discriminated against. An entrepreneur excluded from tendering for a contract with the Italian railways (FS)
connected this fact to the presence of a notoriously "well-connected" competitor: "[W]e realized immediately that the cards, as you might say, had
already been dealt" (PR:85). Afterwards he redoubled his efforts to enter
the restricted circle of corrupters.

The alternative is to abandon the public sector market. When he realized
that it was indispensable to pay bribes in order to work with the provincial
administration of Bari, for example, Paolo Giuliesi "ceased to present tenders and since he absolutely refused to grease palms on the sole occasion
that work was awarded, he has still not been paid what is due to him"
(TRIB:258). Barriers to poor administration are in fact increasingly weakened by the expulsion or marginalization of those protagonists most hostile to corruption, since the risk of complaints to the authorities diminishes.
It also reinforces the belief—widely held among politicians and entrepre-

neurs—that corruption is inevitable. Mario Chiesa has claimed: "There was a feeling of impunity in the air. It might seem incredible, but I've never asked for a penny from anyone in my life. Not because I was particularly decent and honest; it just wasn't necessary. If you came to me proposing to sell me 100 million worth of equipment and I smiled you would have said: 'This is the sum at your disposal' " (*Panorama* 13 December 92, p. 46). Thus, *the attempt to bypass the inefficiency and arbitrariness of the state by purchasing individual protection is destined to fail*. It spreads and consolidates the very distrust underlying it in an ever wider spiral of corruption.

Summarizing, on the one hand, as indicated in Figure 9.1, the investigations into political corruption have showed very clearly how misadministration (sometimes resulting from inertia, sometimes from able maneuvering) increases the discretional and arbitrary power of the administrators in each phase of the process leading to the "purchase" of public measures by bribery: from the creation of artificial demand to the contamination of the system of adjudication and the weakening of controls (see Chapters 5 and 7). In such a context, the generalized inefficiency of public structures, for which the functionaries themselves are in part responsible, permits them to "privatize" and sell the resources of their office in exchange for bribes. The discretional power accompanying administrative inefficiency can be used to further the interests of aspiring corrupters: thus, corruption feeds on inefficiency. When long delays in carrying out certain procedures become the rule, even a functionary who limits himself to performing his job within the time foreseen by the regulations can demand a *tangente* in exchange for this by now unanticipated "service."

Corruption, in turn, not only produces but also promotes inefficiency. First, corruption has social costs: "The damage to the public administration caused by the necessity for entrepreneurs, drained to the profit of the accused, to make up the losses sustained from extortion and the consequent elevation of the costs, poor execution of the work, proliferation of price revisions, execution of noncontractual work, and the requirement for supplementary technical evaluation, has been very serious" (TRIS:434). Moreover, if one of the objectives of functionaries is to collect bribes, they have an interest in fostering the conditions of procedural delay, viscosity, and unpredictability that widen the margins for corrupt transactions. Misadministration causes a growth of mistrust in the public administration,

misadministration → mistrust in implementation of citizens rights
→ search for protection → propension for paying bribes
→ (demand of) corruption → selective inclusion
→ increased (perception of) maladministration

Figure 9.1. Vicious circle between misadministration and corruption.

and of pessimistic expectations concerning the effective enjoyment of rights sanctioned by law, on the part of citizens and entrepreneurs. As a result, privileged channels of access to public decisions are sought, irrespective of whether they refer to enjoyment of a service or competition for a public contracts, jobs, etc. The necessity for privileged channels increases the willingness to "buy" access by paying bribes, in other words, the demand for corruption. Through the diffusion of corrupt practices, in fact, a selective inclusion of those who pay is realized. Corruption therefore increases inefficiency, recommencing the vicious circle.

2.2.   The Vicious Circle between Clientelism and Corruption

If "misadministration" increases demand for corruption, *clientelism*—another typically Italian phenomenon (Graziano 1980)—increases the supply. The Italian politicians involved in illicit activities appear to have possessed notable networking capacity—that is, particular ability in creating contacts, developing bonds of trust, and forming ties of mutual obligation and favor—to which was added a "patrimonialistic" conception of public goods as private assets. Both these characteristics, undoubtedly useful in organizing a system of illegal exchange or for successfully introducing oneself into an existing one, also favor the construction of a network of personal support formed both of clients and "friends" in the local elite. As mentioned in Chapter 3, various testimony emphasizes the ability of many defendants to distribute favors to a large number of individuals, privileging sectors and groups who could provide the greatest compensation in terms of electoral backing and collusion. In synthesis, it can be said that corrupt politicians reinforce their electoral and collusionary fiefs by developing both traditional forms of clientelism, based on localized patron-client relations, and client networks anchored in broader institutional contexts; both patron brokerage and organizational clientelistic brokerage, to use the definition of Eisenstadt and Roniger (1984:243–45).

Besides, it is precisely the desire to expand the volume of bribes that induces corrupt politicians to increase the activity and spending of the entities they administer, and with them the opportunities for distributing favors. To collect more bribes, in fact, they must employ an increasing amount of resources and spend an increasing quantity of public money, at least in those sectors where the illicit rewards appear highest and the risks lowest. By reinvesting in politics the money collected from bribes, corrupt politicians are able to organize sophisticated client networks and to acquire political protection. The same resources were invested in order to obtain from the bosses the nomination to public offices. As a Milan politician confessed, "With the bribes, I paid the membership cards and controlled 'bundles of votes.' . . . When my position in the public office had to be renewed or I needed a new appointment, I put those bundles of votes and membership cards on the table of the party" (MPM:160). Finally, by distributing favors the corrupt politician can achieve the complicity in the public administration necessary for his activities.

Our research seems to indicate that this simultaneous presence of corruption and clientelism is not casual but rather that it is related to the complementarity between the two phenomena and the similarity of their causal dynamics. Although it is true that various forms of corruption are to be found in more "ideologized" political systems, it can be concluded that the "pragmatic," "apolitical," "open-minded" conception of political activity described by corrupt administrators favored the construction of broad client networks.

It can be added that, as is it shown in Figure 9.2, clientelism and corruption converge to form a rising spiral, the diffusion of the one easing that of the other and vice versa. In the first place, the spread of vote buying—linked to the presence of clientelism—raises the cost of politics, forcing politicians to seek material resources to invest in the quest for power. As Mario Chiesa recalled: "The requests for money on the side of the comrades became unbearable" (Andreoli 1993:126). Clientelism and vote buying boost the incentives to seek funds by unlawful means, that is, to "allow" oneself to be corrupted. Moreover, they render more competitive corrupt politicians, who can reinvest payoffs more or less directly in buying votes: "Certainly—a Milanese politician stated—the race for power is a race for money. So that, often, placing a member of your own party fraction as president or councillor of the administrative council of this or that public enterprise means an additional financial source. And therefore a new share of power not only in terms of votes, but also in terms of money" (*Panorama*, 25 October 1992, p. 57). The number of politicians willing to "purchase" votes and backing, particularly through strategies of "individualistic mobilization" (Pizzorno 1980), therefore increases.

clientelism → increase of exchange votes
→ increase in the cost of politics → (supply of) corruption
→ availability of money for politicians
→ incentives to buy votes → clientelism

Figure 9.2. Vicious circle between clientelism and corruption.

2.3. The Vicious Circle between the Mafia and Corruption

To the vicious circles already described, others are added, particularly in the south of the country. The presence of *organized crime* reinforces the sta-

(politically protected) organized crime → votes and (violent) protection for
corrupt politicians → increasing power of corrupt politicians → public works and
legal protection for organized crime → increasing power of
(politically protected) organized crime

Figure 9.3.   Vicious circle between organized crime and corruption.

bility of the illegal deals that underpin political corruption and widespread misadministration (see Figure 9.3). In certain areas, political corruption and common crime have fed off each other, weakening the market,
the state, and the society. The presence of resources of a violent nature consolidates corrupt exchange, and the latter in its turn favors the spread of
those conditions of generalized illegality that protect organized criminal-
ity. The criminal groups strengthen the position of corrupt politicians
through the blocks of votes they control and the use of violence. In their
turn, corrupt politicians use the power they possess to offer services
enhancing the power and reputation of the criminal organizations that
back them (della Porta and Vannucci 1995). Moreover, by guaranteeing
impunity and control of the territory, often secured through the regulation
of public contracts, corrupt politicians have reinforced the power of organized crime itself. The very presence of resources of violence that are not
legitimate (that is, under the control of the state) is therefore a resource that
can be easily bought by corrupt politicians and entrepreneurs and used to
impose the implementation of corrupt exchanges. In its turn, the presence
of corruption increases the demand for the services of organized crime,
strengthening its grip on civic society and on the institutions.

It can be added that the relationships between organized crime and corrupt politicians were favored by the existing state of misadministration,
and in their turn contributed to making it worse. Misadministration has
also increased the dependence of ordinary citizens on crime. As the Parliamentary Anti-Mafia Committee has warned,

> Where the public administration is inert or inept and administrative controls
> fail to operate, almost automatically a favorable situation is created for the
> mixing of organized crime and politics. Often, it is no longer a question of
> mixing but of the occupation of public institutions by emissaries of Mafia
> groups, who administer power on behalf of the 'family' to which they
> belong, against the interests of the public and, on occasion, undisturbed by
> the organisms of control, whether administrative or juridical. In these areas,
> small communes on the whole, the Mafia has created a microsystem that
> conditions the daily life of citizens in a particularly oppressive way; the level
> of degradation is profound, and there is no right of any importance that can
> be exercised without Mafia mediation. (CPMF:18)

Concluding, to the economic damages of corruption we have to add its
dangerous consequences at the political level. In particular in democra-

cies, corruption undermines the very principles on which the regimes are based: equality of citizens' rights and transparency of the political decision-making process. In fact, bribes open the way for privileged access to the state for those who are willing and can pay the price: this leaves the other citizens with the belief that one "counts" only if one has the right personal contacts with those who occupy the state (Pizzorno 1992). At the same time, because of its illegal nature, corruption increases the range of public decisions that are taken in secrecy. Moreover, the diffusion of corruption influences the very nature of the most important actors of intermediation between the state and the citizens: the political parties lose in fact their capacity to articulate collective demands and are transformed into machines for the organization of remunerative economic business. The political personnel change accordingly, with the creation of a class of "business" politicians, who understand politics as the means for a rapid, and often illegal, economic enrichment, and use the money they obtain via corruption for buying votes and thus extending their power in the political arena. The effect of these changes is the decline of the capacity of the administrative system to satisfy general demands and produce public goods. All these processes converge to delegitimize democratic institutions while, at the same time, the weakening of the democratic institutions reproduces corruption. In fact, since with the diffusion of corruption, citizens' rights are transformed into favors, the more generalized corruption is, the more the citizens need to find a political protector—and therefore are ready to pay for this protection.

3. THE FALL OF A CORRUPT SYSTEM: LESSONS FROM THE ITALIAN CASE

Moving from single-cause explanations to an analysis of the interaction between the different phenomena allows a better understanding of the dynamics of what Italian media and politicians have called the "crisis of the regime," largely determined by the *mani pulite* judicial inquiry. The collapse of the system of corruption was not determined by a rebellion of its direct "victims": it was not those paying bribes who attacked the system in the first instance; the regime was not rocked by conflicts between corrupters and corrupted, nor even between "honest" and corrupt entrepreneurs. Rather, it collapsed through a crisis of legitimacy produced by the complex interlinkage of corruption, clientelism, and misadministration represented by political protection of organized crime.

In fact, the corruption, clientelism, and misadministration characterizing Italian postwar development have created a vicious circle, reducing diffuse support (that is, a consensus toward the political regime and its institutions) for the system and increasing the need for specific support (that is, support for a single component of the system—for instance, corrupt politicians).[17] During the reconstruction of the 1950s, the existence of a polarized political culture, the climate of the cold war and the direction taken in economic development prevented the spread of diffuse support. As a consequence, there has been a tendency to substitute "specific" support—directed, that is, toward those holding power at a given moment in time (Mastropaolo 1987). This can explain an apparent paradox: the fact that Italy has, if compared with other Western countries, a very high rate of electoral participation, and, at the same time, a very low confidence in its governing institutions (Morlino and Montero 1994).[18] Rather than by civic spirit, electoral participation could therefore be explained by ideological stances or by the clientelistic incentives that were used to capture specific consent. In the long term, however, this solution contributed to further undermine generalized support. In fact, "the clientelistic practice, based as it is upon a personalized use of power, impedes the dissociation between the roles and the role-holders that is the first characteristic of institutionalized authority. Being based upon the antibureaucratic principle of the 'consideration of the person,' it undermines confidence in the 'rules of the game' and in those institutions that should enforce them" (Graziano 1980:53).

Moreover, the decision of the Constituent Assembly not to give any one organ precedence over the others—in other words, to create a weak parliament, weak executive branch, and weak head of state—led to political fragmentation and a massive recourse to the practice of *lottizzazione* (see Chapter 4) on the part of coalition governments (Pasquino 1991:49). This enlarged the space available for the creation of a class of professional politicians, who found ample leeway for surviving the vicissitudes of elected office in the administration of public entities. It must be added that this progressive occupation of society and the economic system has not been translated into increased efficiency; on the contrary, the inefficiency of the administrative system has constantly grown while the possibility of gaining diffuse consent has shrunk as a consequence. As an indicator, we can refer to the national debt, which constantly increased from 456,031 billion lira (71.9 percent of the GNP) in 1983, to 1,673,574 million (111.4 percent of GNP) in 1992 (Mershon and Pasquino 1995:223). Thus, a spiral has been created in which the absence of diffuse consent has extended the parties' occupation of civil society, and this colonization has, in its turn, produced state crime and misadministration, reducing the capacity of the system to inspire a diffuse consensus.

Three factors were involved in precipitating the crisis of the system. First, a difficult economic conjuncture, added to the inflationary mechanisms internal to corruption itself, made the cost of political illegality unsustainable. Second, the Maastricht Agreements—which expanded markets to firms of EEC countries—heightened the expectations of citizens and entrepreneurs and, in the case of the latter, the fear also of being unable to withstand international competition. Finally, the chronic lack of diffuse consensus produced its most dramatic effects when the basis of legitimization of the party systems—founded (not only in Italy) on the division of the world into two blocs—disappeared with the collapse of the socialist regimes of East Europe.

Thus, a kind of "virtuous circle" was set in motion. Dissatisfaction with the growing inefficiency of public services led to a fall in consensus. In the political election of April 1992, electoral support for the two previously hegemonic parties—DC and PSI—dropped from 34.3 to 29.7 percent, and from 14.3 to 13.6 percent, respectively. The electoral defeat, together with judicial investigations against their leaders, led to their collapse: in 1994 the DC got 11.1 percent and PSI 2.2 percent. The delegitimization of the political class provided an impetus to investigations of corruption, and the results of the latter further strengthened the process of delegitimization. Consequently, judicial inquiries into offenses against the public administration spread like wildfire, laying bare also the buying and selling of votes and the organic relationships between certain politicians and organized crime. The *mani pulite* investigations undermined the authority of the party bosses—such as Arnaldo Forlani and Bettino Craxi, leaders of the DC and the PSI—and the most influential centers of power, curtailing their capacity to sanction those breaking the previously all-prevailing conspiracy of silence. The loss of political protection also began to weaken some sectors of organized crime. In turn, their difficulties led to a further loss of power on the part of the politicians they backed.

These political conditions eased the task of the magistrates conducting the inquiries. Mario Chiesa, arrested with a bribe in his pocket a few weeks before the elections of 1992, was not supported by the PSI leadership—after a weak initial attempt at proposing the thesis of a "political move" by the judges. Exploiting the favorable circumstances, as the inquiries proceeded, the magistrates of the *mani pulite* pool successfully pushed individuals involved toward collaboration: the latter less and less frequently anticipated threats from powerful politicians implicated as a result of compromising revelations or rewards for remaining silent: "The news of the full collaboration of Chiesa with the investigating judge . . . determined some public administrators to abandon their offices and assume an attitude of collaboration with the judiciary" (CD, 31 July 1992, no. 81, p. 3).

The magistrates also contributed to the strengthening of incentives to collaborate. Their actions showed the awareness of the need to influence the conditions in which those under investigation decide whether to collaborate, encouraging the choice to confess. The investigative strategy followed from the beginning of the inquiry confronted suspects with the pressing decision of whether to confess, sowing suspicions that others had already talked and raising the prospect of spending at least a period of preventive custody in prison in case of remaining silent or, vice versa, being released immediately in the case of a confession (a situation analogous to the archetypal of the famous "prisoner's dilemma").[19] Moreover, there has been a spreading of information about the chain of confessions taking place behind the closed doors of the magistrates' offices. For a prisoner, confession may appear the most convenient decision either when other potential codefendants have already confessed, or when he is still unaware of what they have done, and it is in his interest to preempt them. Isolation in prison was critical to prevent suspects from learning of the confessions of others: in this way reaching agreements of the "I won't talk if you don't" kind was no longer possible. Roberto Mongini, vice-president of SEA and one of the first to be arrested in 1992, recalled thus the entrepreneurs' confessions that followed his arrest: "A Mongini in San Vittore [the Milan prison] is something very different from a free Mongini. For instance, with me in prison, if the newspapers had reported that I was confessing (as in fact several dailies did, after the first interrogation, where I had really added no new information), maybe some entrepreneurs who had worked with SEA, would have been scared, and run to the public persecutor before the *carabinieri* could run for him" (Mongini 1992:13). Awareness of the ever-increasing mass of information in the hands of the magistrates spread increasingly rapidly, creating a veritable race to confess before others.[20] The support offered by public opinion, at the same time, prevented the political leadership from obstructing the work of the magistrates. The system of overlapping complicity thus crumbled like a house of cards, greatly accelerating the rhythm of the inquiry's development.

Summarizing, the breakdown of the corrupt system was set in motion by some *exogenous factors*. The fall of "actually existing socialism" in Eastern Europe delegitimized a party system that had been built upon the struggle between communist and democratic regimes. This can explain why, rightly after 1989, a series of scandals in most European countries increased the distance between political parties and the citizens—the Spanish *desencanto* as well as the German *Parteiverdrossenheit*. The progressive integration of the European markets was another factor that destabilized the national system. The main causal explanations for the breakdown of the corrupt system are however *endogenous* ones. In a democratic system, corruption erodes the legitimacy of the political system. The market as well as the actors of political mediation degenerate. Corruption feeds misadministration, thwarting the production of public goods: the sum of individual vices does not produce public virtues. As any illegal market, political corruption needs the development of an alternative system of protection, but it is unable to implement it; it needs stability, but produces insecurity. In a democratic system with countervailing forces, even systemic corruption seems to be destined, therefore, to undergo violent crises. The actors that set these crises in motion can be different ones: the political opposition, the press, the judiciary. In Italy, thanks to their high degree of independence from the political parties, the judges played the major role in the breakdown of the corrupt regimes.

If the judiciary investigation started a "virtuous circle" that is significantly modifying the Italian political system, recent events have indicated, however, that the illegal networks created during corrupt exchanges tend to be very persistent. Notwithstanding the flourishing of the investigations and the first condemnations of corrupt political leaders, the fight against corruption is far from being won. In this context, the *mani pulite* inquiry, which has temporarily curbed the perverse ascending spiral of corruption and inefficiency, undoubtedly had beneficial effects. Nonetheless, the prospects for the future remain uncertain. In fact, the action of the magistrates has broken only one of the rings in the chain of reciprocal causality by increasing enormously the subjective perception of the risks involved in corruption. Organized crime influence, clientelistic networks, exasperating slowness, unjustified delays, normative complexity, and the procedural quagmire—in other words, the components of structural inefficiency in public activity—continue to be present. In-depth reforms are necessary to prevent, once the storm has passed, the market of corruption from ever expanding again.

For some time now, the debate on the legislative changes required to cut down the endemic illegality existing within the state has been intensifying. Looking, either explicitly or implicitly, at the variables influencing individual calculations of the costs and benefits of participation in corrupt exchange, many of the solutions proposed in Italy, as elsewhere, aim to transform the utility function of corruption. The probable costs of corruption can be raised by increasing the penalties and improving controls on the public administration.[21] A series of proposals have been made in different countries in this area: the creation of commissions of inquiry independent of the parties (Pinto-Duschinski 1977);[22] a reduction in the discretional powers of the public administration (Gardiner and Olson 1974); an increased coordination between its various branches (Banfield 1975); the institutionalization of various kinds of accountability mechanisms (independent office for public auditing; independent investigating agencies; offices of local ombudsmen with the power to control local bureaucracy; citizens' watchdog committees providing information and monitoring services) (Bardhan 1997:1338). In a comparative analysis the opportunity of "a change in the rules of the game between politicians and bureaucrats" has also been suggested, "[in such a way that] bureaucratic elites offset the power of politicians, the bureaucratic structures become more independent of political intrusion and party politics, with the consequent withdrawal of bureaucratic resources from the political context" (Etzioni-Halevy 1989: 302; on the same theme, see Pippig 1990). Higher wages to bureaucrats, or even an incentive pay structure in public administration, should deter malfeasance (Becker and Stigler 1974).[23] An increase in the salaries of local administrators might raise the level of "professional competence " of aspiring candidates, their social status, and, at the same time, the costs of illegal activity. The risks of being implicated in judicial proceedings would then include the loss of a greater income and more prestigious social position. Containing the cost of politics, particularly through controlling the level of electoral expenses, might lower the propensity of politicians to seek (sometimes illegal) financing.[24] The introduction of competition between different bureaucratic structures would allow curbs on the monopolistic power that public agents usually find themselves exercising (Rose Ackerman 1986). Competing or overlapping jurisdictions between multiple officials can in fact facilitate "exit" from the corrupt exchange on the one hand, and raise the costs and uncertainty for the corrupt project on the other. Control on corruption may also be facilitated by involving the citizens in the diagnosis of corruption: "Ways of consulting them include carrying out systematic client surveys; setting up citizens' oversight bodies for public agencies; involving professional organizations; consulting with village and borough councils, and using telephone hot-lines, call-in radio shows, and educational programs" (Klitgaard 1998:4).

However, it seems necessary to go beyond the single causes of corruption to consider the complex interconnections between political illegality and other phenomena. From what has been said up to now, it follows that, alongside measures influencing individual costs and benefits, it is necessary to act on those macrophenomena that favor the spread of corrupt practices. The control of corruption will be all the more difficult if, at the same time, the problems connected with administrative inefficiency, an electoral system favoring the buying and selling of votes, and political protection of organized crime are not also confronted.[25] Among the changes to the "rules of the democratic game" that can favor competition within and between different centers of power and render more transparent public decision-making procedures are those relative to the division of tasks, with precise government responsibilities for those who win the elections and control responsibilities for those who become the opposition,[26] a more rigorous separation between political functions and administrative functions, a reduction in the parasitic rents connected to state intervention, and the conditions for a real competition among the enterprises present in the public market. A profound reform of the public administration appears equally necessary, one that would lead to a greater accountability on the part of the public bureaucracy, the fixing of strict time limits for fulfilling administrative tasks, an increase in the technical and professional competence of functionaries, and the introduction of serious controls on their efficiency. In a perspective of reform, the controls on public procedures should untie the knot that links illicit activities and administrative inefficiency. For instance, in the procedures for public contracts, a system of incentives in which the penalties for the corrupters grows more than proportionally to the price of the public contract would reduce the incentives to illegal activities (Rose Ackerman 1978:124). The severity of the controls should also be proportional to the size of the contracts. For the corrupted politicians and bureaucrats, sanctions and the frequency of controls should be related to the amount of resources they administer, so that the additional gains from corruption are more than balanced by an increase in their expected costs.[27] Investigations of corruption should start in every instance in which the results of contractual activities are not satisfactory. These forms of control should be sufficient to fight simultaneously the negative effects of corruption and inefficiency.[28]

Many of these proposals have been elaborated by a special committee studying the prevention of corruption (CSPC) set up on September 1996 by the president of the chamber of deputies: The control of political corruption implies a simplification of the legal system, in order to avoid the presence of contrasting norms; an increased visibility of public procedures; a reduction of public controls on private activities; a limitation of the parties' budgets and an increase in their transparency; a clear separation of power between the public bureaucracy and the politicians; a general definition of the conflicts of interest as well as a regulation of the practices of "pantouflage" (the practice of high-level public bureaucrats retiring and taking consultancy jobs in the private sector) and insider trading; the reduction of the parties' power to nominate their candidates to the leadership of public and semipublic bodies as well as to intervene in the recruitment of public employees; an increase in the technical capacities as well as in the prestige of the public administration; the promulgation of codes of behavior for those with frequent contacts with the public administration; control on the patrimony of a sample of public employees; the introduction of higher degrees of transparency in the various phases of the procedures for public tenders; a shift from procedural control to control over the quality of the final product.

Regarding the public tendering system in particular, the proposed responses aim to break the vicious circle between corruption and inefficiency through a series of measures: provision of funding should be dependent on the formulation of a preliminary program on the part of the public administration and a procedure should not begin without a detailed and reliable plan of execution; maximum visibility of tendering and the widest possible participation should be favored (with a simplification of public tendering notices and the adoption of open procedures); a maximum of transparency in the decision-making process should be ensured (making access to information easier, adopting criteria of evaluation that reduce discretionary power, and eliminating restrictions on information); a clear distinction should be made between those involved in planning (dealt with by technically qualified staff) and execution; a system of observers should be instituted, and they should be armed with database information; vigorous rather than simply formal controls on the conduct of both public administrators and private contracting parties (to measure the efficiency of the services rendered and ensure the regularity of the budget) should be instituted and reinforced; instruments for the rapid resolution of disputes between the public administration and private sector contractors should be adopted.

Other measures are more specifically designed to combat the more diffuse sources of inefficiency in the sector: the legal framework should be reviewed and tightened up; the execution of tenders should be dependent on the existence of sufficient funding; the number of decision-making centers involved in contracting procedures should be reduced and their respective powers more precisely defined; insurance coverage and the payment of deposits should be used to protect both the public administration and the winner of the contract against nonfulfillment, unanticipated difficulties burdens, or other unforeseen circumstances; qualification for participation in tendering should be on a technical and financial basis; public diffusion of information on the objectives, expected duration, costs, and outcomes of any public activity should be favored.

It remains to be seen whether the bureaucratic and political elite (notwithstanding the drastic renewal of the latter) will be capable of radically reforming public procedures and behavior, relinquishing the incomes, power, and privileges they have acquired, often by taking part in corrupt exchanges. The capacity of parliaments and governments to develop and implement an appropriate response to corruption will be a good indicator of the capacity for self-reform in democracies—a characteristic that is usually considered as a sign of the superiority of the democratic regimes. For this reason, a failure to face this challenge would not merely produce a new increase in corruption, but would trigger a profound delegitimation of our polical system.

NOTES

1. This notion of social norms or "conventions," proposed by David Hume and taken up more recently by Sugden (1986:32), refers to the idea of an equilibrium among a number of actors continually interacting. A stable equilibrium can be seen as a norm that, although not the only one possible, it is convenient to respect because the others respect it.

2. The spontaneous emergence of a norm in no way implies that its effects are desirable, even for those who respect it. In the case considered above, for example, when *all* entrepreneurs respect the bribery "rule," the benefit to be had for each of them tends to cancel out (MacRae 1982). Nevertheless, even in this case generalized corruption has an intrinsic robustness: no one has an interest in evading or defying the system, even when they are aware of its ruinous consequences for the collectivity. This is even more so for individuals outside the group in which the conventions are formed and observed and who suffer the consequences.

3. "The formation of spontaneous orders is the result of their elements following certain rules in their responses to their immediate environment. . . . Society can thus exist only if by a process of selection rules have evolved that lead individuals to behave in a manner that makes social life possible" (Hayek 1973:43–44). This principle applies on a smaller scale to the "social life" of the market for corruption. Francesco Saverio Borrelli, Milan's chief prosecutor, suggested that "[the system of corruption] is something that has grown spontaneously over time. Once it was recognized that the interests of those governing and the interests of those who wanted to do business could easily be married in this way, that a bargain could be struck and opposition silenced, the phenomenon grew on its own, gaining momentum day after day" (PM:48–49).

4. Naturally, other norms are possible. If it is expected that the others will inform the authorities of any attempt at corruption, then sharing that honesty is the best strategy.

5. The moment in which newcomers, having revealed their intentions, are introduced to the "rituals" of corruption is accompanied by an elevated risk of judicial involvement. This risk can be reduced by a suitable "socialization" of the rules in force (Sherman 1980:480) An essential role in this process is played by political leaders, who influence "the trust, loyalty, and personal integrity of their followers." If they are corrupt, therefore, they "allow their corruption to spread from one institution to another" (Werner 1983:149–50). As we noted (in particular in Chapters 3 and 4), the political parties played this socialization role in Italy.

6. This is confirmed by Maurizio Prada: "The mechanism of enterprises giving us money was so well consolidated that it was no longer necessary to ask. It was well known that the award of a contract required this and it was automatic, once a contract was gained, to quantify the sum to be given to the parties" (MPM:148).

7. It can be expected that unlike an "honest" politician, a "corrupt" one who has not been adequately compensated will seek to punish the businessman. If the latter knows with certainty to which category a politician belongs, his decision is an obvious one: pay who is "corrupt" and not who is "honest." On the other hand, if he does not know exactly a politician's category then even a small probability that he is corrupt is sufficient to make it worthwhile paying every time (if the reprisals feared are serious enough). See Kreps and Wilson (1982).

8. Matteo Carriera, ex-president of IPAB of Milan similarly stated: "Whether or not you believe it, I never asked for anything. The money arrived anyway. Sometimes I didn't even know the reason" (*Il Giornale*, 21 July 1992, p. 7).

9. An entrepreneur with liquidity problems, for example, or a politician urgently needing funds for an approaching election campaign will be in a weaker negotiating position.

10.   These costs are particularly high in illegal exchange because they include the danger of legal sanctions. This would explain, for example, the annoyance of one entrepreneur, De Mico, with the attitude of the director of works in the construction of the Venice prison. Contrary to the situation with other corrupt officials it "was never possible to find an arrangement to avoid continual disagreements. For four or five years I had to pay according to his will and inclinations" (PROM:649–50).

11.   On the other hand, if the overall system of rules governing decision-making is efficient and the system of controls ensures that agents' actions produce the expected results, then corruption of necessity generates inefficiency. If an illegal exchange modifies an agent's conduct, then the latter deviates from expected behavior (efficient by definition). If it does not, the costs associated with rent-seeking still need to be taken into account.

12.   In many cases, however, corruption almost certainly has the opposite effect: creating greater inefficiency. In the examples above, it is possible that someone who has no right to it obtains a benefit by corruption or that an agent is paid to delay or block a decision that is appropriate but undesirable to the corrupter.

13.   More generally, public officials may have an incentive to influence organizational decisions to their benefit: "This influence activity can be costly to the organization in a number of ways. First . . . it may lead to decisions being taken that are inefficient from the organization's point of view. Second the time and effort spent on influence activities (and in dealing with them) are resources with valuable alternative use" (Milgrom and Roberts 1988:S156).

14.   As Rose Ackerman remarks, "A corrupt system of government services has the distributional disadvantage of benefiting unscrupulous people at the expense of law-abiding citizens who would be willing to purchase the services legally" (1978:8).

15.   Between 1977 and 1992 the number of cases brought before the Regional Administrative Courts (TAR) increased by 169 percent, clear indication of a greater demand for justice in the administrative field (Arabbia and Giammusso 1994:283). The overburdening of the courts, indicative of more frequent conflict between public and public administration, has led to a larger number of outstanding cases and longer intervals before the courts arrive at a decision. This in its turn has increased mistrust of the efficacy of the judicial system and the recourse to forms of political protection.

16.   According to a shopkeeper in Rome, "[O]iling the necessary wheels is like having to pay an additional tax. But it's worthwhile because administrative procedures that would take years get done in a few weeks. It costs. But I don't see any alternative for those who want to work in this city" (FIPE 1992:7).

17.   For the distinction between diffuse and specific support, see Easton (1975).

18.   In 1982, different opinion polls indicated that only 31 percent of Italian citizens trusted the parliament, as against 53 percent in the United States and Germany, 48 percent in France, and 40 percent in Great Britain; only 28 percent of the Italians trusted the public bureaucracy as against 64 percent in Great Britain, 55 percent in the United States, 50 percent in France, and 35 percent in Germany (Rose 1984). See also Eurobarometer opinion polls in Chapter 1: the percentage of Italian citizens who are "not at all satisfied" or "not very satisfied" with the working of democracy in Italy has never been below 60 percent since 1973.

19.   In an interview, Judge Davigo stated: "We have to introduce an incentive for the denunciation of the crime, foreseeing, within a very limited time span from the moment of the crime, a nonliability to punishment. With this 'premium' we introduce an asymmetry: we give those who confess an advantage over those who do not confess" (Davigo 1993:15). The text of a reform proposal on the persecution of corruption crimes, presented in September 1994 by the *mani pulite* judge is based upon those very same principles: increased penalties (art. 1), the confiscation of sums and profits obtained through corruption (art. 5), and, above all, nonliability to punishment for those who, within three months after the corrupt exchange, confess their crimes and provide information on the others responsible (artt. 6, 7) (*L'Unità*, 5 October 1994, p. 3).

20.   In this way, Mongini recalls the arrests of the first entrepreneurs: "It is not difficult to imagine what happened after that day. Agitated telephone calls among politicians, among entrepreneurs, and between politicians and entrepreneurs. . . . It did not take long to realize that those arrested had started to talk" (Mongini 1992:21).

21.   Actually, a policy approach based only on penalties may produce undesired consequences: Mookherjee and Png's (1995) model shows that small increases in penalties may raise bribery, while larger increases will reduce it.

22.   In Hong Kong, after a major scandal in 1976, the establishment of an independent committee against corruption brought about a dramatic increase in both denunciation and condemnation for corruption charges (for instance, Manion 1996).

23.   According to empirical evidence, in fact, there is a negative relationship between the level of wages for public employees and corruption across less developed countries (Goel and Nelson 1996; Rijckeghem and Weder 1997).

24.   Many other measures of reform within public administration have been suggested: "cutting down on the proliferating functions of government departments . . . ; making supervisors answerable for gross acts of malfeasance by their subordinates; well-established procedures for 'whistle-blowers' and guaranteeing their anonymity; authorization of periodic probing of ostensible but 'unexplainable assets' of officials; working in teams (for example, in Singapore customs agents were asked to work in pairs) . . . so that there is some check in the bargaining process; well-defined career paths in civil service . . . ; periodic job rotation" (Bardhan 1997:1338).

25.   These considerations have been fully confirmed by the recent reform of the public contract system, which had revealed itself to be among the most vulnerable to illegalities. Approved on 11 February 1994, Law 109 fully took on board the requirement for transparency: procedures with a greater level of discretionality were drastically limited, while the preparation of projects, the direction of the work, and the activities of supervision and control were given, in the first instance, to the internal technical divisions of local administrations, with the object of reducing recourse to modifications and amalgamations of the original projects. On the basis of the arguments developed in this book, a reform of this kind represents a strong bastion against corrupt practices, drastically reducing the opportunities for committing abuses and illegalities. However, the law confronted only one aspect of the problem, the need to combat corruption, without considering the inefficiency and the limited qualitative and quantitative resources of the administrative

structure. This created the undesired effect of an almost complete "standstill" in public contracts, caused by the inability of public agencies to handle the responsibilities foreseen by the legislation and, then, a return to the old norms, whose vulnerability to corruption and exponential growth in costs has been "historically" proven.

26.   The main institutional changes after the *mani pulite* investigation were those brought about by the new electoral laws for the national elections, passed in 1993 (Laws 276 and 177), which introduced several elements of the "first-past-the-post" model. Reform of the local electoral system went in the same direction. However, the reform appears incomplete. Galeotti and Merlo (1994), presenting empirical evidence from a sample of nine Western European countries, argue that proportional representation elicits political collusion and determines conditions for the endogenous emergence of corrupt behavior on the part of the elected government. However, as Lijphart observed, in ideologically inhomogeneous societies the majoritarian model has negative effects when the minorities feel excluded and lose confidence in the political regime (Lijphart 1984).

27.   Moreover, there should be no inverse relationship between the established penalty and the probability of being discovered.

28.   In more general terms, radical reforms and intense anticorruption policies should be preferred to "incrementalist" approaches when considering the possibility of multiple equilibria in the corruption system (see Chapter 1). In fact, only radical reform can determine a "jump" from a high-level to a low-level corruption equilibrium, while incremental changes will probably induce marginal adjustments in the decisions of individuals involved in corrupt practices. For an analysis of the characteristics—political context, stimulus, objective, strategy, and political consequence—of corruption cleanups see Gillespie and Okruhlik (1991).

List of Archival Documents from Court Records and Government Investigations (in Order of Investigation)

Verona, *Cespugli d'oro:*

PRV	Public Prosecutor at the Court of Verona, PPC for Firou-zabadi +44, 10/12/1991
VIV1-12	Public Prosecutor at the Court of Verona, Reports of Evidence of 12 Interrogations, October–November 1990
DSV	Public Prosecutor at the Court of Verona, Ordinance of Judicial Attachment to Montagnana Italo, no. 1367/90
MCV	Public Prosecutor at the Court of Verona, Request for Application of Precautionary Measures, no. 1367/90
OCV	Court of Verona, Judge for the Preliminary Investigations, Order of Provisional Arrest, no. 3743/90, 22/10/1990
PTV	Command of the Excise and Revenue Police of Verona, Communication of Information of Crime, no. 8402/IIII/9110, 28/6/1990
GFV	7th Legion Revenue Guard Corps of Verona, Elaboration of "File Seg" Confiscated to Montagnana Aldo
AGFV	7th Legion Revenue Guard Corps of Verona, Delegated Investigation, no. 829/90
IGFV	7th Legion Revenue Guard Corps of Verona; Investigation of the Implementation of Major Road Works, no. 43/I/UG, 23/3/1990
RPV1–RPV2	Reports of the Expert at the Court of Verona
QV	Questura of Verona, Response to Note 40/88, no. 1/89, 24/1/1989

Milano, *Mani Pulite*

CDM	Chamber of Deputies, doc. IV, no. 6, Domanda di autorizzazione a procedere, 2/6/1992
CDRM	Camera dei Deputati, doc. IV, no. 6-A, Report of the Giunta per le autorizzazioni a procedere, presented at the presidency 3 July 1992
TNM	*Tangentopoli. Le carte che scottano* (pp. 65–86, Excerpt from the "Richiesta di autorizzazione a procedere nei confronti dell'on. Bettino Craxi," 12/1/1993), Supplement to *Panorama*, February 1993

MPM   E. Nascimbeni, A. Pamparana, *Le mani pulite*, A. Mondadori, 1992
TM   A. Carlucci, *Tangentomani*, Baldini & Castoldi, 1992 (this and the preceding book are published reports of evidence from interrogations)
PM   *Mani Pulite*, supplement to *Panorama*, October 1992
SDM   Senate of the Repubblic, doc. IV, no. 13, Domanda di autorizzazione a procedere, 12/6/1992
CDEM   Public Prosecutor at the Court of Milan, Domanda di autorizzazione a procedere, 8/10/1993, *Avvenimenti* 42, November 3, 1993
MF   Tribunal of Milan, Report of Evidence of the Interrogation with Leonardo Sciascia, 22/12/1994 (in *Le mazzette della Fininvest*, Milano, Kaos Edizioni, 1996)
SLM   Tribunal of Milan, Report of Interrogation of Silvano Larini, no. 6380/91, R.G. notizie di reato, no. 671/92, R.G.G.I.P., March 13, 1993

Milan, ICOMEC
PRIM   Public Prosecutor at the Court of Milan, PPC, JP no. 990/83 against Rodi Luciano +29
TRIM   Court of Milan, SC no. 3182/89, 22/12/1989

Milan, CODELFA
PRCM   Public Prosecutor at the Court of Milan, Writ of Subpoena, JP no. 5805/85, 28/8/1989
VICM   Public Prosecutor at the Court of Milan, Report of Evidence of the Interrogation with Mura Giovanni, JP no. 5805/85
PCCM1-3   Public Prosecutor at the Court of Milan, Richiesta di autorizzazione a procedere nei confronti di Gangi Giorgio, Sirtori Francesco, Natali Antonio, JP no. 5805/85,

Milan, *Carceri d'oro*
PROM   Public Prosecutor at the Court of Milan, PPC, JP nos. 2537/88A and 2620/88A, 12/2/1991
CPDM   Centro Nazionale di Prevenzione e Difesa Sociale: *Il sistema degli appalti. Un'analisi dei problemi di pianificazione e controllo, Rapporto finale del primo anno di ricerca*, research report, edited by Gherado Colombo, January 1990

Milan, Lombardia Informatica
PRLIM   Public Prosecutor at the Court of Milan, PPC, JP no. 6009/90, Mod.21, 21/4/1992

Milan, ATM
TAM   Court of Milan, SC no. 1891/91, 15/5/1991

Milan, Duomo Connection
PRDM   Public Prosecutor at the Court of Milan, PPC, JP no.
             16645/90/21 R.G., 20/3/1991
TRDM   Tribunal of Milan, SC no. 764+769+1207+1486/91 R.G.,
             25/5/1992

Milan, Other
TFM   Court of Milan, SC 11/3/1980, *Il Foro Italiano* II:525–27, 1980

Bari, *Consiglio Provinciale*
UIB   Court of Bari, IMBI no. 7641/80 R.G.P.M., 6/4/1985
TRIB   Court of Bari, SC no. 861/85, 29/11/1985

Savona, *Clan Teardo*
UIS   Court of Savona, IMBI, JP no. 1019/81 R.G.P.M., 24/8/1984
TRIS   Court of Savona, SC no. 145/85, 8/8/1985
CCS   Supreme Court of Cassation, SC no. 1852/89, 10/6/1989
GFS   Report of Colonel Niccolò Bozzo from the Revenue Guard
             Corps of Savona, 1984

Rome, *Lenzuola d'Oro*
PR   Public Prosecutor at the Court of Rome, PPC, JP nos.
             10726/88A and 6302/88A R.G.P.M., 20/2/1991

Roma, *Orta. coop*
PRTR   Public Prosecutor at the Court of Rome, PPC, JP no.
             4541/90A R.G.P.M., 1/10/1990
RSR   Revenue Guard Corps of Rome, Service Report

Roma, Lockheed
CCR   Constitutional Court, SC 2/8/1979, no. 221, *Il Foro Italiano*
             II:2193–2289, 1979

Roma, Asbanane
TBR   Court of Rome, SC 11/5/1964, *Il Foro Italiano* II:409–12, 1964

Turin, Zampini
QGT   Court of Turin, SC against Zampini +19, 15/3/1986, excerpts
             in *Questione Giustizia* 2:356–97, 1987

Florence, Villa Favard

QGF   Court of Florence, SC against Falugi +4, 28/2/1986, excerpts
             in *Questione Giustizia* 2:337–55, 1987

Palermo, Siino case

PRP   Public Prosecutor at the Court of Palermo, Request for
             Application of Precautionary Measures, no. 2789/90 N.C.

Palermo, Ciancimino case

UIP   Court of Palermo, IMBI against Baio Giuseppe +8,
             30/6/1990
TP   Court of Palermo, SC no. 2395/88 R.G., 20/7/1990
TRP   Court of Palermo, SC no. 411/90 R.G., 17/1/1992

Palermo, Other

TRMP   Court of Palermo, SC no. 1941/84, 20/7/1984
DAP   Public Prosecutor at the Court of Palermo, Domanda di
             autorizzazione a procedere contro il senatore Giulio
             Andreotti, 27/3/1993, *Panorama*, 11/4/1993
PP   Memoria by Public Prosecutor at the Court of Palermo, JP
             no. 3538/94, no. R., against Giulio Andreotti (published
             as *La vera storia d'Italia*, Napoli, Tullio Pironti, 1995)
DAPDDA   Public Prosecutor at the Court of Palermo. District Anti-
             Mafia Direction. *Memoria by* Public Prosecutor at the
             Court of Palermo, JP no. 3538/94 VIII Vol. (published in
             Avvenimenti, supplement, 1/2/1995)

Caltanissetta

LCC   Legion Carabinieri of Palermo, Judicial Report of Charges
             against Cosentino Francesco +73, R.G. no. 2215/11-1-
             1988, 23/2/1989
LCAC   Legion Carabinieri of Palermo, Enclosures nos. 1–60 to the
             R.G. no. 2215/11-1988, 23/2/1989
LCPC   Legion Carabinieri of Palermo, Judicial Report on the Inves-
             tigations about the Charges against Cosentino Francesco
             +73, R.G. no. 2215/11-1-1988, 11/7/1989
PRC   Public Prosecutor at the Court of Palermo, PPC, JP no.
             78/A/91, 31/12/1991

Naples

PRN   Public Prosecutor at the Court of Naples, PPC, JP no. 370/88
             R.G.G.I. against Galasso Sabato +11, 5/8/1989
APN   Richiesta di autorizzazione a procedere, 7/4/1993, supple-
             ment to *La Repubblica*, 15/4/1993

PRTN   Public Prosecutor at the Court of Naples, PPC, JP no. 2291/85 R.G.G.I. against Scotti Pasquale +33, 15/5/1986

UIN   Court of Naples, IMBI, PJ no. 1873/84 R.G.G.I. against Lorenzo Nuvoletta +29, 28/7/1989

TN   Court of Naples, SC in JP against Roberto Pepe +8 (draft), 21/12/1989

Pisa, Pretura Viareggio

IPI   IMBI, JP. no. 400/88AS, 27/2/1990

TPI   Court of Pisa, SC in JP no. 2853/88 R.G.P.M., 13/12/1990

VPI 1–48   Public Prosecutor at the Court of Florence, Reports of Evidence of 48 Interrogations, March 1987–April 1989

DPI 1–25   Court of Pisa, Reports of Evidence of 25 Interrogations in the Court, November–December 1990

Catania, USL 35

PCA   Public Prosecutor at the Court of Catania, Request of Subpoena, JP no. 3755/87 R.G., 11/6/1988

ACA   Court of Appeal of Catania, SC in JP no. 5463, 10/7/1991

Gioia Tauro, Centrale ENEL

PRG   Public Prosecutor at the Court of Palmi, Ordinance of precautionary judicial attachment in JP no. 100/90R.G., 8/2/1990

MDG   Comune of Rosarno, Defense Memoire of the Attorney Giacomo Saccomanno in the Appeal to the Court of Cassation, 21/9/1990

TCG   Civil Court of Palmi, Appeal ex art. 700 C.P.C. of the Commune of Rosarno, represented by the attorney Giacomo Saccomanno, 15/6/1988

Trapani, masonic lodges

PRT   Public Prosecutor at the Court of Trapani, PPC, JP no. 725 A. P. M. and 39/87 G.I., 27/11/1989

TPT   Court of Trapani, Transcription of the Hearing of 20/3/93, JP no. 24/91 against Grimaudo Giovanni +7, in Rome, Rebibbia

Venice, De Michelis-Bernini

APV   Richiesta di autorizzazione a procedere nei confronti degli on. Gianni De Michelis e Carlo Bernini, in *Avvenimenti*, 2 settembre 1992, pp. 14–19

Parliamentary Documents

CSPC   Committee for the Prevention of Corruption, Final Report to the President of the Chamber of Deputies, 23 October 1996

CPMF   Parliamentary Committee of Inquiry on the Mafia, Final Report on Mafia and Politics, approved on April 6, 1993 (supplement to *La Repubblica*, 10/4/1993)

CPDT   Parliamentary Committee of Inquiry in the Reconstruction after the Earthquake in Basilicata and Campania on November 1980, Final report approved on January 27, 1991, Vol. I

CD   Chamber of Deputies, Domanda di autorizzazione a procedere in giudizio, doc. IV

MPU   Evidence of Witnesses Tommaso Buscetta, Leonardo Messina, and Gaspare Mutolo before the Parliamentary Committee of Inquiry on the Mafia, in *Mafia e Potere*, supplement to *L'Unità*, 15/4/1993

CP2   Parliamentary Committee of Inquiry on the P2: Relazioni finali ed allegati, doc. XXIII, no. 2

Documents of the City Council of Florence

CCFI   City Council of Florence, *Verbale della seduta straordinaria d'urgenza del 7 dicembre 1982;* and *Verbali delle sedute del consiglio comunale del 27 e 30 gennaio, 24 e 28 settembre, 8, 15 e 24 ottobre, 5, 7 e 12 novembre 1984.* Florence, manuscript

Documents of the Tuscany Region

RGRT   Reports of the Ombudsman of the Tuscany Region, years 1991, 1992, and 1993

State Auditors' Department

CC   Report to the Parliament for the years 1987–1992

CCL   Report to the Parliament about the Local Authorities for the Year 1991

Interviews

I-1/60   Interviews with Experts (Politicians, Judges, Lawyers, Entrepreneurs, etc.)

Legend

JP   Judicial Proceeding
IMBI   Investigating Magistrate's Bill of Indictment
PPC   Public Prosecutor's Charge
SC   Sentence of Court

References

Aberbach, J. D., Putnam, R. D., and Rockman, B. A. (1981). *Bureaucrats and Politicians in Western Democracies*, Cambridge, MA: Harvard University Press.

Acemoglu, D. and Verdier, T. (1997). *The Choice between Market Failures and Corruption*. Discussion paper 6, Ecole Normale Superieure-Delta, Paris.

Ades, A. and Di Tella, R. (1995). *Competition and Corruption*. Discussion Paper 169, Institute of Economics and Statistics, University of Oxford.

Ades, A. and Di Tella, R. (1997a). "National Champions and Corruption: Some Unpleasant Competitiveness Arithmetic." *Economic Journal* 107:1023–42.

Ades, A. and Di Tella, R. (1997b). "The New Economics of Corruption: A Survey and Some New Results." Pp. 80–99 in *Political Corruption*, edited by P. Heywood. Oxford: Blackwell.

Adonis, A. (1997). "The UK: Civic Virtues Put to the Test." Pp. 103–17 in *Democracy and Corruption in Europe*, edited by D. della Porta and Y. Mény. London: Pinter.

Akerlof, G. (1970). "The Market for 'Lemons': Qualitative Uncertainty and the Market Mechanism." *Quarterly Journal of Economics* 84:488–500.

Akerlof, G. (1980). "A Theory of Social Custom, of Which Unemployment May Be One Consequence." *Quarterly Journal of Economics* 94:749–75.

Alam, M. S. (1990) "Some Economic Costs of Corruption in LDCs." *The Journal of Development Studies* 27:85–97.

Alam, M. S. (1995). "A Theory of Limits on Corruption and some Applications." *Kyklos* 48(3):419–35.

Alatas, S. H. (1990). *Corruption: Its Nature, Causes and Functions*. Aldershot: Averbury.

Alberoni, F. (ed.) (1967). *L'attivista di partito*. Bologna: Il Mulino.

Alexander, H. E. (1985). "Organized Crime and Politics." Pp. 89–98 in *The Politics and Economics of Organized Crime*, edited by H. E. Alexander and G. E. Caiden. Lexington, MA: Lexington Books.

Amato, G. (1980). *Una repubblica da riformare*. Bologna: Il Mulino.

Amato, G., Cassese, S., Coen, F., and Galli della Loggia, E. (1983). "Tavola rotonda su 'Affarismo e politica': quali risposte alla questione morale." *Mondoperaio* 4:2–13.

Amick, G. (1976). *The American Way of Graft*. Princeton, NJ: Center for Analysis of Public Issues.

Andreoli, M. (1993). *Andavamo in Piazza Duomo*. Milano: Sperling & Kupfer.

Andvig, J. C. (1991). "The Economics of Corruption." *Studi economici* 46:57–94.

Andvig, J. C. (1995). "Corruption in the North Sea Oil Industry: Issues and Assessments." *Crime, Law and Social Change* 23:289–313.

Andvig, J. C. (1996). "Corruption and Softening of Government: The International Dimension". Paper presented at the International Conference on Corruption in Contemporary Politics, University of Salford, November.

Andvig, J. C. and Moene, K. O. (1990). "How Corruption May Corrupt." *Journal of Economic Behaviour and Organization* 23:63–76.

Arabbia, A. G. and Giammusso, V. (1994). "Profilo statistico della pubblica amministrazione." Pp. 271–87 in *L'amministrazione pubblica italiana: Un profilo,* edited by S. Cassese and C. Franchini. Bologna: Il Mulino.

Arlacchi, P. (1983). *La mafia imprenditrice.* Bologna: Il Mulino.

Arlacchi, P. (1988). "Saggio sui mercati illegali." *Rivista Italiana di Sociologia* 29(3):403–37.

Arlacchi, P. (1992). *Gli uomini del disonore.* Milano: Mondadori.

Arrow, K. (1972). "Gifts and Exchanges." *Philosophy and Public Affairs* 1(4):343–62.

Axelrod, R. (1984). *The Evolution of Cooperation.* New York: Basic Books.

Bachrach, P. and Baratz, M. S. (1970). *Power and Poverty. Theory and Practice.* New York: Oxford University Press.

Baget Bozzo, G. (1985). "Il principe della Liguria." *La Repubblica,* July 28–29.

Bakker, H. E. and Shulte Nordholt, N. G. (eds.) (1996). *Corruption and Legitimacy.* Amsterdam: SISWO.

Balassone, F. (1991). "Efficienza nelle gare d'appalto per le opere pubbliche." *Economia Pubblica* 12:659–69.

Banfield, E. C. (1958). *The Moral Basis of Backward Society.* New York: Free Press.

Banfield, E. C. (1975). "Corruption as a Feature of Governmental Organization." *Journal of Law and Economics* 18:587–605.

Banfield, E. C., and Wilson, J. Q. (1967). *City Politics.* Cambridge: Cambridge University Press.

Barbacetto, G. (1992). "Il sistema Milano." *Micromega* 3:65–72.

Barbacetto, G. and Veltri, E. (1991). *Milano degli scandali.* Bari: Laterza.

Barbagallo, F. (1997). *Napoli fine novecento.* Torino: Einaudi.

Barca, P. (1994). *Imprese in cerca di padrone.* Bari: Laterza.

Bardhan, P. (1997). "Corruption and Development: A Review of Issues." *Journal of Economic Literature* 35:1320–46.

Barzel, Y. (1989). *Economic Analysis of Property Rights.* Cambridge: Cambridge University Press.

Baumol, W. J. (1990). "Entrepreneurship: Productive, Unproductive and Destructive." *Journal of Political Economy* 98:893–921.

Bayley, H. D. (1966). "The Effects of Corruption in a Developing Country." *Western Political Quarterly* 4:719–32.

Beck, J. P. and Maher, M. W. (1986). "A Comparison of Bribery and Bidding in Thin Markets." *Economic Letters* 20:1–5.

Becker, G. S. (1968). "Crime and Punishment. An Economic Approach." *Journal of Political Economy* 76:169–217.

Becker, G. S. and Stigler, G. J. (1974). "Law Enforcement, Malfeasance, and the Compensation of Enforcers." *Journal of Legal Studies* 3:1–18.

Becquart-Leclercq, J. (1989). "Paradoxes of Political Corruption: A French View." Pp. 191–210 in *Political Corruption. A Handbook,* edited by A. J. Heidenheimer, M. Johnston, and V. T. LeVine. New Brunswick, NJ, and Oxford: Transaction.

Becquart-Leclercq, J. (1993). *Corruption politique: à la recherche des victimes.* Paper presented at the Joint Sessions of the European Consortium for Political Research, Leide, April.

Beenstock M. (1979). "Corruption and Development." *World Development* 7:15–24.

Belligni, S. (1987). "Corruzione e scienza politica: una riflessione agli inizi." *Teoria Politica* 1:61–88.

Belligni, S. (1995). "Die 'Schmutzigen Jahre.' Die Ent-Institutionalisierung der italianischen Parteien." Pp. 167–87 in *Politische Institutionen im Wandel,* edited by B. Nedelmann. Westdeutscher Verlag: Opladen.

Ben-Dor, G. (1974). "Corruption, Institutionalization and Political Development." *Comparative Political Studies* 7:63–83.

Benassi, I., and Sganga, S. (1994). "Sviluppo, criminalità e corruzione: i resoconti delle interviste." *Qualeimpresa* 7:40–54.

Benson, G. C., Maaren, S. A., and Heslop, A. (1978). *Political Corruption in America.* Lexington: Lexington DC.

Benson, B. L. (1988). "Corruption in Law Enforcement: One Consequence of 'Tragedy of Commons' Arising with Public Allocation Processes." *International Review of Law and Economics* 8:75–84.

Benson, B. L. (1990). *The Enterprise of Law. Justice Without the State.* San Francisco: Pacific Research Institute for Public Policy.

Benson, B. L. and Baden, J. (1985). "The Political Economy of Governmental Corruption: the Logic of Underground Government." *Journal of Legal Studies* 14:391–410.

Berg, L., Hanh, H., and Schmidhauser J. R. (1976). *Corruption in the American Political System.* Morristown, NJ: General Learning Press.

Bettin, G. and Magnier, A. (1989). *Il consigliere comunale.* Padova: Cedam.

Bettin, G. and Magnier, A. (1991). *Chi governa la città?* Padova: Cedam.

Blankenburg, E., Staudhammer, R., and Steinert, H. (1989). "Political Scandals and Corruption Issues in West Germany." Pp. 913–31 in *Political Corruption. A Handbook,* edited by A. J. Heidenheimer, M. Johnston, and V. T. LeVine. New Brunswick, NJ, and Oxford: Transaction.

Bliss, C. and Di Tella, R. (1995). *Corruption with Small Corrupt Agents.* Economics discussion paper 105, Nuffield College, Oxford.

Bliss, C. and Di Tella, R. (1997). "Does Competition Kill Corruption?" *Journal of Political Economy* 105:1001–23.

Block, A. (1991a). *Perspectives on Organized Crime.* Dordrecht: Kluwer Academic.

Block, A. (ed.) (1991b). *The Business of Crime.* Boulder, San Francisco, Oxford: Westview.

Bobbio, N. (1980). "La democrazia e il potere invisibile." *Rivista Italiana di Scienza Politica* 10:181–203.

Bocca, G. (1983). "La banda di Teardo che inquina la Liguria." *La Repubblica,* September 7.

Botta, A. (1983). "Vieni in loggia . . ." *L'Europeo,* September 24.

Bouckaert, B. (1995). "Istituzioni e morale." *Biblioteca della libertà* 31(137):33–55.

Bouissou, J. M. (1997). "Gifts, Networks and Clienteles: Corruption in Japan as a Redistributive System." Pp. 132–47 in *Democracy and Corruption in Europe,* edited by D. della Porta and Y. Mény. London: Pinter.

Boycko, M., Shleifer, A., and Vishny, R. (1995). *Privatizing Russia*. Cambridge, MA: MIT Press.

Bryce, J. (1921). *Modern Democracies*. London: Macmillan.

Buchanan, J. M. (1980). "Rent Seeking and Profit Seeking." Pp 3–15 in *Toward a Theory of the Rent Seeking Society*, edited by Buchanan, J. M., Tollison, R. D., and Tullock G. College Station: Texas A&M University Press.

Buchanan, J. M., Tollison, R. D., and Tullock, G. (eds.) (1980). *Toward a Theory of the Rent Seeking Society*. College Station: Texas A&M University Press.

Caciagli, M., Anastasi, A., D'Amico, R., Gentile, M. R., Gori, N., Mattina, L., and Nociforae, E. N. (1977). *Democrazia cristiana e potere nel Mezzogiorno. Il sistema democristiano a Catania*. Firenze, Guaraldi.

Cadot, O. (1987). "Corruption as a Gamble." *Journal of Public Economics* 33:223–44.

Caiden, G. E. and Caiden, N. J. (1977). "Administrative Corruption." *Public Administration Review* 37:301–8.

Canosa, R. (1996). *Storia della magistratura italiana*. Milano: Baldini & Castoldi.

Canosa, R. and Federico, P. (1974). *La magistratura in Italia dal 1945 a oggi*. Bologna: Il Mulino.

Cartier-Bresson, J. (1996). "Corrupción institucionalizada y neo-corporativismo, con ejemplos del caso frances." *Nueva sociedad* 145:110–25.

Cartier-Bresson, J. (1997a). "Le grilles de lecture." Pp. 21–37 in *Pratiques et controle de la corruption*, edited by J. Cartier-Bresson. Paris: Montchrestien.

Cartier-Bresson, J. (1997b). "The Economics of Corruption." Pp. 148–66 in *Democracy and Corruption in Europe*, edited by D. della Porta and Y. Mény. London: Pinter.

Cassese, S. (1983). *Il sistema amministrativo italiano*. Bologna: Il Mulino.

Cassese, S. (1989). "L'efficienza della pubblica amministrazione e i suoi costi." *Rivista trimestrale di scienza dell'amministrazione* 4:71–75.

Cassese, S. (1992). "Corruzione e inefficienza." *La Repubblica*, August 23/24.

Cassese, S. (ed.) (1993). *I controlli nella pubblica amministrazione*. Bologna: Il Mulino.

Cassese, S. (1994). "Il sistema amministrativo italiano, ovvero l'arte di arrangiarsi." Pp. 11–18 in *L'amministrazione pubblica italiana: Un profilo*, edited by S. Cassese and C. Franchini. Bologna: Il Mulino.

Cazzola, F. (1988). *Della corruzione. Fisiologia e patologia di un sistema politico*. Bologna: Il Mulino.

Cazzola, F. (1991). *Periferici integrati. Chi, dove, quando nelle amministrazioni comunali*. Bologna: Il Mulino.

Cazzola, F. and Morisi, M. (1995). "Magistrature et classe politique: Aux delà les urgences de la crise italienne." *Politix* 30:76–89.

Cazzola, F. and Morisi, M. (1996). *La mutua diffidante Magistratura e politica in Italia*. Milano: Feltrinelli.

CENSIS (1992). *Dossier illecito*. Milano: Franco Angeli.

Chafuen, A. and Guzman, E. (1996). *Economic Freedom and Corruption*, mimeo. Hartfield: Atlas Economic Research Foundation.

Chambliss, W. (1978). *On the Take. From Petty Crooks to President*. Bloomington: Indiana University Press.

Chevallier, G. and Loshak, D. (1982). *Introduzione alla scienza dell'amministrazione*. Rimini: Maggioli.

Chibnall, S. and Saunders, P. (1977). "Worlds Apart: Notes on the Social Reality of Corruption." *British Journal of Sociology* 28:138–54.

Chiesi, A. M. (1995). "I meccanismi di allocazione nello scambio corrotto." *Stato e Mercato* 43:127–62.

Chubb, J. and Vannicelli, M. (1988). "Italy: A Web of Scandals in a Flawed Democracy." Pp. 122–50 in *The Politics of Scandal*, edited by A. S. Markovits and M. Silverstein. New York, Holmes and Meier.

Ciconte, E. (1994). "Ludovico Ligato." Pp. 99–183 in *Cirillo, Ligato e Lima. Tre storie di mafia e politica*, edited by N. Tranfaglia. Bari and Roma: Liguori.

Clarke, M. (1983). *Corruption: Causes, Consequences, and Control.* New York: McMillan.

Clinard, M. B. (1952). *The Black Market: A Study of White Collar Crime.* New York: Rinehart.

Clinard, M. B., and Yaeger, P. C. (1980). *Corporate Crime.* New York: McMillan.

Coase, R. H. (1937). "The Nature of Firms." *Economica* 4:386–405.

Coisson, F. (1983). "Avanti Savona." *L'Espresso,* June 26.

Colajanni, N. (1888), *Corruzione politica.* Catania: Filippo Tropea.

Colby, W. and Forbath, P. (1981). *La mia vita nella CIA.* Milano: Mursia.

Coleman, J. W. (1987). "Toward an Integrated Theory of White Collar Crime." *American Journal of Sociology* 93:406–39.

Coleman, J. S. (1990). *Foundations of Social Theory.* Cambridge, MA, and London: Belknap Press of Harvard University Press.

Colombo, G. (1996). *Il vizio della memoria.* Milano: Feltrinelli.

Commissione delle Comunità Europee (1997). *Una politica dell'Unione contro la corruzione.* Comunicazione della Commissione al Consiglio e al Parlamento Europeo, Bruxelles, May 21.

Cornwell, R. (1983). *God's Banker: An Account of Life and Death of Roberto Calvi.* London: Victor Gollancz.

Cotta, M. and Isernia, P. (eds.) (1996). *Il gigante dai piedi d'argilla.* Bologna: Il Mulino.

Cressey, D. R. (1953). *Other People's Money: A Study in the Social Psychology of Embezzlement.* Belmont, MA: Wadsworth.

Cubeddu, R. (1994). "Democrazia, liberalismo, corruzione." *Ragion Pratica* 3:12–25.

D'Auria, G. (1993). "Modelli di controllo nel settore pubblico: organi, parametri, misure." Pp. 201–38 in *I controlli della pubblica amministrazione*, edited by S. Cassese. Bologna: Il Mulino.

Dahl, R. (1961). *Who Governs? Democracy and Power in an American City.* New Haven, CT: Yale University Press.

Dahl, R. (1967). *Introduzione alla scienza politica.* Bologna: Il Mulino.

Dasgupta, P. (1989). "La fiducia come bene economico." Pp. 63–93 in *Le strategie della fiducia,* edited by D. Gambetta. Torino: Einaudi. [First published in English as "Trust as a commodity." In *Trust: the Making and Breaking of Cooperative Relations,* edited by D. Gambetta. Oxford: Blackwell, 1988]

Davigo, P. (1993). "Tempo per un nuovo inizio," interview by C. Dematté. *Economia & Management* 2:9–17.

de Winter, L. (1997). "Facilitators of political corruption in Belgium." Paper presented at the Conference on "Political Corruption in Europe and Belgium," Brussels, 12 December.

de Winter, L., della Porta, D. and Deschouwer, K. (1996). "Comparing Similar Countries." Pp. 215–36 in *Partitocracies Between Crisis and Reform: The Cases of Italy and Belgium*, edited by L. De Winter, D. della Porta, and K. Deschouer. *Res Publica* 2(Special issue).

Del Gaudio, M. (1992). *La toga strappata*. Napoli: Tullio Pironti.

della Porta, D. (1990). "Risorse e attori della corruzione politica. Appunti su tre casi di governo locale in Italia." *Polis* 4:499–532.

della Porta, D. (1992). *Lo scambio occulto. Casi di corruzione politica in Italia*. Bologna: Il Mulino.

della Porta, D. (1993). "Milan: Immoral Capital." Pp. 98–115 in *Italian Politics*, edited by G. Pasquino and S. Hellman. London: Pinter.

della Porta, D. (1996a). "Actors in Corruption: Business Politicians in Italy." *International Social Science Journal* 149:349–64.

della Porta, D. (1996b). "The System of Corrupt Exchange." Pp. 221–33 in *The New Italian Republic: From the Fall of Communism to the Rise of Berlusconi*, edited by S. Gundle and S. Parker. London: Routledge.

della Porta, D. (1997). "The Vicious Circles of Corruption in Italy." Pp. 35–49 in *Democracy and Corruption in Europe*, edited by D. della Porta and Y. Mény. London: Pinter.

della Porta, D., and Mény, Y. (eds.) (1997a). *Democracy and Corruption in Europe*. London: Pinter.

della Porta, D., and Mény, Y. (1997b). "Democracy and Corruption: Towards A Comparative Analysis." Pp. 166–80 in *Democracy and Corruption in Europe*, edited by D. della Porta and Y. Mény. London: Pinter.

della Porta, D., and Pizzorno, A. (1996). "The Business Politicians: Reflections from a Study on Political Corruption." *Journal of Law and Society* 23:73–94.

della Porta, D. and Vannucci, A. (1994). *Corruzione politica e amministrazione pubblica. Risorse, attori, meccanismi*. Bologna: Il Mulino.

della Porta, D. and Vannucci, A. (1995). "Politics, the Mafia, and the Market for Corrupt Exchange." Pp. 165–84 in *Italian Politics. Ending the First Republic*, edited by C. Mershon and G. Pasquino. Boulder, San Francisco, and Oxford: Westview.

Dente, B. and Regonini, G. (1987). "Politica e politiche in Italia." Pp. 83–121 in *Stato e regolazione sociale. Nuove prospettive sul caso italiano*, edited by P. Lange and M. Regini. Bologna: Il Mulino.

Derlien, H. and Mayntz, R. (1988). *Einstellungen der politisch-administrativen Elite des Bundes 1987*. Bamberg.

Deysine, A. (1980). "Political Corruption. A Review of the Literature." *European Journal of Political Research* 8:447–62.

Di Pietro, A. (1991). *Criminalità mafiosa e tessuto economico produttivo*. Paper presented to the S. A. P. Conference, Milano.

Di Palma, G. (1978). *Sopravvivere senza governare. I partiti nel parlamento italiano*. Bologna: Il Mulino.

Dobel, J. P. (1978). "The Corruption of a State." *American Political Science Review* 72:958–73.

Doig, A. (1984). *Corruption and Misconduct in Contemporary British Politics*. Harmondsworth: Penguin.

Doig, A. (1996). "From Lynskey to Nolan: The Corruption of British Politics and Public service?" *Journal of Law and Society* 23:36–56.

Dorman, M. (1972). *Payoff: The Role of Organized Crime in American Politics.* New York: David McKay.

Duverger, M. (1961). *Les partis politiques.* Paris: Colin.

Easton, D. (1975). "A Reassessment of the Concept of Political Support." *British Journal of Political Science* 26:435–57.

Eigen, P. (1994). "Corruption: A Catastrophe to Developing Countries." Pp. 65–70 in *Corruption & Democracy,* edited by D. V. Trang. Institute for Constitutional & Legislative Policy, Budapest.

Eisenstadt, S. N. and Roniger, L. (1984). *Patrons, Clients and Friends. Interpersonal Relations and Structure of Trust in Society.* Cambridge, Cambridge University Press.

Elster, J. (1989a). *Nuts and Bolts for the Social Sciences.* Cambridge, Cambridge University Press.

Elster, J. (1989b). "Social Norms and Economic Theory." *Journal of Economic Perspectives* 3:97–117.

Epko, M. (1979). *Bureaucratic Corruption in Sub-Saharan Africa. Toward a Search of Causes and Consequences.* Washington DC: University Press of America.

Etzioni-Halevy, E. (1989). "Exchanging Material Benefits for Political Support: A Comparative Analysis." Pp. 287–304 in *Political Corruption. A Handbook.* edited by A. J. Heidenheimer, M. Johnston, and V. LeVine. New Brunswick, NJ: Transaction.

Eurobarometer, *Trends 1974–1995.* Brussels.

Falcone, G. (with M. Padovani) (1991). *Cose di Cosa Nostra.* Milano: Rizzoli.

Fava, C. (1991). *La mafia comanda a Catania. 1960/1991.* Bari: Laterza.

Feinstein, J. S., Block, M. K., and Nold, F. C. (1985). "Asymmetric Information and Collusive Behavior in Auction Markets." *American Economic Review* 75:441–60.

Ferraresi, F. (1980). *Burocrazia e politica in Italia.* Bologna: Il Mulino.

Federazione Italiana Pubblici Esercenti (FIPE) (1992). *Malati di tangente.* Dossier.

Fituni, L. (1996). "I padrini della nazione. Il ruolo delle mafia nella crisi russa." Pp. 7–32 in *Mafie e antimafia. Rapporto 1996,* edited by L. Violante. Bari and Roma: Laterza.

Fleisher, D. (1997). "Political Corruption in Brazil." *Crime, Law and Social Change* 25:297–321.

Fougére, L. (1984). "Les voies et moyens de la corruption." *Pouvoirs* 31:13–18.

Franzini, M. (1993). "La corruzione come problema di agenzia." Pp. 120–54 in *Teoria economica delle istituzioni,* edited by R. Artoni. Bologna: Il Mulino.

Freddi, G. (1978). *Tensioni e conflitto nella magistratura. Un'analisi istituzionale dal dopoguerra al 1968.* Rome and Bari: Laterza.

Freddi, G. (1992). "La pubblica amministrazione: perché funziona in modo così deludente." Pp. 215–39 in *Dentro la politica,* edited by G. Urbani. Milano: Il Sole–24 Ore Editore.

Friederich, C. J. (1972). *The Pathology of Politics.* New York: Harper and Row.

Frognier, A. P. (1986). "Corruption and Consociational Democracy: First Thoughts on the Belgian Case." *Corruption and Reform* 1:143–48.

Furebotn, E. G. and Pejovich, S. (eds.) (1974). *Economics of Property Rights.* Cambridge: Ballinger.

Galasso, A. (1993). *La Mafia Politica.* Milano: Baldini & Castoldi.

Galeotti, G. and Breton, A. (1986). "An Economic Theory of Political Parties." *Kyklos* 39:47–65.

Galeotti, G. and Merlo, A. (1994). "Political Collusion and Corruption in a Representative Democracy." in *Public Finance and Irregular Activities.* Supplement to *Public Finance/Finance Publiques* 49:232–43.

Galli, G. (1966). *Il bipartitismo imperfetto. Comunisti e democristiani in Italia.* Bologna: Il Mulino.

Galli, G. (1983). *L'Italia sotterranea. Storia, politica, scandali.* Bari and Roma: Laterza.

Galli, G. (1991). *Affari di Stato.* Milano: Kaos.

Gambetta, D. (1993). *The Sicilian Mafia.* Cambridge, MA, and London: Harvard University Press.

Gambetta, D. and Reuter, P. (1995). "Conspiracy among the Many: The Mafia in Legitimate Industries." Pp. 116–36 in *The Economics of Organized Crime,* edited by G. Fiorentini and S. Peltzman. Cambridge: Cambridge University Press.

Gardiner, J. A. (1993). "Defining Corruption." *Corruption and Reform* 7:111–24.

Gardiner, J. A. and Lyman, T. R. (1978). *Decisions for Sale. Corruption and Reform in Land-Use and Building Regulation.* New York: Praeger.

Gardiner, J. A. and Olson, D. J. (eds.) (1974). *Theft of the City.* Bloomington: Indiana University Press.

Gaxie, D. (1973). *Les professionels de la politique.* Paris: Seuil.

Geis, G. (1968). *White-Collar Criminal. The Offender in Business and the Profession.* New York: Atherton.

Giglioli, P. P. (1996). "Political Corruption and the Media: The Tangentopoli Affair." *International Social Science Journal* 149:381–94.

Gillespie, K. and Okruhlik, G. (1991). "The Political Dimensions of Corruption Cleanups." *Comparative Politics* 24:77–95.

Goel, R. K. and Nelson, M. A. (1996). *Corruption and Government Size: A Disaggregated Analysis.* Department of Economics, Illinois State University, mimeo.

Goel, R. K. and Rich, D. P. (1989). "On the Economic Incentives for Taking Bribes." *Public Choice* 61:269–75.

Golden, M. A. (1995). *A Comparative Investigation of Political Control in the Bureaucracy: A Preliminary Review of the Italian Case.* Paper presented at the APSA Meeting, Chicago, August 31–September 1990.

Goldstock, R. (1993). "Organized Crime and Corruption." *Corruption and Reform* 7:137–45.

Good, D. (1989). "Individui, relazioni interpersonali e fiducia." Pp. 41–62 in *Le strategie della fiducia,* edited by D. Gambetta. Torino: Einaudi.

Gould, D. J. (1980). *Bureaucratic corruption and underdevelopment in the Third World. The case of Zaire.* New York: Pergamon.

Gould, D. J., and Amaro-Reyes, J. A. (1983). *The Effects of Corruption on Administrative Performance. Illustrations from Developing Countries.* Working paper no. 580, Washington, D.C., World Bank Staff.

Grau, E. R. and Gonzaga de Melo Belluzzo (1996). "Brasil y el Circulo Corrupto." *Nueva Sociedad* 145:174–84.

Gray, C. W. and Kaufmann, D. (1998). "Corruption and Development." *Finance & Development* 35(1):7–10.

Graziano, L. (1980). *Clientelismo e sistema politico. Il caso dell'Italia*. Milano: Angeli.

Groenendijk, N. (1996). *A Principal-agent Model of Corruption*. Paper presented at the International Conference on Corruption in Contemporary Politics, University of Salford, November.

Guarnieri, C. (1989). "Burocrazia e magistratura." Pp. 223–40 in *Scienza politica*, edited by L. Morlino. Torino: Edizioni della Fondazione Agnelli.

Guarnieri, C. (1991). "Magistratura e politica: il caso italiano." *Rivista Italiana di Scienza Politica* 21:3–32.

Guarnieri, C. (1992). *Magistratura e politica in Italia*. Bologna: Il Mulino.

Guccione, V. (1993). "Controlli ex-ante e controlli ex-post nella normativa pubblica." Pp. 23–36 in *I controlli della pubblica amministrazione*, edited by S. Cassese. Bologna: Il Mulino.

Hall, C. D. (1996). *The Uncertain Hand: Hong Kong Taxis and Tenders*. Shatin: Hong Kong Center for Economic Research, Chinese University Press.

Harendra, K. D. (1989). "The Genesis and Spread of Economic Corruption: A Microtheoretic Interpretation." *World Development* 17:503–11.

Harris, P. (1989). "Socialist Graft: The Soviet Union and the People's Republic of China." Pp. 513–33 in *Political Corruption. A Handbook*, edited by A. J. Heidenheimer, M. Johnston, and V. T. LeVine. New Brunswick, NJ, and Oxford: Transaction.

Hayek, F. A. (1973). *Rules and Order*. vol. I of *Law, Legislation and Liberty*. London: Routledge and Kegan Paul, 1973–1979.

Heidenheimer, A. J. (ed.) (1970a). *Political Corruption: Readings in Comparative Analysis*. New Brunswick, NJ: Transaction.

Heidenheimer, A. J. (1970b). "The Context of Analysis." Pp. 3–28 in *Political Corruption: Readings in Comparative Analysis*, edited by A. J. Heidenheimer. New Brunswick, NJ: Transaction.

Heidenheimer, A. J. (1996). "The Topography of Corruption: Explorations in a Comparative Perspective." *International Social Science Journal* 149:337–48.

Heidenheimer, A. J., Johnston, M. and LeVine, V. T. (eds.) (1989). *Political Corruption. A Handbook*. New Brunswick, NJ, and Oxford: Transaction.

Herzog, D. (1975). *Politische Karriere. Selektion und Professionalisierung politischen Führungsgruppen*. Berlin: Westdeutscher Verlag.

Heywood, P. (1995). "Sleaze in Spain." *Parliamentary Affairs* 48:726–37.

Heywood, P. (1997). "From Dictatorship to Democracy: the Changing Forms of Corruption in Spain." Pp. 65–84 in *Democracy and Corruption in Europe*, edited by D. della Porta and Y. Mény. London: Pinter.

Hillman, A. L. and Katz, E. (1987). "Hierarchical Structure and the Social Costs of Bribes and Transfers." *Journal of Public Economics* 34:129–42.

Hirschman, A. (1970). *Exit, Voice and Loyalty*. Cambridge, MA: Harvard University Press.

Hirschman, A. (1982). *Shifting Involvements*. Princeton, NJ: Princeton University Press.

Hobbes, T. ([1651] 1968). *Leviathan*. Harmondsworth: Penguin.

Holmes, L. (1996). *Corruption and the Crisis of Post-Communist State*. Paper presented at the International Conference on Corruption in Contemporary Politics, University of Salford, November.

Holzner, B. (1972). *Reality Construction in Society*. Cambridge, MA: Schenkman.

Hopkins, J. (1996). *Political Entrepreneurs and Political Corruption: The Party as Business Firm*. Paper presented at the International Conference on Corruption in Contemporary Politics, University of Salford, November.

Huntington, S. P. (1968). *Political Order in a Changing Society*. New Haven, CT: Yale University Press.

International Chamber of Commerce (1996). *Extortion and Bribery in International Business Transactions*. Document No. 193/15, March 26, Paris.

Iwai, H. (1986). "Organized Crime in Japan." In *Organized Crime: A global Perspective*, edited by R. J. Kelly. Totowa, NJ: Rowman and Littlefield.

Jacquemin, A. and Slade, M. E. (1989). *Cartels, Collusion, and Horizontal Merger*. Pp. 415–73 in *Handbook of Industrial Organization*, edited by R. Schmalensee and R. D. Willig. New York: Elsevier Science.

Jagannathan, N. V. (1986). "Corruption, Delivery Systems, and Property Rights." *World Development* 14:127–32.

Jiménez Sanchez, F. (1995). *Detras del escandalo politico. Opinion publica, dinero y poder en la Espana del siglo XX*. Barcelona: Tusquets.

Jiménez Sanchez, F. (1996a). *Political Scandals in Spain (1990–1995). Some Reflections on the Role of Public Opinion in Democracy*. Paper presented at the International Conference on Corruption in Contemporary Politics, University of Salford, November.

Jiménez Sanchez, F. (1996b). "Possibilities and Limits of Political Scandals as a Form of Social Control." *Revista Espanola de Investigaciones Sociologicas* (English edition):49–76.

Johnson, O. E. G. (1975). "An Economic Analysis of Corrupt Government with Special Application to LDC's." *Kyklos* 28:47–61.

Johnson, C. (1995). *Japan: Who Governs? The Rise of a Developmental State*. New York: Norton.

Johnston, M. (1982). *Political Corruption and Public Policy in America*. Monterey, CA: Brooks/Cole.

Johnston, M. (1986). "Corruption and Democracy in America." Pp. 137–50 in *Trend, Waste and Abuse in Government*, edited by J. B. McKimey and M. Johnston. Philadelphia: ISHI.

Johnston, Michael (1994). "Comparing Corruption: Conflicts, Standards and Development," paper presented at the XVI World Congress of the International Political Science Association, Berlin, August.

Johnston, M. (1996). "The Search for Definitions: The Vitality of Politics and the Issue of Corruption." *International Social Science Journal* 149:321–36.

Jones, C. and Menezes, F. M. (1995). *Auctions and Corruption: How to Compensate the Auctioneer*. Working paper in Economics and Econometrics, Australian National University, 11 August.

Katz, R. S. (1986). "Party Government: A Rationalistic Conception." Pp. 31–71 in *Visions and Reality of Party Government*, edited by F. G. Castles and R. Wildenmann. Berlin: De Gruyter.

Katz, R. S., and Mair, P. (1995). "Changing Models of Party Organization and Party Democracy." *Party Politics* 1:5–28.

Kaufmann, D., and Siegelbaum, P. (1997). "Privatization and Corruption in Transition Economies." *Journal of International Affairs* 50:419–59.

Key, V. O. (1936). *The Technique of Political Graft in the United States.* Chicago: University of Chicago Press.

Kirchheimer, O. (1957). "The Waning of Opposition in Parliamentary Regimes." *Social Research* 24:127–56.

Klitgaard, R. (1988). *Controlling Corruption.* Berkeley: University of California Press.

Klitgaard, R. (1998). "International Cooperation against Corruption." *Finance & Development* 35(1):3–6.

Knight, F. (1921). *Risk, Uncertainty and Profit.* Boston: Houghton Mifflin.

Kopp, P. (1996). "Dinero de la droga y lavado financiero." *Nueva Sociedad* 145:80–91.

Kramer, J. M. (1977). "Political Corruption in the U.S.S.R." *Western Political Quarterly* 15:213–24.

Kregar, J. (1994). "Deformation of Organizational Principles: Corruption in Post-Socialist societies," Pp. 47–60 in *Corruption & Democracy,* edited by D. V. Trang. Institute for Constitutional & Legislative Policy, Budapest.

Kreps, D. (1990). *A Course in Microeconomic Theory.* Hemel Hempsted: Harvester Wheatsheaf.

Kreps, D. and Wilson, R. (1982). "Reputation and Imperfect Information." *Journal of Economic Theory* 27:253–79.

Kurer, O. (1993). "Clientelism, Corruption, and the Allocation of Resources." *Public Choice* 77:259–73.

Landesco, J. (1968). *Organized Crime in Chicago.* Chicago: University of Chicago Press.

LaPalombara, J. (1964). *Interest Groups in Italian Politics.* Princeton: Princeton University Press.

LaPalombara, J. and Poggi, G. (1975). "Clientela e parentela nella burocrazia." Pp. 474–83 in *La burocrazia,* edited by F. Ferraresi and A. Spreafico. Bologna: Il Mulino.

Leff, N. (1964). "Economic Development Through Bureaucratic Corruption." *American Behavioural Scientist* 8:8–14.

Leonard, W. N. and Weber, M. G. (1978). "Automakers and Dealers: A Study of Criminogenic Market Forces." In *White Collars Crime,* edited by G. Geis and R. F. Meier. New York: Free Press.

Leone, R. (1988). "Tra risanamento e normalizzazione. Inchiesta sulla situazione della Dc a Catania." *La Sicilia,* November 6, 8, 10, 11.

Lerner, G. (1983). "Il metodo Teardo." *L'Espresso,* October 16.

Levi, M. and Nelken, D. (eds.) (1996). *The Corruption of Politics and the Politics of Corruption.* Oxford: Blackwell.

LeVine, C. (1975). *Political Corruption: The Ghana Case.* Stanford, CA: Hoover Institute Press.

Licandro, A. and Varano, A. (1993). *La città dolente. Confessioni di un sindaco corrotto.* Torino: Einaudi.

Liebermann, Y. and Syrquin, M. (1983). "On the Use and Abuse of Rights. An Economic View." *Journal of Economic Behaviour and Organization* 4:25–40.

Lien, D. D. (1986). "A Note on Competitive Bribery Games." *Economic Letters* 22:337–431.

Lien, D. D. (1990). "Corruption and Allocation Efficiency." *Journal of Development Economics* 33:153–64.

Lijphart, A. (1975). "The Comparable Cases Strategy in Comparative Research." *Comparative Political Studies* 7:687–93.

Lijphart, A. (1984). *Democracies. Patterns of Majoritarian and Consensus Government in Twenty-One Countries.* London: Yale University Press.

Little, W. (1992). "Political Corruption in Latin America." *Corruption and Reform* 7:41–66.

Little, W. and Posada-Carbò, E. (eds.) (1996). *Political Corruption in Europe and Latin America.* London: Macmillan.

Liu, A. P. L. (1989). "The Politics of Corruption in the People's Republic of China." Pp. 489–511 in *Political Corruption. A Handbook,* edited by A. J. Heidenheimer, M. Johnston, and V. T. LeVine. New Brunswick, NJ, and Oxford: Transaction.

Loïma, A. (1993). "Les embûches de la transition en Russia: corruption et pratiques mafiouses." *Le Courrier des pays de l'Est* 381:20–36.

Lui, F. T. (1986). "A Dynamic Model of Corruption Deterrence." *Journal of Public Economics* 31:215–36.

Macdougall, T. (1988). "The Lockheed Scandal and the High Cost of Politics in Japan." Pp. 193–229 in *The Politics of Scandal,* edited by A. S. Markovits and M. Silverstein. New York: Holmes and Meyer.

MacRae, J. (1982). "Underdevelopment and the Economics of Corruption: A Game Theory Approach." *World Development* 10:677–87.

Magatti, M. (1996). *Corruzione politica e società italiana.* Bologna: Il Mulino.

Magnolfi, L. (1996). *Networks di potere e mercati illeciti. Il caso della loggia massonica P2.* Messina: Rubettino.

Magone, J. M. (1996). *Political Corruption and Sustainable Democracy in Small Countries: The Portuguese Case in Comparative European Perspective.* Paper presented at the International Conference on Corruption in Contemporary Politics, University of Salford, November.

Majone, G. (1988). "Efficienza o efficienze della pubblica amministrazione? Problemi di allocazione, produzione, distribuzione e sviluppo nei pubblici servizi." *Rivista Trimestrale di Scienza dell'Amministrazione* 4:81–87.

Malec, K. L. and Gardiner, J. A. (1987). "Measurement issues in the study of official corruption: a Chicago example." *Corruption and Reform* 2:267–78.

Maltz, M. D. (1985). "Toward Defining Organized Crime." Pp. 21–35 in *The Politics and Economics of Organized Crime,* edited by H. E. Alexander and G. E. Caiden. Lexington, MA: Lexington Books.

Manion, M. (1996). "La experiencia de Hong Kong contra la corrupcion. Algunas lecciones importantes." *Nueva Sociedad* 145:126–37.

Manzetti, L., and Blake, C. (1996). "Market reform and corruption in Latin America: New Means for Old Ways." *Review of International Political Economy* 3:662–97.

Markovits, A. S. and Silverstein, M. (1988). "Introduction: Power and Process in

Liberal Democracies." Pp. 1–13 in *The Politics of Scandal*, edited by A. S. Markovits and M. Silverstein. New York: Holmes and Meier.

Massarenti, A. (1996). "Spezzare la collusione." *Biblioteca della libertà* 137:77–84.

Mastragostino, F. (1993). *L'appalto di opere pubbliche. Norme interne e disciplina comunitaria*. Bologna: Il Mulino.

Mastropaolo, A. (1984). *Saggio sul professionismo politico*. Milano: Franco Angeli.

Mastropaolo, A. (1987). "Scambio politico e ceto politico." *Democrazia e diritto* 27:27–62.

Mastropaolo, A. (1990). *Il ceto politico. Teoria e pratiche*. Roma: La Nuova Italia Scientifica.

Mauro, P. (1995). "Corruption and Growth." *Quarterly Journal of Economics* 110:681–712.

Mauro, P. (1996). *The Effects of Corruption on Growth, Investment, and Government Expenditure*. IMF Working Paper WP/96/98.

Mauro, P. (1998). "Corruption: Causes, Consequences and Agenda for Further Research." *Finance & Development* 35(6)1:11–14.

McChesney, F. S. (1987). "Rent Extraction and Rent Regulation in the Economic Theory of Regulation." *Journal of Legal Studies* 16:101–18.

Médard, J. F. (1997). "France-Afrique: Within the Family." Pp. 22–35 in *Democracy and Corruption in Europe*, edited by D. della Porta and Y. Mény. London: Pinter.

Médard, J. F. (1982). "The Undeveloped State in Tropical Africa: Political Clientelism or Neo-Patrimonialism." Pp. 177–92 in *Private Patronage and Public Power*, edited by C. Clapham. London: Frances Pinter.

Mershon, C. and Pasquino, G. (eds.) (1995). *Italian Politics. Ending the First Republic*. Boulder, CO, San Francisco, and Oxford: Westview.

Mendras, M. (1997). "Rule by Bureaucracy in Russia." Pp. 118–30 in *Corruption and Democracy*, edited by D. della Porta and Y. Mény. London: Pinter.

Mény, Y. (1992). *La Corruption de la République*. Paris: Fayard.

Mény, Y. (1996). "'Fin de Siecle' Corruption: Change, Crisis and Shifting Values." *International Social Science Journal* 149:309–20.

Mény, Y. (1997). "France: The End of the Republican Ethic." Pp. 7–21 in *Democracy and Corruption in Europe*, edited by D. della Porta and Y. Mény. London: Pinter.

Merton, R. K. (1957). *Social Theory and Social Structure*. New York: Free Press.

Merton, R. K. (1972). "The Latent Functions of the Machine." In *Urban Bosses. Machines and Progressive Reformers*, edited by M. S. Bruce. Washington, DC: Heath, Lexington.

Messina, S. (1992). *Nomenklatura*. Milano: Mondadori.

Milgrom, P. and Roberts, J. (1982). "Predation, Reputation and Entry Deterrence." *Journal of Economic Theory* 27:280–312.

Milgrom, P. and Roberts, J. (1988). "An Economic Approach to Influence Activities in Organizations." *American Journal of Sociology* 94(supplement):S154–79.

Mogiliansky, A. (1994). *Corruption in procurement: The economics of regulatory blackmail*. Research paper in Economics, Department of Economics, University of Stockholm, May 5.

Mogiliansky, A. (1995). *Corruption and Networks: An Example of Multified Contacts*. Research paper in Economics, Department of Economics, University of Stockholm, December 1.

Mola, A. (1992). *Storia della massoneria italiana dalle origini ai giorni nostri.* Milano: Bompiani.

Mongini, R. (1992). *Gli impuniti.* Milano: Sperling & Kupfer.

Montias, J. M. and Rose Ackerman, S. (1980). "Corruption in a Soviet Type Economy: Theoretical Considerations." Pp. 53–83 in *Economic Welfare and the Economics of Soviet Socialism: Essays in Honor of Abram Bergson,* edited by S. Rosenfielde. Cambridge: Cambridge University Press.

Mookherjee, D. and Png, I. P. (1995). "Corruptible law enforcers: How should they be compensated?" *Economic Journal* 105:145–59.

Morisi, M. (1991). "Gli stadi di 'Italia'90' come esperienza di governo locale." *Rivista trimestrale di Scienza dell'Amministrazione* 2:3–57.

Morlino, L. and Montero, J. M. (1994). "Legittimità, consolidamento e crisi nell'Europa meridionale." *Rivista italiana di scienza politica* 24:27–66.

Mortara, V. (1974). "Tendenze conservatrici e rapporti con la politica degli alti burocrati." Pp. 259–65 in *L'amministrazione pubblica in Italia,* edited by S. Cassese. Bologna: Il Mulino.

Murphy, K. M., Shleifer, A., and Vishny, R. W. (1991). "The Allocation of Talent: Implications for Growth." *Quarterly Journal of Economics* 105:503–30.

Murphy, K. M., Shleifer, A., and Vishny, R. W. (1993). "Why is Rent-Seeking So Costly to Growth?" *American Economic Review Papers and Proceedings* 83:409–14.

Myrdal, G. (1968). *Asian Drama: An Enquiry into the Poverty of Nations.* New York: Twentieth Century.

Nas, T. F., Price, A. C., and Weber, C. T. (1986). "A Policy-Oriented Theory of Corruption." *American Political Science Review* 80:107–19.

Nelken, D. (1996a). "A Legal Revolution? The Judges and Tangentopoli." Pp. 191–206 in *The New Italian Republic: From the Fall of Communism to the Rise of Berlusconi,* edited by S. Gundle and S. Parker. London: Routledge.

Nelken, D. (1996b). "The Judges and Political Corruption in Italy." *Journal of Law and Society* 23:95–112.

Neppi Modona, G. (1993). "Ruolo della giustizia e crisi del potere politico." *Quaderni di sociologia* 37:6–30.

Nicolosi, S. (1989). *Il caso Catania. 1965–1988: i fatti e i perché dei fatti.* Catania: Tringale.

Njaim, H. (1996). "Clientelismo, mercado y Liderazgo partidista en America Latina." *Nueva Sociedad* 145:138–47.

Nye, J. S. (1967). "Corruption and Political Development. A Cost-Benefit Analysis." *American Political Science Review* 61:417–27.

Organization for Economic Cooperation and Development (1997). *OECD Actions to Fight Corruption.* Note by the Secretary General to the OECD Council at Ministerial Level, Paris, May 26.

Oldenburg, P. (1987). "Middlemen in Third-World Corruption: Implications of an Indian Case." *World Politics* 39:508–35.

Olson, M. (1965). *The Logic of Collective Action.* Cambridge: MA: Harvard University Press.

Olson, M. (1993). "Dictatorship, Democracy, and Development." *American Political Science Review* 87:567–75.

Organized Crime Task Force (1988). *Corruption and Racketeering in the New York City Construction Industry.* Interim report. New York: ILR Press.

Ouchi, W. G. (1980). "Markets, Bureaucracies, and Clans." *Administrative Science Quarterly* 25:129–41.

Padioleau, J. C. (1975). "De la corruption dans les oligarchies pluralistes." *Revue francaise de sociologie* 16:33–58.

Pansa, G. (1987). *Lo sfascio.* Milano: Sperling & Kupfer.

Pansa, G. (1994). *I bugiardi. L'Unità* (supplement), 12–14 March.

Pantaleoni, M. (1984). *L'industria del potere.* Bologna: Cappelli.

Paoli, L. 1995, "The Banco Ambrosiano Case: An Investigation into the Underestimation of the Relations between Organized and Economic Crime." *Crime, Law and Social Change* 23:345–65.

Pareto, V. (1916). *Trattato di sociologia generale.* Catania: G. Barbera Editore.

Pasquino, G. (1985). "Partiti, società civile e istituzioni." Pp. 1–30 in *Il sistema politico italiano,* edited by G. Pasquino. Bari-Roma: Laterza.

Pasquino, G. (1987). "Regolatori sregolati: partiti e governo dei partiti." Pp. 53–81 in *Stato e regolazione sociale. Nuove prospettive sul caso italiano,* edited by P. Lange and M. Regini. Bologna: Il Mulino.

Pasquino, G. (1990). "Partitocrazia." Pp. 774–77 in *Dizionario di politica,* edited by N. Bobbio, N. Matteucci, and G. Pasquino. Torino: Utet.

Pasquino, G. (1991). *La repubblica dei cittadini ombra.* Milano: Garzanti.

Paul, C. and Wilhite, A. (1994). "Illegal Markets and the Social Costs of Rent-Seeking." *Public Choice* 79:105–15.

Pelinka, A. (1988). "Austria: The Withering of Consociational Democracy." Pp. 166–89 in *The Politics of Scandal,* edited by A. S. Markovits and M. Silverstein. New York: Holmes and Mayer.

Pérez-Diaz, V. (1996). *Espana puesta a prueba. 1976–1996.* Madrid: Alianza.

Perrone, N. (1991). *Il dissesto programmato. Il sistema delle partecipazioni statali.* Bari: Dedalo.

Philp, M. (1997). "Defining Political Corruption." Pp. 20–45 in *Political Corruption,* edited by P. Heywood. Oxford: Blackwell.

Pinheiro, P. S. (1994). "Corruption in Brasil." Pp. 37–40 in *Corruption & Democracy,* edited by D. V. Trang. Institute for Constitutional & Legislative Policy.

Pinto-Duschinsky, M. (1977). "Corruption in Britain." *Political Studies* 25:274–84.

Pippig, G. (1990). "Verwaltungsskandale. Zur Korruption in der Öffentlichen Verwaltung." *Aus Politik und Zeitgeschichte* (supplement to *Das Parlament*):7:11–20.

Pizzorno, A. (1971). "I due poteri dei partiti." *Politica del Diritto* 2:197–209.

Pizzorno, A. (1980). "I ceti medi nei meccanismi del consenso." Pp. 67–98 *I soggetti del pluralismo,* edited by A. Pizzorno. Bologna: Il Mulino.

Pizzorno, A. (1992). "La corruzione nel sistema politico." Pp. 13–74 in *Scambio occulto,* edited by D. della Porta. Bologna: Il Mulino.

Pizzorno, A. (1993). *Le radici della politica assoluta.* Milano: Feltrinelli.

Pizzorno, A. (1996). "Vecchio e nuovo nella transizione italiana." Pp. 253–85 in *Il paese dei paradossi,* edited by N. Negri and L. Sciolla. Roma: La Nuova Italia Scientifica.

Poggi, G. (ed.) (1968). *L'organizzazione partitica del Pci e della Dc.* Bologna: Il Mulino.

Popescu-Birlan, L. (1994). "Privatization and Corruption in Romania." *Crime, Law and Social Change* 21:375–79.

Procura di Milano (1996). *Prospetto riepilogativo di "mani pulite,"* updated to October 10.

Pujas, V. (1996). "Political Scandals: The Illegal Financing of Political Parties in France, Spain and Italy." Paper presented at the International Conference on Corruption in Contemporary Politics, University of Salford, November.

Putnam, R. D. (1973). "Atteggiamenti dell'alta burocrazia nell'Europa occidentale." *Rivista italiana di scienza politica* 39(1):145–86.

Putnam, R. D. (1993). *Making Democracy Work: Civic Traditions in Modern Italy.* Princeton, NJ: Princeton University Press.

Qizilbash, M. (1994). *Corruption, Temptation and Guilt: Moral Character in Economic Theory.* Discussion papers in Economics and Econometrics, University of Southampton, no. 94-19.

Rashid, S. (1981). "Public Utilities in Equalitarian LDC's: The Role of Bribery in Achieving Pareto Efficiency." *Kyklos* 34:448–60.

Rasmusen, E. (1990). *Games and Information.* Oxford: Blackwell.

Rasmusen, E. and Ramseyer, J. M. (1994). "Cheap Bribes and the Corruption Ban: A Coordination Game among Rational Legislators." *Public Choice* 78:305–27.

Reed, S. R. (1996). "Political Corruption in Japan." *International Social Science Journal* 149:395–406.

Rehren, A. (1997). "Corruption and Local Politics in Chile." *Crime, Law and Social Change* 25:323–34.

Reuter, P. (1983). *Disorganized Crime.* Cambridge, MA, and London: MIT Press.

Reuter, P. (1985). "Racketeers as Cartel Organizers." Pp. 49–65 in *The Politics and Economics of Organized Crime,* edited by H. E. Alexander and G. E. Caiden. Lexington, MA: Lexington Books.

Reuter, P. (1987). *Racketeering in Legitimate Industries. A Study in the Economics of Intimidation.* Santa Monica, CA: Rand.

Reuter, P. (1993). "The Commercial Cartage Industry in New York." In *Crime and Justice: A Review of Research,* volume 18, *Beyond the Law: Corrupt Organizations,* edited by A. Reiss and M. Tonry. Chicago: University of Chicago Press.

Rhodes, M. (1996). "Financing Party Politics in Italy: A Case of Systemic Corruption." Paper presented at the International Conference on Corruption in Contemporary Politics, University of Salford, November.

Ridley, F. F. and Doig, A. (eds.) (1995). *Sleaze: Politicians, Private Interests & Public Reaction.* Oxford: Oxford University Press.

Righettini, S. (1995). "La politicizzazione di un potere neutrale. Magistratura e crisi italiana." *Rivista Italiana di Scienza Politica* 25:227–65.

Rijckeghem, C. and Weder, B. (1997). *Corruption and the Rate of Temptation: Do Low Wages in Civil Service Cause Corruption?* IMF paper no. 73.

Robinson, M. S. (1985). "Collusion and the Choice of Auction." *Rand Journal of Economics* 16:141–45.

Rogow, A. A. and Lasswell, H. D. (1966). *Power, Corruption and Rectitude.* Englewood Cliffs, NJ: Prentice Hall.

Rose, R. (1984). *Understanding Big Government.* London: Sage.

Rose Ackerman, S. (1975). "The Economics of Corruption." *Journal of Public Economics* 4:187–203.

Rose Ackerman, S. (1978). *Corruption. A Study in Political Economy.* New York: Academic Press.

Rose Ackerman, S. (1986). "Reforming Public Bureaucracies through Economic Incentives?" *Journal of Law, Economics and Organization* 2:131–61.

Rose Ackerman, S. (1994). "Corruzione e concorrenza: il caso dell'europa orientale." *Ragion Pratica* 2:63–73.

Rose Ackerman, S. (1996). "Democracy and 'Grand' Corruption." *International Social Science Journal* 149:365–80.

Rosenthal, M. (1989). "An American Attempt to Control International Corruption." Pp. 701–15 *Political Corruption. A Handbook,* edited by A. J. Heidenheimer, M. Johnston, and V. LeVine. New Brunswick, NJ: Transaction.

Rossi, E. (1993). *Capitalismo inquinato.* Bari: Laterza.

Roth, R. (1989). "Eine korrupte Republik? Konturen politischer Korruption in der Bundesrepublik." Pp. 201–33 in *Anatomie des politischen Skandals,* edited by R. Ebbighausen and S. Neckel. Frankfurt am Main: Suhrkamp.

Rothacher, A. (1996). *Structural Corruption in a Gift Culture.* Paper presented at the International Conference on Corruption in Contemporary Politics, University of Salford, November.

Rowley, C. K., Tollison, R. D., and Tullock, G. (eds.) (1987). *The Political Economy of Rent Seeking.* Boston: Kluwer.

Rubin, P. (1973). "The Economic Theory of the Criminal Firm." Pp. 155–66 in *The Economics of Crime and Punishment,* edited by S. Rottenberg. Washington, DC: American Enterprise Institute.

Ruggiero, V. (1996a). *Economie sporche. L'impresa criminale in Europa.* Torino: Bollati Boringhieri.

Ruggiero, V. (1996b). "France: Corruption as Resentment." *Journal of Law and Society* 23:113–31.

Saba, R. P. and Manzetti, L. (1997). "Privatization in Argentina: The Implication for corruption." *Crime Law and Social Change* 25:353–69.

Sands, B. N. (1990). "Decentralizing an Economy. The Role of Bureaucratic Corruption in China's Economic Reforms." *Public Choice* 65:85–91.

Santino, U. and La Fiura, G. (1990). *L'impresa mafiosa.* Milano: Angeli.

Sartori, G. (1979). *Logica e metodo in scienze sociali.* Milano: SogarCo.

Sartori, G. (1982). *Teoria dei partiti e caso italiano.* Milano: SogarCo.

Sartori, G. (1987). *The Theory of Democracy Revisited.* Chatham, NJ: Chatham House.

Sapelli, G. (1994). *Cleptocrazia. Il "meccanismo unico" della corruzione tra economia e politica.* Milano: Feltrinelli.

Scaccioni, A. and Marradi, A. (1994). "Sviluppo, criminalità e corruzione: interviste in profondità." *Qualeimpresa* 7:37–40.

Schelling, T. (1967). "Economics and Criminal Enterprise." *Public Interest* 7:61–78.

Schelling, T. (1984). "What Is the Business of Organized Crime?" Pp. 179–94 in *Choice and Consequence,* edited by T. Schelling. Cambridge, MA: Harvard University Press.

Scheuch, E. K., and Scheuch, U. (1992). *Cliquen, Klügel und Karrieren.* Hamburg: Rowohlt Taschenbuch.

Schwartz, C. A. (1979). "Corruption and Political Development in the U.S.S.R."
    Comparative Politics 12:425–43.
Scott, J. C. (1972). *Comparative Political Corruption.* Englewood Cliffs, NJ: Prentice
    Hall.
Seibel, W. (1997). "Corruption in the Federal Republic of Germany Before and in
    the Wake of Reunification." Pp. 85–102 in *Democracy and Corruption in Europe,*
    edited by D. della Porta and Y. Mény. London: Pinter.
Serio, J. (1992). "Organized Crime in the Soviet Union and Beyond. " *Law Intensity
    Conflict and Law Enforcement* 1()2:127–51.
Sherman, L. W. (1978). *Scandal and Reform: Controlling Police Corruption.* Berkeley:
    University of California Press.
Sherman, L. W. (1980). "Three Models of Organizational Corruption in Agencies of
    Social Control." *Social Problems* 27:478–91.
Shleifer, A. and Vishny, R. W. (1993). "Corruption." *Quarterly Journal of Economics*
    107:599–617.
Simis, K. (1982). *USSR: The Corrupt Society.* New York: Simon and Schuster.
Solivetti, L. M. (1987). "La criminalità d'impresa: alcuni commenti sul problema
    delle cause." *Sociologia del diritto* 1:41–77.
Somjee, S. (1974). "Social Perspectives of Corruption in India." *Political Science
    Review* 13:180–86.
Somogyi, G. (1992). "L'economia della corruzione." *Mondoperaio* 11:76–80.
Stoppino, M. (1982). *Potere e teoria politica.* Genova: Igic.
Sugden, R. (1986). *The Economics of Rights, Cooperation and Welfare.* Oxford: Black-
    well.
Sutherland, E. H. (1983). *White Collar Crime.* New Haven, CT: Yale University Press.
Sutherland, E. H. and Cressey, D. R. (1974). *Criminology,* 9th edition. Chicago: Lip-
    pincott.
Tanzi, V. (1994). *Corruption, Governmental Activities, and Markets.* IMF working
    paper 94/99, August.
Taylor, M. (1987). *The Possibility of Cooperation.* Cambridge: Cambridge University
    Press.
Teodori, M. (1986). *P2: la controstoria.* Milano: SogarCo.
Theobald, R. (1996). "Can Debt Be Used as a Weapon in the War against Corrup-
    tion (the Uganda Plan)?" Paper presented at the International Conference on
    Corruption in Contemporary Politics, University of Salford, November.
Thompson, D. F. (1993). "Mediated Corruption: The Case of the Keating Five."
    American Political Science Review 87:369–81.
Tilly, C. (1985). "War Making and State Making as Organized Crime." Pp. 169–91
    in *Bringing the State Back In,* edited by P. B. Evans, D. Rueshmeyer, and T.
    Skocpol. Cambridge: Cambridge University Press.
Tirole, J. (1986). "Hierarchies and Bureaucracies: On the Role of Collusion in Orga-
    nizations." *Journal of Law, Economics and Organization* 2:181–214.
Tirole, J. (1996). "A Theory of Collective Reputation (with Applications to the Per-
    sistence of Corruption and to Firm Quality)." *Review of Economic Studies*
    63:1–22.
Tranfaglia, N. (1992). *Mafia, politica e affari. 1943–92.* Bari and Roma: Laterza.

Tranfaglia, N. (1994). "Mafia, politica e affari. Tre storie esemplari." Pp. 3–29 in *Cirillo, Ligato e Lima. Tre storie di mafia e politica*, edited by N. Tranfaglia. Bari and Roma: Liguori.

Transparency International and Göttingen University. (1995–1997). *Corruption Index, 1995–1997*. http://www.transparency.de.

Tullock, G. (1980). "Rent-Seeking as a Negative-Sum Game." Pp. 16–36 in *Toward a Theory of the Rent-Seeking Society*, edited by J. M. Buchanan, R. D. Tollison, and G. Tullock. College Station: Texas A&M University Press.

Tullock, G. (1984). "The Backward Society: Static Inefficiency, Rent Seeking, and the Rule of Law." Pp. 224–37 in *The Theory of Public Choice*, edited by J. M. Buchanan and R. D. Tollison. Ann Arbor: University of Michigan Press.

Tullock, G. (1989). *The Economics of Special Privilege and Rent Seeking*. Boston, Dordrecht, and London: Kluwer Academic.

Tullock, G. (1990). "The Costs of Special Privilege." Pp. 195–211 in *Perspectives on Positive Political Economy*, edited by J. E. Alt and K. A. Shepsle. Cambridge and New York: Cambridge University Press.

Turone, S. (1992). *Politica ladra. Storia della corruzione in Italia 1861–1992*. Bari and Roma: Laterza.

Ullman-Margalit, E. (1977). *The Emergence of Norms*. Oxford: Oxford University Press.

Van Rijckeghem, C. and Weder, B. (1997). *Corruption and the Rate of Temptation: Do Low Wages in the Civil Service Cause Corruption?* IMF discussion paper no. 97/73.

Van Outrive, L. (1996). "The Political Role of the Judiciary: The Belgian Case." *Res Publica* 38:371–84.

Van Duyne, P. C. (1997). "Organized Crime, Corruption and Power." *Crime, Law and Social Change* 26:201–38.

Vannucci, A. (1993). "Scambi e collusioni: analisi di un caso." *Il Progetto* 74:75–86.

Vannucci, A. (1997a). *Il mercato della corruzione*. Milano: Società Aperta.

Vannucci, A. (1997b). "Corruzione, partiti e competizione politica: osservazioni sul caso italiano." *Quaderni di scienza politica* 4(1):121–70.

Vannucci, A. (1997c). "Inefficienza amministrativa e corruzione." *Rivista Trimestrale di Scienza dell'Amministrazione* 29–56.

Vannucci, A. (1997d). "Politicians and Godfathers: Mafia and Political Corruption in Italy." Pp. 50–64 in *Democracy and Corruption in Europe*, edited by D. della Porta and Y. Mény. London: Pinter.

Varese, F. (1994). "Is Sicily the Future of Russia? Private Protection and the Rise of the Russian Mafia." *Archives Européennes de sociologie* 35:214–58.

Wade, R. (1982). "The System of Administrative and Political Corruption: Canal Irrigation in South India." *Journal of Developmental Studies* 18:75–86.

Wade, R. (1985). "The Market for Public Office." *World Development* 13:467–97.

Ward, P. (ed.) (1989). *Corruption, Development and Inequality*. Routledge: London.

Warszawski, D. (1993). "Tangentopolska." *Micromega* 2:94–105.

Waterbury, S. (1973). "Endemic and Planned Corruption." *World Politics* 25:533–55.

Waterbury, S. (1976). "Corruption, Political Stability and Development." *Government and Opposition* 11:426–45.

Weber, M. (1919). *Politik als Beruf.* Monaco and Lipsia: Duncker & Humblot.

Weber, M. ([1922] 1981). *Economia e società.* Milano: Comunità.

Werner, S. B. (1983). "New Directions in the Study of Administrative Corruption." *Public Administration Review* 146–54.

Werner, S. B. (1989). "The Development od Political Corruption In Israel." Pp. 251–73 in *Political Corruption. A Handbook,* edited by A. J. Heidenheimer, M. Johnston, and V. T. LeVine. New Brunswick, NJ, and Oxford: Transaction.

Williams, R. (1996). *Watergate to Whitewater: Corruption in American Politics.* Paper presented at the International Conference on Corruption in Contemporary Politics, University of Salford, November.

Williamson, O. E. (1985). *The Economic Institutions of Capitalism.* New York and London: Free Press–Collier Macmillan.

Williamson, O. E. (1989). "Transaction Cost Economics." Pp. 136–82 in *Handbook of Industrial Organization,* edited by R. Schmalensee and R. D. Willig. New York: Elsevier Science.

Williamson, O. E. (1991). "Che cos'è la teoria dei costi di transazione?" Pp. 231–52 *L'organizzazione economica. Imprese, mercati e controllo politico,* edited by O. E. Williamson. Bologna: Il Mulino. [First published in English as *Economic Organization.* Brighton: Wheatsheaf, 1989.].

Wilson, Richard W. (1991). "Political Pathology and Moral Orientations." *Comparative Political Studies* 24:211–30.

Wolf, E. R. (1966). "Kinship, Friendship, and Patron-Client Relations in Complex Society." Pp. 1–22 in *The Social Anthropology of Complex Societies,* edited by M. P. Banton. London: Tavistock.

Wolfinger, R. E. (1973). *The Politics of Progress.* Englewood Cliffs, NJ: Prentice Hall.

Zampini, A. (1985). *Il faccendiere.* Torino: Edizioni Zeta.

Zampini, A. (1993). *Io corruttore.* Napoli: Tullio Pironti Editore.

Zink, H. (1930). *City Bosses in the United States: A Study of Twenty Municipal Bosses.* Durham NC: Duke University Press.

Zuluaga Nieto, J. (1996). "Cuando la corrupcion invade el tejido social." *Nueva Sociedad* 145:148–59.

Author Index

303

Subject Index